Resisting
Radicalization

Resisting Radicalization

Exploring the Nonoccurrence of Violent Extremism

edited by
Morten Bøås, Gilad Ben-Nun,
Ulf Engel, and Kari Osland

LYNNE
RIENNER
PUBLISHERS

BOULDER
LONDON

This work is being made available under the Creative Commons Attribution-Non-Commercial-No Derivatives 4.0 International License (CC BY-NC-ND 4.0). To view a copy of this license, visit https://creativecommons.org/licenses/by-nc-nd/4.0/.

Published in the United States of America in 2025 by
Lynne Rienner Publishers, Inc.
1800 30th Street, Suite 314, Boulder, Colorado 80301
www.rienner.com

© 2025 by Lynne Rienner Publishers, Inc. All rights reserved

Library of Congress Cataloging-in-Publication Data
A Cataloging-in-Publication record for this book is available
from the Library of Congress.

ISBN: 978-1-962551-54-0 (hc: alk. paper)
ISBN: 979-8-89616-016-8 (pb: alk. paper)

British Cataloguing in Publication Data
A Cataloguing in Publication record for this book is available
from the British Library.

Printed and bound in the United States of America

∞ The paper used in this publication meets the requirements
of the American National Standard for Permanence of
Paper for Printed Library Materials Z39.48-1992.

5 4 3 2 1

In memory of Kjetil Selvik, our dear friend, colleague, and contributor, who passed away during the production of this book

Contents

Acknowledgments ix

1 Most People Are Not Radicalized 1
   Kari Osland, Morten Bøås, Ulf Engel, and Gilad Ben-Nun

Part 1 Exploring the Nonoccurrence of Violent Extremism

2 Enabling Environments 17
   Morten Bøås and Kari Osland

3 The Entrepreneurs of Violence 33
   Abdoul Wakhab Cissé and Henrik Vigh

4 Measuring Social Cohesion and Resilience 51
   Ulf Engel

Part 2 Cases from North Africa, the Middle East, and the Balkans

5 Islamists and the Choice Not to Take Up Arms: Algeria and Egypt 67
   Georges Fahmi and Djallil Lounnas

6 Religious Resilience and the Guardian State: Morocco and Jordan 85
   Gilad Ben-Nun and Nizar Messari

7 Ethnonationalism and Religious Radicalization: Serbia and Bosnia and Herzegovina 103
   Edina Bećirević and Predrag Petrović

viii Contents

8	Exporting Radicalization and Strengthening Resilience: Tunisia and Kosovo *Simeon Estatiev, Andreas Lind Kroknes, and Francesco Strazzari*	119
9	Regime Survival and Mobilization: Iraq, Mali, and Syria *Colin Powers, Luca Raineri, and Stéphane Lacroix*	143
10	Traditional Authority and Local Community Resilience: Bosnia and Herzegovina, Iraq, and Syria *Kjetil Selvik, Dlawer Ala'Aldeen, Ahmad Mhidi, Diana Mishkova, and Kamaran Palani*	161
11	External Donors and the Marketing of P/CVE: Niger, Tunisia, and Syria *Laura Berlingozzi, Silvia Carenzi, and Daniela Musina*	179

Part 3 Conclusion

12	P/CVE Policies of Europe and the United States *Dylan Macchiarini Crosson, Pernille Rieker, Tatjana Stankovic, Steven Blockmans, and Elsa Lilja Gunnarsdottir*	197
13	Implications for Policy and Future Research *Ulf Engel, Gilad Ben-Nun, Morten Bøås, and Kari Osland*	225

List of Acronyms	233
References	237
The Contributors	269
Index	275
About the Book	281

Acknowledgments

The PREVEX Project, the work and findings of which are the foundation of this book, received generous funding through the European Union's Horizon 2020 research and innovation program under grant agreement No. 870724. It is, therefore, imperative for us to thank the EU for the grant, support, and trust in allowing us to study thoroughly the issue of preventing violent extremism in the Balkan and Middle East and North Africa regions. A hearty thanks goes to all who participated in the project over these exciting years, including the contributors and those who have been involved in the field or from their offices.

We thank all of PREVEX's partners: the Atlantic Initiative (Bosnia and Herzegovina), the Alliance for Rebuilding Governance in Africa (Mali and Niger), Al Akhawayn University (Morocco), the Belgrade Centre for Security Policy (Serbia), the Centre for Advanced Study (Bulgaria), the Centre for European Policy Studies (Belgium), the Centre for International Studies (Paris), the European University Institute (Italy), the Group of Legal and Political Scholars (Kosovo), the Institute for Democracy and Mediation (Albania), Leipzig University (Germany), the Middle East Research Institute (Kurdistan Region of Iraq), the Norwegian Institute of International Affairs (Norway), Sant'Anna School of Advanced Studies (Italy), and the University of Copenhagen (Denmark). We also thank Lynne Rienner Publishers and the excellent folks there for their support, trust, care, and patience. It is a great privilege that our research and endeavor may gain reach through such a bastion of critical scholarly publishing.

We would also like to thank Andreas Lind Kroknes and Kristian Lefdal for their excellent assistance during the last hectic days of editing in Oslo.

—*Morten Bøås, Gilad Ben-Nun, Ulf Engel, and Kari Osland*

1

Most People Are Not Radicalized

*Kari Osland, Morten Bøås,
Ulf Engel, and Gilad Ben-Nun*

SINCE THE SEPTEMBER 11, 2001, ATTACKS IN THE UNITED STATES, a significant amount of literature has helped us to understand the processes of radicalization (Borum 2004; Sageman 2004; Moghaddam 2005; McCauley and Moskalenko 2008; Farhadi 2022). This literature also provides insights into the operations of groups that promote and conduct violent extremism (see, for instance, Beaujouan et al. 2024; Busher, Malkki, and Marsden 2024; McLaughlin 2024; Pilkington 2024). However, this focus on the manifestation of violent extremism has also weakened researchers' awareness of the fact that most people are not radicalized, even in environments that are conducive to radicalization. By using refined conceptual and empirical analyses, in this book we investigate why some communities are less susceptible to violent extremism than others.

Precarious living conditions across the Balkans, the Middle East, and North Africa can make these regions fertile ground for radical ideas. Nonetheless, despite genuine grievances and legitimate reasons for anger, most people who live in these areas do not succumb to radicalization, nor do they embrace ideas that lead to acts of violent extremism. With the goal of increasing our understanding of local community resilience in the face of violent extremism, the authors of this volume investigate not only the occurrence of violent extremism but also the nonoccurrence of violent extremism in so-called enabling environments. They also ponder why some communities are more or less likely to experience violent extremism than others. Their work is based on empirical studies conducted by researchers involved in the Preventing Violent Extremism in the Balkans and the MENA (PREVEX) project, which has been funded since 2020 by the European Union (EU).[1] PREVEX draws on diverse voices, and research is coproduced across the Global North and Global South. Scholars based in the project regions and Europe have conducted fieldwork in the Western Balkans, the Middle East, North Africa, and the Sahel.

While giving due regard to local and regional context sensitivity, the researchers are united around the findings that individuals' journey into violent extremism that culminates in joining groups or insurgencies rarely starts because of religious convictions or political ideologies (UNDP 2017, 2023). Instead, genuine material grievances concerning unemployment, lack of educational opportunities, and lack of possibilities for social mobility mainly fuel extremism. This is not to say that religion does not factor in, but we think it matters differently from what is often assumed. Our findings suggest that insurgents use religion as an ideology and a branding technique at different times and for various reasons. However, if it is the case that people are primarily recruited on the basis of root causes, not religious convictions, it has important implications for how we ought to think about preventing and countering violent extremism (P/CVE) programming in the future.

Although we are concerned herein with the emergence of violent extremism, a key innovative feature of this book is its emphasis on nonoccurrence. We have observed that most research on violent extremism focuses on answering the question of *why* people take up arms rather than the reverse question: Why do people living in enabling environments often choose *not* to become involved in political violence and why do they frequently seek to resist it, either openly or more subtly?

This investigation of nonoccurrence fills a gap in the scholarly literature on violent extremism. It also has important policy implications in that it can provide finely tuned, context-sensitive, and practical suggestions for preventing violent extremism by strengthening societal resilience. Several key concepts are instrumental to the analysis in this book. Because the chapters further explore them, here we only briefly explain these ideas and provide the background of the volume's subject matter.

Background and Key Concepts

The September 11, 2001, terrorist attacks in the United States have shaped the political strategy for the fight against terror in not only the United States but also the European Union and several other countries (see, for example, Bøås and Jennings 2005; Perl 2005). Yet, as these strategies and policies were being developed and refined, the destructive impact of violent extremism continued to take a toll, generating adverse shocks across international borders. The wars in Iraq and Syria, along with the rise of the Islamic State (IS), have framed subsequent US and EU policies (see, for example, ICG 2016; Bruneau 2015). The "foreign fighters" phenomenon, which has gained considerable attention in Europe and its neighborhood, is linked to several large-scale terrorist attacks, including those in Paris in 2015; in Brussels, Berlin, and Nice in 2016; and in Manchester, London, and Barcelona in 2017. Violent extremism is, therefore, of eminent concern to the EU and neighboring states. With the Islamic State facing territorial defeat, there is the potential for a wave of returning foreign fighters (see Lounnas 2018). Therefore, preventing violent extremism within and beyond Europe has become a significant objective of the EU since it adopted the Counterterrorism Strategy in 2005 (Council of the EU 2005) and its elaborations (Council of the EU 2011, 2015, 2017; EEAS 2016).

Violent extremism is not codified in international law, and even the United Nations Secretary-General's Plan of Action (UNSG 2016) states that it is a diverse phenomenon without clear definitions. Indeed, despite widespread use in security discourses, the term *violent extremism* lacks a precise definition, as was the case for *radicalization* and *terrorism*, the words violent extremism as a concept was designed to replace or enrich. This constitutes a significant problem because the absence of a clear definition of violent extremism paves the way for human rights abuses when authoritarian regimes exploit this ambiguity to delegitimize political adversaries.

Recent scholarship also highlights the fact that the concepts of radicalization and violent extremism remain ill-defined and imprecise (Schmid 2013) in narratives, framings, and policies that fluctuate between cognitive (Kepel 2005) and behaviorist epistemologies (Neumann 2006; UNDP 2017, 2023). In practice, this ambivalence has contributed to sweeping policies that have criminalized nonviolent groups and stigmatized entire communities considered at risk (Kundnani 2012; Heath-Kelly 2017; Osland and Erstad 2020). The current popular discourse in Mali that young Fulani herders of the Sahel are particularly prone to involvement with armed jihadist movements shows all too well how counterproductive this can be, in this case leading to a heavy-handed, indiscriminate state response (see Ba and Bøås 2017; Benjaminsen and Ba 2018, 2021, 2024). Moreover, most theories of violent extremism are built on abstract Western-based models (Macaluso 2016), and the lack of context sensitivity means they cannot capture local specificities (Coolsaet 2016).

In consideration of local and regional contexts, we understand *violent extremism* to be violence with a political or religious agenda. Agents of violent extremism are often involved in criminal activity locally, nationally, or transnationally, but it is not their sole motivation to extremism (Kalyvas 2003; Bøås, Cissé, and Mahamane 2020). Regarding *radicalization*, we follow Utas and Vigh (2017) in distinguishing between leader cadres and rank-and-file support. An understanding of radicalization considers not only religious beliefs and political ideology but also livelihoods and political possibilities afforded to the people in question. Thus, we take a clear stance and disagree with much of the work on this issue, which bases violent extremism in mental transformation theories (see Rambo 1993; Silber and Bhatt 2007; Horgan 2008; Borum 2011), where some preexisting grievance that leads to increased contact with and inclusion in a radicalized environment results in a person's complete commitment to the objectives of the radical group (see Silber and Bhatt 2007). The radical persona is seen to be totally absorbed by and committed to the radical idea, and the person is transformed from a discontented to an extremely dangerous individual.

Fundamental to our analytical framework is the concept of an *enabling environment*, which can be understood as an area in which various factors create a situation conducive to the expression of violent extremism. These factors, or drivers, might include poverty, marginalization, alienation, religious or ideological indoctrination, heavy-handed state responses, precarious masculinities, and appropriation-of-rights-based grievances.

When one or more of these drivers exist, an individual might experience a *decisive moment*, the moment when an extremist idea can be transformed into violence and violent acts. Although it is crucial to understand these moments, it is equally, if not more important to understand why a situation does not reach a decisive moment even in an enabling environment.

Therefore, we give due attention to *nonoccurrence* of violent extremism because it may very well tell us much more about how to prevent violent extremism than would focusing only on why it occurs. We ask: Why do some communities more than others display much greater resilience in the face of violent extremist ideologies? What role do local community leaders, including religious leaders, play in this resistance to extremism? Understanding why violence does not occur is often more relevant for strengthening resilience and designing preventive measures than is understanding why it occurs. We define *resilience* as the ability of political systems and (in)formal governance arrangements to adjust to changing political and social conditions while keeping their structures intact (Carpenter 2006).

Violent extremism rarely emerges in a vacuum. In the study regions, the usual factors and drivers of violent extremism are present. Poverty is widespread, and many communities experience economic and political marginalization. This may lead people to feel alienated from a state that has neglected their well-being for years. Youths and young men are particularly prone to perceived and real marginalization that could set them on a path to alienation, and alienation may make them more susceptible to extremist religious-ideological indoctrination (see, for instance, Dzhekova et al. 2016). We also know from our previous studies that the chances for radicalization increase in the presence of two other factors: (1) rights-based grievances that, if expressed, are met with (2) heavy-handed state responses (Bøås 2015; Bøås, Cissé, and Mahamane 2020; Doboš, Riegl, and Hansen 2019).

Under such circumstances, *competing authorities* may emerge. This happens most commonly in fragile states, where the government lacks the capacity or willingness to care for and protect its citizens and citizens view the state not as benevolent but as dysfunctional and corrupt. Then, competing authorities, including proponents of extremist views, exploit or appropriate citizens' grievances (Kilcullen 2015). The competing authorities that we are concerned with in this volume are those we define as *entrepreneurs of violence*. These nonstate actors combine their political agenda with income-generating activities. They rule by force and violence, but they also distribute resources, provide some level of order, and offer protection to (at least parts of) the population in the areas they control or attempt to control.

Entrepreneurs of violence primarily, but not exclusively, are local in origin and may have *local-global connections* (Bøås and Dunn 2017). The violent extremists we observed in the study regions originated locally and had global connections. But we found a need to distinguish between groups that used their local-global connections deliberately, purposefully, and strategically to become active operational brands in more extensive global networks of extremist ideology (for example, al-Qaeda or IS) and those that mainly employed such connections as a branding exercise, to appear more powerful, global, and omnipotent than they are (Bøås, Cissé, and Mahamane 2020).

Case Selection, Methods, and Methodology

To better understand violent extremism, we oriented the research for this book toward detailed empirical studies with a substantial fieldwork focus. The chapter authors use an interdisciplinary methodology informed by grounded theory and a mixed-methods approach.

In conducting comparative investigations of violent extremism in regions as diverse as the Balkans and the broader Middle East and North Africa (MENA), our research held a delicate balance between underlining similarities and recognizing differences. We carefully selected cases that illustrate the challenges of violent extremism in the studied regions. These micro case studies are connected to the country analyses that form the backbone of comparative country analysis in each region; we then initiated interregional comparisons of the Balkans and MENA. The research is case-based and comparative within and across regions.

We define the two regions as follows. The Balkans cases are divided into two broad linguistically divided areas: the Slavic cases, such as those form Bosnia and Serbia, and the Albanian-speaking cases, such as those from Kosovo. The MENA cases include those from Algeria, Egypt, Iraq, Jordan, Morocco, Syria, and Tunisia as key cases of concern for this volume.

Because the violent extremism in North Africa is interconnected with violence in the bordering Sahel, we have also included two cases from the Sahel, namely, from Mali and Niger. The main reason we extended the definition of the MENA region to include the Sahel is because what happens in the Sahel and the actors involved in violent extremism there impact the evolution of this phenomenon and can influence prevention strategies in crucial North African areas such as Algeria, Libya, Morocco, and Tunisia (see Bøås 2015, 2017; Strazzari 2015; Raineri 2018b).

With a context-sensitive orientation, we collected primary empirical data at the individual, community, regional, and national levels using qualitative, participatory research methods, lab-in-field experiments, and quantitative mapping and surveys. The qualitative methods include interviews, focus group discussions, and participation in informal and formal interactions.

Our methodological approach has four fundamental aspects. The first is interdisciplinary considerations: we combined an institutionalist approach with a bottom-up approach that draws on peace and conflict studies supplemented with expertise from anthropology and area studies. This brings together two important strands of research that, unfortunately, have not had much interaction. We believe that insights from peace and conflict studies, anthropology, and area studies can help us understand the phenomenon of violent extremism and how it can most effectively be prevented, while insights from institutionalist studies help us understand how states and institutions react to this phenomenon. This completes the current empirical puzzle, enhances the policy relevance of our research, advances the science in this area, and enables a much more context-sensitive approach to preventing violent extremism.

The second fundamental aspect of our methodological approach is the employment of *critical conjunctures* in investigating the drivers of violent extremism (see Bourdieu 1977; Johnson-Hanks 2002). Such a processual approach allows us to see the shifting ways in which social structure, political formations, and life-worlds may connect to radical movements and ideologies. We approach violent extremism and resilience analytically by researching the aggregation of political events, perspectives, and precarity—the critical conjunctures—that lead people to negotiate or contest ethnonationalist or extremist religious movements. Because one factor in isolation cannot explain violent extremism, understanding must be found in how social and political forces combine to afford access to perceived better personal and collective futures. The focus is on how the intersection of different factors (their presence or absence) explains the outcome, namely, violent extremism. In other words, rather than searching in vain for a single overarching explanation of violent extremism, we have worked from the perspective that there are different pathways to violent extremism, each a different combination of factors. The factors leading to radicalization are "rarely coherent, fixed in direction or clear in outcome" (Johnson-Hanks 2002, 865). Presuming them to be so resonates poorly with social and political life and blurs the picture of intersecting forces and aspirations at play.

The third aspect of our methodology is our context-sensitive approach, which allows us to make paradigmatic as well as systematic comparisons, that is, to look at phenomena of a similar order (radicalization and nonradicalization) and juxtapose the specific structures and events that bring them into being in their various instances. Although, for example, poor livelihoods and a Salafi-based interpretation of Islam cannot by themselves explain violent extremism, they may be important vectors, along with social conditions, in the occurrence of extremism (see Roy 2017b). That is, they form one supposed pathway. Another assumed pathway, as evidence shows, involves youths from wealthy backgrounds who experience another factor, such as social alienation (see Khosrokhavar 2021). Although different factors may explain the same outcome in various contexts, not all cases of violent extremism can be explained by a single pathway. The multifaceted nature of violent extremism in the regions under scrutiny suggests that multiple factors play different roles depending on the local and regional context. Hence, a single explanatory framework can encompass various independent and interrelated pathways. We analyzed the relationship of precarity, social options, and political processes in the different regions to detect such critical conjunctures.

This approach suggested that a fruitful way to embark on this research was to identify *decisive moments* as events that enable and afford affiliation with or distance from radical ideas and agendas. Ideological radicalization and hate speech are widespread; more effective prevention of violent extremism entails better understanding the decisive moments when behaviors such as these are transformed into violence. What leads to these decisive moments, and what is their potential for turning violent? Research conducted mainly in France found that ideologically radicalized individuals who turn violent and violent expressions that are later framed in an ideologically radicalized discourse (Roy 2017b) may have a mutually constitutive and opportunistic relationship. The reality is that people can have an unsettled connection to radical environments (Jensen and Vigh 2018); they appear to connect and disconnect in tune with social and political changes. Grievances about injustice, "the system," and lack of opportunity may lead to social anger that can find direction in radical ideologies—this is obvious in the Balkans and the broader MENA region. However, to study this relationship, we must explain under which circumstances these factors combine, how, and why. Rather than basing it on an apparent threshold of radicalization, our approach is premised on the argument that being radical is not a stable status but a position an individual can engage with and inhabit in specific situations. The researchers contributing to this book have studied both individuals' trajectories and narratives, and the contexts and groups in which these individuals may be radicalized to engage in violent extremism.

The fourth fundamental aspect of our methodology is its approach to scale. Because the nature of violent extremism necessitates studies that integrate analyses of global discourses, root causes, and conflict dynamics, several types of actors must be examined (Hansen 2021). Our research moves across scales, ranging from individuals to communities, regional dynamics, and global movements. Using this strategy to move across scales, we were better able to identify critical conjunctures and decisive moments by comparing circumstances in different field sites. Moving from minor to major institutions and aggregations enabled us to gain insights into the specific landscapes of incapacity and closure, possibilities, and affordances that agents are forced by circumstance to navigate. It enabled us to empirically demonstrate how these formations may be practically or ideologically connected. Thus, our work to map such connections recognizes the importance of local social institutions, midlevel formations, and international transregional and nonstate organizations, as well as many informal institutions.

The empirical research has the potential to clarify whether local institutions play a preventive role or are counterproductive to prevention. With better knowledge of regional organizations' role, we gain insight into what the EU can do to support regional institution building to prevent violent extremism beyond its current support of increasing security and stabilization capacity. This issue is particularly relevant given that global and regional actors, including the UN Development Programme (UNDP) and the African Union (AU), in their work to prevent violent extremism (e.g., the UNDP 2016 strategy on preventing violent extremism in Africa), are increasingly dealing with regions and communities, and the state per se is playing a less important role.

Before presenting the book's structure, we delve into the background by conceptualizing the state in these regions.

Conceptualizing the State

In the Balkans and the MENA, the modern state's conception of national identity was challenged from both above and below by supranational and subnational identities. Most of the territories in question were historically part of the same imperial structure, the Ottoman Empire (1299–1922), which ruled the Middle East, North Africa, and the Balkans for over six centuries. Despite variations in the depth and length of Istanbul's rule across the territory, the experience left behind elements of a shared legacy

(Brown 1996; Bryant 2016). The transition from empire to territorial states created similar challenges across the post-Ottoman world.

The Ottoman Empire was based on Sunni Islam but allowed various religious communities to govern themselves. Although its military was mainly Turkish, people of different languages could still advance in society. After the empire dissolved and gave way to individual states, language and specific historical accounts became central to nationalist movements. The post-Ottoman (Western) Balkans went through separate processes of state formation and later disintegration. In the wider MENA region, the shift toward modern statehood was complicated by colonial powers, which led nascent states to resist Western influence. Secular ideologies played a significant role in anti-imperialist movements, but as nationalism and modern statehood failed in the broader MENA, political Islam gained prominence.

The post-Ottoman legacy has significantly influenced most parts of the two regions under study, except for the Sahel and Morocco. The two main regions are home to a spectrum of states, ranging from strong (e.g., Morocco, Egypt, and Serbia) to weaker (e.g., Kosovo) and fragile (e.g., Libya, Mali, and Iraq). Additionally, states in these regions have undergone various transformations with varying degrees of involvement from the international community. These transformations include authoritarian resurgence (e.g., Syria, Turkey, Egypt, and Saudi Arabia) and complex transitions to liberal statehood (e.g., Tunisia and Bosnia). The states under scrutiny also differ significantly in terms of state capacity, social legitimacy, and extent to which social, economic, cultural, and environmental shocks have impacted the role of the state and its social contract with the population. In the case of the Sahel, we can observe how increased climatic variability has led to detrimental livelihoods and heightened social unrest.

In the broader MENA region, we have observed that local conflicts rooted in rights issues can turn violent in areas where states lack capacity and legitimacy and where international responses are inconsistent, ad hoc, or seriously underfunded. These lacks create opportunities for violent insurgencies inspired by radical ideologies to occur and exploit local conflicts (Bøås 2015, 2017). This has occurred in Mali, and similar situations exist across the broader MENA region. In parts of the Balkans, such as Kosovo, the state's role and its status in relation to Serbia is controversial. Here, local conflicts have also been exploited by other actors, including those driven to some extent by radical ideology. However, it's interesting to consider why more people have not become radicalized (Kursani 2018c). This brings us to the significance of understanding the reasons why violent extremism does not occur. What can external stakeholders such as the EU learn about societal resilience from such cases?

Notwithstanding the significant differences within these regions, particularly between the Balkans and the multifaceted MENA region, at least five conceptual commonalities can be observed, all of which may operate in a circular fashion.

First, even if the degree of state weakness and fragility differs considerably between the states in question, our research assumes that all states can be exposed to an internal or external shock. Violent extremism can be seen as constituting such a shock, and thus, what matters more is the state's response capacity. Can the state respond adequately, or if it cannot do so on its own, can it effectively utilize external assistance? The state needs a certain amount of administrative capacity (to act single-handedly or to effectively absorb external assistance) and at least some popular legitimacy. So, although the state can be an integral part of the solution, it can also be a driver of violent extremism, causing an initially minor phenomenon to explode into a much larger problem due to ill-defined and heavy-handed state responses.

Second, these regions are characterized by unsettled states or questionable social contracts. Arising from previous conflicts, the state's form and content (e.g., it territoriality and borders) are, to at least some extent, disputed. In states where the social contract is questioned, social spaces are opened for new (radical) ideologies, be they nationalist or religious, to emerge and to (re)claim legitimacy based on certain ideational narratives pushed forward at the expense of established understandings.

Third, if the state lacks a minimal consensus on what constitutes the polity, it becomes more vulnerable and open to the influence of transnational, regional, or global powers. Key actors in these regions include states and intergovernmental organizations (e.g., United States, Russia, Turkey, Iran, the UN, EU, World Bank, and NATO), as well as nongovernmental transnational forces, such as Salafi-inspired jihadi groups and actors involved in transnationally organized crime. Some, but not all, are connected through the flow of powerful ideas about people, belonging, and the politics of place, articulated through secular democratic visions of place as well as ethnonationalist and Salafi discourses.

Fourth, competing identities characterize these regions. An assortment of ideas exist regarding how to settle the state in terms of nationalism, religion, polity, and belonging.

Fifth, even though these regions circle the EU, they seem to be experiencing a waning of EU soft power, reduced in proportion to their increased geographical distance from the enlargement area.

In both regions under study, many people, lacking a sense of long-term security, feel their lives are insecure and reliant on precarious livelihoods. This lack of a long-term understanding of security, not least its gendered components, is an important dimension that we must tease out from beneath the manifest drivers of violent extremism. It should be acknowledged that the preceding conceptual commonalities are phrased in general terms because they vary significantly between countries and regions.

The Structure of the Book

Part 1: Exploring the Nonoccurrence of Violent Extremism

In the first part of the book, we examine the key concepts guiding this research. Morten Bøås and Kari Osland start in Chapter 2 by exploring enabling environments, factors fueling violent extremism, and local community resilience. In this chapter, the aim is twofold: first, to present and define the concept of an enabling environment, and second, to ask how it can be operationalized in systematic studies on the ground that bring to the fore not only the occurrence of violent extremism but also its nonoccurrence, thereby illuminating local community resilience even in areas seen as prone to radicalization and violent extremism. The chapter explores different varieties of nonoccurrence, from open resistance to more subtle versions. It discusses the foundations of local community resilience to violent extremist ideologies and actors.

In Chapter 3, Abdoul Wakhab Cissé and Henrik E. Vigh delve into definitions of extremism and the role of violent entrepreneurs. They make the point that individuals may approach who or what they identify as extremist or radical figures or formations looking for opportunities to attain socially or culturally defined goals. The authors describe the specific affordances of violent extremism in Mali, Burkina Faso, and Niger and ponder the underlying motive behind the witnessed move to violence. This piece examines characteristics, agendas, modes of negotiating violent extremism, and the opposition to such movements.

In Chapter 4, Ulf Engel interrogates the relevance of the social cohesion concept to the study of nonoccurrence of violent extremism and terrorism (VET) in otherwise enabling environments. He first defines *social cohesion* so that the concept can be applied across world regions and empirical PREVEX cases. He then questions whether it is possible to scientifically measure social cohesion comparatively across world regions without falling into conceptual Eurocentrism. He focuses on four key initiatives that have operationalized social cohesion for development and peacebuilding interventions: the Social Cohesion and Reconciliation (SCORE) project, the Bertelsmann Social Cohesion Radar (SCR), the related UNDP approach, and a project pursued by the German Development Institute. The chapter author concludes that "social cohesion" is a socially constructed time- and space-specific term. The universalist understandings discussed in this chapter are based on Western historical experience and epistemologies of the Global North, which need to be contextualized, deconstructed, and decolonized to become relevant. Recent debates on southern Africa indicate that insight into local context, belief systems, and cosmologies may be an avenue for further fruitful inquiries.

Part 2: Cases from North Africa, the Middle East, and the Balkans

This second part of the book focuses on how nonoccurrence and resilience have played out in our case countries. In Chapter 5, Georges Fahmi and Djallil Lounnas analyze Islamists and the choice to take up arms in Egypt and Algeria. In Egypt, after the military intervention against the rule of the Muslim Brotherhood in July 2013 and the new regime's decision to classify the movement as a terrorist organization, many voices warned that nonviolent Islamists would shift their tactics to include the use of violence, as was the case in Algeria in 1992 when the Algerian authorities decided to cancel the results of the elections after the victory of the Islamists. However, unlike their Algerian counterparts, only a minority among the Muslim Brotherhood and its supporters have decided to do so. This chapter compares the case of the Muslim Brotherhood in Egypt after 2013 to that of the Armed Islamic Group in Algeria after 1992 to understand the drivers that might lead some Islamists to take up arms while others do not.

In Chapter 6, Gilad Ben-Nun and Nizar Messari examine religious resilience and the guardian state in Jordan and Morocco. They focus on the emerging division in approach toward Islamic violent extremism in the MENA region. Some states have relied exclusively on confronting violent extremist groups using traditional security tools, whereas other states, including Jordan and Morocco, have created spaces for political dialogue and deradicalization. Morocco and Jordan consciously and affirmatively offer protected and enclosed spaces for dialogue with violent extremists in their practice. This chapter examines how these countries construct such dialogue spaces and the differences between Jordanian and Moroccan approaches to the practice. The conclusion suggests why the differences between Morocco and Jordan exist and why both countries largely adhere to a pro-dialogue approach, which sets them apart from the majoritarian group of MENA states.

In Chapter 7, Edina Bećirević and Predrag Petrović discuss various forms of violent extremism in Serbia and Bosnia and Herzegovina. They interrogate the origins, drivers, and threat levels of violent extremism. The focus is on Islamist extremism as well as far right extremism. Furthermore, they analyze the effectiveness of legal and institutional frameworks for addressing extremism and terrorism, while raising the question of why Islamist and far right extremism are treated differently in Serbia and Bosnia and Herzegovina. In the concluding section of the chapter, they revisit questions of reciprocal radicalization, the mutual influence of extremisms on each other, the normalization of the far right, and weak responses of state institutions to the far right.

In Chapter 8, Simeon Estatiev, Andreas Lind Kroknes, and Francesco Strazzari focus on the export of radicalization in Kosovo and Tunisia.

Tunisia and Kosovo are often referred to as *countries of origin* from which a significant number of radicalized Islamic militants—following UN definitions—have become foreign terrorist fighters by joining the ranks of jihadist organizations abroad, such as the Islamic State (IS) and some al-Qaeda affiliates. Both states are sometimes given as examples of externalization of the problem. In repressing and persecuting radicalized individuals and in showing a degree of externally assisted institutional solidity, Tunisia and Kosovo have created an environment that encourages militants' departure. The return of foreign fighters after the defeat of IS in the Middle East and the demise of the self-proclaimed Caliphate have, in turn, given rise to a host of new challenges. The connection between the emigration–return of radicalized individuals and domestic political stability is at the core of this chapter. The authors ask two main questions: first, why do secular nation-states in regions as different as North Africa and the Western Balkans produce a relatively high number of jihadis? And second, what are the shared factors or markers of resilience that lead to the nonoccurrence of violent extremism? The authors argue that because of external (securitization) and internal (the Muslim community and its institutions) pressure, radicalized individuals and groups in Tunisia and Kosovo have adopted a strategy to merge into the locally embedded tradition (domestication).

In Chapter 9, Colin Powers, Luca Rainer, and Stephane Lacroix argue that jihadism has provided an ideological focus around which to rally grievances against incumbent regimes in deeply fractured societies. In countries like Syria, Mali, and Iraq, jihadist organizations have managed to trigger, fuel, or contribute to large-scale insurgencies among disenfranchised social groups. The authors explain why jihadist mobilization patterns are uneven despite common structural challenges facing local societies: jihadist mobilizations tend to reproduce the lines of sectarian (tribal, ethnic, etc.) divides, whereby deep horizontal and vertical inequalities contribute to political polarization. At the same time, sectarianism can explain the limits of jihadist mobilizations in the three countries. Local rulers in Syria, Mali, and Iraq have managed to instigate balancing operations by deploying paramilitary formations in areas of limited statehood while they rely on large-scale stabilization and counterinsurgency interventions sponsored by foreign hegemonic actors. The analysis of the complex interactions of terrorism and counterterrorism thus suggests that foreign protection and domestic divide-and-rule tactics have contributed to shoring up local rulers and entrenching their grip on power, fueling authoritarian backsliding, contributing to patronage politics, and perpetrating abuses against civilians in Syria, Mali, and Iraq alike.

In Chapter 10, Kjetil Selvik, Dlawer Ala'Aldeen, Ahmad Mhidi, Diana Mishkova, and Kamaran Palani analyze traditional authority and local community resilience in the cases of Bosnia, Iraq, and Syria. More specifically, they compare how traditional Hanafi Sunni leaders and local community resilience in Bosnia, Iraq, and Syria relate to the phenomenon of *foreign terrorist fighters* (FTFs). The chapter systematically interrogates the role of "moderate Islam" among Muslims in preventing violent extremism. In contrast to Iraq and Syria, the authors argue first that, in the specific Western Balkan context, traditional Muslim identity acts as the main "brake" on adopting radical versions of Islam. Second, and related, is the indispensable role of religious officials, such as muftis or imams, in creating close-knit communities, where radical elements are easily identified, and in preventing, countering, and raising awareness of violent extremism.

In Chapter 11, Laura Berlingozzi, Silvia Carenzi, and Daniela Musina examine the role of external donors and how preventing and countering violent extremism is marketed to them in the cases of Niger, Tunisia, and Syria. More than twenty years after the September 11 attacks and the start of the War on Terror, the counterterrorism agenda has shown its limitations. Traditional hard enemy-centric military approaches have been coupled with softer population-centric approaches, namely, P/CVE, to achieve better results. External donors have devoted enormous amounts of funding to the P/CVE agenda in so-called fragile countries. Thus, on the basis of three case studies—Niger, Tunisia, and Syria—the authors look at how states have attracted economic assistance by portraying themselves as—at least to some extent—proactive upholders of successful P/CVE policies. The authors also highlight how constructing the image projected externally is functional in building internal political consensus.

Part 3: Conclusion

The final part looks at policy and policy implications. In Chapter 12, Dylan Macchiarini Crosson, Pernille Rieker, Tatjana Stankovic, Steven Blockmans, and Elsa Lilja Gunnarsdottir compare the preventing and countering violent extremism policies of the European Union and the United States. The literature primarily emphasizes the EU's counterterrorism- and P/CVE-*specific* focus on using security to address the challenges of violent extremism, arguing that security has taken precedence over good governance and social justice, thereby undermining its effectiveness. The US approach has been described as exhibiting similar tendencies. The authors review general concepts discerned from previous research on EU and US counterterrorism and P/CVE policies and trace this approach over time. After analyzing key documents and conducting interviews with policymakers, they find that both the EU and the United States—in their words, funding and policy implementation—pay significant and increasing attention to the structural causes of radicalization, violent extremism, and terrorism by mobilizing significant development-oriented resources and diplomatic energy. By doing so, both actors balance security concerns and broader socioeconomic and diplomatic engagement. However, the authors' analysis also reveals that the EU and the United States pay less attention to measures specifically promoting good governance and peacebuilding.

In the final chapter, Ulf Engel, Gilad Ben-Nun, Morten Bøås, and Kari Osland discuss the implications of our findings for policy and avenues for future research.

Concluding Remarks

Literature published since September 11, 2001, has improved our understanding of radicalization processes and how groups that promote violent extremism operate. Despite its usefulness, this bulk of research has obstructed our awareness of the fact that most people are not radicalized, even in areas that provide fertile ground for radical ideas. These so-called enabling environments are places of poverty, where individuals lack social mobility, which makes people feel hopeless about their future.

In this book, the empirical evidence is based on cases from the Balkans, the Middle East, North Africa, and the Sahel. There are commonalities even across such a large universe of cases. Local communities demonstrate different degrees of resilience, but this is often overlooked and misunderstood by international actors, who are much more interested in the occurrence of violent extremism and hard security measures to fight terrorists in accordance with the still-dominant view of a global war on terror that emerged after September 11. In the chapters ahead, we are more interested in the nonoccurrence of violent extremism and why some communities are less susceptible to it than others.

Notes

1. PREVEX (grant number 870724) was funded by the European Union's Horizon 2020 modality. For further information see https://www.prevex-balkan-mena.eu/.

2

Enabling Environments

Morten Bøås and Kari Osland

Violent extremism is like a slippery soap—hard to grasp. Most of us have our views about what violent extremism is, what type of acts of violence qualifies, and what types of ideas, ideologies, and belief systems we would say promote it. The challenge, however, from an academic angle is that this is almost exclusively subjective. What we deem as violent extremism may be perfectly justifiable in the eyes of others. For example, indiscriminate violence may be used as part of a strategy of asymmetrical warfare against a stronger opponent or may be deemed legitimate used against someone seen as an enemy, intruder, or unbeliever. These individuals are considered sinful enemies of God who deserve whatever punishment those on the right side of religion (and thereby history) see fit to expose them to. Therefore, people disagree about what constitutes violent extremism, making it hard for states to reach a consensus on a universally accepted definition (see Amit and Al Kafy 2022; Stephens, Sieckelinc, and Boutellier 2019). Consequently, international law does not codify violent extremism (Bøås 2024; OHCHR 2008).

Although no universally accepted definition exists, violent extremism is commonly associated with certain specific features. Most often, it involves nonstate armed groups that either employ asymmetrical tactics of warfare, including attacks on civilian targets and populations, or inspire others not necessarily parts of the group to conduct such attacks. As a field of inquiry associated with insurgencies and groups defined as terrorists, violent extremism has been examined since the dawn of war studies, and the academic field of terrorist studies appeared already in the early 1970s (see, for example, Jenkins 1975).

The shock of the September 11 attacks, however, created an intense focus on the manifestations of violent extremism, on the actors involved, and on the attacks they had perpetrated. This led to extensive and important literature that provided valuable insights into the history and dynamics of groups such as al-Qaeda and the Islamic State (IS) (Kepel 2005; Neumann 2006; Hegghammer 2010; Lacroix 2011; Byman 2015; Hegghammer and Nesser 2015; Roy 2017b). However, the intense focus on the manifestations of violent extremism also contributed to the creation of a blind zone. The literature neglects the very fact that most people are not radicalized, and even in what has been defined as areas conducive to violent extremism—what we call enabling environments—most people are not radicalized.

This suggests that many local communities harbor a high level of resilience against violent extremist ideas and the groups behind those ideas. Therefore, this chapter aims to establish a framework for understanding the relationship of drivers of violent extremism in enabling environments, determinants of occurrence, and nonoccurrence in enabling environments. To understand the latter, we need to focus on local community resilience, what constitutes the basis of local community resilience, and why it can be present in one local community but not in another within the same enabling environment. In this regard, we have drawn some inspiration from Anderson and Wallace's (2013) volume that discusses why people and communities opt out of war and subsequent strategies to prevent violent conflict.

Enabling Environments

We define the *enabling environment* as an area where the combination of specific factors present creates a situation where expressions of violent extremism are likely to occur. The factors supposed to facilitate the emergence of violent extremism are usually listed in the literature as well as in policy documents as resource scarcity and poverty, high unemployment, few educational opportunities, and a sense of alienation and marginalization from the state, often in combination with heavy-handed counterterrorism measures from state security forces (see UNDP 2016).

To varying degrees of severity, these factors are present in the regions of interest in the Western Balkans, the Middle East, North Africa, and the Sahel. There are enormous differences between these regions, but distinct similarities are also present, as spelled out in the introduction to this volume. The states in these regions are all, to varying degrees, fragile. Albeit on very different scales, they face economic constraints and challenges, high unemployment and underemployment that particularly affects youths, educational sectors in crisis, and parts of the population feeling alienated by the state they are supposed to belong to.

Although acts of violent extremism tend to be justified on religious or political grounds, the path to participate in extremism often starts with more basic material grievances, usually issues concerning lack of security, lack of employment, and other economic problems. The state may be perceived as playing a role in creating these grievances, while, in some cases, it is also too weak to control local conflicts, which leaves a space that violent extremists can exploit. This creates a local environment in which violent groups inspired by extremist ideologies can find ways to integrate into local communities (Bøås 2015), for example, by offering protection and support in local struggles over land rights and access to water. This is the case in the Sahel, where most states are relatively weak and local militia groups exert quite a high degree of social, if not always territorial, control that allows them to present alternative ideas about how life should be on the basis of their interpretation of religious texts and practices (Bøås 2025).

Nonetheless, even in an environment conducive to violent extremism—an enabling environment—most people are not radicalized. An important question that this chapter will attempt to clarify is, therefore, what turns an enabling environment into one where violent extremist ideas and groups supportive of these ideas gain traction to the extent that they dominate the social sphere and gain acceptance for violent actions? However, we must also investigate the other side of this equation and thereby ask why some communities remain resilient even if all the factors supposed to be conducive to the manifestation of radicalization and violent extremism are present. To achieve this, we first elaborate on the enabling environment framework, highlighting that cases of both occurrence and nonoccurrence of violent extremism are possible. We then delve into the drivers of violent extremism, with examples from North Africa and the Sahel, the Middle East, and the Western Balkans. Third comes a section where we explore further the issue of nonoccurrence in enabling environments by looking at cases in the Sahel and the Western Balkans before we end the chapter with concluding comments regarding policy prescriptions and further research.

The Enabling Environment and Cases of Occurrence and Nonoccurrence

We defined the *enabling environment* as a space where the socioeconomic conditions caused by a combination of specific factors create a situation where violent extremism is likely. In these environments, disadvantaged communities or individuals may become so disenfranchised by the state and society that they could be susceptible to supporting, joining, or implementing organized violence inspired by political or religious extremist ideology.

If this happens, the enabling environment has become a site of various deep-seated grievances that provide the precursors of such ideologies with emotional entry points to garner support (see Rupesinghe and Bøås 2018). This can happen, for example, if an armed group approaches those who are (or feel) most vulnerable in society and offers them the means of escaping a situation of despair and lack of direction in favor of the dead certainty of violent resistance (see Bøås and Dunn 2013a). Recruiting among the poorest and least educated is a well-proven insurgency tactic: targeting destitute young men (but also women) who are considered more malleable to indoctrination by the group targeting them. Those targeted by violent extremist groups may be in a life situation where they feel that they have little, if anything at all, to lose by joining or supporting an extremist group.

This can happen in an enabling environment, but we stress that there is no path dependency between living in an enabling environment and becoming a violent extremist. An enabling environment means that most of the factors that, according to the literature, are conducive to the occurrence of violent extremism are present. Whether violent extremism manifests and gains social traction depends on several factors we conceptually define as *decisive moments*, cases of occurrence and nonoccurrence of violent extremism and the effect of preventive measures (see Figure 2.1). Together, this constitutes the enabling environment framework.

The first core feature is the decisive moment. Although ideological radicalization bordering on hate speech may be widespread, it is crucial to

Figure 2.1 The Enabling Environment

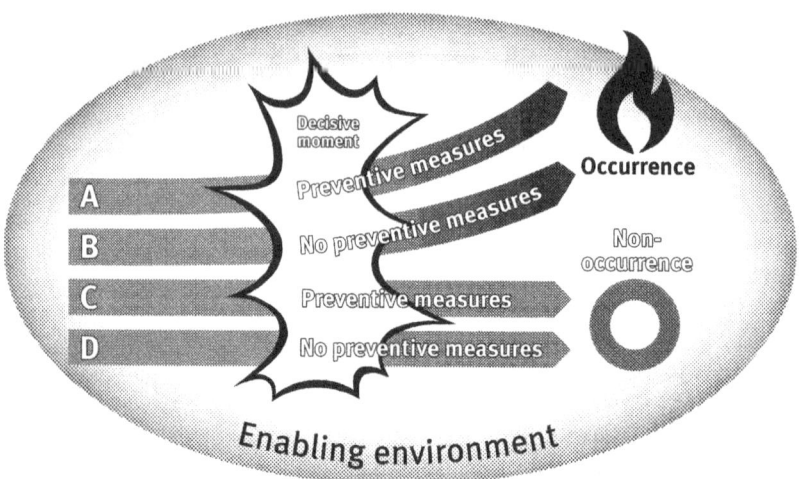

understand the moments in which this is transformed into violence. What leads to these decisive moments, and what is the potential for violence? Sometimes, the nonoccurrence of violent extremism in an enabling environment that has reached a decisive moment—a potential tipping point—is due to a successful intervention by a local or external stakeholder.

The second core feature of the analytical framework is the occurrence or nonoccurrence of violence. We pay particular attention to instances of nonoccurrence of violence in the enabling environment (Raets 2017). Why do some communities display much greater resilience to violent extremist ideologies than others? What role do local community leaders, including religious leaders, play? Do women play a particular role in these situations? Understanding why violence does *not* occur is often more relevant for strengthening resilience and devising preventive measures than understanding why it does happen. Therefore, looking at this feature helps us understand with greater precision the factors that make individual communities more resilient.

This leads us to the third core feature of the enabling environment model, which is the effect of preventive measures. Cases B and C in the model show the usual anticipated outcome of prevention or no prevention. However, in some cases, we are faced with evident preventive measures, but violence still occurs (see case A in the model). In other cases, no visible preventive measures are taken, but anticipated violence still does not happen (see case D in the model). This feature of the model sheds light on when and where preventive measures are working so that we can prescribe what works or does not. We assume that an improved understanding of how different drivers of violent extremism operate and why extremism escalates into violence in some places but not in others is the key to identifying effective prevention strategies.

Therefore, this model's key innovative aspect is our strong focus on nonoccurrence. We observed that most research on violent extremism focuses on answering the question of why people take up arms rather than on answering the reverse question of why people living in enabling environments often choose *not* to become involved in political violence. Frequently cited factors—such as political grievances, socioeconomic deprivation, and deeply conservative religious views (see, for example, UNDP 2022)—should, in theory, have led to much broader populations joining violent groups. However, despite concerted attempts by violent extremists to recruit more broadly, the overall majority of those living in enabling environments remain resilient.

Thus, the most relevant questions for future research are: What prevents decisive moments from tipping over into violence, and what prevents radicalization in the first place? Cragin (2014, 337) argues that it is impossible to understand pathways to radicalization or to design policies to preempt them without a complementary knowledge of why individuals resist the influence of violent extremism. Policies designed to prevent violent extremism need to work on both levels: weakening the factors pushing for violence while strengthening the factors resisting such a path. Hence, policies designed to prevent violent extremism must incorporate knowledge of why individuals and groups resist such influence, even in enabling environments.

Drivers of Violent Extremism

Violent extremism does not occur in a social vacuum, and in the regions of the world that this volume is concerned about, most of the usual factors attributed to the manifestations of violent extremism are present. Poverty is widespread in the Middle East and North Africa, and in the Western Balkans; many communities experience economic and political marginalization. This may lead people to feel a sense of alienation from a state that they think has never cared much for their well-being, safety, and security. Youth and young men are particularly prone to perceived and real marginalization that could set them on a path to alienation, which could make them more inclined to accept extremist religious-ideological manipulation and indoctrination (see also UNDP 2016). We also know from our studies that the chances that this will happen increase with the presence of two other factors: rights-based grievances that, if expressed at times, are met with very heavy-handed state responses (see Bøås 2015; Bøås, Cissé, and Mahamane 2020).

What this means is that, although rising poverty and increased inequality, dysfunctional and deteriorating educational systems, and a sense of living in an insecure environment matter as potential drivers of violent extremism, we cannot ignore the role and responsibility of the state. This suggests that the real driver of violent extremism often is the state, not only indirectly through its inability to give its inhabitants a sense of meaning, belonging, and economic safety but also directly through heavy-handed responses to expressions of radicalism and resistance against a life that for many seems relatively meaningless because it does not give them even the faintest promise of upward social mobility. Both these expressions of state complicity in the spread of violent extremism are vividly visible in the case of the Sahel; therefore, this is the place in this chapter's universe of cases where we start our inquiries before moving on to the Middle East and the Balkans.

Under such circumstances, what often emerges is a scenario of competing authorities. This happens most frequently when state authority is weak and the state lacks legitimacy. Because the state lacks the capacity or willingness to care for and protect its citizens, the latter view the state as dysfunctional and corrupted. This leads to grievances against the state that can be instrumentalized by violent entrepreneurs using extremist ideologies and discourses. The competing authorities that we conceptualize as violent entrepreneurs (see Chapter 3 for a deeper discussion) are nonstate actors that use violence. They have some form of political agenda, but it works in tandem with different types of income-generating activities. They rule by force and violence, but they also distribute (some) resources, provide some level of order, and offer protection to (at least parts of) the population in the areas they control or attempt to control. Their presence among rural communities in the Sahel and parts of the Middle East is often more substantial than that of international community actors and their national allies (Bøås 2015). These nonstate actors are less visible in North Africa and the Western Balkans, but even there, we find them in specific rural or urban settings.

Most of the violent entrepreneurs we are concerned with are local in origin, but some may have solid local-global connections. By this, we mean that the form of violent extremism we study in this volume's empirical universe is local but with global connections. We, therefore, need to distinguish between local-global connections, where groups deliberately, purposefully, and strategically navigate to become active operational entities in more extensive global networks of extremist ideology, and those violent entrepreneurs that mainly employ such strategies as a branding exercise to look more powerful, international, and omnipotent than they are (Bøås and Dunn 2017).

The Sahel is increasingly presented as the new global frontier of jihadi-inspired violent extremism (Council on Foreign Relations 2023; Demuynck and Böhm 2023). Although the most important nonstate armed groups are inspired by the religious doctrines of al-Qaeda or Daesh, this does not mean that they have become operational branches of global jihadi networks. Their struggle is almost exclusively local and regional. Although an ideologically convinced leadership exists, the evidence we present later in this chapter suggests that the majority of those who join these groups are recruited less based on religion and more based on grievances concerning lack of employment, education, and social mobility and the prevalence of violent conflict and subsequent lack of security in the area where they live.

When all these factors are present, we may be confronted with so-called decisive moments. These are the moments when extremist ideas are transformed into violence and violent acts. Typically, this may be a situation where chaos erupts as a result of unforeseen incidents, which create a cloud of uncertainty about the events that have transpired. Central to this chaos is often the belief that an act has been committed against "Us"—a perception of a situation that may or may not be accurate. The critical aspect is that people feel an existential threat, a profound sense of injustice, or deep insecurity. A pertinent example from the Western Balkans is the Kosovo riots of March 17–19, 2004.

After the 1999 war, Kosovo experienced a period of relative stability (Bátora et al. 2018). However, on March 17, 2004, rumors started circulating that Serbs were allegedly responsible for the drowning of three young Albanian children (Human Rights Watch 2004). This sparked ethnic Albanians to violently riot against Serbs and other non-Albanians, which caught many off-guard, including the substantial international presence of the North Atlantic Treaty Organization (NATO)-led Kosovo Force (KFOR), the UN Interim Administration Mission in Kosovo police (UNMIK police), and the Kosovo Police Service. Around 4,100 Serbs, Roma, Ashkali, and other non-Albanian minorities were displaced, and 550 homes and 27 Orthodox churches and monasteries were burned (Human Rights Watch 2004). Though surprising, this incident manifested in underlying ethnic tensions linked to security and group status (Kelmendi and Skendaj 2022). It was also proof of the gap between the hopes held by the majority Kosovo-Albanian population just after the NATO intervention, which ended the war in 1999, and the experienced reality five years later (Visoka 2017).

This is an example of a decisive moment in an enabling environment, where preventive measures had been established but were insufficient to prevent the outburst of riots—although the rioting lasted only for a limited period. This case also illustrates how the enabling environment model, discussed earlier, is an ideal-typical model, with most real-world instances falling in between. Although it is crucial to understand these moments in which an idea is transformed into violence, it is equally, if not even more pertinent to comprehend why a situation does not reach its decisive moment even in an enabling environment where all the factors discussed here are present. Therefore, we must also give due attention to the cases of nonoccurrence because these may very well tell us more about how violent extremism can be prevented than focusing postfactually only on why it occurred.

Corruption and State Fragility

While the differences among and level of diversity of the case studies are significant, there are also important similarities regarding drivers of violent extremism. State fragility, corruption and bad governance, an education system that does not work, heavy-handed state security approaches, and misplaced international interventions are present from the Western Balkans to the Middle East, North Africa, and the Sahel.

If we want to understand the drivers of violence and the occurrence of violent extremism in the Sahel, the situation in central Mali offers a vivid illustration. Here, the region of Mopti is situated at the crossroads of the North and the South of Mali. Whereas most of the population are Muslims, the region is also a melting pot of all major ethnic groups in Mali. It is densely populated and not only ethnically diverse but also socioeconomically diverse, with various economic groups: pastoralists (Fulani and Tuareg), sedentary farmers (Bambara, Dogon, Malinke, and Songhay), and fishermen (Bozo). Thus, what the inner delta brings together is three different types of livelihoods—herders, farmers, and fishers—who have entirely different interests in using the scarce water and land resources. That is, water and land are resources these groups have fundamentally different functional interests in. In the Inner Delta, these issues of scarcity have never been easily reconciled. As population pressure increases, traditional authority wanes and state authority is increasingly dysfunctional and corrupted. Because these resources are essential for survival, the right to access them must be defended using all means necessary. Because the French intervention of 2013 (first Operation Serval and later Operation Barkhane) failed to defeat the jihadi rebellion (see Bøås 2015), one jihadi faction—the Katiba Macina—started to operate in the Mopti region. When a heavy-handed security response followed this in the form of state security forces profiling young Fulani herdsmen as "jihadis" and "terrorists," the situation in Mopti reached a decisive moment. Not only did support and acceptance of the Katiba Macina grow among parts of the Fulani population in the region but also, consequently, other ethnic groups also started to organize and arm their militias to provide security for their local communities.

What emerged was a cocktail of armed nonstate groups of jihadi insurgents and ethnic self-defense groups. Consequently, the relations between various local communities that traditionally used to be at least cordial, if not exactly friendly, were fragmented and polarized. The self-defense groups of the Songhay and the Dogon—respectively, the Donzos and the Dana—are widely understood by the Fulani community as driven by the aim of expelling and killing every Fulani in the region and claiming their land and cattle. As one local Fulani leader expressed it:

> Their goal is to create disorder to seize and steal our properties. Once we have left the area and abandoned our hamlets, they will take our properties. Their goal is to exterminate every Fulani and take our land. (Bøås et al. 2021, 13)

Dogon and Songhay communities in Mopti see the Donzos and the Dana as defenders, and they claim that the Katiba Macina are violently forcing them to submit to an extreme version of Sharia theology. To Songhay and Dogon communities, the Katiba Macina represents not only a new and unknown danger that hides in forest bases and roams the region on motorbikes but also an attempt to establish Fulani hegemony in Mopti. Because Fulani and Dogon communities, therefore, increasingly seem to stand on opposite sides in violent conflicts, it is easy to conclude that an ethnic element has been added to an already complex conflict. However, interestingly, both Fulani and Dogon respondents to our fieldwork survey reacted to this supposition. In their view, this is "neither a religious conflict nor an ethnic one, but an economic conflict caused by bad governance" (Bøås et al. 2021, 18). This suggests that the root causes are not necessarily extremist ideology or religious views but a conflict over scarce resources that has exploded into violence because of desperation and fear of losing access to the primary resources of land and water that are essential for the survival of their local communities.

Going more deeply into the ethnographic details of our fieldwork in Mali, the conflict over scarce resources becomes quite clear and underlines the complex micropolitics that can create a decisive moment. A snapshot of our fieldwork data from the commune of Bandiagara in Mopti reveals how intercommunal conflicts over access rights and the use of resources can drive a community to collaborate with jihadi insurgents: After the 2016 municipal elections in Bandiagara, the losing candidates from the ADEMA-PASJ party were worried about being excluded. They feared losing their representation in the municipality assembly, which would preclude them from voicing their concerns on land rights issues. Consequently, two prominent leaders from the area brokered a deal with the Katiba Macina in the hope of gaining by force what they had lost in the elections. Using Bandiagara as a base, the Katiba Macina started attacking neighboring villages and taking control of fertile land that their new allies in Bandiagara could utilize (Bøås et al. 2021).

These findings dovetail with those of previous studies. For example, Bøås, Cissé, and Mahamane (2020) argue that a key strategy of jihadi-inspired Sahel insurgencies is for violent extremists to appropriate local conflicts, usually related to land usage, as a way to integrate locally. In the Bandiagara case just described, we also see that the opposite can be true: local opportunists may exploit the presence of armed groups in the vicinity to reverse local power configurations. Poorly managed conflicts cultivate a spirit of revenge, and in the region of Mopti (but also elsewhere in the Sahel), communities have turned to extremist groups to take revenge and to protect themselves and their property. This is the case not only in some Fulani communities but also in Dogon, Bambara, and Songhay communities in Mopti.

The complex drivers of the violent extremism equation outlined here are not unique to Mali and the Sahel. We also find similar micropolitical dynamics at play in the Middle East. Iraq, for example, continues to suffer from fragility, instability, and conflict, which in the past has enabled the occurrence of violent extremism across the country. However, as studies from our colleagues at the Middle East Research Institute (MERI) in Erbil have shown, there are huge variations at the local provincial level, and Nineveh, for example, suffers from tensions between urban and rural areas that are exacerbated by conflicts between some groups in Nineveh and in Baghdad fueled by geopolitical tensions (see Ala'Aldeen, Mohammed, and Wirya 2022). The liberation of Nineveh from IS in 2017 did not offer a solution to these long-standing conflicts. Instead, the forces that have dominated post-IS Nineveh have played a prominent role in feeding these conflicts, limiting the attempts that have been made to build local resilience against violent extremism.

The political elite that captured and since 2017 has dominated the local administration in Nineveh is backed by the Shia Popular Mobilization Units. The minority Christian groups have received generous international economic grants compared to other religious communities. In contrast, the Sunni Arab minority has once again been marginalized and suffers from the stigma of association with IS. It is, therefore, no surprise that Sunni Arabs' trust in state institutions, let alone their ability to achieve peace and stability in the province, remains at its lowest.

This means that not only is this part of Iraq very much still an enabling environment but also a new decisive moment may materialize once more. Local government administration in Nineveh is still based on sectarian power-sharing and characterized by discrimination based on religion and ethnicity, which opens social spaces for agents of violent extremism to operate. Widespread and increasing corruption becomes the hallmark of governance and, thereby, drives further rivalry and conflict in the governorate. Limited access to education in the post-2017 phase is another concern, because this is another key feature of an enabling environment. The defeat of IS was not accompanied by measures aimed at returning children and youths to school. This is particularly evident in the camps where IS members' families have been held since the military defeat, where many who should have been to school do not have access to any educational facilities (Ala'Aldeen, Mohammed, and Wirya 2022). This combined with the lack of appropriate programs for reintegrating these children and youths into the public school system leaves them completely excluded from access to education. Lack of education and, we would say, lack of opportunity to engage socially with children and youth from other ethnic and religious communities in school will continue to make them vulnerable to agents of violent extremism, who will have a substantial pool of disadvantaged and alienated youths to recruit from.

Unemployment and youth unemployment are top concerns in Nineveh. The disastrous economic consequences of IS occupation exacerbated an economic decline of the governorate that was already dire because of high levels of corruption through a patronage system organized around the key political parties. Nineveh's economic recovery continues to be hampered by bad governance and persistent conflict and displacement.

As was the case in Mali, also in this part of Iraq, the state, the state's security forces, and the militarization of society that nearly always follows on the heels of such behavior by the state are barriers to stabilization, peacebuilding, and the fight against violent extremism. As one group either arms themselves or is armed by the government, other groups begin to believe that security can be provided only by an armed group (see Ala'Aldeen, Mohammed, and Wirya 2022). In Nineveh, the militarization of society occurred in parallel to the fight against IS that was consolidated after the liberation of the governorate. These groups include the 30th Brigade, composed mainly of the Shabak; the Babylonian Brigades, with a Christian minority and an Arab (Sunni and Shia) majority, most of whom are not originally from Nineveh; the Nineveh Plain Protection Units (mainly Christian); the Sinjar Protection Units, consisting of Yezidi fighters; a Shia Turkmen majority group; and the Tribal Mobilization Forces of Sunni Arabs. Although perceived differently by different communities in the governorate, the consequence of this militarization of society based on ethnoreligious groups widens the gap between and within communities and further delegitimizes and weakens state authority and control. This represents yet another key feature of an enabling environment that could turn into a decisive moment for the recruitment of violent extremist groups that promise to restore order and control based on an extremist religious and social script.

Following these lines of argument, we can see that local rights-based conflicts turn violent in areas where states lack capacity and legitimacy and where international responses are haphazard, ad hoc, and seriously underfunded. Such circumstances open social spaces and physical landscapes onto which violent insurgencies inspired by radical ideology can maneuver to appropriate local conflict (Bøås 2015). This is, for instance, what has happened in Mali, and there are several relatively similar situations across the broader Middle East and North Africa (MENA) region. In parts of the Balkans, for example, in Kosovo, the state's role and status in relation to Serbia are contentious. There, local conflict has also been appropriated by other actors, including, to a certain extent, those motivated by radical ideology.

Despite the absence of violent extremism in the Western Balkans since the Yugoslav War of the 1990s, it remains crucial to maintain vigilance in the region for several reasons. First, from a historical perspective, the phenomenon of foreign fighters first emerged during the Yugoslav War in the 1990s. During this period, foreign fighters from the Middle East joined the conflict to support Muslim fighters, known as mujahidin, particularly in Bosnia and Herzegovina and Kosovo (Duyvesteyn and Peeters 2015). Additionally, there were reports of Russian fighters aiding Serb forces and European fighters supporting Croat forces (Popovic 2021; Mishkova et al. 2021, 11). Postwar, many mujahidin were granted citizenship, leading to the establishment of several Salafi communities. These groups actively attempted to propagate their ideology within the local communities (Mishkova et al. 2021, 23–24). Second, as a probable consequence of these developments, many foreign fighters from this region joined conflicts in Iraq, Syria, and Ukraine (Azinovic 2018; Global Initiative Against Transnational Organized Crime 2023). Third, the Western Balkans host several communities in what could be described as enabling environments. These are areas where underlying factors may predispose the community to violent extremism and where a single triggering event, a decisive moment, could potentially ignite violent extremism.

In the Western Balkans, such underlying factors are overlapping division lines in ethnicity and religion, frozen conflicts with competing narratives about the war, high unemployment and scarcity of resources, low degree of horizontal and vertical trust, relative deprivation, and few opportunities for social mobility (Mishkova et al. 2021). Furthermore, studies have shown that in the Western Balkans, radical Islamist ideology and radical ethnonationalist or far right ideologies both inflame and maintain each other (see Bećirević 2018; Stojkovski and Kalajdziovski 2018). Thus, as the in-depth studies of violent extremism in Kosovo by Shpend Kursani (2018a, 2018b, 2018c) suggest, the intriguing question should be centered on why even more people in the region have not been radicalized. Also, Georges Fahmi (2017), an expert on the Muslim Brotherhood, posed a similar question related to this group in 2017. These observations take us back to the importance of understanding the logic behind cases of nonoccurrence in enabling environments.

Cases of Nonoccurrence in Enabling Environments

Although it might seem naive to discuss cases of nonoccurrence in environments as enabling as those in Mali and Iraq, this perspective gains depth when we explore people's perceptions of the reasons why acquaintances join groups like the Katiba Macina in Mali or IS in Iraq. It is, in fact, quite remarkable that we find such similar motivations for joining extremist groups in two countries as different as Iraq and Mali. Despite their only primary commonality being they are Muslim-majority countries, research reveals a fascinating trend: In surveys conducted by Ala'Aldeen, Mohammed, and Wirya (2022; in Iraq) and Bøås et al. (2021; in Mali), only 10 to 15 percent of the respondents believed that acquaintances who joined violent extremist groups did so because of religious conviction. Instead, a majority indicated issues such as state repression, poverty, unemployment, and lack of education as the primary drivers.

Some of the respondents in Mali who had intimate knowledge of people who had joined the Katiba Macina pointed to a feeling of being abandoned by the state as the decisive moment for the individual in question (Bøås et al. 2021). This is noteworthy because it suggests that when extremist ideas manifest in local communities in Mopti, this should be seen not as a sign of an anti-state rebellion but rather as a craving for a state that would work for them.

This insight is important because it challenges the prevailing notion in mainstream scholarship about the primary motivations for joining violent extremist insurgencies. If extremist beliefs are not the primary driver, these conflicts must be rooted in material conditions more than previously thought. This revelation also highlights the likelihood of more moderate religious views being prevalent in these societies than commonly assumed. This indicates that, despite a minority who join insurgencies with extremist ideology, local communities may still exhibit significant resilience against extremist ideas.

Findings by Mishkova et al. (2021, 71) indicate that, for the Western Balkans, two types of factors have strengthened communities' resilience against violent extremism. The first category includes religious counternarratives, social cohesion, and civic values linked to what the authors call "the radicalization wave" (from 2011 through 2014). The second category includes the hard approach by state institutions and the soft response by international donors and civil society organizations, which is linked to the period after the radicalization wave (from 2015 onward).

As for the first category, the prevalence of moderate Islam in the Balkans is significant. Muslim communities primarily adhere to the Hanafi Sunni tradition, which differs from radical Islamic interpretations. The region's history of communism has also nurtured a secular mindset, leading to a unique, less conservative Islamic practice than the religion practiced on the Arabian Peninsula. Furthermore, through their studies, Mishkova et al. (2021, 76–83) found that entrepreneurs of violence carefully analyze communities before advancing their agendas. They avoid targeting mosques, communities, or religious leaders who have a history of actively addressing and combating violent extremism. Muftis and imams play a crucial role in fostering tight-knit communities where radical elements can be readily detected. They are key in efforts to prevent and counter extremism and raise awareness about these issues (87).

As for the second category, Mishkova et al. (2021, 83–84) identify that the way violent extremism is met matters. First, they point to rigorous state actions against violent extremism that have confined extremists' activities to propaganda, disrupted group organization as a result of heightened visibility, and projected legal risks onto the group. Second, they also identify the effects of the softer approach, led by civil society organizations and supported by international bodies, that focuses on preventing and countering extremism. Such an approach includes referral systems, capacity building, awareness campaigns, and community-level projects to bolster grassroots resilience.

Our research findings from Mali corroborate results of our Balkan research, particularly the role of traditional and religious leadership. Segou, the region neighboring Mopti, has shown much more resilience toward the forces of violent extremism. Although the region is slightly closer to Bamako, there are also clear indications that the jihadi insurgents have met more discursive resistance in Segou than what has been the case in Mopti. The question is why. Our research indicates that the relative nonoccurrence of violent extremism in Segou can be explained by stronger social cohesion (see Bøås et al. 2021). The region has experienced fewer access-based conflicts between farmers and herders than Mopti. This suggests that traditional authority is less likely to be eroded by this potentially violent competition and has, therefore, been able to maintain traditional values that reduce causes of conflict within and between local communities. Another important factor is that Segou has been exposed to a different land dynamic from that of Mopti. Ever since the 1930s, agricultural production in Segou has been export-oriented, which has created an environment prone to investment and has encouraged an entrepreneurial mindset to which the "liberation" semantics of the violent extremist groups under the guise of Islam and "jihad" seem to have less appeal. This is supported by a historical tradition in Segou of being an important center of Sufism and Islamic teaching.

Contrary to other places in Mali and the Sahel, Sufism has here seen a revitalization of traditional praxis resulting from the development of new Sufi figures who stand at the crossroads of charismatic leadership and the newly emerging stylistic trends of youth movements (Bøås et al. 2021). What we can draw from this is that, first, the absence of local conflict that forces of violent extremism can appropriate is essential to resilience. The local traditional authority can maintain its position as an institution of arbitration that earns local respect and legitimacy as it continues to provide public goods. Second, suppose this also contributes to an economy with a certain level of inclusivity, as seems to be the case in Segou, which fosters an environment of economic entrepreneurship and peaceful activities. Both conditions may be important sources of local resilience against violent extremism.

Conclusion

Despite the very distinct characteristics of communities in the Sahel, the Middle East, and the Western Balkans, some driving forces toward violent extremism arc similar in these regions, making them each an enabling environment: there is high unemployment, lack of resources, weak governments, and few possibilities for social mobility, especially among the youth. Furthermore, although people living in these enabling environments have many good reasons for being angry, few become radicalized to the extent of taking up weapons. We find that most people are not radicalized and that many of these communities have a high level of resilience.

What can external stakeholders learn about societal resilience from such cases? Although the importance of contextual understanding cannot be overemphasized, our cases have the following characteristics in common: First, they have a long history of moderate religion and ideology. Second, respected local leaders, families, or individuals who protect the tradition of moderation are present. Third, these leaders are seen as noncorrupt and deliver or do something that the local community sees as valuable.

Last, and in conclusion, the finding that extremist beliefs are not the primary motivation for joining violent insurgencies in regions like Iraq and Mali or becoming foreign fighters from the Western Balkans has significant implications. It challenges the dominant academic perspective and suggests that these conflicts are more materially based. It also points to a more widespread presence of moderate religious views in these societies than previously recognized. For policymakers, this emphasizes the importance of addressing underlying material issues such as state repression, poverty, unemployment, and lack of education. It also underlines the potential effectiveness of reinforcing and supporting the inherent resilience of local communities against extremist ideologies. To do so, we need to understand the context of the case in question and then support and strengthen the local community leaders so that they can continue to contribute with something that is seen as valuable in their community. To do so and to avoid delegitimizing these local actors of resilience, outside actors must have the lightest possible footprint. Local leaders must be their own agents, not any outside actor's agents. Thus, to prevent violent extremism from happening, we need to understand not only why it happens but also why it does *not* occur in what we have called enabling environments.

3

The Entrepreneurs of Violence

*Abdoul Wakhab Cissé and
Henrik Vigh*

Long-term ethnographic research on militant youths commonly highlights how mobilization and radicalization are entangled into larger social worlds. Rather than being isolated from the mundane, as extremism dislodged from everyday life, such studies are attentive to how extremism is seen to provide alternative states of order and rights and how mobilization is seen to afford life chances and security. Who are identified as extremist or radical figures or formations by figures in power may be locally approached for their potential in providing opportunities to attain socially or culturally defined goals. Building on a comparative mixed methods study from the Sahel—that is, Mali, Burkina Faso, and Niger—in this chapter we look at the social contingency of radicalization and extremism and detail how people may mobilize into such movements to survive and maintain viable existences.

The point of departure is twofold. On the one hand, we highlight how so-called extremist groups and tenets crosscut national boundaries and political entities. Militant groups and movements in the Sahel have profoundly regional rather than merely national dynamics. On the other, it becomes clear from the ethnography that violent extremism emerges in relation to unjustly distributed or directly lacking states of order. Rather than merely being forces of disorder, such movements gain traction in countries where the existing order is seen to benefit only a tiny part of the population or in zones where the governing order is perceived as predacious and rapacious.

The three field sites covered in this chapter can be comprehended as intertwined within a larger region, sharing cultural, social, and political dynamics and deep-seated disgruntlement regarding the distribution of resources, power, and, not least, suffering. The states in question are perceived to have serviced a small elite at the expense of the population. The state has been either minimally or negatively present in the areas where violent extremism has gained a foothold. Extremism is understood as a movement aimed at destroying the existing order through violence and, if necessary, gaining backing in social systems that are unable to guarantee the well-being of their populations. In politically, economically, or socially disadvantaged areas, as well as in poor neighborhoods and slums, calls for radical change, destruction, and the establishment of new systems often seem necessary for achieving basic levels of influence, resources, and recognition.

The point is perhaps a bland one, yet in a period when radicalization and violent extremism are, at least in the Global North, predominantly associated with Islamist movements, it seems pertinent to point out the obvious, namely, that one is hard-pressed to find examples of violent Islamic extremism that does not emerge upon a background of existing radical exploitation and oppression. In other words, the institutionalization of, for example, sharia is commonly predated by predatory regimes, where sharia stands out as a more just and benevolent order, just as violent extremism most often overturns not a benign order but a brutal one. The latter instigates a sequence of violent societal changes; the former, an encompassing body of rights.

Radicalization, as a particular trajectory into violent extremism, is, in this perspective, simultaneously a move away from a life deemed lacking in worth and a move toward an envisioned better state of being. Extremism emerges within crises rather than merely being a phenomenon that is conducive to crises (Vigh 2008). Extremist groups often end up being as repressive as the forces they overturn. Yet, they gain their initial support by proclaiming themselves to overturn wrongs and provide better futures for the people they identify with. The remainder of this chapter describes the specific affordances of violent extremism in the crises-struck field sites in question. In it, we ponder the underlying motive behind the witnessed move to violence and the decision not to engage in or to disengage from such. We discuss characteristics, agendas, modes of negotiating violent extremism, and the opposition that such movements conjure.

Empirical Point of Departure

All violent extremist groups may be related to an experience of exploitation and repression in one way or another, be it the class struggle and the downtrodden masses, the local or global fate of Muslim population groups, regionalist or nationalist insurgence, or more political experiences of grief and grievance (Collier and Hoeffler 2004; Bøås, Cissé, and Mahamane 2020).

The prolific emergence of violent extremist movements in the Sahel is no exception (Cissé 2021). With a focus on Mali, Burkina Faso, and Niger, it becomes clear that all three Sahelian countries have been ruled by political groups that worked to privilege specific parts of the population at the expense of others and that used violence and repression to maintain control. We are looking at not new lines of conflict but novel intensifications of long-term fault lines. Multisecular conflicts between pastoralists and farmers, between ethnic groups, and between rival political communities have existed in the region and have taken violent forms before (cf. Bisson et al. 2021). However, within the last few decades, we have seen more organized militant formations emerge in response to shifting political dynamics and compound critical states of affairs. Since 2015, modes of violence using religious rhetoric, as well as groups seeking to counter such Islamist and jihadist-defined militancy, have gained a clear presence in the region. Militant proselytizing takes place, and various insurgent groups have materialized in response.

This is the case in Burkina Faso, Mali, and Niger, which form the empirical basis for this chapter. In Burkina Faso, our fieldwork was concentrated on regions such as the Boucle du Mouhoun, the Northeast, and localities that have been heavily impacted by the activities of violent entrepreneurs, such as Toéni, Barsalgho, and Kongoussi. We picked Mopti, Segou, and Ansongo as localities for scrutiny in Mali. And in Niger, we conducted a survey in the Diffa region and two others in the Tillabéri region. The criteria for selecting these localities were defined in terms of proximity to areas under the control of violent extremist groups, levels of insecurity, and proximity to similarly affected areas in neighboring countries (Ansongo in Mali bordering Niger, Toéni in Burkina Faso bordering Mali, and Tillabéri and Ayourou in Niger close to the border with Mali). We selected these to capture more regional dimensions of the issue.

In all cases, we are looking at areas where armed actors work through a political agenda that seeks to unsettle or disrupt existing (dis)orders and institute new regimes of authority, resource distribution, and income-generating activities. The empirical material was collected primarily through qualitative methods. Using interview guides, a questionnaire, and focus group interviews structured around precise information to be gained, we conducted research over four years in different localities in the three countries. The research involved various stakeholders (i.e., local populations, administrative and customary authorities, civil society organizations, youth organizations, and herders' organizations). Three field surveys were carried out in Mali and Niger in addition to two surveys in Burkina Faso. After each collection, a feedback workshop bringing together the research assistants who had carried out the fieldwork and the principal researcher was organized to present the data and discuss the methodology, the salient findings, and the difficulties encountered. This reflexive and participatory phase of our fieldwork enabled us to rephrase and adapt research guides to the specific settings at hand, to shape the particular questions meaningfully to the local context, and to identify and address different categories of actors—such as state agents, local elected representatives, traditional authorities, and so forth—that were seen to play a role in the occurrence and nonoccurrence of violence, and the support and resilience toward it. More specifically, we designed individual questionnaires to acquire knowledge of people's perceptions of such violent extremism in the areas. A total of 250 individual questionnaires were administered in Niger (Tadress, Tilla Kaina, and Kabia) and Mali (Niono, Sirifila Boundi, Diabaly, Nampala, Dogofry, Sokolo, Siribala, Dialloubé, Tenenkou, etc.). In Burkina, we collected data in various parts of the country (eastern region, Tapoa Province, etc.) and carried out around one hundred interviews over four years of fieldwork in the country.

The context of insecurity and suspicion prevailing in the survey areas prevented us from carrying out many focus groups. Despite this, a few were, notably, conducted in Burkina Faso and Niger. Criteria of occurrence and nonoccurrence of violent extremism were used to select the localities where the interviews occurred. For example, the choice of Tadress in Niger is justified by the fact that this site is home to people who are victims of violent extremism. In the case of Tilla Kaina, also in the Tillabéri region of Niger, the area has never been directly affected by the phenomenon yet functions as an enabling environment and space for recruitment.

In each locality, we approached community leaders and village chiefs and explained the reasons for the research to gain their trust. We explained that we needed to interview elders, men and women, young people, and so on. Although such an approach may reaffirm existing power hierarchies, it is necessary to gain access. Respondents were selected according to their availability and trust. The environment is characterized by solid distrust, and as a result, we had to present and make ourselves visible numerous times to gain the respondents' trust before interviewing them. Sometimes, the intervention of chiefs facilitated rapport, making it possible to carry out interviews because respondents were assured they were not exposed to any risks by participating. In these situations, we communicated the anonymous nature of the interviews, which helped to overcome the obstacles of reticence and mistrust, and we methodically requested oral consent before interviews.

Extremist Order

Researching the presence and emergence of armed groups in a situation of crisis and (dis)order, such as in the Sahel, is a challenging task. Yet the importance of doing so is evident: it provides a window to a better understanding of the phenomenon of violent extremism in the specific region and broader terms. The ethnographic focus on movements that seek change by violent means and formations that rule by force clarifies how locals inhabit unstable and fluctuating political landscapes and how people and politics adjust their presence and alliances accordingly (Vigh 2006; Sardan 2023). Understanding how violent extremist groups operate vis-à-vis local populations is crucial to national, regional, and international attempts to stabilize the Sahel and, hence, is vital for shaping policies and responses accordingly. Three dimensions of violent extremism became intelligible through the fieldwork undertaken, namely, (1) the internal orders that it seeks to instantiate, (2) the oppositional order it represents, and (3) the oppositional striving for order that it spurs.

About the former, what characterizes violent extremist groups is, rudimentarily, their use of violence and coercion in seeking to establish rule and govern population groups. Yet we know relatively little about how this is accomplished concerning jihadist or Islamist movements in the Sahel. Besides narratives centered on reigns of terror and violence—often articulated within a tiresome narrative of the perpetual perpetration of African politics—we have little insight into the strategies of consolidation and the roads to legitimization that such groups make use of.

What surfaces with a closer look is that these groups are less monolithic than we imagine and that a redistribution of resources, provision of order, and offers of protection are part of their presence. Whereas the violence is apparent, the reality on the ground is particularly challenging for any attempted categorization because forces are multiple and variable. While some may proclaim to work via an order given to them directly by God, that is, sharia law, the picture on the ground is less clear-cut and often of a more complex nature. "The ways in which jihadist insurgents in the Sahel govern is rarely considered in the academic literature," Rupesinghe and Bøås 2019, 1) states, continuing:

> They have often been portrayed as "Islamic terrorists," who achieve their objectives by using brutal force against the civilian population and who finance their activities through criminal networks and activities. However, scattered empirical evidence reveals a different picture. Jihadist insurgents, like other insurgent groups, often use a variety of strategies to rule territory and populations. The scale, character, and form of how such groups govern differs not only between countries but also at the subnational level within the same group.

As it becomes apparent when doing fieldwork in such situations, and in conflict zones more generally, such politics are defined not by the absence of governance but rather by the coexistence of various modes of governance. As Bøås and Dunn (2017) argue, armed insurgencies may be seen as part of emerging arrangements that do not exist in isolation from the political, social, and economic dimensions of local governance systems nor do they necessarily eclipse such other dimensions. They are part of shifting and, often, unstable landscapes of authority and rule as "governance assemblages" or "figurations." In some cases, armed insurgencies are one manifestation of competing governance systems. In other situations, they may be consolidating their presence, yet there is a complex interaction between modes of governance at various stages of power (Bøås and Dunn 2017).

Furthermore, rather than being a singular movement or emergence, the range of, for example, Islamist insurgencies in the Sahel consists of groups with vastly different modes of governing and governance capacities. Sharia may be proclaimed as an implementation of a universal order, but the reality on the ground is far more diverse than this totalitarian discourse suggests. Still, some groups can provide a certain degree of sovereign order, while others are roaming groups without much territorial control (Olson 2000). Between these two poles, we find insurgencies that provide what we may call "sporadic governance" (Utas and Vigh 2017) as a type of political ordering that fluctuates between *potentia* and *presentia*. Not all groups seek to gain more permanent territorial control but aim for social control of a targeted population or over an economic niche, often through unpredictable coercive activities and the intermittent provision of some governance services. Suppose the formal power of the state cannot prevent the coercive activities of an insurgency or offer governance services of usable quality. In that case, the considerable social grip that violent extremists may have over local populations is facilitated.

The reduction of dominant governance capacity, particularly but not only in peripheral areas, thus opens new spaces where distinct groups of actors can seek local integration and legitimacy through the establishment of different types of violent and repressive order. All this takes place in what we define as an enabling environment, that is, in areas where the combination of economic recession, changing livelihood possibilities, unemployment, low and declining levels of education, and the impact of climate change cause disadvantaged communities or individuals to become so alienated from the powers that be that they become inclined to support, join, or implement violent extremist agendas (cf. Breen 2019). Although extremist groups are defined by their use of violence, this does not mean they are void of legitimacy when seen locally. The structural factors that constitute enabling environments translate into an array of deep-seated grievances that provide the harbingers of such ideologies with the social and emotional entry points that allow them to garner support (Merton 1938; Rupesinghe and Bøås 2019).

A field-based approach is therefore needed to understand the finer dynamics of the phenomenon, not only to illuminate the social anchoring of such movements but also equally to nuance standard descriptions of state-centric and methodologically nationalist approaches. As Rupesinghe and Bøås (2019, 5) make clear in their work on the issue, "The focus on stable territorial control, institutions and delivery of services, does not illuminate the diverse practices which foster social embeddedness of insurgents in local communities, how they regulate and control social behavior, their implantation in and regulation of local political economies and clientelist logics which connect insurgents to the local population and other elites."

So, when looking at the social, economic, and political orders that define violent extremism in the Sahel, we may summarize that we are concerned with groups that seek to mobilize an organized force to promote an alternative order of governance in response to an already critical situation. These are actors who resort to violence (weapons), work with a more or less defined political agenda, and set an alternative set of rights (e.g., sharia-based politicoreligious order, control of local resources). And the allure of this agenda is associated with imaginaries and practices set on alternative resource-distributing activities (Della Porta 1995). What also becomes clear is that people who resist or desist from such mobilization commonly have viable alternatives to violence. Those who resist can access other subject positions and choose different forms of inclusion than those who engage. Resistance points our attention to the processual aspects of such affiliations, where what was formerly necessary has become voluntary.

Emerging Islamist Groups

Our work resonates with a social movement theory of violent extremism (Della Porta 1995). Yet, it does so by looking at more significant regional, transnational, and global dynamics and their localized responses. Such a theoretical point of departure enables us to move beyond the notion of innate violence and institutional failure and look instead at how violent extremism comes into being and what it brings into being—what it does and how. Violent extremism commonly represents, in this perspective, an oppositional order that works through and produces politics in its own right, seeking to construct legitimacy and authority in the process (cf. Lund 2006).

From a more social scientific perspective, the conflicts researched in our survey areas can in part be explained in generational and class terms by a desire to challenge social status on the part of individuals who might be called "social cadets" (Bayart 1978).[1] A range of scholars have raised this point using different idioms centered around generational positions and youth, yet all direct our attention to the social construction of forced immobility and subservience within societies (cf. Vigh 2003). They illuminate the struggle for social status and the quest for viable beings that are found at the lower echelons of society. Individuals who are dominated and structurally disadvantaged—slaves, herdsmen, youths, migrant populations groups, et cetera—are, in this perspective, particularly prone to being mobilized into supporting revolutions and partaking in violent rebellions because they stand most to win from dismantling the established system. It is an aspect of disgruntlement that connects many groups examined in our work. What sets those who take action apart from those who do not is that the former have fewer or more positively imaginable paths available. The legitimacy of collective violence is often rooted in the unbearable or unsustainable nature of the status quo.

The example of the Rimaibés, or cattle herders, can be given. In the commune of Toéni in Burkina Faso, the interviews revealed that cattle owners employed herders to guard their herds. The latter began to resent their status as subservient herders, a position without positive prospects. They took advantage of their positions to seize the herds entrusted to them before joining the groups of violent entrepreneurs operating in the cross-border area with Mali (Gaye 2020). Interestingly, the frustration of the herders has, furthermore, served as a reason for enlisting in jihadist groups, militant formations also offering the possibility of change yet even further legitimized. The same situation can be observed in the central region of Mali and the Tillabéri or Diffa area of Niger (Benjaminsen and Boubacar 2009; Idrissa and Isambourg 2020). The more militant interpretations of Islam may thus provide both the impetus and the ideological justification for violent extremism. Such interpretations may provide the medium through which such imaginaries are articulated and alternative politicoreligious practices instituted as they afford legitimacy, community, and a script for order. In the three fieldwork countries, Islam is a widely practiced religion. In Niger and Mali, Islam of Sufi origin (e.g., Qadiriyya, Tijaniya) has dominated the market of religious offerings. Currently, reformist Islam, which is influenced by Saudi-supported and financed Salafism, is becoming increasingly prominent in these three countries. It is in fierce competition with the traditional beliefs within the faith, which Salafists position as being less "pure" as a result of their accommodation of certain traditional practices specific to the communities in question.

Within the novel Islamist movements, preaching is used to gain support from communities, to challenge previously adopted religious practices, and to impose a new code of life and "performance" of ingroup community ("skipped" pants, mandatory hijab wearing for women and beards for men, etc.). Similarly, as a singular claim to legitimacy, Islam is highjacked into advocating direct attacks on competing, foreign, or formerly dominant systems of value. The public school of the French language is, for instance, a target because it is considered by such groups to convey socioreligious ideas and values defined as *haram*—that is, prohibited. Schools are closed, and teachers and traditional administrative authorities are threatened or assassinated as transmitters of Western rather than Islamist values.

The Group for the Support of Islam and Muslims (JNIM) provides an interesting example. It operates in the eastern region of Burkina Faso and central Mali. It is a violent extremist organization of Salafist ideology created on March 1, 2017, during the Malian security crisis. It was born from the merger of Ansar Dine, al-Qaeda in the Islamic Maghreb forces, and the Al-Mourabitoune Katiba. Its leader is Iyagh Ghali, a Malian, and the group's emir in the eastern region of Burkina Faso is Jaffar Dicko, a Burkinabè, brother of Malam Dicko, the first jihadist leader in the Sahel region. The group is active in Burkina Faso, in the provinces of Gourma (Nassougou and Matiacoali), and in Kompienga and Komanjoari. The armed groups of Hamadoun Kouffa's Katiba of Macina, allied with the JNIM, are directly present in Mali in the communes where surveys were conducted (Dialloubé, Tenenkou, Douentza, etc.).

Another such example of an Islamically anchored violent extremist group is the Islamic State in the Greater Sahara (ISGS), a terrorist organization with a Salafist ideology that emerged on May 15, 2015, from a split in Al-Mourabitoune caused by the allegiance of one of its commanders, Adnane Abou Walid al-Saharaoui (killed in a French Army bombing). This group reports its presence in Burkina Faso in the provinces of Komandjari, Tapoa, and Yagha in the Sahel. In Mali, their presence is known in Ansongo on the border with Niger. However, it has recently been reported that ISGS is moving toward central Mali and is competing with (JNIM), with violent confrontations taking place in a feud over the same religious claim to power. Finally, the ISGS is the leading violent extremist group in Niger, where it operates mainly in the Tillabéri region (cf. Rupesinghe and Bøås 2019). All three groups manage to fuse local grievances with more significant ideological movements, and in this way Islam becomes both a placeholder for a broad range of complaints and concerns, a connector, and a discourse that lends itself to performative opposition.

Islam, or religion more generally, does not seem viable as a single motivating force toward extremism. First, traditions vary, readings and interpretations of scriptures differ, and minor interreligious differences may become conflictual divides. Second, the imposition of a singular order on a diverse field is often as repressive as the orders sought to be replaced! Instead, such movements need to benefit from an intersection of authority on different levels to maintain momentum. The ability of violent entrepreneurs to create, manipulate, or interfere in local conflicts and tensions varies. Still, those among them who have the opportunity to be "embedded" locally are more likely to establish and maintain authority. Their capacity to resonate with local grievances and social cleavages, such as land disputes, disputes over trade rights, or transhumance, is needed to secure their integration into local communities. For instance, in the Tillabéri region of Niger, most actors interviewed said that violent extremists have support among the population: "they benefit from the complicity of widowed women, those frustrated by bad governance, certain traditional authorities, and traders" (cf. Hassan 2020). Likewise, in Diffa, the Boko Haram sect has support from various socioprofessional groups (herders, fishermen, youths, traders, women, marabouts, etc.), refugees, and internally displaced persons. It achieves this through coercion (threats, terror, intimidation of the population), but also because the dissatisfaction with the status quo is, in fact, broadly shared, the money the group distributes and material donations it makes—such as motorcycles given to young people—and the internal security it provides showcase alternative orders that are perhaps not yet realized or considered comparable in terms of the suffering Boko Haram produces.

However, jihadist groups not only exploit local cleavages but also work with a strategy of actively creating them. In addition to violent attacks resulting in the death of men and massive displacement of populations, a tactic is to progressively embark on territorial occupation in several regions of Burkina Faso, notably in the Boucle du Mouhoun, the East, the Sahel, the North-Central region, the North, and recently in the Cascades and the Hauts-Bassins. These occupations begin, most often, with violent incursions into villages, and sometimes they carry out targeted executions to increase the scale of the terror and push the population to flee or to collaborate. Gradually, they establish themselves and set up a blockade on the villages or groups of villages under their administration. This strategy can also be observed in Mali and Niger. In these villages, it is not the laws of the republic that govern the daily life of the population, nor local customs, but rather the laws of armed individuals.

The most emblematic cases are Mansila and several villages in the Sahel; Madjoari in the East, Sollé, and other communes in the northern region of Burkina Faso; and Somadougou and Mondoro in Mali. In most of these areas under terrorist occupation, the population is subject to sharia law. Men must wear beards and short pants, while women must wear veils. French language education is replaced by preaching and or Koranic teaching. The sale of alcoholic beverages and music is prohibited. In short, the armed groups have imposed new modes of social regulation on the population, which has no choice but to suffer or flee. In some communes, local authorities have decided to negotiate with them to avoid attacks. This is sometimes an initiative of local elected officials and religious or customary leaders. In the Mopti region of Mali, for example, local communities (Djénné, Somadougou, Safourlaye, etc.), including Fulani and hunters, have signed peace agreements in several communes, thereby agreeing to cease all hostility toward each other.

The actions of violent extremist and particularly jihadist groups such as the JNIM and ISGS have promoted a radical change in community life in their preferred territories. From Diffa to Tillabéri in Niger, from Kongoussi in Burkina Faso to Dialloubé in Mali, the presence of these groups has weakened the state presence in terms of delivery of essential social services. This greatly affects already marginal communities. For example, the transhumant cross-border herders of the region are forced to remain in set areas even when there is a fodder and water deficit, the triggers that would typically make them move their herds. Markets are no longer lively along the borders. Access to schools, water points, and health centers is becoming problematic, and schoolteachers are threatened with death or sometimes killed. Thus, the attacks clarify the weakness of the state. Unless the insurgent movements promptly provide social services and security, they very quickly risk being identified as the cause of rather than the alleviation of suffering.

The complex strategies of providing better opportunities, dividing communities, and inciting unrest can be seen in central Mali and the areas of Burkina Faso where our surveys were conducted. Violent extremist groups take advantage of the lack of job opportunities and training for young people as well as local dissatisfaction with government services such as water and forestry management in central Mali, and the suspicions of corruption and slow administrative processes as well as the state's counterterrorism efforts in Burkina Faso. Land conflicts, exacerbated by climate change, which are numerous in local communities, feed the breeding ground. "To be honest, these are the same Fulani who were with us here," an interlocutor told us when he was describing who mobilized into such groups. He continued:

> The same people with whom we formed a family, the same people who were guarding our cattle, disappeared with the cattle. They came to see me personally with the following message: "We cannot be considered herders and find ourselves guarding your cattle; your cattle should be our property because you are farmers, and we are herders."
>
> The Fula here were considered our employees because they keep our animals, and in addition, they do not cultivate. Logic would dictate that instead of being farmers, they own animals. However, the reality is quite different; not only do they not cultivate and therefore depend on what they produce, but they also do not own the animals they keep. In other words, they have nothing. This frustration has led many to become involved in terrorism.[2]

Self-Defense Groups

Terrorist attacks have, as such, been directed at destroying the state, public services, and alliances by targeting their symbols or leaders. This has been observed in all three countries of fieldwork. Several local elected officials have been assassinated or have only barely escaped the ambushes of armed terrorist groups. In all regions under the influence of violent extremist groups, the local administration—both deconcentrated and decentralized (prefectures, town halls, schools, health centers, police stations and gendarmerie brigades, water, and forestry posts, etc.)—have practically ceased to exist. The various technical services are closed. Local elected officials and municipal or deconcentrated service agents have had to withdraw to the provincial or regional capitals. In the northern region of Burkina Faso, for example, more than fifteen mayors have taken refuge in the regional council, where they occupy an office with their agents—a telling sign of the state virtually disappearing from several communes in the Boucle du Mouhoun, East, Center-North, North, and Sahel regions.[3] In addition, armed terrorist groups seem to focus on undermining all local legitimacy that could help build community resilience by carrying out targeted assassinations. These include the assassinations of the Chief of the Land of Yirgou (also a municipal councilor and moral supporter of the Koglweogo in his zone) and members of his family (January 1, 2019) and Sheikh Werem Issoufi of Arbinda (March 31, 2019). In the East, local imams were coldly executed, an atrocity followed by attacks on Catholic and Protestant churches in the Sahel (Silgadji, April 28, 2019), Center-North (Dablo, May 12, 2019), and North (Toulfé, May 27, 2019) regions.

This targeting of religious and customary practices and actors pits communities against each other. It provokes clashes and lasting disruption of social cohesion and peaceful cohabitation between ethnic groups that have traditionally lived in relative harmony. In some cases, terrorist attacks have indeed provoked monstrous reprisals. Examples include the intercommunity clashes in Yirgou, where dozens of people were killed (49 according to the government; more than 200 victims, according to the collective against impunity and the stigmatization of communities, which was formed after the Yirgou tragedy), and in Arbinda, where about sixty people were killed. Although religious communities have shown relative resilience in the face of this attempted opposition by terrorist groups, the fact remains that terror has invaded several regions and villages. There has been a gradual shift from spectacular attacks with high media profiles to acts of intimidation and mass exactions that force people to flee their villages to urban centers or to areas that were seen as less exposed.

However, given the poor security situation in areas under the influence of terrorist groups, East, North-Central, North, and Boucle du Mouhoun in Burkina Faso, for example, communities have organized to ensure their protection by creating *self-defense groups*. In some regions, notably in the far west of Burkina Faso, secret societies (such as the Dozos) have armed and organized, which only generates additional groups of violent entrepreneurs. Here, recruitment is often voluntary or by initiation and driven by a commitment to defend their land, their communities, and their property.

Furthermore, such groups may be seen as a response to the targeting of traditional authorities, such as customary chiefs, imams, priests, and village chiefs, by violent extremist groups, who consider these to be supporters of the state they are fighting against.

Yet, the nature of such attacks varies. In Diffa, Boko Haram infiltrated customary authorities through money or parental affinity. In the region of Tillabéri, dozens of village chiefs have been forced to flee with their family members to avoid being killed. Local elected officials in Burkina Faso were forced to hold municipal council meetings in their place of refuge. The Islamist groups in the region have thus shattered traditional or modern state structures of power and provision. As an interlocutor described, he had never "personally" been "threatened":

> But in some communes, some village chiefs have been threatened, such as in the commune of Bourra or the commune of Fafa. Just recently, the village chief of Monsonga received threats from an armed group; to guarantee his safety, his children took him to Bamako, but the rest of the family remained in Monsonga.

As both traditional authority and the presence of the state are increasingly limited, the defense and security forces have, in places, bolstered the state's mission to fight terrorism. In central Mali, prefects, sub-prefects, and magistrates have been almost totally absent until recently when the state claimed "an increase in the power of the FAMA [Malian Armed Forces]." Yet, at times, such security forces themselves become semidetached in their attempt to counter jihadist groups, and parts of them continue to convert the organized force at their disposal to gain alternative systems of resource and power distribution. The development of such relatively rogue security forces concurs with other groups seeking to reinstate weakened sociopolitical orders and groups that arise as self-defense groups, for example, in opposition to other violent extremists. Whereas extremist groups seek to unsettle existing orders and impose new ones, the defense and security forces seek to restore, reinstate, or preserve the order that formerly served as the guarantor of their lot. The primary objective of self-defense groups is, more specifically, to protect the communities that have created or mandated them.

Such groups highlight the fact that violent extremism is not merely an Islamist issue. Extremists can be found in all the outer regions of political orientations. Furthermore, extremists are not just interned and imprisoned but also emerge from such processes in a response to punishment interpreted as persecution. In other words, looking at the Sahel, it seems clear that oppression and persecution, despite it being counterterroristic and regardless of who is perpetrating these strategies, may lead to extremist responses. State repression and corruption led to the onset of jihadist violence in the Sahel, causing the process of escalation—a circuitous dynamic—where Islamist violence leads to a reaction in the shape of counterterrorism and what we may call counterextremism—a violent extremist feedback loop.

Militias and self-defense groups have, for this reason, become numerous in central Mali. Working under names such as GATIA, Dozo Hunters, Dana Ambasagou, Coupeurs de Route, and Foirail Robbers, these groups are varied in terms of ethnicity, religion, and livelihood—just as their defined enemies and political aims may vary—yet they connect in seeking to protect their community or livelihood (for example, Bambara, Bozo, and Bella). In the three countries under scrutiny, such informal defense forces are usually made up of police, gendarmes, and military personnel and fighters associated with them. They meet the criterion of violent extremism insofar as their counterterrorism strategy seeks to restore order, yet this is done brutally and often with disregard for the rule of law. In pursuing this agenda, such groups sometimes become implicated in atrocities similar to those of the groups they resort to perpetration and coercion against. Self-defense group dynamics become even more apparent when we briefly describe some examples of the forces involved.

The Rougas

The National Union of Rougas, created in 2012, based in Fada N'gourma in eastern Burkina, is a group primarily made up of Fulani, but there are also Mossis and Gourmantchés. Traditionally, the Rougas were representatives of Fulani herdsmen present in all three of our field sites. This group of "herdsmen," responsible for representing all herders in the area, are mainly present in the East, North, Center-North, and Sahel parts of Burkina Faso. They formed an interesting group in terms of violent extremism because they turned into a defense force in reaction to the disruptive developments that came to impact their lives and livelihoods. Their mission currently consists of preventing and settling conflicts and ensuring good conditions for pastoral practices in their competence areas.

The Rougas are divided into four main groups: the *rougas* themselves, who are chiefs; the *dogorèh*; the *warssgho*; and the *larmèh*. The *larmèh* constitute the female part of the *rougas*, the *dogorèh* are constantly with the *rougas*, and the *warsgoh* guard the herds during transhumance. Traditionally, they were called to action in the event of cattle theft and relied on information networks throughout the country to apprehend the alleged thief or thieves. Elected by a college of wise men, according to a certain number of criteria—the main one being that he or she has never been found guilty of theft—the *rougas* do not impose fines on suspected thieves or possess weapons. However, within a context of growing insecurity, in which they have become targeted by terrorist groups as well as defense and security forces, their organization has changed, and parts of the group have become militarized. Some have migrated to the cities for fear of being killed; others formed an intelligence network for the defense and security forces, with whom they collaborate to inform about the movements of terrorists; and others have evolved into a militant defense force set to protect and reinstall their tradition livelihoods and ways of life (Bisson et al. 2021).

The Koglweogos and Donzo Hunters

The *Koglweogo*, a Mooré term meaning "guardians of the forest," were established in the 1990s with a mission to protect the environment and agricultural property, and the traditional livelihoods associated with them.[4] Today, they are present throughout the country, except in the west of Burkina Faso and the Cascades. Their members are called on to intervene in cases of theft or looting. They are made up of mainly farmers and herders but also former thieves who have repented and decided to side with the general population. Each zone in the area has a *Koglweogos* leader. The *Koglweogos* were formerly armed with traditional hunting rifles, but they now have weapons of war to deal with terrorist attacks. The *Koglweogos* have set up a court where they judge alleged thieves and wrongdoers.

In 2015, faced with the resurgence of organized crime and terrorist attacks in some areas of the country, they changed not only their mission but also their name. Rather than protectors of ecological niches and livelihoods, they became a militia, or self-defense group, that mobilized to compensate for the lack of manpower in the defense and security forces. Consequently, since the beginning of terrorist attacks in eastern Burkina, the *Koglweogos* have become targets of armed groups, and being unable to deal with the sophisticated weapons of the terrorists, many *Koglweogos* have fled to larger towns to escape the killings. However, according to testimonies, some *Koglweogos* with sophisticated weapons are now at the forefront of the fight against terrorism under another name: the VDP, or Volunteers for the Defense of the Homeland.

Volunteers for the Defense of the Homeland

The VDP were established by a bill on December 26, 2019, signed into law on January 21, 2020. Recruited volunteers receive fourteen days of military training and sign a contract with the state. They are hired for one year on a renewable contract, with a maximum of five years of legal duration. Volunteers are recruited in villages that are burdened by jihadist aggression and supervised by the defense and security forces. The VDP intervenes alongside the Burkinabè army for surveillance, information, and protection missions. They act as guides and trackers and are often engaged in combat.

Organized around a local leader and divided into distinct groups—namely, intelligence groups and combat groups—they monitor the movements of people in the territory and identify incoming "foreigners." In the event of a terrorist attack, they are generally on the front line, and the defense and security forces are alerted afterward.

The defense and security forces in Burkina Faso do not always respond to terrorist attacks. This was the case in the terrorist attack in Solhan on June 5, 2021, which resulted in the death of more than 130 civilians. The defense and security forces that were alerted were unable to come to the rescue of the volunteers and civilians, highlighting the need for the VDP to remain vigilant and ready to defend their community. The VDP has repelled terrorist attacks in certain localities, such as Koaré, located a few kilometers from the city of Fada N'gourma. Yet, the Volunteers for the Defense of the Homeland are not merely reactive and have carried out military actions in the eastern region. Areas once under siege by jihadist groups have been liberated by the VDP, as in the case of Mouroudeni, located five kilometers from Tanwalbougou in the department of Fada N'gourma. National opinion in Burkina Faso is divided over the establishment of the VDP. Although part of the population supported their creation, large parts opposed it because of the likelihood of perpetration of violence by the volunteers, instances of which have indeed been reported.

Diverse Extremism in the Sahel

It is essential to underline that all the described militant groups operate within an arena that goes beyond the traditional delineation of state. Some operate locally, others are regionally anchored, and still others are squarely focused on protecting groups or factions within the state rather than the population at large. Yet, despite these differences, we argue that three types of violent extremist groups exist in the Sahel: (1) state security forces, (2) Islamist groups, and (3) self-defense groups, and they share several traits despite their many differences. All three types of militant formations can concurrently be found in the Sahel, and all recourse to or use violence and coercion—in opposition, as resistance, or in relation to attaining an alternative societal or religious order. The simultaneous presence of these different forces in the region means that the populations of conflict-affected areas are often trapped by confrontations of state security forces, jihadist groups, and self-defense forces. Burkina Faso currently has more than one million internally displaced persons.[5] The massive displacement of people in the Tillabéri region has prompted the Nigerien government to strengthen security in the region and to encourage people to return to their homeland. The number of displaced persons from the Mopti area to Bamako is also significant. One of the major challenges linked to these massive population displacements remains the reconstitution of living together in a post-conflict period. Yet, once again, we see violent extremist groups capitalize on social cleavages and grievances to recruit to their cause.

The recruitment methods of extremist groups vary according to the group's nature—that is, state security, jihadist, or self-defense—but most entice new members by offering promises of order and social possibilities and self-worth, which is otherwise missing in people's lives. In addition to religious discourse, terrorist groups use promises of increased status and autonomy to recruit from the communities under their influence. This is the case, for example, for the Fulani who herd the animals of other ethnic groups in several of the regions concerned. In exchange for joining the ranks of a group, such herders are pushed to break ties with their patrons to become owners of the herds under their care. Caste systems are also denounced as an injustice as a way to mobilize the youths of ethnic groups that are dominated by such social hierarchies. Although the groups in question may have different beliefs and ideological attunements, they share a modus operandi of taking advantage of social injustices in crisis situations. To further convert poverty-stricken youths to their cause, they offer security, mobility, goods, capital, and status—motorcycles, sums of money, and hope for a better life. The deterioration of the security situation and the multiple and protracted crises (community, land, local governance, climate change, etc.) that the conflicts have exacerbated make youths particularly vulnerable and leave them at risk of being exploited by violent extremists. As such, armed terrorist groups (ATGs), as they are called in Niger, most often use strategies based on social, cultural, political, and economic offerings and inclusion to penetrate communities and convince people to join them.

Conclusion

The changes underway in the Sahelian region are unprecedented in terms of the destabilization of state, social structures, and community relations. The actions of violent extremist groups not only challenge territorial security and the institutional foundations of states and political structures but also breed and feed the fragility of the latter and amplify it as they encourage populations to reject the status quo. Violent extremism is defined by its use of force and coercion. It resorts to collective violence to unsettle, dismantle, or overturn political orders and institutionalize new ones. However, this chapter, seeking insights beyond that, highlights that the insecurity induced is only the visible face of deeper grievances and aims whose contours and consequences must be analyzed from a short-, medium- and long-term perspective.

What and how the situation will change from here is difficult to predict and prejudge. However, while there is ample uncertainty about whether the destabilization capacities of violent extremism, the capacities of state structures, and the resilience of communities to safeguard relations of peace and bearable coexistence will be reduced or reinforced, the potential for disruption prevails. Violent extremism in the Sahel currently induces local and regional disorder while violent extremists gain support as purveyors of order and from global positions proclaiming to supply it. The Sahel is a region caught in a flux that transcends local feuds and national dissidence and that is reinforced or attenuated by geopolitical concerns beyond local actors' control.

Notes

1. Writings, including those of Georges Balandier, Claude Meillassoux, and Bayart, have referred to "social cadets" as the set of dominated social categories (youths and women) as opposed to their "social elders," who have authority linked to their age, their position in the lineage, and the possession of symbolic and material resources.

2. Interviews with Toéni, Burkina Faso, September 2020.

3. Nevertheless, there is a clear desire on the part of the state to reclaim areas that are beyond its control. This is notable in the Malian and Burkinabe cases in recent months.

4. Mooré is Burkina Faso's main national language.

5. Recently, armed jihadist groups in Burkina Faso have given ultimatums to evacuate people from specific sites. Some explain that these evacuation ultimatums aim to control mining sites, pressure the state, and the like.

4

Measuring Social Cohesion and Resilience

Ulf Engel

The aim of the Preventing Violent Extremism in the Balkans and the MENA (PREVEX) research network is to "contribute to more effective policies that prevent violent extremism through strengthening societal resilience."[1] The intellectual puzzle the project addresses is why violent extremism (VE) does not occur in places that would otherwise be conducive to its flourishing. These enabling environments include the existence of past grievances, detrimental economic conditions, the lack of options for better livelihoods resulting from unemployment, young median ages, and other structural conditions favorable to the rise of VE (see Chapter 2, this volume). The research interest is why, under these conditions, individuals and groups show resilience toward violent extremist ideologies. The empirical findings from our collaborative research (see, for instance, Mishkova et al. 2021; Bøås et al. 2021; Skare et al. 2021a, 2021b; Ben-Nun and Engel 2022a, 4) indicate that "resilience towards VE concerns the relationship between stable and socially credible governance structures that provide long-term betterment of economic conditions, which builds upon strong politico-religious legitimacy of government."[2]

Some scholars and international organizations use the terms *resilience* and *social cohesion* almost interchangeably (see World Bank 2022), but most treat social cohesion as a precondition, or a necessary component, for building resilient collectives and institutions. In general, resilience, first, is discussed regarding individuals, groups of people, companies, or societies and, second, about very different phenomena—including climate change, drought, famine, technological change, psychological trauma, urban change, or violent conflict (see, for instance, the literature reviews by

Bhamra, Dani, and Burnard 2011; Martin-Breen and Anderies 2011; Barrett et al. 2020).[3]

This chapter aims first to contribute to the question of whether it is possible to define the concept of social cohesion so that it works across world regions and can be applied to very different empirical cases. Second, I discuss whether it is possible to measure social cohesion comparatively across world regions without falling into the trap of conceptual Eurocentrism (on the notion, see Amin 1988; Blaut 2000; Hobson 2012). If this is feasible, then deeper insights into social cohesion's emergence, maintenance, and contestation across historically and culturally distinct world regions might be possible.

It is almost impossible to do justice to the wealth of literature on social cohesion that academics, think tanks, and international organizations have published. Therefore, this chapter broadly discusses four key initiatives that implement social cohesion for "development" and "peacebuilding" interventions. The first project reviewed is Social Cohesion and Reconciliation (SCORE), which has been developed since 2009 through a partnership between the United Nations Development Programme's Action for Cooperation and Trust (UNDP ACT) and the Brussels-based Centre for Sustainable Peace and Democratic Development (SeeD); funding comes from the US Agency for International Development (USAID). Second, in 2012, the Bertelsmann Stiftung, an independent foundation established in 1977 and based in Gütersloh, Germany, began the development of the Social Cohesion Radar. Third, around the same time, the UNDP started to develop a conceptual framework for social cohesion (Lefko-Everett 2017). Fourth, the German Development Institute in 2020 established a research focus on social cohesion for the German Federal Ministry for Economic Cooperation and Development (BMZ) and developed an indicator system for Sub-Saharan Africa.[4] Of course, there have been numerous other attempts to operationalize an idea of social cohesion, but they have been less sustainable, less sophisticated, or less well-documented.[5]

This chapter is organized as follows: In the second section, a brief overview of the central dynamics in the debate on social cohesion is given. The third section discusses different definitions of social cohesion, as provided by the aforementioned four initiatives. The fourth section examines their attempts to measure and compare social cohesion across different societies. Particular attention is paid to how conceptual Eurocentrism is discussed, if at all. In the fifth section, the observations on definition and measurement are taken up again from a perspective of postcolonial reasoning. This includes a brief discussion of other proposals on how best to build social cohesion indices (SCIs). The examples are from African cases (Rwanda, South Africa, and Kenya). The implicit hope is that at least some offer an epistemology inspired by experiences and concepts different from those of the (nongeographical but epistemologically defined) Global North. A conclusion follows this.

Social Cohesion in Academic Debate

Social cohesion has been discussed in the humanities and social sciences for many years.[6] There seems to be a general understanding that social cohesion "makes communities and states more resilient in the face of crises and facilitates change processes that benefit everyone" (Leininger et al. 2021, 1). It is the "glue that holds societies together and is connected to numerous positive social outcomes" (Moustakas 2022, 1). In international peacebuilding and conflict prevention, it is regarded as a critical concept (see United Nations and World Bank 2018). Often, authors place their concepts intellectually in a historical line with European sociologists such as Ferdinand Tönnies (1885–1936), D. Émile Durkheim (1858–1917), and, to a lesser extent, Georg Simmel (1858–1918) and Max Weber (1864–1920). Looking at the academic debate that developed in the late nineteenth and early twentieth centuries, Hooghe (2011) identifies a distinctly European and a North American approach. The former stresses how social exclusion, inequalities, and marginalization undermine social cohesion and how the state must play a role in mitigating these dynamics, whereas the latter highlights the importance of individual behavior and beliefs (see also Langer et al. 2011, 323f.). The term is used in descriptive, normative, prescriptive, and analytical ways.

Based on a bibliometric analysis of 5,027 journal articles listed in the Web of Science (WoS), Moustakas (2022, 4) shows that "there has been a substantial growth in publications since 1994, with over 55% of publications originating between 2016–2020 alone."[7] The list of the twenty "most prolific countries and institutional affiliations regarding social cohesion-related research" is dominated by the United States (20.02 percent) and the United Kingdom (14.81 percent). The highest-scoring non-Western countries among the top twenty are South Africa (2.92 percent) and China (2.27 percent) (5). Following the WoS categories, Moustakas identifies public occupational, environmental health, sociology, environmental studies, educational research, and interdisciplinary social sciences as the most relevant disciplines where the concept is used most widely, "together accounting for just over 40% of all research" (7). Moustakas furthermore identifies three dominant research clusters within this body of research. The first is exploring "how social and structural factors, such as inequality, economic development, or education, impact social cohesion at the city, national, or regional level"; a part of this cluster discusses "how education can mediate social cohesion in different contexts" (see also Burchi and Zapata-Román

2022). The second cluster interrogates "how identity or diversity, be it ethnic, religious, or class level, mediates social cohesion or its specific dimensions, such as social relations, civic participation, or trust." The third cluster highlights "how (perceived) social cohesion in neighborhoods or other geographic settings impact various measures of health, quality of life, and wellbeing" (Moustakas 2022, 12–13). These findings emphasize the vague nature of the term *social cohesion* and its use in response to very different empirical situations, predominantly in contexts in the Global North.

Closer to the research agenda of this collaborative effort (see Bøås, Osland, and Erstad 2019, 7f.), in the literature on the "de-radicalization" of violent extremists and terrorists (on the concept, Ashour 2009; Rabasa et al. 2010), one can also find traces of the term *social cohesion* (see, for instance, COAR 2022; Mercy Corps 2022a). This literature is written from a social engineering perspective to programming conflict interventions by actors based, or trained, in the Global North (for an overview, see Grip and Kotajoki 2019).

Defining Social Cohesion

Attempts by academics, think tanks, and international organizations to define social cohesion overlap and intersect. An element of intertextuality has yet to be uncovered more systematically (and bibliometric analysis would be an exciting tool to do so). In the policy realm, the concept of social cohesion rose to prominence more than twenty years ago: in 1998, the Canadian government established a Social Cohesion Network; in 2004, the European Council adopted a Social Cohesion Strategy; in 2005, the government of New Zealand adopted a Social Cohesion Framework; in 2011, Organisation for Economic Co-operation and Development (OECD) drafted a social cohesion policy to close the widening gap between economies of the Global North and the Global South, to name but a few.[8]

To illustrate the variety in the debate, two examples from international organizations should suffice. Introducing the Social Cohesion Policy Reviews tool, the OECD formulated its concept directly referencing Durkheim's "The Division of Labor in Society" (the French sociologist's doctoral dissertation, 1893). Accordingly, a society is "'cohesive' if it works toward the well-being of all its members, fights exclusion and marginalization, creates a sense of belonging, promotes trust, and offers its members the opportunity of upward social mobility" (OECD 2011, 51). Social cohesion was imagined as a triangle comprising social inclusion, social capital, and social mobility (54).[9] A decade later, UNDP published a note on social cohesion approaches' conceptual framing and programming implications. It stated that social cohesion "is the extent of trust in government and within society and the willingness to participate collectively toward a shared vision of sustainable peace and common development goals" (UNDP 2020, 16).[10] This ambiguity on the meaning and scope of social cohesion is characteristic of much of the debate in think tanks and academia.

To come to the four institutions analyzed in more detail in this chapter, SCORE is focusing on four dimensions whose absence would undermine social cohesion: governance and human security; intergroup relations and identity formation; psychosocial functioning and community bonding; and civic attitudes and behaviors (SeeD 2018, 2022a; see SCORE 2022). It aims at supporting what is labeled "resilient social cohesion." On its website, SeeD reflects on the "sharing and transferring [of] knowledge, ensuring national experts can use evidence-based strategies to design community-level peacebuilding and conflict prevention projects and approaches" (SeeD 2022b). Therefore, part of SeeD's methodology lies in establishing national reflection groups. The principle of "inclusive national ownership" has an epistemological dimension and can be a way to avoid the simple transfer of Eurocentric concepts. Still, it is not in itself a guarantee. However, in identifying the lack of evidence-based research as a challenge, that is, the "unvalidated theories of change based on expert assumptions, intuition and habitual practices without robust contextual adaptation" (e.g., the use of liberal peace theories could be an example of unquestioned transference of Western concepts), SCORE shows some awareness of a few pitfalls associated with the use of Western ideas.

A rather influential definition of social cohesion has been provided by the Bertelsmann Foundation in its Social Cohesion Radar (SCR), initially as a reaction to a growing sense of fragmentation within Western societies.[11] Social cohesion, the foundation argues, "is generally agreed to be valuable in and of itself—as the manifestation of an intact society, marked by solidarity and helpfulness, and by a kind of team spirit" (Bertelsmann Stiftung 2013, 8). Explicitly, Bertelsmann's researchers relate to Durkheim (1897) and Tönnies (1887). Sensing some form of consensus in the research community, Bertelsmann defines three domains: a "cohesive society is characterized by resilient social relations, a positive emotional connectedness between its members and the community and a pronounced focus on the common good" (Bertelsmann Stiftung 2013, 13). Deliberately, this definition excludes "material wealth, social inequality and well-being" (14). Interestingly, the UNDP—which will be reviewed shortly—has criticized the Bertelsmann approach precisely on this ground: if you discuss social cohesion or the lack thereof in, for instance, South Africa, "omitting wealth and quality-of-life measures would create an incomplete picture of the state of society" (Lefko-Everett 2017, 23)

Furthermore, the Bertelsmann concept does not rely on the assumption of homogenous values (Bertelsmann Stiftung 2013, 15), but this is not because of cultural relativism. Instead, the opposite holds: with Durkheim, the notion of "organic solidarity" ("which is rooted in diversity and mutual interdependence") and the imagination of European modernity without the need for homogeneity in Western societies is reintroduced (15). The first Bertelsmann Study focused on thirty-four Western countries (see also Dragolov et al. 2016). Case selection, first and foremost, was justified by the fact that these countries "are at a similar stage in their social, political, and economic development" (Bertelsmann Stiftung 2013, 18). The reference to "stages" of "development" indicates a slightly outdated, heavily Eurocentric understanding of history. Not too surprisingly, Bertelsmann finds a strong correlation between high GDP and strong social cohesion (41); likewise, higher levels of income inequality are associated with weaker social cohesion (42). Reviewing this approach five years later, Bertelsmann concludes "that modernization and social cohesion are not mutually exclusive. Successful modernization bolsters social cohesion. When modernization works, societies hold more strongly together" (Bertelsmann Stiftung 2018, 18). On the basis of identification of different "social cohesion regimes" (a Nordic one, one from an English-speaking country, etc.), it is concluded that there is not a single path to cohesion but many different options (see Dragolov et al. 2016, 51ff.). The centrality of "modernization" (and modernity) reflects a specific Western knowledge order in which other world regions are assigned their place.

An opportunity for postcolonial reflexivity arose five years later, when Bertelsmann conducted a similar exercise in Asian countries (Bertelsmann Stiftung 2018). The question was solved by interpreting "the complexity of the economic, social, and political transformation processes that almost all Asian societies have been undergoing" as just another form of "social modernization" (20). Extending its methodology to non-Western world regions hasn't raised any conceptual problems for Bertelsmann; the opportunity to engage with indigenous thinking and longstanding traditions about social cohesion in India, China, South Korea, Japan, and other regions was lost.

UNDP, the third primary social cohesion tool scrutinized here, also refers to Durkheim and Tönnies but comes up with a slightly different taxonomy.[12] Stressing the commonalities, rather than the differences in debate, UNDP argues that social cohesion is "a key element of stability and peace" (Lefko-Everett 2017, 12). It avoids spelling out a clear-cut definition (though it suggests that social cohesion is somehow related to social capital and reflects upon how social cohesion can be achieved). The UNDP proposal for operationalizing social cohesion is reflective to the point that it concludes from the diversity of the African continent in terms of "history, culture, language, governance systems, economic conditions, and human development status" that "without additional supplementary research," existing social cohesion indicators and measures "will be unable to capture [the continent's] complexity and diversity" (9). However, this additional research was not undertaken.

In academic debate, it is generally acknowledged that "while there is a common sense across the literature that social cohesion is a key trait of any society, its definition varies in different disciplines and socio-cultural contexts" (Leininger et al. 2021, 1). As Schiefer and van der Noll (2017, 587) demonstrate, many definitions of social cohesion cut across various epistemological lines. However, in their review of the literature, they also identify some common ground, materializing in six core dimensions: "social relations, identification, orientation towards the common good, shared values, equality/inequality, and subjective/objective quality of life" (595). Close to the Bertelsmann Stiftung, Schiefer and van der Noll frame three essential features of social cohesion: "(1) the quality of social relations (including social networks, trust, acceptance of diversity, and participation), (2) identification with the social entity, and (3) orientation towards the common good (sense of responsibility, solidarity, compliance to social order)" (595).

Explicitly based on Schiefer and van der Noll's literature overview, the German Development Institute has coined the following lean definition: "Social cohesion refers to the vertical and horizontal relations among members of society and the state that hold society together. Social cohesion is characterized by attitudes and behavioral manifestations that include trust, an inclusive identity, and cooperation for the common good." *Horizontal* refers to "the relationship between individuals/groups within a society," and *vertical* refers to "the relationship between individuals/groups and the state/other public institutions" (Leininger et al. 2021, 3). The institute traces the concept's roots back to Durkheim (and a touch of Weber). As in most examples discussed here, there is no serious attempt at an intellectual archaeology of the term. Underlying the whole concept is a universalism the authors are usually unaware of: "The concept of social cohesion presented here is universally applicable. We demonstrate how to apply and operationalize it in Africa" (10).

In the collaborative research that led to this edited volume, many important observations have been made on the nexus between resilience and social cohesion. Regarding the Balkans, social cohesion has been discussed in the context of civic values around the dominant form of the Hanafi school of thought of Sunni Islam (Mishkova et al. 2021, 72–76).[13] Accordingly, "social cohesion refers to the extent of connectedness between individuals and institutions, as well as the homogeneity in society" (72). Social cohesion is also associated with "neighborliness" (75). In North Africa, the Sahel, and the Middle East, social cohesion is associated with peace (Bøås et al. 2021, 70; Skare et al. 2021a, 34). Analyzing EU practices to prevent and counter violent extremism (P/CVE) in the Maghreb and the

Sahel, Raineri et al. (2020) identify a social cohesion narrative underpinning these interventions, particularly in Tunisia and Mali. This narrative, the second most prominent out of a cluster of five narratives, "builds on the idea that existing conflicts fuel violent extremism and that individuals at risk often belong to a specific community (defined by religion, age, social status, ethnicity, etc.). The aim of P/CVE is then to reinforce the overall cohesion of the society, including through peacebuilding and development initiatives, and to have fragile communities acting as gatekeepers against extremism" (3). This research also identified the need to address the challenges of cross-regional and cross-cultural comparison systematically.

In the past decade, a consensus has emerged among academics, think tanks, and international organizations mainly situated in the Global North to define social cohesion based on a few interrelated domains. If and when attempts have been made to search for a theoretical grounding, reference is to a constructed tradition of European sociology (in this ancestral gallery, one will then find Durkheim, Tönnies, Simmel, and Weber). However, the representatives of this tradition are only sparsely quoted in the original. Other than Western philosophical or sociological sources of knowledge production, they are hardly acknowledged. Thus, thinking about social cohesion quickly tends to become a universalized Western enterprise. What does this finding mean for discussing how social cohesion can be measured and compared?

Measuring Social Cohesion

Schiefer and van der Noll (2016) relate the discussion on the standardization of measurement to the purpose of comparison. They argue that "a society's level of social cohesion can only be properly evaluated when it is possible to compare social cohesion across countries." A comprehensive measurement of social cohesion should, therefore, span across time and an adequate set of societies. However, at the same time, they are also skeptical about the limits of comparison when they state: "A possible comparison can be OECD, or EU countries, or countries within continents. Comparing Germany to, for example, India or a central African country is difficult" (595). Why?

The challenges of interregional and intercultural comparison have been extensively discussed (see, for instance, Chabal and Daloz 2005; Middell 2021). Predominantly, concepts of comparison are based on the historical experience of the Global North; the analytical categories derived from this are deeply embedded in a very dominant knowledge order. Yet, the comparison makes little sense and leads to distorted results if the concepts are not neutral, have normative weight, and represent only a Western worldview ("the state," "development," "market," "civil society," "secularity," etc.). Therefore, the following section also explores if and how the academics, think tanks, and international organizations that define and measure social cohesion are reflecting on what has been called the "cognitive empire" (see Ndlovu-Gatsheni 2020), that is, the asymmetries in knowledge orders, the continued dominance of Western thought, and its power effects (also see Inusah 2022).

In the following, the four abovementioned analytical instruments on social cohesion are briefly discussed (for an excellent systematic overview of an even more significant number of tools, see Lefko-Everett 2017, 51–53). First, SCORE was developed as a tool "to diagnose the root causes of conflict and predict which peacebuilding measures would most likely bring about positive conflict transformation outcomes" (SeeD 2022b). It is active in sixteen countries across the world.[14] SCORE constructs case-specific composite indices that are based on nationwide household surveys developed in bottom-up consultative processes and that operate within the boundaries of a "content framework." The latter focuses on four dimensions of "societal functioning": (1) governance and human security; (2) intergroup relations and identity formation; (3) psychosocial functioning and community bonding; and (4) civic attitudes and behaviors. Depending on the country and index iteration, the SCORE index uses different variables. These are shown in "heatmaps," which also illustrate regional differences. For Ukraine, for instance, the 2017 SCORE index is based on a combination of measurements of trust, identity/feeling of belonging, participation, equality/inequality, orientation toward the common good, solidarity, shared values, cooperation, tolerance, connectedness, and other (life skills, civic attitudes, psychosocial assets). For South Sudan, for instance, social cohesion is measured against six primary indicators: intergenerational cohesion, peaceful citizenship, intergroup harmony with outgroups, community cooperation, inclusive civic identity, and readiness for violence.

Second, on the basis of three domains—social relations, connectedness, and common good—the Bertelsmann Stiftung's Social Cohesion Radar assigns three empirical indicators to each of the domains: Social relations represent the networks and interactions between individuals and groups within a community, trust in others, and acceptance of diversity. Connectedness captures the degree to which people identify with the community, their trust in society's institutions, and whether they believe that social conditions are just. Finally, the common good describes actions and attitudes manifesting people's willingness to take responsibility for others and the community. These include solidarity and helpfulness, the recognition of social rules, and participation in society and political life (see Walkenhorst 2018, 2; Bertelsmann Stiftung 2013, 14). The sources used are cross-sectional data from representative comparative surveys, data from international institutions, and expert opinions.

Third, UNDP (i.e., Lefko-Everett 2017) introduces a variety of social cohesion measurements, also making a distinction between those developed outside Africa and those developed on the continent (discussed later). It stresses the strengths and limitations of each of these proposals. Yet this is not done from an explicit position of epistemological reasoning or a more profound understanding of the challenges of cross-regional or cross-cultural comparison—but with a sense that, for some reason, local knowledge and attitudes make a difference. UNDP (Lefko-Everett 2017, 34) proposes six dimensions to measure social cohesion in an African context: (1) inclusion (measured in terms of primarily access and participation in economic and social life, including quality-of-life indicators), (2) belonging (identity, shared norms and values, and feelings of acceptance and belonging in society), (3) social relationships (social networks, trust in individuals, and the acceptance and value placed on diversity in a society), (4) participation (active involvement in political life), (5) legitimacy (trust in institutions and feelings of representation), and (6) security (feelings of safety from political or social violence and crime). The secondary data to investigate these aspects comes from the Afrobarometer, the World Values Survey, the Pew Research Center, the Gallup World Poll, the Strategic Harmonization of Statistics in Africa, and the African Peer Review Mechanism.

Finally, the German Development Institute operationalizes social cohesion using perception-based data generated by the Afrobarometer and empirical data from the Varieties of Democracy Institute (V-Dem). The data selected from these surveys is then coded and aggregated. In some cases, the interpretation of this data, however, is a little irritating. One example is: "High identity scores coincide with countries with strong liberation movements. This is consistent with the fact that liberation shaped national identities after the independence of these states (South Africa, Tanzania, Zimbabwe)" (Leininger et al. 2021, 32). This observation contrasts the social realities in the countries concerned, the levels of resistance to liberation movements in power (or apathy), and the relative weight of the born-free generation (i.e., those born after independence).[15]

What do these SCIs say about the countries PREVEX is dealing with? Very little, actually. Leininger et al. (2021, 39) indicate that in the period 2005–2015, social cohesion in Mali was in decline, but that (in 2014) the society still was characterized by high levels of "trust" (44). None of the other SCIs discussed in this section have addressed the PREVEX case studies.

Discussion

To conclude the last two sections of this chapter on defining and measuring social cohesion, this brief review shows that the term *social cohesion* is a floating signifier (Laclau 2005) that social actors can fill with shifting meanings. It is fluid and has no fixed meaning. Others have called it a "quasi-concept" (Bernard 1999). And this can be an advantage (see Ostiguy and Moffitt 2021). As UNDP (2020, 16) observed: "Much of the value of the concept of social cohesion . . . lies in its adaptability and the thinking, debates, and descriptions that support discussions of its definition, characteristics, and contribution to peace and development." However, apart from the definitional differences in detail, three points stand out: The analyzed SCIs situate themselves in a Western school of sociological thought. They operate with a methodological toolbox that is informed by Western academic practice. And they treat the societies under review as closed national containers. This form of methodological nationalism (see Agnew 1994) easily misses the relevance of cultural transfers, diaspora entanglements, and other transregional influences on individual perceptions and how they may affect group perceptions and identities. However, the main critique is on the first two points.

The previous two sections have highlighted some essential definitional ambiguities. They have also drawn attention to the tension between the pursuit of objectification and the search for general patterns that insist on a universalized order of knowledge, on the one hand, and local or regional knowledge systems that resist these attempts, on the other. The following two examples of non-Western philosophical traits of social cohesion are briefly recalled to challenge the current research agenda.

Discussing the methodology of an SCI for the Arab world, Harb (2017, 10) emphasizes the relevance of the writings of the famous Arab scholar Ibn Khaldūn (1332–1406) for the debate on social cohesion. In the *Muqaddimah* ("Introduction," 1377), Ibn Khaldūn, among others, discusses the concept of 'Asabiyyah and the nature of social ties, or bonds of cohesion, between group members (on the continued relevance of his thoughts, see Abou-Tabickh 2022).[16] In South Africa, the philosophy of *Ubuntu* offers similar traits, particularly about shared beliefs and values. Ubuntu—often translated as "a person is a person in the community with others," or "I am because you are"—is in itself a heterogeneous concept. Also referred to as "African humanness," it is a cosmology, a nonuniversalizing epistemology that makes no difference between the physical and the spiritual, between humans, animals, and objects.[17] Both 'Asabiyyah and Ubuntu thinking impact how social cohesion is imagined—with further consequences on how it then can be measured.

Against this background, the question arises whether African research communities commissioned by their respective governments have seized the opportunity and developed non-Western narratives and probably even specific methodologies on social cohesion. There are three exciting cases where African governments have invited the development of SCIs in societies that have reemerged from trauma: Rwanda after the 1994 genocide, South Africa after the end of apartheid in 1994, and Kenya after the violent elections in 2007–2008 (for an overview of the literature on social cohesion after violent conflict, see Fiedler and Rohles 2021).

Rwanda started publishing opinion surveys on social cohesion in 2005. They are administered by the National Unity and Reconciliation Commission (NURC, established in 2002) and result from a merger of previously separated reports on community courts (*gacaca*), decentralization, and land reform. The national household survey asks how government initiatives affect social cohesion at various spatial layers of governance, that is, cells to provinces (NURC 2008, 8). The NURC questionnaire addresses traditional practices that have been revived to deal with the effects of the genocide, such as the *gacaca* (community) courts or *inyangamugayo* (trustworthy persons who become mediators in their communities). However, it does not lead to methodological innovations that would depart from standard Western practice: NURC has spent little time discussing its epistemology, and the surveys are firmly based on a Western tradition of technological conceptualizations. After the third iteration (2007), the Social Cohesion Index was replaced in 2010 by the Rwanda Reconciliation Barometer (which still contains a wealth of information on social cohesion but does not relate to local concepts or a discussion on other methodological ways to think about society).

Two institutional proposals have been made in South Africa for constructing a Social Cohesion Index (SCI). With funding from the government, the Human Sciences Research Council (HSRC) proposed a Social Cohesion Barometer aligned with government policies and inspired by the South African constitution. The proposal was developed by academics, including Jarè Struwig (Struwig et al. 2013). The data for this endeavor was to come from the South African Social Attitudes Survey (SASAS) regularly conducted by the HSRC. All academic references are to the "cognitive empire." However, the authors also admitted: "The conceptual and empirical work discussed in this chapter represents the formative stages in a longer journey" (418). In the end, the barometer did not materialize. Four years later, the Institute for Justice and Reconciliation (IJR) suggested an SCI based on data from its own South African Reconciliation Barometer (SARB) (IJR 2017). The methodology closely follows Langer et al. (2011) as well as UNDP (Lefko-Everett 2017; see also Burns, Lefko-Everett, and Njozela 2018). Although the IJR at least captured "local" and "national" approaches through an open-ended questionnaire, in both the HSRC and the IRJ proposals, there is no epistemological innovation outside of the dominant Eurocentric tradition previously discussed (cf. Lefko-Everett, Govender, and Foster 2016).

Finally, in 2012, Kenya established a National Cohesion and Integration Commission. It tasked the Kenya Institute for Public Policy Research and Analysis to develop a Kenyan Social Cohesion Index. Like all the other indices, this one also (briefly and superficially) ties in with Durkheim's intellectual tradition (see KIPPRA 2014, 6). On a methodological note, the critical points of reference are Chan, To, and Chan (2006) and Rajulton, Ravanera, and Beaujot (2007) (see Onsomu et al. 2017). Again, nothing new under the sun.

Overall, there are few prospects for developing African SCIs that also relate to local cosmologies and philosophies. The trade of SCIs is firmly in the hands of institutions that are part of the epistemological Global North and its dominant political economy. Admittedly, this conclusion also depends on the extent to which alternative cosmologies and philosophies (such as Ubuntu) have any relevance in real life, and if so, for whom. The discussion can be cut short if they are only assertions rather than social practices.

Conclusion

The presence and degree of social cohesion in society are vital to understanding why some communities are more resilient to violent extremism than others. Against this backdrop, two questions were at the center of this chapter: first, whether it is possible to define the concept of social cohesion to make it usable for the different empirical cases that stretch across several world regions, and second, whether it is possible to measure social cohesion across regions without falling into the trap of conceptual Eurocentrism. The findings are ambiguous.

First and foremost, *social cohesion* is a socially constructed and time/space-specific term (see Blum et al., forthcoming). The universalist understandings discussed in this chapter are based on Western historical experience and epistemologies of the Global North (and, on top, often also lack historicity). They need to be contextualized, deconstructed, and decolonized. Recent research on southern Africa confirms that debates about social cohesion ought to differ from place to place and should not necessarily be bound to discourses within containerized states but have dimensions of transregional entanglements (Blum and Engel 2024). The understanding of the term depends on concrete political negotiations and social discourses on cultural transfers and exchanges. The meaning of social cohesion in one place can change over time (see Engel and Middell 2020). Contributions to this edited volume confirm this assessment: during fieldwork in the various sites analyzed by the multiple contributors, the ambiguity of terms came to the fore.[18] Hence, these dimensions of intertextuality and intertemporality call for more attention.

It is not a matter of throwing out the baby with the bathwater but of taking a closer look at the site-specific cultural and philosophical traditions related to what is discussed today under the term *social cohesion*. The SCORE methodology provides some good guidance in this regard. So, first of all, the concrete conditions under which societies, or groups of people, talk about social cohesion in their language and concepts must be reconstructed discourse-historically. Cultures of remembrance, the arts, and popular culture may serve as promising entry points. Harb's (2017, 16f.) methodological notes on an SCI for the Arab region come closest to this suggestion. This can have very local references and transregional references that arise through interconnectedness (for rural southern Africa, see, for instance, Bank 2021). This investigation should also address how social order is created and legitimized. In this case, the "state" as imagined in the Global North may not necessarily play such a central role (which is partly reflected in the Afrobarometer data). Only then will it be possible to think about measurability.[19] Whether the indicator systems primarily developed in the Global North are then still considered sufficiently context-sensitive can only be reserved for a later discussion. At least regarding the Arab region, Harb (2017, 24) concludes that relying on available opinion polls "is counterproductive and ill-advised" because such polls "do not address any of the [relevant] horizontal (intergroup) variables . . . and are thus unlikely to address questions on social cohesion in the region." Developing a global understanding of social cohesion has only just begun.

Notes

1. With gratitude, I acknowledge the profound comments made on an earlier draft of this chapter by Constanze Blum, Research Institute Social Cohesion (Leipzig University).

2. Regarding Asia, for instance, a similar argument has been advanced by Walkenhorst (2018), Bertelsmann Stiftung (2018), and Croissant and Walkenhorst (2021). "Overall, the study shows that economic development, prosperity, human development (especially education and life expectancy) and gender equality are key factors fostering social cohesion" in South, Southeast, and East Asia (SSEA) (Walkenhorst 2018, 6).

3. Considering the PREVEX research agenda, few operationalizations of the term can be found. About Africa and transnational organized crime (TOC), ENACT (2021, 146) defines *resilience* "as the ability to withstand and disrupt organized criminal activities as a whole, rather than individual markets, through political, economic, legal and social measures. Resilience refers to countries' measures taken by both the state and non-state actors."

4. Renamed in June 2022 as the German Institute of Development and Sustainability (IDOS).

5. This is not to diminish the relevance of the contribution of other pioneers of the debate such as Beauvais and Jenson (2002), Berger-Schmitt (2002), Chan, To,

and Chan (2006), Jenson (2010), Acket et al. (2011), Langer et al. (2011), or Njozela, Shaw, and Burns (2017).

6. The Google Ngram Viewer (https://books.google.com, accessed in 2022) shows a first entry for the term in 1805. The term *resilience* goes back to at least 1500, although was used infrequently.

7. The Google Ngram Viewer indicates that the exponential growth of the term's use occurred somewhat between 1982 and 2004. The same applies to *resilience*.

8. Active social cohesion policies in the Global South are often neglected in this literature (for instance, South Africa since 2008, or Sierra Leone since 2018).

9. The term *social cohesion* is distinct from *social capital* and *social contract*. However, the OECD was not the only one conflating them (see, for instance, UNDP 2020).

10. The lead author of the study is Timothy D. Sisk, who is teaching at the Josef Korbel School of International Studies, University of Denver, Colorado. See also Cox and Sisk (2017).

11. The report was written by Klaus Boehnke, Georgi Dragolov, and Jan Lorenz (all Jacobs University, Bremen), Zsófia Ignácz (Goethe University, Frankfurt/Main), and Jan Delhey (Otto-von-Guericke University Magdeburg). The Bertelsmann methodology has also been applied by, for instance, UNECA (2016).

12. The report was written by Kate Lefko-Everett (submitted June 29, 2016), who at that time worked at the Institute of Justice and Reconciliation in Cape Town. Today she is a freelance consultant.

13. See also the SeeD report on Bosnia-Herzegovina (Guest, Machlouzarides, and Scheerder 2020), which is based on the SCORE methodology.

14. Also in Bosnia and Herzegovina, Iraq, and Mali—but not in any of the other countries analyzed by PREVEX.

15. Tanzania gained independence in 1961, Zimbabwe in 1980, and South Africa held is first democratic elections in 1994.

16. On the importance of high 'Asabiyyah for the formation of sectarian identity, see Goldsmith's (2015) study on the Alawite community in Syria.

17. For recent discussions, see, for instance, Genger (2022), Sartorius (2022), Kaungu (2021), Moyo (2021), Tella (2021), and Nnodim and Okigbo (2023).

18. Exchanges were conducted at a PREVEX project workshop held in Copenhagen, Denmark, May 4–5, 2022.

19. A panel organized at the annual conference of the Research Centre Global Dynamics (ReCentGlobe) on April 20, 2023, in Leipzig, with contributions on Ethiopia (Fana Gebresenbet, Institute for Peace and Security Studies, Addis Ababa) and Côte d'Ivoire (Betrand Baldet, SeeD, Nicosia), demonstrated that this perspective indeed has some potential.

5
Islamists and the Choice Not to Take Up Arms: Algeria and Egypt

Georges Fahmi and Djallil Lounnas

In the 1990s, Algeria and Egypt were among the first Arab states to experience violent extremism.[1] The origins in both cases can be traced to the Afghan jihad of the 1980s, when thousands of young Arabs traveled to Afghanistan after the Soviet invasion to "support" the resistance against the Red Army. Upon return to their home countries, they coalesced with local youth and created jihadi groups to overthrow the regimes in place within the Arab world to replace them with radical Islamist ones instead (Tawil 2011). Under repression, those radical groups experienced splits and divisions, both on the battlefield as well as on the ideological front, leading some of them to renounce violence. In contrast, others continued to wage brutality, often going to extremes.

In Algeria in January 1992, Algeria's authorities canceled the general legislative elections because of fears of the state's takeover should an electoral victory of the Front Islamique du Salut (FIS) ensue. The cancellation of elections, along with the prospect of the takeover, raised fear, and the elections were canceled by the authorities while the FIS's banning led to civil strife, which claimed tens of thousands of lives during the 1990s (Willis 1999; Martinez 2000). Moreover, FIS's outlawing resulted in the emergence of various disconnected (and often competing) jihadi groups, which, by 1994, had regrouped into two major rival factions. On the one hand, Armée Islamique du salut (AIS) remained open to negotiations with the Algerian authorities toward potentially putting an end to the violence. On the other hand, the contrasting Groupe Islamique Armé (GIA) rejected any engagement with the government because it sought to conduct a jihad for the sake of overthrowing the government and replacing it with a revolutionary Islamic state. Whereas the AIS insurgency eventually entered into a truce in 1997 and later disbanded itself in the 2000s, the GIA veered into extreme violence, which ultimately resulted in its demise.

Mirroring the events in Algeria in July 2013, Egypt witnessed a military intervention against the Muslim Brotherhood's rule, with the new regime's decision to classify the movement as a terrorist organization. At that time, many warned that nonviolent Islamists would shift their tactics toward violence, as happened when the Algerian authorities decided to cancel the results of the elections after the victory of the Islamists in 1992. Yet, unlike their Algerian counterparts, only a minority among the Muslim Brotherhood's followers opted to do so.

Correspondingly, this chapter compares these two cases by analyzing the attitudes and actions of Islamist actors who agreed not to resort to violence (or renounced it outright) versus those who marched forward violently. Each case is presented within its respective general country-specific context, which provides clues toward the broader question of occurrence or nonoccurrence of violent extremism across and within the Islamist spectrum of both cases.

Conceptual Approach: Two-Factored Framework for Islamists' Decision to Take Up Arms

To facilitate a deeper understanding of the occurrence or nonoccurrence of Islamist violence, we examine two decisive moments in each country where Islamic groups actively engaged in debates over this issue of picking up arms: Algeria in 1992 and Egypt in 2013. We then set these debates within a two-factored framework. The first debated issue concerns the role of religious ideas in leading or preventing people from taking up arms. The second issue revolves around the calculative rationale of resorting to violence in terms of its projected odds expediency when considered against the regime's anticipated sheer military strength of prospective retaliation. As a former GIA leader who relinquished violence explained, the process of not resorting to violence was based on gauging two elements:

1. The religious-ideological question of whether or not Islamist violent actions would trigger *fitna* (division of the community of believers) and whether or not the killing of civilians en masse is tantamount to *takfir* (apostasy)
2. Consideration of the government's military superiority and its control over all aspects of security in the country

The central concept in radical Islam, called *takfir*, has steered major debates within jihadi groups because it constitutes the basis for the legitimization of the use of violence. The notion of *takfir* is central to jihadists because it is a necessary logical stepping stone for them to enact violence against those classified as enemies (Hafez 2000). For some jihadists, *takfir* can *only* be declared on governments and their supporters, yet *not* on civilians. In contrast, the more extreme groups, such as the GIA, believed that because government stems from populations, these populations were no longer considered as "civilian" and hence had become legitimate targets. It is the more extreme groups that eventually became known as Takfirists or Neo-Takfirists (Alshech 2014).

Mirroring Algerian debates a decade or so earlier, the Egyptian Muslim Brotherhood's youth debated the use of violence against Egypt's security forces, with discussions revolving around two questions: Was it religiously permissible to use violent means? Would such violence achieve its goal of bringing down the regime? In Egypt, many youths answered both of these questions negatively, concluding that violence was neither religiously permissible nor militarily expedient to bringing down the regime.

The Case of Algeria: Jihadi Armed Groups' Internal Conflict 1992–2000: AIS vs. GIA

The FIS's victory in Algeria's 1992 elections, which signaled an increased risk of the establishment of an Islamic state in the country, brought about an intervention of the Algerian Army, which canceled the elections and outlawed the FIS. With most of the FIS leadership exiled or in jail and thousands of its militants arrested, those who did escape repression decided to resort to armed force to directly confront the authorities. The dissolution of the FIS, which hitherto was already divided along two main competing ideological lines, led to the formation of two rival armed groups: the AIS and the GIA, who confronted the Algerian authorities while also engaging in a deadly struggle with one another. This resulted in bloody civil strife that killed tens of thousands of people between 1992 and 2000.

The AIS's origins trace back to the FIS faction known as the Djazara, or the Algerianists, which comprised the FIS's educated political leadership, who demanded the establishment of an Islamic state as sourced from *Algerian* Islamic inspirations rather than *Middle Eastern* influences such as those from the Egyptian Muslim Brotherhood (Labat 1995). The Djazara believed in utilizing political activism rather than violence to reach power. They broadly endorsed a multiparty system with its associated social and political freedoms, yet remained ambiguous on the justification of resorting to violence and the respect of individual liberties such as women's rights (Joffe 2011). By 1994, most Djazara-affiliated armed groups that merged to form the AIS claimed allegiance to the ex-FIS jailed leadership now in jail. Accordingly, the AIS stressed its commitment to abide by the Quran and Sunna and considered the jihad as a means (*wassila*) to establish an Islamic state, albeit it did not see jihad as an end in itself. This implied that other means (e.g., elections, preaching) could create an Islamic state (Hafez 2000). As a former AIS member explained: "The main goal of the AIS was the return to the electoral process of 1992," and violence remained "a response to the canceling of the election."[2] As a mediator between the AIS and the authorities confirmed: "The fact the AIS was structured by former political activists of the FIS, with a certain level of political training, facilitated contacts and potential negotiations with them."[3] Notwithstanding its armed insurgency, the AIS's main agenda was a political one.

Juxtaposed to the AIS stood the GIA, which stemmed from the FIS radical Salafi school of thought. It gathered support from the youths of the impoverished, marginalized suburbs of major cities, especially in Algeria's north, which constituted favorable enabling environments for the spread of the most extreme views of Salafism. Radical and revolutionary, and abhorrent of democracy as a form of disbelief (*kufr*), this faction of Salafi jihadism, now termed "the Islamic Armed Group," or GIA, called for the establishment of a fundamentalist Islamic state in Algeria run strictly according to the tenets of the Quran, Sunna, and sharia (Islamic) law.

The backbone of GIA's earlier guard consisted of Algerian foreign fighters from Afghanistan who, after fighting the Soviet Army during the 1980s, had returned home. Between 1979 and 1989, an estimated one thousand Algerians, answering the calls of Palestinian preacher Abdellah Azzam, joined the "jihad" in Afghanistan, where they received ample military training (Labat 1995). A radical mentor of Osama bin Laden, Azzam called the Arab youths for the jihad in Afghanistan against the Soviet invasion and in support of local Afghan Muslim populations. Once there, the Algerian fighters were dispatched to the various camps led by the Afghan resistance, and many of them received ideological and military training from former Afghan politicians and mujahidin leader Gulbuddin Hekmatyar, the most radical leader of the Afghan resistance.

Once back in Algeria in 1990, following the Soviet withdrawal from Afghanistan, the "Algerian Afghans" recruited youths from the poor suburbs of the cities from which they originated and trained and socialized them toward radical Salafi jihadism (Tawil 2011). This resulted in the establishment of the GIA in 1993, which deemed the Algerian authorities as apostates, hence the announcement that there would be "no negotiation, no cease-fire, no reconciliation, no security, [and] no guarantee with the apostate regime" (Hafez 2000). Moreover, whereas the AIS fight was to take place strictly within Algeria itself, the GIA's war was to be broader in its geographic scope: "Our fight is to free all the Muslim countries, from here

(Algeria) to Palestine" (Sifaoui 2010). In 1994, intending to unify the ranks of all Algerian jihadi groups, the GIA's then leader Chérif Gousmi, proclaimed himself "caliph" and required all to pledge allegiance to him while also declaring the Djazara as a *bidaa* (innovation), which in effect amounted to proclaiming the AIS as a *takfiry* (apostasy) group—in addition to the regime. By adopting such a brutal and uncompromising stance, the GIA effectively escalated into "total war" with all the other actors in the conflict.

The carnage that followed between 1994 and 1997, which is considered the bloodiest years of the Algerian civil war, has been well documented. At its peak, up to a thousand people were killed per day; often no one was spared, including women and children. By 1996, and moving away from Salafism jihadism to takfirism, the GIA effectively declared apostasy against parts of Algeria's civilian population writ large, raiding and massacring remote villages. Even under the most conservative estimates, well over a hundred thousand people died in Algeria between 1992 and 1997.

The Decision to End Violence on the Part of the AIS: The Ceasefire of 1997

On September 1, 1997, Madani Mezrag, the national emir of the AIS, ordered all his troops to stop fighting while calling other groups "attached to the interest of Islam and the Nation" to do the same (Martinez 1998). This decision was motivated by two converging dynamics: the evolution of the security situation, which was favorable (by then) to the Algerian authorities. And the fact that prominent Ulema (religious scholars) now called the violence *fitna* (a division of Islam) rather than jihad—hence, it was religiously illegitimate altogether.

The origins of the 1997 ceasefire can be traced back to the Algerian army's massive offensive of 1995, which pushed back all the armed groups and inflicted heavy losses on both GIA and AIS virtually across the entire country (Martinez 1998; Willis 1999). At the same time, the violent conflict, which had also pitted the GIA against the AIS (since 1994), further depleted the resources of both groups. The GIA's 1996 decision to deliberately target civilians caused further internal struggles while distancing local populations from both the AIS and the GIA; local populations created powerful pro-government groups called the Groupes de Legitime Defense (GLD), or Patriots. These provided additional and decisive support to the army against the various armed groups, especially the GIA (Martinez 2000). In that regard, to describe the situation during those years, a former GLD/Patriot explained that "there was no more State in those areas; they (GIA) killed everyone: paysans [villagers], women, kids . . . destroyed schools . . . they destroyed knowledge. It was a project of death, [so] that's why we decided to combat them, with [the] support of the army."⁴ In this context, the situation was rapidly deteriorating for the jihadi groups, at risk of total defeat. In this context, the AIS leaders had realized that "there had been too many killings, too many deaths, that the country could collapse and this was not their aim at all."⁵ Specifically, a former AIS member explained that the extreme violence of the GIA had put the AIS under extreme pressure to find a (negotiated) solution with the authorities to stop the cycle of violence.⁶ The life of the jihadists in the mountains had become unbearable under the pressure of the army, aggravated as it was by the lack of food and medicine that followed the dismantling of the logistics groups of those jihadi groups and loss of popular support.⁷

Thus, by 1996, direct negotiations between the authorities and the AIS had begun while jailed FIS leadership were only "informed and consulted." Lengthy and complex, the talks lasted well over a year. By the summer of 1997, an agreement was reached, with the AIS groups expected to announce a ceasefire for September that year. To date, the existence and exact content of the agreement remain in question. Yet it is fact that the AIS did agree to a ceasefire, along with another faction (the Islamic League for Predication and Djihad, or LIDD). Overall, nearly 6,000 men stopped fighting in exchange for amnesty, some 2,200 prisoners were released, and economic benefits for social reintegration were provided. However, any return to the political process was precluded. As a former FIS leader put it, this agreement was "purely a 'military one,' nothing more. There was no political component, and it was done without being sanctioned by the FIS."⁸ Nevertheless, one should note that the ex-FIS leaders endorsed the agreement if only to stop violence.

The Role of Ideas in the AIS Ceasefire

One of the significant challenges for the Algerian ceasefire concerned the so-called ideological religious legitimacy conundrum. At its heart, any process of peace between the Islamists and the government they considered a vile enemy of Islam, or even an apostate, required some Muslim theological "squaring" of such efforts as religiously legitimate. In this context, the AIS resorted to a rather extensive religious corpus that was essentially, yet not exclusively, derived from the Egyptian Muslim Brotherhood's religious scholarship; it eventually resulted in the disbandment of insurgency in Algeria. These religious references played a pivotal role in the negotiations and agreements between the AIS-LIDD and the Algerian authorities.

To begin with, there was the resort to precedents and analogies inspired by the actions of the Prophet Muhammad. LIDD leader Ali Benhadjar argued that it was religiously legal to enter into talks and to sign a truce with the Algerian authorities because the Prophet himself had undertaken similar endeavors during his time. Benhadjar explained that the Prophet did not hesitate to negotiate and sign truces with Jewish communities of the Arab Peninsula (with which he had been in conflict at times) as well his archenemies, the Quraishi tribes ruling Mecca, with whom he signed the treaty of Hudaybiyyah. Thus, Benhadjar reasoned, given that negotiations had ensued and pacts were signed with people the Prophet considered "infidels," the Islamist groups in Algeria could do the same with the Algerian authorities. This was further justified by the fact that it was being done for the general good of Muslims across Algeria, rendering Islamist groups as faithful followers of the Prophet's path of reconciling with authorities,[9] also seeing as these authorities had never been considered non-Islamic sensu stricto by the AIS.

As AIS's Emir Madani Mezrag explained, his decision to enter into the negotiations was strongly influenced by the writings of Egyptian Muslim Brotherhood leaders, including Hassan al-Banna, Mahmud Abdel Halim, and the texts of Cheikh Abu Hamid al-Ghazali—one of the most critical thinkers of Islam of the twelfth century (Ashour 2011). Back in the 1930s, the Muslim Brotherhood's founder, al-Banna, had stressed that jihad was a duty for all Muslims. Yet the jihad was meant to resist aggression, not commit one. For al-Banna (2010), the jihad was designed to protect God's message and peace. It was not meant to satisfy private or personal interests. Moreover, al-Banna believed that no atrocities should be committed during wartime under the pretext of jihad, including stealing or killing of women, children, elderly persons, or religious leaders. Still, these very atrocities were being committed by the GIA.

The writings of Mahmud Abdel Halim, a founding father and significant leader of the Muslim Brotherhood, were also cited by Mezrag as having profoundly influenced his thought process. Indeed, Abdel Halim wrote three major books that exposed the organization's history from its very creation in the 1930s to what Abdel Halim called its "darkest hours" in the 1950s and 1960s. The third volume is the most interesting because it covers those "dark years" of the Brotherhood's massive repression by the Nasser regime, as thousands of its members were arrested, tortured, and killed. Back then, despite the repression, Abdel Halim continued to negotiate with former Egyptian president Gamal Abdel Nasser. As he stressed, this was done in accordance with the orientations of the organization's *murshid* (religious leader) al-Hudaybi, who, back in the fifties and sixties, called for moderation and centrism. The talks with Nasser included the possibility of freeing all prisoners and the potential for the Brotherhood's relegalization (Abdelhalim 1973, 288–289). All this perfectly mirrored the AIS negotiations with Algeria's authorities, although back in the sixties, the Muslim Brotherhood–Nasser negotiations eventually failed.

The writings of al-Ghazali, a critical Islamic scholar of the twelfth century, are essential in the sense that he insisted on science and reason as much as religious principles to achieve the goals of Islam. In that regard, while al-Ghazali's writings did deal with the jihad and apostasy, he nonetheless insisted on those following principles in reaching the way of Islam. Finally, one should note that several other highly respected Muslim scholars (in this case, of Salafi obedience) also called for the end of violence in Algeria and the need to put an end to the *fitna* (division) because the jihad had effectively become illegitimate. Among these, one should note shaikhs al-Albani, al-Uthaymeen, and Rabi, who all called for the end of violence in Algeria, issuing fatwas in that regard back in 1999.

The Role of Ideas in the GIA's Refusal to a Ceasefire

Whereas the AIS and other groups entered negotiations with the Algerian authorities to put an end to the conflict, eventually reaching an agreement, the GIA followed the opposite path. Remaining firm and rejecting any dialogue or truce, regardless of the situation on the field, the GIA instead launched a wave of bloody massacres against the Algerian population. The GIA justified this by using more radical and extreme views of Salafi jihadism, eventually drifting toward takfirism. Much like the AIS-LIDD leadership resorted to analogies of the Prophet's actions, Mohammed Mokkdem (journalist and specialist of Algerian jihadi groups) explained that those who rejected any process of negotiations despite military defeat did so by arguing that "the prophet was defeated in the battle of Uhud, [so] it did not prevent him from taking Mecca and winning a few years later, that God was testing their patience and endurance."[10] Thus, for them, the jihad was to continue regardless of the setbacks.

Indeed, in 1996, the GIA issued a communiqué announcing that it remained steadfast on the principle of *wala* and *bara* (loyalty and disavowal). Thus, those who were allied with God and helping the GIA would be spared, whereas those who did not follow the religion of God and helped the *taghout* (tyrant) would enter into conflict with the GIA, which would "kill them" (Sifaoui 2010, 113). In this context, after initially declaring apostasy against the Algerian regime and all those who supported it, from 1996 onward, the GIA declared the *takfir* on the population at large (Hafez 2000, 587–588).

Because foreign-fighter returnees from Afghanistan chiefly created it, the GIA was de facto inspired by the Salafi jihadi doctrine. Thus, among the critical thinkers that influenced this organization was Sayyid Qutb, on the *takfir* of the regimes in place and the need to conduct the jihad against them; another vital thinker from whom the GIA derived thought was Abu

Muhammad al-Maqdisi, whose work covered in many respects the concept of Al Wala wal Bara (see Thurston 2017). The doctrines of Abdellah Azzam and bin Laden on the jihad also played a pivotal role in the ideological framing of the GIA. Therefore, once back in Algeria, foreign-fighter returnees fascinated with those ideas and precepts inculcated them into their recruits, primarily youths from the poor suburbs of major Algerian cities. This helped to decisively frame the ideological orientations of the GIA, which from the onset claimed direct filiation with Salafi jihadism.

Moreover, once the civil strife started, the GIA began to receive support from Salafi jihadi scholars, among whom was Abu Qutada al-Filistini, an extremist imam. In that regard, al-Filistini signed numerous fatwas authorizing the GIA to (among other tasks) kill the families of the members of the security services (Mokeddem 2002). Another one was Abu Mussab al-Suri, a prominent radical Salafi jihadi scholar who framed the thinking of the GIA and helped its newspaper *Al Ansar* get published in London (Atwan 2007). For al-Suri, Islamic states could only be established with "guns, bullets and teeth," which echoed the strategy of the GIA, which he described as "a heroic and powerful organization" (Thurston 2017).

Hence, adopting the hardened Salafi jihadi creed, the GIA refused any talks or negotiations with Algerian authorities and instead called for jihad until victory. In the end, this very line of extremism led the GIA insurgency to fall into takfirism when it launched its policy of extensive massacres against Algerian civilians. In turn, this finally led all the foremost Salafi jihadi scholars (including al-Filistini and al-Suri) to break ties with the GIA. In 2004, the GIA was wholly dismantled by the Algerian security services.

For its part, the Salafist Group for Preaching and Combat (GSPC) was created in 1998 by Salafi jihadi splinter groups of the GIA. The GSPC, claiming to return to the "Puritan Salafi creed," rejected the *takfir* on the population and the extreme violence of the GIA while also rejecting any negotiation with the authorities. In time, by 2007, the GSPC had become al-Qaeda in the Islamic Maghreb (AQIM). On the basis of those very principles of Salafi jihadism and the rejection of takfirism, in 2014 AQIM also refused to join the newly created Islamic State in Iraq and the Levant (ISIS/ISIL) and decided to remain loyal to al-Qaeda instead.

Egypt: The Case of the Muslim Brotherhood After 2013

Since Hassan al-Banna founded the Muslim Brotherhood in 1928, the group has maintained an influential position in Egypt's political scene. The group has a dual structure as a religious evangelizing movement and a sociopolitical organization. After the 1952 military coup, the Muslim

Brotherhood thought it would play a role in shaping the new regime. However, it clashed with Nasser twice in 1954 after an attempt on his life, and in 1965, Nasser accused the Brotherhood of planning a series of terrorist attacks to destabilize his regime. Nasser eradicated the movement by imprisoning many of its leaders and making others leave the country. These repressive measures led to the radicalization of a faction within the Brotherhood. It was during these years that the Muslim Brotherhood figure Sayyid Qutb wrote his book *Milestones*.

This was considered the ideological foundation of the radical Islamic movement in Egypt. The Nasser regime executed Qutb in 1966, but his ideas inspired a violent Islamist insurgency that started in the 1970s. According to Qutb, a society is only Muslim if it lives under God's law, *hakimiyyat Allah*, as revealed in the Quran. He argued that any supposedly Muslim society governed by artificial law is not Muslim, even if it claims to be. Another faction of the Muslim Brotherhood rejected Qutb's ideas. The supreme guide of the movement, Hassan al-Hudaybi, responded to Qutb's ideas in his book *Preachers, Not Judges* (*Du'at la Qudat*), arguing against Qutb's concept of excommunication. In its treatment of the fundamental question of who is a Muslim, al-Hudaybi insisted that anyone who pronounces a declaration of faith in earnest must be considered a Muslim (Zollner 2009).

After Sadat rose to power in 1970, he released the Muslim Brotherhood leaders. He encouraged them to rebuild their movement to counter the influence of Nasserist and leftist groups, particularly inside the universities. This is known as the second foundation of the Muslim Brotherhood. Since the 1980s, the Brotherhood has taken part in almost all parliamentary elections (except in 1990), seeming more like "an informal party" than a religious evangelizing movement (Bianchi 1989, 198). The Brotherhood also succeeded in using democratic processes to achieve electoral victories in almost all professional syndicates. In 2000, it won 17 of the 444 parliamentary seats, a number that jumped to 88 in the 2005 parliamentary election. During the 2010 parliamentary election, together with other opposition parties, the Brotherhood withdrew after the first round when it became clear that the regime would not allow opposition members to gain seats. Only two months later, Egyptians took to the streets against the Mubarak regime. The January 25, 2011, revolution that toppled Mubarak's regime opened up new opportunities for the Muslim Brotherhood, whose activities had until then been relatively restrained by the regime. In April 2011, it established the Freedom and Justice Party. The party participated in the 2011 legislative election and won 46 percent of the seats in Egypt's first free and fair election. In May 2012, the Muslim Brotherhood competed in the presidential election. Its candidate, Mohamed Morsi, who ran against Mubarak's former prime minister,

Ahmed Shafiq, won the second round in June 2012 with almost 51.7 percent of the votes.

During the Muslim Brotherhood's rule, relations between the Islamic movement and non-Islamic political groups were sharply polarized. In his first few months in power, Morsi tried to reach out to the opposition, and he even appointed some opposition figures to his administration. However, it soon became clear to these people that they were only there for show and that political decisions were not made by Morsi at the presidential palace but instead by the guidance office at the Brotherhood's headquarters. The turning point in relations between the regime and the opposition came while writing a constitution. The opposition withdrew from the constituent assembly to put pressure on the president to change his policies. However, Morsi decided to face the crisis, accepted the draft constitution, and called for a referendum. Although the constitution was adopted with 63.8 percent of the votes, three governorates rejected it, including Cairo with 56.8 percent. On a parallel track, tensions also rose between the Brotherhood and Egyptian state institutions, particularly al-Azhar (Egypt's oldest religious institution), the judiciary, and the security agencies, over which the group attempted to tighten its control. Although it was in power, the Brotherhood lacked control of the state apparatus. The more it tried to control these institutions, the more resistance it faced (Al-Anani 2015, 539).

Some institutions rejected what has been called the "Brotherhoodisation of the state" (*akhwanat al-dawla*), referring to the appointment of Muslim Brotherhood members to key positions in the state administration. The crisis peaked on June 30, 2013, when the opposition forces participated in massive demonstrations to demand early presidential elections. Morsi rejected this call and insisted that he was the legitimate president until the end of his mandate. His supporters also took to the streets to support him. In this highly polarized environment, supported by the judiciary, the political opposition, the Coptic pope, and the shaikh of al-Azhar, the military intervened on July 3, 2013, to remove Morsi from power. The Muslim Brotherhood and its supporters refused to accept this and staged sit-ins at Rabaa al-Adawiya and al-Nahda Squares to demand Morsi's return to the presidency. As all political attempts to reach a compromise between the Brotherhood and the new regime came to a dead end, the security forces intervened on August 14, 2013, and dispersed the demonstrators, resulting in the Brotherhood having to operate under even harsher conditions than during the Mubarak era. In addition to thousands of deaths and arrests, the new regime also dissolved the Freedom and Justice Party, confiscated and froze the financial assets of the movement's leadership in October 2013, and classified the Brotherhood as a terrorist organization in December 2013. Members of the Muslim Brotherhood continued to protest the new political rule.

This strategy stemmed from a decision made during a sit-in to use a nonviolent, creative approach to face the new regime. In a speech on July 5, 2013, at the Rabaa al-Adawiya protest, the Brotherhood's supreme guide, Mohammed Badie, stressed, "our revolution is peaceful and will remain peaceful. And our peacefulness is stronger than bullets."[11] However, by the end of 2014, as the regime was consolidating its power, some Muslim Brotherhood youths began to question the utility of this approach to facing the regime, particularly as jihadist groups in Sinai and mainland Egypt that had chosen a violent path were seeking to attract Brotherhood members. Within the Brotherhood, a tense debate ensued on whether to use self-defense tactics to protect protesters from police attacks.

At the end of 2014, Mohammed Kamal proposed a new plan to escalate violent attacks. The plan was intended to pave the way for what he thought might have been an opportunity to bring down the regime. The new leadership framed this strategy within an ideology based on a document called "The Jurisprudence of Popular Resistance to the Coup," issued by a religious committee within the Brotherhood. The document offers religious justification for the use of violence against security forces by underlining the religious concept of "Dafa' al-Sa'el" or "Repelling the Assailant," which, according to this document, is equivalent to the modern idea of the right to self-defense. However, the historical leadership, both in Egypt and abroad, interfered to put an end to this violent approach and accused Kamal of seeking to militarize the Muslim Brotherhood.

Members of the historical leadership represented by Mahmoud Ezzat, the deputy of the supreme guide, and Mahmoud Hussein, the secretary general, rejected Kamal's new strategy to escalate violence and tried to reassert their control over the movement. To decrease the tension between the two groups, Mohammed Kamal agreed to step down as leader of the administrative committee. In October 2015, the two camps decided to form a second administrative committee directed by Mohammed Abdel Rahman, a member of the Guidance Bureau known for being close to the historical leadership. Mohammed Kamal kept his position as a mere member of this new committee. However, this attempt soon failed as Mohammed Abdel Rahman accused the committee of acting without consulting him. In contrast, the committee accused him of blocking all its decisions without explanations.

Throughout 2016, the historical leadership used organizational skills to regain control over the administrative structure. In April 2016, Mahmoud Ezzat declared that the Shura council had met and selected a new administrative committee. A month later, Mohammed Kamal announced his resignation in an audio message from his position as an administrative committee member. He called on all the administrative offices to unite and support the efforts to elect a new leadership. Five months later, security forces assassinated Kamal.

Factors Shaping Youths' Decision Not to Take Up Arms

Although many Muslim Brotherhood youths experienced the wave of political radicalization after 2013, most of them didn't take up arms. Two main factors shaped their decisions on whether to take up arms: (1) ideas and, (2) cost-benefit calculations. Both of these factors were further influenced by the more general presence of legitimate voices that either supported or rejected such decisions.

The Role of Ideas

Youths who went through this wave of political radicalization looked for a conceptual frame to explain the political struggle they were facing, to show the final aim they should struggle for, and to clarify the means allowed to be used in the battle. Although, as many have already argued (Roy 2017a), religious ideas play only a secondary role in the radicalization process, they nonetheless play an essential role in the transition from radicalization to violence. The fact that ideas come later in the radicalization process does not mean that ideas were not influential in shaping the paths of these radical youths. These ideas frame the struggle and identify the final aim and the path toward achieving it. Without these ideas, a decision to take up arms was less likely to take place. A Salafi jihadi frame offered some youths an answer to their questions.

The root of the jihadi doctrine goes back to a similar period of clashes between the Muslim Brotherhood and the Egyptian regime during the 1950s and 1960s. The writings of Islamist thinker Sayyid Qutb in the 1960s offered an inspiring frame for many youths to make sense of the post-2013 political environment. The Muslim Brotherhood, including Qutb himself, was a strong supporter of the 1952 military coup in Egypt, with the idea that it would build a regime based on Islam. However, both the secular and socialist political paths of coup leader Gamal Abdel Nasser left Islamists disappointed.

The regime's persecution of the Muslim Brotherhood during the 1950s and 1960s led Qutb to reconsider the frame of the political struggle in Egypt. He concluded that the battle was neither economic nor political—but religious. Essentially, it was a struggle between beliefs: either unbelief or faith, Jahiliyyah or Islam (Qutb 1987, 176–177). According to Qutb, the enemies of believers may wish to change the nature of the struggle into an economic, political, or racial struggle so that believers become confused concerning the true nature of the battle and the flame of belief in their hearts is extinguished. Believers must not be deceived and must understand that this is a trick. Qutb argued that by changing the nature of the struggle, the enemy intended to deprive them of their weapon of true victory, victory that could take any form, be it the victory of the freedom of spirit, as was the case for believers in the story of the Makers of the Pit, or dominance in the world because of freedom of spirit, as happened with the first generation of Muslims.

It was only after the process of political radicalization, as described in the first section of this chapter, that youths started to look for ideas that fit their radical political approach to make sense of the political crisis they were facing. In most of the cases followed here, the decision to embrace jihadi ideas came only after radical political convictions were deeply rooted. In other words, angry youths looked for ideas to justify their decision to practice violence. They looked for ideas; it was not ideas that were looking for them.

However, these ideas were not merely tools to justify their political radicalization. Once adopted, these ideas had their own impact. For many of these individuals, Salafi jihadi ideas changed their worldview entirely, including the initial trigger of radicalization, and ousted the rule of the Muslim Brotherhood. In the case of one Muslim Brotherhood supporter who had protested against ousting Mohammed Morsi after July 2013, adopting jihadi ideas led him to change his position on Morsi and argue that Morsi entirely deserved what happened to him because he did not rule by what God revealed—he'd resorted to democracy (Arij 2018). Here, the jihadi literature makes out that political violence is not only a normatively accepted choice but also an Islamic duty. Ideas play a primary role in leading an individual to move or not move from political radicalization to violence. All the cases of Egyptian youths who decided to take up arms looked for literature that justified the use of violence. Many of them found what they were looking for in the writings of Sayyid Qutb and Abdullah Azzam.

On the other side, religious ideas represented a barrier to violence among those who were raised rejecting ideas of excommunication. This was the case with many of the Brotherhood youths. Since the 1970s, the Brotherhood had preached against the jihadist groups' doctrine of excommunicating state officials and using violence to achieve their political goals. There were clear orders not to promote any sympathizer to the entire member level if there were doubts over his views on these two issues. Others who had had religious education at an al-Azhar religious institute faced this same ideational barrier. In these cases, their religious ideas played a decisive role in their decisions not to take up arms against other Muslims.

Youths reacted to this ideational barrier differently. Some, indeed, accepted the fact that violence was not a viable option. Others tried to offer a new conceptual frame for the practice of violence. This is the case of one branch of the Muslim Brotherhood. A part of the leadership sought to offer a conceptual frame that would allow Muslim Brothers to practice a limited level of violence in their strategy to resist the political regime. They asked several religious scholars within the Brotherhood to offer an ideational frame that set the conditions for the practice of violence. This committee issued a document called "The Jurisprudence of Popular Resistance to the Coup." It justified the use of violence against security forces by underlining the religious concept of Dafa' al-Sa'el, or Repelling the Assailant, which, according to the document, is equivalent to the modern idea of the right to self-defense.

This ideological framework contained various degrees and choices between nonviolence and fully armed confrontation. According to the religious approach, the assailant should be resisted gradually, starting with the least costly measures (threats/beatings). This new ideological framework was distinct from Salafi jihadist ideology, which relies on the principle of excommunication as the basis for the military struggle against state institutions to achieve Islamic governance. The approach in the document did not excommunicate members of the security forces and underlined that they should be resisted not because of their faith but because of their actions.

Cost-Benefit Calculation

On the basis of the conceptual frame adopted to make sense of their political crisis, youths likely weigh the costs and benefits of taking up arms against state institutions. The decision to take up arms is a challenging one. The Muslim Brotherhood youths who considered this path in the new ideological frame supported by a part of their leadership had two main concerns that led them to renounce violence on the basis of cost-benefit calculations.

The first factor was the power imbalance between them and the security forces they faced, which made it impossible for them to win a military battle. The second factor was the lack of support from Egyptian society. This was the case even within families. One member of the Brotherhood was rejected by a part of his family after he was released from prison. Other members of the Brotherhood were shocked when residents of their neighborhoods attacked them and refused to let their protests pass through those areas (Ramadan 2013). This high level of widespread anger, together with the power imbalance between violent groups and the Egyptian state security forces, rendered the decision to take up arms very costly. At the same time, any benefits were less likely to be achieved.

Some youths who abstained from practicing violence saw violence in this case as a premature option because it did not reflect a strategy. Although they could accept the use of violence in principle, they argued that violence needed to be part of a more comprehensive strategy, and this was not the case. By lack of a strategy, they meant that the approach did not consider the day after the collapse of the regime. It principally appeared to be a mere hopeless option with a lack of other reciprocal political tools such as cultivating channels for negotiation and building alliances to translate gains. Many of these Islamist youths thought that violence would lead nowhere. However, those who followed the jihadi doctrine were not deterred by the sacrifices they had to make and not even by their likely defeat by the Egyptian security forces.

The jihadi doctrine frames the struggle against the political regime as one of believers against nonbelievers, in which jihad is a religious duty regardless of the outcome of the battle. Moreover, the jihadi doctrine frames the meaning of costs and benefits differently. In Sayyid Qutb's own words, life with all its gains and losses is not the main criterion when weighing the costs and benefits, and it does not determine who wins and who loses. In his famous book *Milestones*, Qutb quotes the story of the "Makers of the Pit" as is told in the Surah al-Buruj (The Constellations). This is the story of a group of people who believe in Allah and openly proclaim their belief. They encounter tyrannical and oppressive enemies. In Qutb's words, the faith in the hearts of the believers raised them above all persecution. Belief triumphed over life.

The threat of torture did not shake them; they never recanted, and they burned in the fire until death. They freed themselves from this earth and all its attractions, triumphing over life through a sublime faith. Qutb makes this meaning clear by arguing that life's pleasures and pains, achievements and frustrations do not have significant weight on the scale and do not determine winning or losing. Triumph is not limited to immediate victory but is one of the many forms of triumph. In Allah's scale, the proper weight is the weight of faith. In the "Makers of the Pit," the souls of the believers were victorious over fear and pain, over the allurements of the earth and of life (Qutb 1987). Therefore, the ideational frame adopted by the youths directly affected the cost-benefit analysis they made. Ideas shaped the weight of both costs and benefits and, therefore, determined the rationality of the political decision of whether to take up arms.

The Muslim Brotherhood's post-2013 ideational frame based on armed political resistance led many Brotherhood youths to doubt that using violence against Egyptian state institutions would destabilize the political regime, given the imbalance of power between the two sides. Weighing an unlikely victory against all the sacrifices they had to make, many of them gave up on the armed struggle. The youths who adopted a jihadi approach did not face this dilemma. The jihadi frame also played a role in the decisions of Islamist youths who were never members of organizations but who chose to participate in violence. In their case, they were not interested in a cost-benefit calculation because they did not see violence as a political tool to make gains but, instead, as an act of purification to display devotion to God by standing up against tyranny. Only through violence and the sacrifices that came with it could they fulfill their responsibility before God and their fellow Muslims, and the earthly outcome, winning or losing, was merely God's will, according to their understanding. This was true in the case of an Islamist engineer with no organizational affiliation. He fiercely refused any call to consider the rationality of sacrificing his privileges and his established social stance in favor of going for the unrealistic choice of jihad. According to accounts of his experience, he thought it was a matter of being ethical and a good Muslim to care for supporting the weak and to fight injustice.

This account and similar ones contribute to our understanding of why the jihadi approach was more attractive to individuals who did not have any political project, because it seemed more authentic, pious, and transparent in comparison to other trends that sought material gains from this mighty cause.

Conclusion

The comparative analysis of paths to violent extremism in Algeria and Egypt shows many similarities in the characteristics of mobilization but also in the decision not to resort to violence. In the end, the decision not to resort to violence was motivated by two main factors. First is the realistic consideration of the political/military situations, which the Islamist leaders in Algeria called the Waqii (the reality), and what the youth of the Muslim Brotherhood refer to as the balance of power between their movement and Egyptian security. The second factor is religious ideas, especially the writing of the Ulama about the need to maintain unity and peace among the Muslims and to avoid *fitna* (social strife) at any cost.

These two factors are interdependent. Religious ideas shape actors' perceptions of the balance of power and what they might consider a "rational" action or not. Jihadi ideas could offer a frame to make sense of the political struggle by reducing it to a battle over religious doctrine. Jihadi ideas also shaped the weight of both costs and benefits, leading youths to follow this path despite the imbalance of power between armed groups and the Egyptian security forces.

On the other hand, individuals with a religious background that rejects the concept of excommunication of Muslims, such as those with an al-Azhar religious education and members of the Muslim Brotherhood, were less likely to accept the jihadi frame. When members of the Muslim Brotherhood offered a new ideational frame to justify the use of violence based on ideas such as political resistance and self-defense, the power imbalance between them and the state security forces led them to give up on this violent approach.

These differences could also be found within each case. The key difference among the Muslim Brotherhood, Gamaa Al Islmaliya, AIS, and

GIA is the fall into takfirism. Although the Muslim Brotherhood, Gamaa Al Islmaliya, and AIS did not adopt the concept of excommunication, their political struggle against state institutions had a solid political, not religious, component. In contrast, the GIA, as well as groups like Islamic State (IS) in post-2013 Egypt, followed the path of excommunication, and religious puritanism was more prominent than their political goals.

Notes

1. The authors would like to thank Athina Tefsa-Yohannes, professor at the Al Akhawayn Language Center, for editing the Algeria section of this chapter.

2. Interview with a former member of the Islamic Salvation Army (April 2021).

3. Interview with a former local mediator between the Algerian authorities and the AIS (December 2022).

4. Interview with a former Patriot (January 2023).

5. Interview with a former local mediator between the Algerian authorities and the AIS (December 2022).

6. Interview with a former member of the Islamic Salvation Army (April 2021).

7. Ibid.

8. Interview with a former FIS leader (January 2023).

9. See "The elimination of the Djazara (Mohamed Said and Abderezak Rejam) the day decided the group of Zitouni (GIA)" يوم قرر جماعة الزيتوني (GIA) تصفية (جماعة الجزأرة محمد السعيد وعبد الرزاق رجام), Online: https://www.youtube.com/watch?v=Qc7xpXB9lFA.

10. Interview with Mohammed Mokkdem, journalist and specialist of Algerian armed groups (September 2012).

11. The full speech by Mohammed Badie, the supreme guide of the Muslim Brotherhood, on July 5, 2013, is available in Arabic at the following link: https://www.youtube.com/watch?v=mAuHkmXDIxg.

6

Religious Resilience and the Guardian State: Morocco and Jordan

Gilad Ben-Nun and Nizar Messari

Violent extremism continues to affect global societies and has resulted in confrontations between states and violent extremist groups the world over. This chapter examines two states that have been relatively spared extremist strife despite their evident "enabling environment" characteristics. Morocco and Jordan, two relatively poor states in terms of natural resources, are ruled by two constitutional monarchies. Although both countries have had their share of terrorist attacks over the last two decades, compared to other states in the region, these two countries have shown considerable degrees of immunity and resilience toward violent extremism. In addition, both states have seen their GDP progress in the decade between the commencement of the 2011 Arab unrest and 2021, rendering them somewhat exceptional (Jamal and Robbins 2022).

So why have Morocco and Jordan shown such resilience against violent extremism? We argue that both Morocco and Jordan have succeeded in establishing spaces of dialogue between state and society as well as within society. Despite their unequal traits, it is a dialogue that has allowed—as this chapter illustrates—both youth and society to avoid engaging in violent extremism. Moreover, it has permitted Moroccans and Jordanians who had been actively involved in violence to return to their own countries, face tribunals, and eventually benefit from measures of reintegration into their societies.

To explore these different dimensions of dialogue, we first present the institutions Morocco put in place and the initiatives it has taken to deal with violent extremism. We show that although these initiatives are imbued with overt power dimensions, they have allowed Islamists to participate in the public realm and have allowed youth groups to be heard when they express their qualms. In Jordan, we explore engagement in elections as an explicit act of dialogue in which the state and the Islamists have both made active concessions as they have moved toward one another to establish a distinctly Jordanian space for dialogue, coupled with other mechanisms to reduce social tension, such as community policing, broad distribution of food subsidies, usage of subsidies for societal calming, and usage of electoral allowances that serve as pressure valves for the alleviation of social unrest.

Methodological Justifications of the Moroccan-Jordanian Comparison

The comparison of Morocco and Jordan is methodologically merited because of the countries' several unique characteristics. Both are "Sharifian" kingdoms ("guardian states"), rendering their comparison one of cases most alike. Both countries are defined as Muslim constitutional monarchies. Both draw their religious and governmental legitimacy from the lineage of their royal houses as alleged historical generational extensions stemming back to the Prophet Muhammad. From 2011 to 2021, during the Arab unrest, both successfully maintained relative degrees of peace and social calm within their borders, in sharp contrast to many other Arab states.

In contrast to their Gulf state royal peers, neither Jordan nor Morocco rely on the extraction of fossil fuels for economic viability. In contrast to other countries in the Middle East and North Africa (MENA), whose GDP per capita declined between 2011 and 2021, both Jordan and especially Morocco continued to demonstrate steady GDP growth during these tumultuous years (Ben-Nun and Engel 2022 a, 13–14). Last, both countries decided to rely on meaningful dialogue efforts to alleviate their social tensions vis-à-vis Islamic extremism.

Notwithstanding all these similarities, academic literature has not paid attention to the similarities between Morocco's and Jordan's approaches toward preventing violent extremism (PVE) (Jumet 2019, 394). Yet, whereas academic literature has missed the specialty of the Moroccan and Jordanian cases, Arabic-speaking journalism was keen-eyed enough to notice the countries' success. Four years before his assassination in Saudi Arabia's consulate in Istanbul, the well-respected Jamal Khashoggi praised Morocco's and Jordan's conduct vis-à-vis their popular uprisings. Emphatically titling both guardian states as "successful Arab Spring models," Khashoggi wrote:

> These two non-oil-producing . . . have not resorted to force, oppression, security, and detention; instead, they transferred the Arab Spring's protests and anger into positive energy and reconciliation between the government and the people. (Khashoggi 2014)

The Case of Morocco: Dialogue and Engagement on the Monarchy's Terms– The Rabita Mohamadia and Moussalaha

Morocco's strategy for confronting violent extremism serves as an example of resilience and nonoccurrence in an otherwise enabling environment for the development of violent extremism (Ben-Nun and Engel 2022a). This strategy is based on a top-down approach with three different pillars. The first consists of classical policing and intelligence operations. The second focuses on human development to reduce individual and communal vulnerabilities. The third pillar puts forward a more moderate and tolerant understanding of religion in the face of extremist views. The assumption behind this triple top-down strategy is that violent extremism has multiple causes and that an approach that focuses on one cause while neglecting the others is bound to fail. In other words, the triple Moroccan strategy in dealing with violent extremism can be efficient only if it avoids operating in terms of autonomous silos and, instead, entails coordination among the three pillars.

This raises the question of what facilitated Morocco's success in combating political violence and extremism. To be sure, and notwithstanding the international Global Terrorism Index's specific biases, Morocco is a low-risk country in terms of violence, as evidenced in its being ranked seventy-sixth in terms of terrorism threats in 2022 and then improving to place eight-third in 2023 (IEP 2023). This might point to causal links between Morocco's anti-extremist strategies and its low incidence of terrorist attacks. Nevertheless, despite Morrocco's apparent successes in countering extremism, there are adverse examples of this trend. During the second decade of the twenty-first century, young Moroccans were among the highest numbers in the MENA to have migrated to Syria and Iraq to join the Islamic State in Iraq and Syria (ISIS), second only to Tunisians. According to Moroccan authorities, until 2021, 1,659 nationals joined ISIS ranks in Syria and Iraq (Morocco World News 2023).

So, what explains the relative success of Morocco's strategy in countering violent extremism?

Our hypothesis in this chapter is that Morocco, like Jordan, provides spaces for dialogue that brings extremized individuals back to moderation. We focus on three population groups: youths, returnees from Syria and Iraq, and individuals with jail sentences related to previous terrorist activities. What we term "spaces of dialogue" are both upstream of the struggle against extremism and downstream of that action. Upstream action is that of the Rabita Mohamadia of Oulama, which dispenses significant effort in engaging youths in languages and narratives that are attractive to them and that provide alternative, more nuanced, moderate, and ultimately more mainstream religious views, much in line with established Moroccan norms of Sunni Maliki Islam.¹ As for downstream action, we refer here to the initiative called Moussalaha, which can be translated as "reconciliation." It is an official state-sponsored initiative that engages prisoners and provides them with alternative, more nuanced, more moderate, and ultimately more mainstream religious views. It is relevant to note here that the Rabita Mohamadia of Oulama is also a key partner of Moussalaha.

The Moroccan state's strategy in dealing with Islamist-based contestation forces is twofold, resembling a similar strategy followed by the Moroccan state against left-wing contestations during the 1960s and 1970s. These strategies vary with the individual or group targeted and their inclinations. For those whom the Moroccan state deems sensitive to co-optation, it has sought first to domesticate them and then attract them to the legal political realm. When they eventually started participating in official political spaces, the first type of group, represented today by the main Islamist party, the Party of Justice and Development (PJD), did so under the terms established by the so-called Makhzen.² This co-optation process did not occur overnight; it took almost three decades to complete and culminated with the legislative elections of 2011, which followed the enactment of a new Moroccan constitution in July that year. Consequently, the PJD became the first political party in Morocco whose leader was appointed head of the government (Bergh 2013).

A second group has been less susceptible to co-optation, given its refusal to endorse the Moroccan king's role. Similar to some leftists who had contested the monarchy in the 1960s and 1970s, Islamist groups, and one in particular, Al Adl Wa Al Ihssane (the Movement of Justice and Misericord), which the late Abdessalam Yassine founded, contested the role of the king as Commander of the Faithful, which has consistently been a red line that the regime, the deep state we previously referred to as the Makhzen, has never tolerated. Suspicion about the other side's intentions was mutual between the Makhzen and the abovementioned movement. Indeed, the latter group has also been considering the state's official approaches of co-optation as attempts at indoctrination. In turn, the Moroccan state's approach toward this second group has varied between confrontation and "containment" (Maghraoui 2017; Willis 2012).

A third group might be added, and it would consist of those who were radicalized and who participated in violent acts but who are considered to have redeeming features. In its approach toward individuals in this third group, and after the state confronted them with the traditional security apparatus tools, it—the deep state, the Makhzen—also ended up resorting to dialogue and eventually prevention. In this chapter, we focus on the third group and the spaces of dialogue created by the state with this group through two distinct institutions: the Rabita Mohamadia of Oulama and the Penitentiary Administration. The Penitentiary Administration, in collaboration with the Rabita Mohamadia and other institutions, has initiated the Moussalaha program. Indeed, Rabita Mohamadia plays a crucial role in educating new religious leaders, or imams, and in reaching out to the youth through establishing spaces of dialogue with them to impact their understanding of Islam. The action of the Rabita aims to prevent radicalization by offering spaces of dialogue to youths. The second initiative, Moussalaha, aims at deradicalizing detainees who have participated in violent activism. More details are given later, but through Moussalaha, detainees engage in a three-and-a-half-month program in which they venture into spaces of dialogue with their religion and with themselves, after which they can apply for a significant reduction of their sentence or even freedom. In summary, these two initiatives create separate platforms for engaging with vulnerable youth and individuals who have already been radicalized, albeit aiming for the same objective: countering violent extremism.

A caveat is necessary here. In Morocco, political violence is not the exclusive act of the marginalized, on the left or the right. Political violence has also been an act of the state (imprisonment of journalists, crackdowns on human rights, repression of peaceful demonstrations, among others). These state-led actions have established a political environment that has pushed the youth to desperate actions: some dream of fleeing the country and others do flee. Violence as a reaction to desperate conditions takes different forms. For instance, the "Ultras," which are violent groups of soccer team supporters, represent one response by youths to the limited opportunities for freedom in Morocco. Similarly, those who turn to violent extremism demonstrate another response to the oppressive actions of the state. In Morocco and many other regions, people respond to state violence and systematic oppression.

Three-Prong Strategy for Dealing with Extremism

In the next part of this discussion, and as previously mentioned, we analyze the three pillars of Morocco's strategy in dealing with violent extremism.

The first pillar involves using traditional police and intelligence methods that follow a three-step process known as "location, identification/isolation, and eradication." This approach relies on gathering intelligence to locate insurgent groups (location), then separating them from their supporters by disrupting their activities and exposing the threat they pose (identification/isolation). Finally, the strategy involves taking action to attack and arrest these groups (eradication). Over the first two decades of the twenty-first century, approximately 2,000 terrorist cells have been dismantled, and over 3,500 individuals in Morocco with links to terrorist activities have been arrested. This efficiency of Morocco's preemptive strategy results from a wide net of informants throughout the country, which was reinforced by Moroccan intelligence's permanent efforts to infiltrate the suspected groups and gather information from within them (Maghraoui 2009). But even as data exists on dismantled cells and arrested individuals, there is scant information about the whereabouts of detained individuals, their judgments, and their eventual sentencing (Mostafa, Nakagawa, Matsumoto 2016; Wainscott 2017).

The assumption behind the second pillar is that although poverty, joblessness, and lack of economic perspectives are not directly conducive to violent extremism, these conditions represent a fertile field for recruiting would-be terrorists. To deal with these root causes of the insurgency, Morocco launched the National Initiative on Human Development (INDH, from its French name) in 2005 to foster and focus on human development, but with a substantial side effect of limiting the fertile camp for recruiting terrorists. But in fifteen years, Morocco's Human Development Index (HDI) has improved only modestly. In 2005, when INDH was officially launched, Morocco's HDI was 0.580. By 2019, it had reached 0.686. Simultaneously, while Morocco's ranking according to its HDI back in 2005 was 128, in 2019, that ranking was 121. For comparison, during the same period, Botswana, for instance, improved from 0.601 to 0.735 and moved from 123rd to 100th in the ranking. In sum, although Morocco made some relative progress in terms of its human development performance, that evolution was not only modest, but it paled when compared to similar states. King Mohammed VI underlined the limitations of INDH in a speech in 2015. In 2019, he appointed a national commission intending to revamp Morocco's development model to make it more robust and allow it to respond to the needs of the Moroccan population and the challenges facing the country. This shows a significant concern at the top of the political pyramid about the challenges facing Morocco's development and the need to tackle them.

It is possible to argue, however, that the central innovative aspect of Morocco's strategy in dealing with the insurgency is what we call here the third pillar, that is, the one that consists of reforming the religious field. The reform, composed of several parallel initiatives, advocated for Morocco's traditional understanding of Islam: a moderate Sunni and Maliki understanding. One of the main initiatives was to intervene in the education of new imams and the retool those who were already acting, with the same objective: reinforce what is referred to in Morocco as the spiritual strength of Moroccans through the reaffirmation of a moderate understanding and interpretation of Islam. The education of new imams began in 2004. In 2014, the Mohammed VI Institute for Imams was established. It expanded to educate not only Moroccans but also imams from other parts of the world. The institute's significant mission to train both male *and* female religious guides marked a major turning point in the process.[3] Indeed, in 2014, the institute hosted 150 male future imams and 50 female *mourchidates* (women preachers); in 2015, the number of *mourchidates* increased to 100, and currently, women represent 40 percent of the total number of students. As a result, by 2019, more than 777 *mourchid* and *mourchida* (i.e., men and women), including imams from thirty-two countries from Africa, Asia, and Europe, have studied in the institute and were preaching its moderate understanding of Islam throughout the world (Ordioni 2019). The curriculum of studies consists of a one-year program, with an average of thirty weekly hours of studies in which these future imams, men and women, study different disciplines such as religious studies, human rights, foreign languages, and information technology.

The Rabita Mohamadia of Oulama, which is the League of Religious Scholars, is another significant contributor to the reformation of the religious sphere in Morocco, especially concerning the issue of violent extremism. Not only do many of its contributions and publications tackle that issue, but it also has an active and dynamic online presence, which allows it to reach the youth. The Rabita also contributes to initiatives such as Moussalaha, which we describe later. The Rabita Mohamadia explicitly aims at reaching out to youths, mainly through its website, and it resorts to languages and narratives the youth are used to. It offers a platform of multilingual online videos of conferences and talks by theologians. The objective of these interventions is consistently to *deconstruct* the narratives of violent extremism and offer moderate and rational alternatives to the youth. As such, these initiatives represent a space of interaction and dialogue between scholars and youths. The latter connect with listening ears and open-minded scholars who help them veer from the language of extremism. The work of the Rabita is long term because it must gain the trust of the youth before it can deconstruct the language of extremism.

Moussalaha is another space of dialogue in which the Rabita plays a significant role. The program was developed in 2017 by the Moroccan Penitentiary administration in close cooperation with the Rabita Mohamadia of Oulama and the National Council on Human Rights (CNDH), with the support of eminent specialists from different fields. The objective of Moussalaha is to reintegrate detainees sentenced for extremism and terrorism. It acts on the spiritual immunization of detainees and is itself based on three pillars: reconciliation with oneself, reconciliation with the religious text, and reconciliation with society. Selected detainees participate in a unique multiweek program that typically lasts three and a half months. Successful completion of the program qualifies them for sentence reductions or release. Two hundred thirty-nine detainees have benefited from this program since 2017. Initially, the program targeted only male detainees, but now it addresses female detainees as well. With Moussalaha, Moroccan authorities demonstrate their willingness to listen to detainees, address their needs for redemption of past acts, and reintegrate them into society. The program provides that space of dialogue that grants detainees a ticket to be readmitted to society. Moussalaha has a good index of nonrepeat, that is, those who benefit from the program seldom return to violent extremism.

It is also important to note that, as opposed to many other states, including European states, Morocco has been opening the gate for Moroccans previously engaged in Syria as fighters to return home. The Parliamentary Committee on Foreign Affairs and Moroccans Living Abroad has prepared a report on Moroccans who are combatants in Syria and who remain stranded in conflict zones. Of the 1,659 Moroccans who went to Syria and Iraq since the emergence of ISIS, close to 300 were women and more than 628 were children or minors, and Morocco has been readmitting them.

In sum, Moroccan authorities have shown an openness to listening to the needs of the youth and those already radicalized. They opened spaces for dialogues with the objective of deconstructing the pernicious narratives of extremism, thanks to the work of the Rabita Mohamadia of Oulama, and have allowed for the reintegration into society of detainees sentenced for terrorist acts and of combatants who are willing to return home from war zones. This shows Morocco's flexibility in dealing with different situations; Moroccan authorities can offer options almost à la carte to those susceptible to extremism as well as those already victims of extremism but who are willing to reintegrate into society. Of course, a dialogue is a two-way street. In contrast, initiatives such as Moussalaha, as well as others by the Rabita Mohamadia of Oulama, cannot be adequately called dialogues, even if they cannot be described as monologues either. This is because the dialogue takes place over two stages. In the first, Moroccan authorities listen to the youth, the already radicalized, and the combatants. After the listening phase, authorities subject these individuals and groups to a "reeducation," a deconstruction, that convinces them of what is considered the right path. That has allowed Morocco to diversify the tools it uses to address extremism efficiently. Rabita Mohamadia of Oulama, for example, utilizes languages and narratives that resonate with the youth and relies on the internet to convey its messages. This is the same space in which the youth are radicalized initially. The Rabita Mohamadia of Ulama also analyzes the root causes of youth radicalization so that it can address those specific underlying factors. In this sense, the Rabita—and through it, the Moroccan authorities—has adjusted its language and narrative because it listened to the youth.

So, the Rabita provides young people with a discourse tailored to their needs and expectations, using language that shows respect and consideration. Similarly, Moroccan authorities do not ignore or ostracize those Moroccans who have already been radicalized—both combatants willing to return to Morocco and detainees jailed for violent actions. They engage with them in a dialogue where individuals can express their position, and only after are they offered paths to redemption. Even then, those who choose not to participate are not forced to do so. Only those who are willing and receptive are accepted into the program.

Morocco has significantly low incidences of violent extremism. This fact is backed by data and by Moroccans' feeling of safety. The state's approach is based on a policy to combat violent extremism that rejects sole focus on security measures. Instead, policy includes initiatives for human development, promotion of a moderate interpretation of Islam, and efforts toward reconciliation. Some of these tools are more efficient than others: INDH has not been as effective as it was expected to be, and a small but substantial minority of religiously pious Moroccans refuse to be part of what they consider an indoctrination endeavor. Finally, a critical characteristic of Morocco's response to violent extremism is its creation of dialogue spaces presented here. The combination of these initiatives pays off and allows Morocco to offer its citizens a safe and stable space.

The Case of Jordan: Limited Dialogue and Embedded Policies to Alleviate Social Tension

Jordan's mixed legacy of accommodation and confrontation with Islamist groups dates back to the kingdom's independence in 1946, which coincided with granting the right of incorporation to the Jordanian branch of the Egyptian-affiliated Muslim Brotherhood in the kingdom. Over the years, and in stark contrast to their Egyptian counterparts, Jordanian Islamists have generally supported the Hashemite dynasty through the many challenges to the legitimacy of its rule that this noble house has faced. The Brotherhood's siding with the crown against the obstacles to King Hussein's regime in 1956, and again during the Palestinian challenge to Hashemite rule during Black September (1970), further cemented the "mutually acquiescent relationship" between Islamists and the Jordanian regime, at least until the 1990s (Ghadbian 1997, 25n23).

Since the mid-1990s, the challenges posed by Islamism to the Jordanian regime have grown. The return of Wahabi-educated Jordanians from the Gulf states following Saddam Hussein's debacle during Iraq's 1990–1991 occupation of Kuwait (ambivalently supported by the Jordanian monarchy), together with the return of Jordanian foreign fighters from their anti-Soviet campaign in Afghanistan, contributed to turning the kingdom into a hotbed for radically violent but well-trained Islamists. As scholars have noted:

> The paradox of Jordan is that from the 1980s to 2017, it was also a hotbed for jihadi recruitment to fight in Afghanistan, Iraq, and Syria. . . . Abdallah

Azzam, Abu Mus'ab al-Zarqawi, Abu Muhammad al-Maqdisi, and Abu Qatada al-Filastini were all part of the first wave of Jordanian "global jihadists" who went to Afghanistan. (Skare et al. 2021a, 18)

From the 2000s onward, Jordanians were seen as both suppliers of foreign fighters and key ideologues of Islamist Salafi forces in both Iraq and eastern Syria, where they played significant roles in both al-Qaeda and ISIS. And yet Jordan itself has, by and large, been spared any noteworthy "spillover" effect of violent Islamic terrorism in its territory. Jordan has certainly had its share of violent Islamist-inspired terrorist attacks, such as the Amman hotel bombings in 2005 and the major attacks on Jordanian security forces in 2016, which were officially claimed by ISIS (Sweis 2016).

In attempting to explain the conundrum of Jordan's significant role as a breeding ground for violent Islamic extremists as opposed to the relatively few attacks and Islamist violence the country has suffered, critical scholarship has pointed to the Jordanian regime's dual approach of "calibrated repression" (Nesser and Gråtrud 2019). Unlike Egypt and Algeria, Jordan has chosen not to adopt an unwavering and across-the-board military approach toward all Islamists. Instead, in an ideological echo of Morocco's strategy, it has combined the application of harsh military measures against certain Islamists with structured state-controlled efforts at societal dialogue with other Islamists. The latter has even included a degree of co-optation of prominent Salafi Islamists such as Abu Muhammad Maqdisi, Abu Qatada al-Filastini, and Iyad al-Qunaybi, who at times were released from state detention in exchange for support of the monarchy (Skare et al. 2021a, 20).

In a similar vein to Morocco, Jordan has been engaged in reforms of its Islamic institutions, as carried out by the Jordanian Unit to Combat Violent Religious Extremism and Terrorism, under the general umbrella of the kingdom's Ministry of Education, Higher Education and Religious Endowments (Waqf). In addition to training, a significant effort to replace extremist clerics, especially in cities where there had been a proliferation of radical (*takfiri*) clerics, such as Maan, Zarqa, Rusayfa, Irbid, Salt, and Kerak, has resulted in a massive shortage of some 3,300 imams and no less than 700 muezzins (Skareet al. 2021a, 19). The context of this shortage had to do with a more general framework of religious reform in Jordan, which also resulted in retraining programs for Muslim clerics and the screening of those deemed too extremist or retrograde in their views of Islam (Abu Rumman 2021, 247).

However, such measures, which resemble certain aspects of Morocco's work with the Rabita, are only one aspect of Jordan's recourse to "dialogical logic" in confronting the challenges of Islamic extremism. In addition to these measures, Jordan has relied on two significant sets of state practices that, in addition to the more direct reform of Islamist clerical circles, enhance our understanding of how the Jordanian regime communicates with both its grassroots public and its midlevel Islamist social leadership.

Jordan's Specific Measures to Counter Violent Extremism

Jordan's response to the challenges posed by violent Islamic extremism emerges as a comprehensive structure based on state repression interlocked through applying a three-tiered societal dialogue structure that includes direct and indirect features of government–society communication.

This three-tiered structure's most direct dialogue component, as in Jordan's direct dialogue programs for clerical reform, has already received ample research attention (Skare et al. 2021a, 19–20). These direct efforts consist of programs in which the government engages in frontal and face-to-face communication with Islamists, either in the form of clerical reforms or training programs for imams and muezzins. Another facet of this direct dialogue route emerged in February 2015 with the execution by ISIS of a Jordanian Air Force pilot, Moaz al-Kasasbeh, by burning him alive. Seeking to drive a wedge between the ISIS leadership and the senior echelons of Jordanian Salafist clerics, the government released several of the prominent ideologues from prison and placed them under house arrest in what appears to have been an exchange of dialogue. In return, the released clerics, including Abu Muhammad al-Maqdisi and Abu Qatada al-Filastini, clearly called for the pardon of al-Kasasbeh and, after his execution by ISIS, swiftly condemned the excessive violence of their former comrade-in-arms Abu Musab al-Zarqawi for executing a Muslim war prisoner (Hamming 2022, 196n91). At present, a status quo seems to have been reached whereby Abu Muhammad Maqdisi, Abu Qatada al-Filastini, and Iyad al-Qunaybi, though they have not renounced their extremist views, have nevertheless chosen to refrain from any official and openly accessible attacks on the Jordanian regime, either on their websites or, more broadly, in their openly followed sermons. In return, none of the three were sent back to prison. This latter fact points to some dialogue-based co-optation between the regime and the extremists, some kind of mutual deescalation of tensions between them.

The second measure of dialogue used by the Jordanian regime in its relations with society, and especially with the supporters of the Muslim Brotherhood in the kingdom, concerns the conduct of parliamentary elections. Because this aspect of the Jordanian regime's dialogue with society has received less scholarly attention, the following sections are intended to fill this research gap.

The educated reader might wonder how such a rudimentary practice of democracy as the conduct of elections could be related to societal dialogue. But in Jordan, a country whose first four decades after independence were marked by the harsh imprint of martial law, the very idea of holding elections at all or suspending them, and the processes of gradual negotiation and political bargaining that have accompanied each stage of the country's electoral reforms, all amount to nothing less than a broad societal dialogue between the regime and its citizens. This is especially true considering that, out of all the political factions, the Muslim Brotherhood has been the most vocal advocate for elections for many years. Far more politically substantive than the Salafist fringe of extremist clerics such as Maqdisi, Qatada, and Qunaybi, the Brotherhood's electorate is undoubtedly a force to be reckoned with. With roots in Jordan dating back to the kingdom's independence and its long history of support for Jordan's monarchical regime—unlike the Egyptian Brotherhood, which has at times supported and threatened the regime's existence—the Jordanian Brotherhood is not a force that can be easily overlooked or brushed aside.

After Jordan's first full parliamentary elections in 1956, there was a failed coup attempt April 13–20, 1957. Following this event, significant developments in the Palestinian West Bank city of Nablus led to Jordan's strong opposition to holding elections for many years. On April 22, 1957, two days after the failed coup, the deposed Palestinian Jordanian prime minister, Suleiman Nabulsi, officially launched Jordan's so-called Patriotic Congress (*al mu'tamar al watani*). The open air of this congress convened by Nablusi's coalition, which included his own National Socialist Party (NSP—its name explicitly referring to its Nazi ideological origins), the Baath, the Communists, and the independents associated with the Palestinian Mufti Haj Amin al-Husseini, was to challenge the regime in Amman and force its capitulation by mobilizing massive street uprisings (Dann 1991, 60).

By the time of Black September in 1970, when Baathist-backed Palestinians once again attempted to overthrow his Jordanian monarchy, Hussein's total retaliation came to the fore. The irreversible expulsion of the Palestine Liberation Organization (PLO) leadership from Jordan (never to return) and his firm alignment with the US-led Western powers would cement the Hashemite regime's endurance for years to come.

No elections were held in Jordan between 1956 and 1989. In 1989, Jordan held its first parliamentary elections in forty-three years in response to public unrest sparked by an economic downturn and demands for constitutional reform in the kingdom, albeit under the constraints of martial law. With the collapse of the Soviet bloc in 1989 and the subsequent discrediting of communist-leaning pan-Arab Baathism in the early 1990s, the only real force left to challenge Jordan's monarchical regime was Islamism, both in the form of the Muslim Brotherhood and, later, under the guise of hardline Wahhabi Salafism.

Over the past thirty years, from the 1993 elections to the most recent ones in 2020, there has been a discernible pattern of indirect dialogue regarding Jordan's electoral procedures. Parties associated with the Muslim Brotherhood, such as the Islamic Action Front (IAF), have been advocating for the government to hold open and fair elections. They prefer a "bloc voting" system, which in 1989 already disproportionately favored Islamist candidates. On the government side, the regime has made multiple constitutional changes to the electoral system. This includes introducing a "one man, one vote" system in the 1993 elections, implementing a quota system reserving seats for women and ethnic minorities (Circassians, Chechens, and Christians) in 2003, and increasing the size of the elected parliamentary assembly from 80 seats in 1989 to 110 and now 130. Accordingly, most of Jordan's martial laws were lifted in 1991 (*New York Times* 1991).

A signal feature of Jordan's evolving electoral system has been the gradual introduction of procedural changes before each new round of elections, which are usually accompanied by lengthy debates as to whether the Islamists would accept the proposed changes and participate in the forthcoming election or boycott the election while claiming the government was deliberately tilting the playing field. Thus, the Islamists decided to run in the 1989 and 1993–1994 elections, but the shift to one person, one vote led to a partial boycott of the 1997 elections by Islamists. In 2003, when the new electoral guidelines included quotas for women, there was a recurring pattern of Islamist boycotts. By contrast, the 2007 elections, which required each party to have at least five hundred registered members in at least five of Jordan's constituencies, saw the IAF fully participate in the elections. In 2010, another round of changes to the electoral law led to another boycott of the elections by the Muslim Brotherhood.

The "dialogical nature" of Jordanian electoral politics emerged in the run-up to the 2016 elections. The regime's pressure to sever the Jordanian and Egyptian chapters of the Muslim Brotherhood following the upheavals of the Arab Spring from 2011 onward and the retention of the Jordanian chapter while exorcising its Egyptian counterpart serve as a masterclass of dialogical balancing, between being attuned to legitimate Islamist societal sentiments and the maintenance of state security (Magid 2016). Following the onslaught against the Muslim Brotherhood across the Middle East, and particularly after the Egyptian army's coup that overthrew the Islamist-elected President Mohamed Morsi, the Jordanian regime saw it as high time to rein in its Muslim Brotherhood once and for all. The adopted strategy was to create a clear split between the Brotherhood's Egyptian and Jordanian branches. The technical way this was done was through the electoral registration of parties. In 2014, a new registry was established that required all political parties intending to participate in the 2016 elections to register. Although the older Egyptian-affiliated Jordanian Muslim Brotherhood party was duly registered in 1946 and 1953, its registration was revoked and a new, uniquely Jordanian chapter of the Brotherhood, with no ties to its Egyptian counterpart, was duly registered. As tensions mounted against the Jordanian regime for allowing the Jordanian chapter to register while denying the Egyptian-affiliated parts of the movement the right to run for office, the Jordanian government carried out a major coordinated overnight raid on all Brotherhood offices in Amman and later throughout the kingdom (Malkawi 2016; Sweis 2016). With the transfer of assets (real estate, bank accounts, etc.) to the new, uniquely Jordanian Muslim Brotherhood branch, the Jordanian regime dealt a lethal blow to the influence of external Egyptian Islamism over internal Jordanian religious affairs (Magid 2016).

Use of Indirect Dialogue

A clear pattern of indirect dialogue emerges when analyzing Jordanian electoral mechanisms over the thirty-four years between 1989 and 2023. In retrospect, it was through the technical electoral process that the government's will for Islamist participation, but perhaps not for victory, was reconciled with the Islamists' will to assert their political power and challenge the regime, albeit without completely "smashing all China." At times, both the regime's crossing of societal red lines and the Islamists' behavior to that same effect caused one side or the other to pull back, bringing this dialogue system to a standstill and requiring reunification of voices in which each side gave a little to return to cooperative terms of discussion in the run-up to the next elections. As such, over the past thirty-five years, dialogue between the Jordanian government and the Islamists has often revolved around haggling over seemingly procedural electoral issues, albeit ones that have significantly impacted election results. As administrative lawyers are wont to reiterate, when it comes to constitutional elections, procedure can often be more important than substance. Accordingly, electoral haggling should be seen for what it is: political dialogue par excellence, albeit through the back door of the Jordanian society.

The third aspect of Jordan's dialogical thinking concerns what can be broadly described as embedded measures of social tension reduction. Drawing on new cutting-edge research published by Stanford and Cambridge University in 2022, a new picture of a third domain of dialogue has emerged that is more in line with the notion of "the everyday politics of authoritarian rule in Jordan" (Yom 2023). In short, all three of the following monographs provide explanations for aspects of the Jordanian conundrum of nonviolent extremism, which one wise and eminent scholar has described as an

> easily ignored reality: Life under autocratic rule which is predicated not solely on fear or violence but on the creative accommodation of state power. (Yom 2023, 2)

The first monograph, which looks at the politics of protest in Jordan, reveals a regime very much attuned to its society's need for protest and the venting of social discontent. As Schwedler (2022) shows, specific locations in Amman and other cities, such as known streets, certain roundabouts, and even known vacant lots, routinely serve as sites for demonstrations. These are tolerated by the government, which channels people's anger to be vented in these "controlled environments," but the regime also sends government officials to these places during demonstrations to register and record the grievances of the people demonstrating there. Throughout this insightful monograph, Schwedler shows how the information collected by these government officials often moves up to higher levels of government. This turns the spatial geography of controlled protests into a channel for dialogue and communication between the government and grassroots society.

The second recent novelty concerns the rise of community policing in Jordan. In contrast to the General Intelligence Department (the Mukhabarat secret police), the Public Security Directorate (PSD), with its nearly sixty thousand personnel, serves as Jordan's civilian police, charged with the normal maintenance of public order and the prevention of nonpolitical crimes (theft, domestic violence, speeding, assault, murder, etc.). As Watkins (2022) aptly demonstrates in her monograph with the self-explanatory title "Creating Consent in an Illiberal Order: Policing Disputes in Jordan," the PSD still promotes "customary traditions for dispute management," which is a euphemism for the continued practice of tribal courts, whose official function was abolished back in 1976, but which nevertheless continue to exert considerable influence in Jordan's still semi-tribal society (Watkins 2022, 133–137). Much the same can be said of the PSD's Family Protection Department, which essentially deals with domestic and marital abuse and which, in many cases, recommends that victims consult government-run "reconciliation committees" before resorting to family court proceedings (Watkins 2022, 163–166).

The third and most innovative of these new contributions concerns Jordan's securing and controlling the supply of traditional flatbread (*khubuz 'arabi*) in the kingdom. As Martinez (2022) aptly demonstrates, the "politics of bread" in Jordan often has to do with social cohesion and how the state demonstrates its preference for its Jordanian citizens beyond the needs of more than one million Syrian refugees that the country has received who also still need to be fed and cared for. The state's shift from supporting general wheat bread subsidies at the bakery level to allocating direct cash payments on an individual human basis to Jordanian citizens becomes a classic social dialogue measure between the regime and its society. The new way of distributing subsidies forces the poor to deal directly with the government to get the food support they need. This is different from the old system, where anyone, regardless of their wealth or citizenship status, could get the same subsidy at the bakery. As Martinez notes, the Jordanian regime's provision of bread "will continue to form the fabric of experience within which political authority is produced . . . welfare—whether in the form of cash or food—is and will remain a source of the state's vitality, a key condition for its presence, a source of its astonishing ability to subsist and reproduce" (Martinez 2022, 231).

Conclusion

One would be hard-pressed to deny the almost prophetic future Jamal Khashoggi, writing back in 2014, envisioned of what would transpire in Yemen, Iraq, Syria, and Libya:

> Jordan and Morocco are two models—those who did not miss the train. The countries that missed the train are those that have dragged themselves into a civil war like Syria, countries that are about to witness a war like Yemen and Libya, or fragmentation like Iraq. Reforms are no longer useful in these countries. They need an external intervention to contain the damage caused in each of them. The longer they are neglected, the more their situation will crumble and the more it will drag its neighbors into their turmoil. (Khashoggi 2014)

A signal feature linking Morocco and Jordan is their approach to the threat of violent Islamic extremism. Both states rely heavily on their powerful security apparatuses to counter these threats. However, unlike many other Arab regimes that rely solely on repression, Morocco and Jordan demonstrate a strong ability and a genuine willingness to engage in government-structured, regime-controlled dialogue with Islamist groups. To be sure, such efforts at dialogue are anything but equal. On one side are potent states. On the other are groups that depend heavily on social support for survival. At no point since the beginning of the Arab unrest in 2011 did Islamist groups, be they extreme Salafists or more moderate Muslim Brotherhood protagonists, challenge the Hashemite monarchy's staying power, a fortiori for Morocco's monarchy, which is even more powerful, entrenched, and long-lasting compared to Jordan's.

This similarity in approach to extremism is also reflected in other ways. Morocco and Jordan see themselves as guardian states (Sharifian kingdoms) whose rulers trace their lineage to the Prophet Mohammad. Both were seen as partial enemies of the Baathist regimes of the 1970s, and both suffered military coup attempts during that period. Both have remained strong allies of Western military powers, and both have adopted what could be broadly defined as liberal-capitalist state economic modalities. Over time, both kingdoms have gradually opened to the idea of holding elections and allowing nominated governments and cabinets to play an increasing role in running the state, albeit under the continued and tight control of the king. Morocco's engagement with elections dates back to the mid-1970s; the kingdom has since then held regular local and legislative elections without interruption. Like Jordan, 1990s Morocco also saw the unofficial and discrete acceptance of Islamists in the electoral process, albeit under the cover of another party.

Since the 2011 unrest, first in Tunisia and then across the Middle East, both Morocco and Jordan have been largely spared the political and social ruptures that have engulfed other Arab states. Correspondingly, their economies have not experienced significant declines in economic output, in stark contrast to most Arab states whose GDP per capita in 2021 was lower than before 2011 (Jamal and Robbins 2022).

A key puzzle here concerns the plausible link between Morocco's and Jordan's monarchical Sharifian nature and their relative stability under the challenges of both Islamic extremism and the 2011 unrest. Contrary to the record of many Arab countries with long pan-Arabist legacies (e.g., Egypt, Syria, Tunisia, Algeria, Libya, Iraq, and Yemen), the monarchies of both kingdoms appear to have demonstrated considerable political resilience. Both royal houses have explicitly and officially insisted that there is a direct and causal link between their precise measure of stability and their so-called divine destiny. The Moroccan royal house habitually reiterates that the king is the Commander of the Faithful (Amir al-Mu'minin). In Jordan, the state's very name (Hashemite, meaning descended from the tribe of Hashem of the Prophet Mohammad) carries this signal.

Whether there is a causal link between the Sharifian composition of Morocco and Jordan and their apparent relative political stability deserves further study. What cannot be denied is the degree of self-confidence these two monarchies possess, which allows them to enter dialogue with Islamists, even hardliners, without apology. For better or worse, Morocco and Jordan are two of the very few Arab countries that have repatriated their foreign fighters from the ISIS battlefields in Syria and Iraq. Although these individuals will be prosecuted and imprisoned upon their return, it is remarkable that their home countries are willing to take them back in the hope of reintegrating them into society. This stands in stark contrast to the policies of European and other Arab countries that have chosen to leave their ISIS nationals in Iraqi detention camps indefinitely.

Notes

1. Absent a religious hierarchy, Morocco placed a state organ—the Rabita Mohamadia of Oulama, composed of recognized experts of Sunni Islam—to provide nonbinding guidance on emergent religious questions.

2. *Makhzen* refers to the state's authorities and the monarchy's royal entourage. Historically, the Bled al Makhzen was formally and effectively under the king's rule, whereas regions devoid of state authority were called Bled Siba—"the country of disorder." Nowadays, *Makhzen* implies the channels, formal and informal, through which the monarchy rules (Waterbury 1970; Claisse 1987).

3. See "The Mohammed VI Institute for the Training of Mourchidine and Mourchidat Imams," on the Mohammed VI Foundation of African Ulema website (https://www.fm6oa.org/fr/linstitut-mohammed-vi-pour-la-formation-des-imams-mourchidines-et-mourchidates/).

7

Ethnonationalism and Religious Radicalization: Serbia and Bosnia and Herzegovina

Edina Bećirević and Predrag Petrović

Although the framework of the Preventing Violent Extremism in the Balkans and the MENA (PREVEX) project distinguishes between ethnonationalist (far right) and religiously motivated violent extremism, these extremist motivations are not entirely distinct in the Western Balkans—both because the far right ethnonationalism that led to war in the 1990s nurtured an enabling environment for imported religious extremism to emerge in the postwar period and because ethnonationalist extremism is tightly interwoven with clerico-fascism, which is now reflected in a global far right trend of "ethnoreligious nationalism" (see Fisher-Onar 2022; Johnson 2018; Halilović and Veljan 2021).

This intersection between ethnonationalism and religion in the Western Balkans was evident during the wars of the 1990s and has left a lasting impact on the sociopolitical landscape of both Bosnia and Herzegovina (BiH) and Serbia. Ethnonationalist forces are deeply intertwined with the region's religions, Serbian Orthodoxy, Islam, and Catholicism, and extremist rhetoric is far too often expressed even in the "mainstream" religious and political realms. Nonetheless, it was the Islamist extremism that sprang from ideologies that arrived in BiH during the war, brought by Muslim fighters from Asia—including Salafism, Wahhabism, and jihadism—that long dominated the literature on violent extremism in the Western Balkans (Bećirević 2016). The presence of these ideologies in the region gained particular international attention after the emergence of the so-called Islamic State in Syria and Iraq (ISIS), which attracted over a thousand foreign fighters from the area (Rehabilitation and Reintegration of Returning Foreign Terrorist Fighters [RFTFs]). Thus, in 2012, security-oriented researchers in the region began looking closely at postwar radicalization and extremism with a one-sided focus on

Salafi jihadism because this was the year that fighters from the Balkans (and elsewhere) began departing for Syria and Iraq.

Meanwhile, the ethnonationalist extremism that reached its zenith during the Yugoslav Wars in the 1990s never really faded away and has been on the rise again in recent years. And though scholars have studied quite extensively how ethnonationalist radicalization in political and public debate contributed to those wars (Carmichael 2012), much less attention has been paid to postwar ethnonationalist extremism and radicalization in former Yugoslav states. Indeed, ethnonationalism has been mainstreamed into the political life of these countries to such a degree that it is rarely even labeled as extremism, even in texts dedicated to national defense and counterterrorism.

That is a fundamental reason why this chapter focuses on the intricate dynamics of various extremisms in BiH and Serbia, where almost nothing can be explained in simple terms or straightforward concepts. For instance, in some parts of BiH and Serbia, different strains of extremism function in a reciprocally radical relationship, but in others, this does not seem to be the case. And notably, much of what drives the reciprocal extremism of certain groups is shared narratives, meaning the mutual reflectivity of Serb ethnonationalism and Salafism, for example—as seen in narratives of victimhood, the existential threat of "others," and the need for self-protection through exclusion—is itself mutually reinforcing.

Still, because academic study responds to geopolitical circumstances, the threat posed by the Islamic State was understandably prioritized, and few people predicted that extreme ethnonationalism would rise again to become a "new normal" or a significant security threat. The growing prominence of far right political figures in Europe and the United States, coupled with a proliferation of extreme right organizations and an increase in terrorism motivated by their ideology, has only recently refocused attention on this issue. In the Western Balkans, these events have unfolded against the backdrop of Russia's invasions of Ukraine, highlighting extensive research on Russian influence, especially in Bosnia and Herzegovina and Serbia. The central role of the Russian Orthodox Church in these efforts has alerted academics to focus on the risks of religious radicalization beyond Islamism.

This chapter examines these various strains of extremism in BiH and Serbia and the extremist movements that are currently most prevalent in both countries while unraveling the enduring impact of historical conflicts in the Western Balkans and analyzing how current geopolitical dynamics affect the region's sociopolitical landscape.

Ethnonationalism and the Far Right

The project of far right extremists across the Western Balkans is, in many ways, a continuation of the wars of the 1990s. That is, a prominent theme of their rhetoric relates to the redrawing of state borders along exclusively ethnoreligious lines. Extending from this, ethnonationalist groups view the multicultural and multidenominational tradition of BiH as a dangerous aberrance and fear that European Union (EU) membership for countries in the region will undermine ethnonational identities intertwined with religion. Extremist groups with an Orthodox Christian or Catholic identity promote narratives claiming that Christianity and Christians, that is, Serbs and Croats, are under threat. Similarly, Salafist groups claim that Islam and Muslims, that is, Bosniaks, are under threat (Kelly 2019). This rhetoric has leaked beyond the edges of the most radical fringe and has increasingly become normalized even among many political forces that call themselves moderate.

The aspirations of dismantling the Bosnian state have persisted among Serb and Croat nationalists. These ambitions have resurfaced recently as Western international actors, fatigued by crises in the Western Balkans, show increasing willingness to accept local autocratic and nationalistic leaders as legitimate partners. Noticing this shift, Russia has intensified its efforts to destabilize the region by "ensuring that its proxies obstruct [the state-building] process" in BiH (Ruge 2022).

Postwar BiH and the Legacy of Dayton

It is notable that the Bosnian War was the first time since the end of World War II "that fascist and Nazi symbols were used openly in Europe and within official military units without consequence. Nationalist actors viewed historical revisionism, ethnonationalism, and genocidal policies as legitimate means for achieving political goals" (Turčalo and Karčić 2021). This rhetoric, and the impunity with which it has been employed for decades, is a catalyst for far right radicalization across the region. But in BiH, where the "peace" declared in 1995 led to something much more like a frozen conflict than anything resembling restorative reconciliation, the political instrumentalization of extremist ethnonationalism narratives carries significantly heightened risks (United Nations 2021).[1]

It is fair to say that the political figure who has most successfully instrumentalized these narratives in BiH is Bosnian Serb leader Milorad Dodik. For several years, in the immediate postwar period and especially just after he took power in the Republika Srpska (RS) in 2006, Dodik was a reliable ally of the West in efforts to rebuild the Bosnian state and restore interethnic relations. However, deteriorating economic conditions, along with ethnonationalist influences from Serbia and Russia, have led him over the past decade to adopt stringent Serb nationalism, advocating for the dissolution of the Bosnian state. Dodik's rhetoric and tactics have now been adopted by the Croat far right—which promotes narratives centering on the "dysfunctionality of the Bosnian state" and has proposed an even deeper ethnic dis-integration of BiH by calling for the establishment of a third entity exclusively for Croats, on the premise that they are otherwise increasingly threatened as an "unprotected" minority (Prelec and Pradhan 2021).

Alexander Clapp summarized some of the fundamental mistakes of the 1995 Peace Agreement with sharp but appropriate cynicism, noting, for instance, that it "stemmed from a misunderstanding of why the war had broken out in the first place." Ultimately, Clapp argues that the system it created "punishes electoral moderation, erodes political accountability and all but rewards extremism," and the fact that "both entities essentially operate as their states . . . doesn't so much quench the desire for autonomy as dangle it before them" (Clapp 2017). In other words, the Dayton Agreement itself has empowered the ethnonationalist political structures that have prevented its implementation, and the resulting power structures and paralysis have driven extremism in BiH.

Serb Nationalism and the Far Right

The 1990s wars and genocide were driven by ethnonationalism, with Serbian and Bosnian Serb leaders aiming to create a Greater Serbia. They mobilized Serbs through years of indoctrination by political religious figures, and the media, portraying Serbs as threatened by other groups and advocating for an ethnically exclusive Serb state. This exaggerated threat was used to justify aggression against non-Serbs.

The rise of nationalism in (the Republic of) Serbia in the late 1980s was a response by political elites to growing pressure for democratization and liberalization of the economic and political system of the former Yugoslavia. The dominant critique of Yugoslav socialism by Serbian nationalist intellectuals was not focused so much on its economic inefficiency or authoritarian tendencies as on how it had "destroyed" the Serb nation (Pešić 1996, 5–7). Thus, in the new official narrative, social class as a unifying principle was replaced by the ethno-nation, understood not as a political but a biological entity (Kuljić 2002).

Throughout the 1990s, the Milošević government successfully imposed Serb nationalism as the official ideology, and the territorial objectives of ethnonationalists to expand Serbia and Croatia were presented as part of the process of Yugoslav dissolution (Stakić 2016, 133–135). Yet, this would only create two nationally homogenous states by dividing BiH and erasing it from the map. It was this expansionist goal that fueled the series of ethnic conflicts that ensued, including the war against BiH and the genocide and crimes against humanity committed there.

After the fall of Milošević, Serbia began a transition toward democracy via a series of reforms, and new discourses emerged regarding Europeanization, human rights, transitional justice, neoliberalism, and more. Still, even if the hegemony of nationalist discourse was challenged in this process, political and intellectual elites never made a radical break from ethnonationalism. So, it not only has survived but also has remained the dominant and, in some sense, official discourse of Serbia (Stakić 2016, 135). The government of Aleksandar Vučić, the onetime Minister of Information under Milošević, has, in fact, consolidated support partly by using ethnonational narratives to amplify the risk of external threats to Serb unity, as reflected in a recent survey in which nearly four in ten Serbian respondents (39 percent) identified "foreign powers" as among the factors "most responsible for existing tensions between different ethnic groups" in the country (Center for Insights in Survey Research 2022, 152). Vučić was nonetheless able to maintain strong and positive relations with Europe for quite a few years, which prompted European leaders to push Serbia forward as the next Balkan member. But this has recently been questioned against still unresolved talks with Kosovo. Some analysts wonder whether the Serbian president is willing to prioritize the criteria of accession or is simply more concerned with remaining in power "by restricting political opposition and controlling the judiciary, security apparatus, public sector, and media in ways that defy the EU's basic values" (Barber 2023).

All the groups that make up the Serbian far right, whether authentic or fake, old or new, contribute to spreading values and ideals that align with those of the current government—which aims to unite Serbs politically and culturally in an imagined "Serbian World" and seeks to securitize matters such as migration (Petrovic 2024, 84–85). For example, the rhetoric of far right extremists, which is "deeply rooted in the idea of a need to protect Serbia's 'national identity' from perceived enemies" and has designated various entities as "the enemy" as the context demands, increasingly frames "migrants and refugees . . . as the entity whose culture and values threaten the Serbian people and their identity" (Lažetić 2021, 3). This not only reinforces the policy ambitions of the government but also draws the attention of voters away from governance failures, including corruption and economic instability. For these reasons and others, some Serbian policymakers have actively resisted considering far right ethnonationalism in the context of efforts to prevent violent extremism or terrorism, and the government has implemented no activities as part of its counterterrorism strategy to combat political and ethnonational extremism (European Commission 2021, 47).

Serb Nationalist Ideology

Ideologically, the ethnonationalism of today's Serbian elites is grounded mainly in Saint Sava nationalism (Bešlin 2021), which emerged in the 1930s and is considered to have been founded by Nikolaj Velimirović, bishop of the Serbian Orthodox Church.[2] Its essence lies in a combination of Serb nationalism and Orthodox clericalism, wherein the "sacralization of the nation" and the "nationalization of religion" raise the status of the Serb nation to that of a saint and make Orthodoxy a national rather than a universal religion (Falina 2007). Saint Sava nationalism advocates for the establishment of an Orthodox monarchy within historical Serbian borders, with the king as an inviolable and unlimited ruler, and its most ardent supporters resolutely reject Western culture, globalization, democracy, liberalism, human rights, republican values, the anti-fascist tradition, and ecumenism.[3] Although it cannot be said that every far right political party and movement in Serbia, or every Serb ethnonationalist group (inside and outside the country), supports a monarchy per se, most do prefer the rule of a "firm hand" and close ties with the Orthodox Church (Petrović and Hercigonja 2022).

Other essential features of contemporary Serb nationalism include the mighty symbolic and narrative power surrounding Kosovo as the secular and spiritual "cradle of Serbia," for which many Serbs were sacrificed in clashes with Ottoman forces, to whom they eventually had to abandon the territory. In this context, the death of Serbian Prince Lazar in a battle against Ottoman forces has been reframed as both sacrificial and sanctifying (see Bieber 2002). Historical revisionism of World War II likewise plays a role in Serb ethnonationalist rhetoric, which denies any wartime collaboration by the nationalist Chetnik movement with Nazi occupiers or portrays it as a necessary evil to which the Chetniks only conceded to protect Serbs.

In the nationalist narrative, the fact that Serbs have historically suffered significant casualties and have been the victims of genocide means they have always been on "the right side of history." There is considerable mobilizing power in this framing because it simultaneously centers the grievances and moral superiority of Serbs. This is a clear theme of the far right neo-Chetnik movement, for instance, which denies the genocide committed against Bosniaks in Srebrenica while highlighting genocidal acts committed against Serbs in World War II (Turčalo and Karčić 2021). Logically, this has led to the glorification of civilian and military leaders convicted of war crimes in the 1990s and previous wars.

Bosnian Serb Extremism

Numerous neo-Chetnik groups, as well as other far right groups in BiH today, are registered as civil society organizations that promote "national customs, traditions, religious values, and culture." Their exclusivist narratives and genocide denial align with the rhetoric of leading Bosnian Serb political parties, which have repeatedly obstructed efforts to label Chetnik organizations as fascist and ban them. However, in June 2022, the state-level Appellate Court of BiH did sentence three members of Chetniki Ravnogorski Pokret to five months in jail on counts of inciting national, racial, and religious hate, conflict, and intolerance in Višegrad and the surrounding areas. According to the ruling, the defendants sang songs encouraging violence, with lyrics that celebrated mass atrocities committed against Bosniaks in Eastern Bosnia during World War II, as well as crimes committed during the 1992–1995 conflict. The prosecution also charged them with participating in a military formation and using military language, meaning that they behaved as an illegal paramilitary organization (*Pripadnici četničkog pokreta u BiH*).[4]

Besides this network of neo-Chetnik organizations, far right Serb nationalist groups with origins in Serbia also have affiliates in the RS. Most of these RS-based groups (e.g., the Night Wolves, Saint Georgie-Loncari, Eastern Alternative, and many others) receive support from Russia and share the same agenda as their counterparts in Serbia. (See Radio Free Europe 2023; Euronews 2023.)

Croat Nationalism and the Far Right

Over the last century, Croat nationalist extremism has mainly drawn on the fascist ideology of the Ustasha movement, which came to power in 1941 as the installed leadership of the Independent State of Croatia (NDH), a puppet regime of Nazi Germany.[5] In the early Bosnian War, the Croatian Defence Force was loyal to Bosnia and Herzegovina. However, in 1993, with the establishment of the separatist Croatian Republic of Herceg-Bosnia, far right Croat nationalism shifted toward greater antagonism of Bosniaks and BiH, sometimes making them the primary enemy of Bosnian Serb and Serbian forces.

Croat nationalist extremism operates mainly under the cover of non-governmental organizations and associations with official agendas promoting culture and "the homeland," as well as business and football associations and informal groups attached to Catholic parishes or specific priests. Groups in BiH that adhere to a Ustasha ideology are almost all connected to a parent group in Croatia or another country with a Croat diaspora. However, the unique Bosnian state structure arguably gives these groups a greater degree of relevance in BiH (Ristic et al. 2020), which makes it even more notable that they seem to be in lockstep with the official politics of both the Croatian Democratic Union BiH (HDZ-BiH) and the Croat National Assembly (HNS, a platform for Croat parties in BiH).

Croat far right extremism in BiH aims to establish a "third entity" for Croats, revive the wartime Croatian Republic of Herceg-Bosnia, and rehabilitate Ustasha and Catholic clergy from World War II, echoing similar revisionism seen in Serbia and RS. This movement involves war crimes denial by leading politicians in HDZ-BiH and Croatian HDZ, specific media figures, and some Catholic Church officials. (See Jegic 2020; "Sarajevo Mass for Pro-Nazi WWII Collaborators" 2020; Milekic 2019.)

Croat far right groups, including football hooligans like the Ultras-Zrinjski Fan Club, are prone to violence. They attack anti-fascist events and critics of HDZ politics. The Ultras, formed by Croatian Defence Council members in Mostar during the war, have a history of violence at matches and targeting leftist and civic party members during certain holidays. The Ultras have four to five hundred permanent members and can mobilize additional allies from the HDZ-BiH youth wing. There are credible suspicions that the Interior Ministry of Herzegovina-Neretva Canton tolerates or even protects the group (Ristic et al. 2020).

The Catholic Church and Far Right Croat Extremism in BiH

For obvious reasons, the Catholic Church admits no role in supporting Croat far right groups in BiH, and any church activities that could be interpreted as supportive of these groups are framed as the independent actions of local clergy. Yet, specific examples make it hard to believe that the Catholic hierarchy does not at least look the other way or, at worst, sanction collaboration by the church with the Croat far right. For instance, the parish in Široki Brijeg sponsors youth sports competitions that include teams named explicitly for Ustasha units, such as the Black Legion. This serves to normalize far right extremism, and it gets no pushback from religious or municipal authorities because it aligns with the values that have been mainstreamed through many educational institutions across Herzegovina, which either imply or assert that support for the Ustasha is a form of Croat patriotism.[6]

Moreover, in 2020, the Catholic Churches of BiH and Croatia held a mass in Sarajevo to commemorate tens of thousands of Nazi-allied Croatian troops and civilians who were killed in Austria in 1945. The annual commemoration is usually held in Austria but has been canceled because of measures imposed in response to the pandemic. It was then organized in BiH under the auspices of the Croatian parliament—Croatia has been a state sponsor of the event for years, despite briefly stepping away from this role in 2012 "amid criticism that it was rehabilitating the Nazi-allied Ustasha regime" ("Sarajevo Mass for Pro-Nazi WWII Collaborators" 2020).[7] Indeed, along with their Ustasha collaborators, the Croatian troops honored in the commemoration exterminated nearly all of Sarajevo's Jews and many Serbs for crimes that have never been denounced and with victims who have never been remembered by the church (Dervisbegovic and Kovacevic 2020).

Still, this rather public association with the revisionism that drives the Croat far right is not typical of the Catholic Church in BiH, which has generally been quite cautious in recent years about endorsing Croat nationalism or any other form of fascism that emerges among Bosnian Croats, particularly in comparison to the lack of restraint exhibited by the Serbian Orthodox Church, which has openly supported Serb ethnonationalist extremism among

Bosnian Serbs. That is not to say the Catholic Church has avoided wading into Bosnian politics, however. Its leaders have consistently emphasized the minority status of Croats in BiH and have advocated during election seasons for new leadership that will ensure "people in every part of the country . . . enjoy human rights and religious freedom, and feel represented," as well as calling for "a normal state" (Luxmoore 2018). The Croatian and Bosnian Catholic Churches are not the same, nor are they monoliths in themselves. Vjekoslav Perica has referred to the Croatian church as "the most influential anti-liberal social force" keeping Croatia from achieving a true democracy. In essence, Perica argues that "the so-called 'Church of the Croats' and the HDZ party have virtually co-ruled" the country (Perica 2015, 7–8). Thus, the position of the Catholic Church in BiH and its relationship with Croat extremism call for further research, particularly considering that the church almost certainly plays a role in shaping the political platforms of the HDZ-BiH and other far right Croat political parties.

Salafi Extremism in Bosnia and Herzegovina

Salafi (or Salafi-jihadist) extremism is part of a global Islamist, rather than a regional ethnonationalist, phenomenon. Salafism in BiH is also intertwined with the 1992 to 1995 war in a way that newer forms of Bosniak extremism are not because it was the scope of the atrocities committed against Bosniaks during the conflict that motivated hundreds of foreign mujahidin to come and defend Bosnian Muslims (Duyvesteyn and Peeters 2015).[8] It was clear from the start of the war that Bosniaks would be its primary victims, mainly because they had no "backup state" in the way that Bosnian Croats and Bosnian Serbs did.

The war was tragic for all Bosnians, and war crimes were committed not only against Bosniaks but also against ethnic Croats and Serbs. Still, even where the Army of the Republic of BiH (ARBiH) did commit war crimes, it did not do so as methodically as the forces it opposed.[9] And the mujahidin who arrived in BiH to defend Bosniaks against this mass violence brought a conservative Islamic doctrine with them. After the fighting ended, foreign fighters who remained in BiH established several Salafist communities, along with alternative Muslim congregations known as *para-jamaats*. This was complemented by the efforts of Saudi Arabia and other Gulf states to mainstream the conservative ideology of Wahhabism and Salafism in BiH, often under the guise of humanitarian aid. For the most part, these Gulf channels of influence are no longer operational after intervention by the state. Still, they inspired Salafist congregations and communities across the country, spreading a hyper-conservative and intolerant form of Islam that is at odds with the teachings of the official Islamic Community (IC) of BiH.

It is for this reason that only a tiny minority of Muslims in the country practice Salafism, but it has nonetheless become a cudgel of far right Serb and Croat extremists against all Bosnian Muslims. This has especially been true since fighting broke out in Syria and Iraq, which drew some Bosnians to join foreign, and later terrorist, units. Among the key recruitment centers for foreign fighters in BiH were Salafist *parajamaats*, and for several years, the phenomenon of foreign fighter departures put a spotlight on BiH as a potential "hotbed" of Muslim extremism in Europe, a "threat" played up in the political rhetoric of ethnonational parties and latched on to by the media. However, this has never manifested, and even the return of dozens of former fighters and their radicalized family members in multiple waves has not been linked to an increased risk of violence (IEP 2020).[10]

Salafi Extremism in Serbia

Islamist extremism in Serbia is geographically linked to the southwest Sanjak region, which has a predominantly Muslim population. The International Crisis Group (ICG) traces the origins of *takfiri*-inspired extremism in Sanjak to 1997 and the arrival of an imam who preached Salafism at a local mosque in Novi Pazar (the largest town in Sanjak), where the ideology was initially rejected by the local community (ICG 2005, 25). Initially, Salafist adherents in Novi Pazar thus kept a low profile, attracting little attention. However, since 2000, they have gradually become more visible and influential. In 2007, a split in the (moderate) Islamic Community in Serbia opened space for external, fundamentalist influences to take hold (Petrović and Ignjatijević 2022a, 7–8).

Hence, just as far right extremists from Serbia have fought on Ukrainian battlefields, Islamist extremists from Serbia traveled to Syria and Iraq to fight alongside terrorist groups such as ISIS and Al-Nusra. According to police estimates, forty-nine people from Sanjak departed to Syria (Luković 2017), seven of whom were later convicted in Serbian courts for crimes related to terrorism. However, in the context of growing *non*violent extremism in the region, it is concerning that "the Sanjak community is polarized inter-ethnically (between Bosniaks and Serbs), intra-ethnically (between different Bosniak political parties) and religiously (between two Islamic communities)" (Halilović Pastuovic, Hülzer, and Wylie 2023, 21). This could impact community resilience at a time when individuals and groups are promoting extreme ideas, even if they are not engaging in extreme behavior (i.e., openly inciting or committing violence), making some people potentially susceptible to becoming further radicalized into violence in certain socioeconomic or political circumstances.

Common Factors of Radicalization

Across the region, certain common factors contribute to ethnonationalism and religious radicalization, including socioeconomic and political instability. In Serbia and BiH, however, extremism can also be directly linked to the educational systems as well as to a persistent "brain drain" that is weakening the democratic transition of these countries.

Economic Fragility and Political Corruption

In both Serbia and BiH, citizens face several social and political factors that increase their vulnerability to extremism, including poor socioeconomic conditions, high unemployment, low trust in institutions, and high levels of institutional corruption. The fact that political corruption is endemic in both countries means that the distribution of already scarce social, material, and financial resources is unequal, which leaves a large segment of the population, especially young people, unable to meet their needs and achieve their aspirations through official institutions (Kostić, Simonović, and Hoeflinger 2019, 67). In other research, respondents across BiH cited "corruption generally and corrupt politicians specifically, unreliable institutions and the brain drain" as the biggest challenges facing their communities (Veljan and Turčalo 2018, 23). In a more recent survey, an overwhelming majority of all respondents (85 percent) in BiH agreed the country is headed in the wrong direction, a sense that was much more pronounced in BiH than in Serbia (Center for Insights in Survey Research 2022, 11).

Over a decade ago, Teets and Chenoweth (2009, 170) found that "corruption . . . produces more favorable conditions under which terrorists conduct attacks." Ruge (2020) has detailed how "the problem of Dayton . . . stems from the fact that nationalist parties are primarily interested in consolidating their political grip over institutions and undermining the system's capacity for checks and balances rather than creating structures that can work through compromise. State capture lies at the heart of this problem."

In Serbia, these risk factors are most present in the Sanjak region, where higher than average rates of poverty are compounded by high rates of unemployment—which average 15 percent across Serbia but are as high as 60 percent in the region's largest town of Novi Pazar (where, according to some estimates, 70 percent of the unemployed are young people). Sanjak is also somewhat remote from the rest of the country, which can leave its citizens feeling marginalized (Petrović and Ignjatijević 2022a, 9–16).

People who are dissatisfied with the general conditions in their country may be more susceptible to accepting narratives that identify an external cause for their misfortunes, whether this is another ethnic group or "the West." As Dušanić (2020) explains, the theory of displaced aggression interprets intolerance toward another group as a defense mechanism through which accumulated frustrations are directed at a scapegoat. The dissatisfaction accumulated by people in the region because of historical grievances and the betrayed expectations that the state should have fulfilled may thus be redirected to "easy targets" and new enemies. Extremists play a helpful role for political elites in the region by redirecting the frustrations of citizens from failures of the ruling regime to these perceived "enemies."

Education and Emigration

A flawed educational system in Serbia is also among the factors contributing to radicalization in the country because poorly educated citizens who lack critical thinking and analytical skills are more likely to accept extremist worldviews and conspiracy theories. The system is seen as inert and difficult to reform, and because it fails to encourage critical engagement or offer options to gain practical skills, young people in Serbia feel ill-prepared for the job market. Moreover, religious education is of poor quality. It is organized separately for Bosniak and Serbian children in multiethnic communities such as Sanjak because it is aimed at creating loyal believers of concrete confession rather than presenting information about all religions from different perspectives (Petrović and Ignjatijević 2022a, 22–24; Petrović and Ignjatijević 2022b).

In BiH, ethnic segregation is common in towns across the country, and in some places, schools also remain divided along ethnic lines. This, even though the "two schools under one roof" system has been condemned for years. In a 2018 report, the Organization for Security and Co-operation in Europe (OSCE) Mission in BiH emphasized that these schools "segregate children, and through this segregation teach them that there are inherent differences between them. In post-conflict BiH, this increases mistrust among members of different national groups, impedes reconciliation, and is a long-term threat to stability, security, and economic prosperity" (OSCE Mission in BiH 2018, 4). In a survey conducted by the Atlantic Initiative team in 2020, 57 percent of respondents identified the "two schools" system as a security threat (Halilović and Veljan 2021, 25).

Mass emigration, particularly of young people, is another factor that may increase the vulnerability of communities to extremist influences. By shrinking the labor force and tax base, the phenomenon has real economic impacts. According to Ruge (2020), the labor force in BiH shrank by over 10 percent between 2015 and 2020, which "places additional strains on the public budget, as pressure on pension payments . . . increases, foreign loans come due, and the private sector stagnates." This is a formula for even broader socioeconomic marginalization, greater levels of dissatisfaction among the population, and even lower levels of trust in government—all of which are known drivers of violent extremism.

Geopolitics and the War in Ukraine

The Russian invasion of Ukraine has given a solid tailwind to far right groups and political parties in Serbia and in the RS, which have supported the aggression. When a pro-Russia crowd of several thousand gathered in Belgrade on March 4, 2022, in a rally, the slogans heard from protesters included "Serbs and Russians are brothers forever," "Crimea is Russia, Kosovo is Serbia," and "Serbia, Russia, we do not need [the European] Union." Rallies were also held in other cities throughout Serbia as well as in BiH (Petrović and Ignjatijević 2022a).

Members of the People's Patrol (*Narodna patrola*)—the group chiefly responsible for initiating these rallies in support of the Russian invasion—and their leader, Damnjan Knežević, spent time in Moscow in 2022 as guests of leading Russian media outlets, including *Russia Today*. During the visit, members of the group toured the Saint Petersburg headquarters of the Wagner Group, the state-funded paramilitary organization that has been active in Ukraine. This close alignment of Serbian nationalists with the Russian political regime is grounded in narratives of shared history, culture, and religion. Still, Russia has long viewed Serbs as a strategic bulwark against the North Atlantic Treaty Organization (NATO) and the EU and has therefore built up the image of Moscow as a strong defender of Serbia and its "sacred holy land" in Kosovo. To that end, Russia supports Serbia in the international arena by opposing independence for Kosovo and blocking Kosovar membership in international organizations.

According to Alexandar Dugin, Putin's main ideologist, a complete turn to the West would mean the end of Serbia because it could never regain Kosovo and would not even succeed in preserving its territorial integrity within existing borders. He claims that "this is only possible in the multipolar world he promotes, which Putin is attempting to achieve in practice" (Petrović 2024, 80–82). Russia's ability to play an increasingly destabilizing role in the Western Balkans by relying on extremists has been well documented and includes comprehensive efforts in Northern Macedonia, Serbia, and Montenegro (Stronski and Himes 2019; Đorđević 2021; Bechev 2019).

Still, it is BiH that Moscow has consistently viewed as a geopolitical tool over which it gains the most excellent control by fostering internal dysfunction and political conflict. Lately, it has made a specific priority of destabilizing the Bosnian state. It has done this mainly through efforts that strengthen the forces of Serb (and at times Croat) nationalism while undermining democratic development and the legitimacy of state institutions

(Stronski and Himes 2019; Đorđević 2021; Domi and Stradner 2021). In some areas, it has been joined in these efforts by China (for example, in opposing the nomination of Christian Schmidt as the new UN High Representative for BiH), because both Russia and China have come to see the Western Balkans as a region where they may be able to "sell" the superiority of authoritarian over liberal models of government.

Many analysts have started asking whether BiH can still count on unconditional support from Turkey for its Euro-Atlantic aspirations as well as how Ankara's new alliance with Russia may influence Turkish politics in the region more broadly (see Vuksanovic 2021).

State Responses to Extremism

The relationship of Serbian authorities to nationalism and far right groups has always been pragmatic and tolerant. No government in Belgrade has rejected ethnonationalism or unequivocally distanced itself from the far right (Ejdus and Jureković 2016), which has only had more room to operate since the Serbian Progressive Party (SNS) came to power in 2012. The SNS was established by former high-ranking officials of the Serbian Radical Party (SRS), an ultra-nationalist party closely allied to Slobodan Milošević and a strong proponent of the unification of all Serbs into a unitary ethnonational state. This mainstreaming of extremism in Serbian politics means that the far right and Serb ethnonationalists are not regarded as a threat (Petrović 2024, 93–94).

The foreign fighters who saw combat in Syria against the Assad regime have been convicted as terrorists. At the same time, those who fought in Ukraine on the Russian side have been prosecuted on lesser charges (as foreign fighters) and have received milder sentences. Experts agree that the current legal framework in Serbia *is* sufficient for addressing (violent) extremism; the problem is an unprincipled and unequal treatment of Islamist versus far right extremism by Serbian authorities (see Stevanovic 2021). This benevolence of the state to far right groups not only contributes to the spread of values that are incompatible with democracy but also feeds the grievances of non-Serb populations in the region, especially Muslims.

In BiH, support for ethnonationalist agendas varies widely, even within microcommunities. This complicates efforts to counter radical political narratives, especially when combined with foreign influence tactics. Additionally, battling extremism fueled by grievance and threat narratives, exploiting memories of past violence, poses significant challenges in a nation where many citizens have endured or witnessed mass violence tied to their identities.

Conclusion

Because there are so many enabling factors in the Western Balkans that intersect to open space for extremism, we contend that future research into this topic should give greater focus to the active role of regional political actors in manipulating and polarizing public discourse and mechanisms of governance. Foreign influences—especially Russia—seek to exploit these regional dynamics to radicalize national politics further, deepen instability, and weaken the fragile Bosnian state. That said, researchers must not repeat past mistakes by focusing exclusively on any one agent of radicalization in the Western Balkans because this kind of research myopia legitimizes a similar singular focus in policy and strategy at the state level.

Essentially, foreign and regional efforts to destabilize states like BiH can only thrive if domestic factors enabling radicalization persist. This necessitates a commitment to addressing economic, social, sectarian, and corruption issues to neutralize extremism in the Western Balkans. Effective strategies in BiH and Serbia require educational reforms that promote critical thinking, reject revisionism, and present unified historical narratives. As Popović (2020, 13) notes, "in order for collective meaning-making to take place . . . there needs to be a common narrative," and one that the public "accepts and treats as their own."

This will require a holistic approach that allows civil society to take the lead in many cases, for example, "to create and amplify grassroots-based alternative narratives" (Barzegar, Powers, and El Karhili 2016, 9). Such an approach prioritizes resilience building at the community level alongside more functional and restricted security sector collaboration, recognizing that the collaborative security projects commonly implemented by Western countries in the region are likely to produce only short-term results in the fight against extremism unless they are accompanied by initiatives to empower civil society and rebuild trust among citizens and between citizens and state authorities. It is only by addressing the root causes of extremism and dismantling mechanisms of division in the Western Balkans that antidemocratic actors, organizations, and states will be deterred from working to exacerbate instability in the region. In practical terms, the only durable means of countering extremism in BiH and Serbia is to meaningfully support their transitions into full and viable democracies.

Notes

1. Even UN officials have referred to conditions in BiH as a "de facto frozen conflict" (United Nations 2021).

2. Saint Sava lived at the turn of the thirteenth century. There is nothing in his work to support the ideology that emerged seven centuries later bearing his name, and he is known for renouncing the throne in favor of monastic life and for providing autocephaly to the Serbian Orthodox Church. He is also celebrated in Serbia as an educator. According to historian Milivoje Bešlin (2021), Saint Sava was both modern and pragmatic, as well as political, during his time. "He understood the time, understood the international context, acted even [as a] revolutionary, destroying established principles and church canons themselves."

3. For example, see (in local language) the program of the "Monarchist Club Carostavnik": https://carostavnik.blogspot.com/p/blog-page_21.html.

4. Media widely reported on this judgment, for example, "Court of BiH: 'Ravnogors' Punished by Five Months in Prison for Spreading Hatred" (https://www.klix.ba/vijesti/bih/sud-bih-ravnogorci-kaznjeni-sa-po-pet-mjeseci-zatvora-zbog-sirenja-mrznje/221220183).

5. "While the Catholic Church attempted to justify this, independent media in Croatia, as well as other media across the region, published photographs of a local priest with young children wearing T-shirts adorned with the symbol of the 'Black Legion.'" See more: https://www.index.hr/vijesti/clanak/foto-na-nogometnom-turniru-u-organizaciji-crkve-djeca-nosila-majice-s-natpisom-crna-legija/980284.aspx; https://visoko.ba/promocija-ustastva-u-sirokom-brijegu-djeciji-tim-crna-legija/; https://www.nezavisne.com/novosti/gradovi/Maloljetnici-u-Sirokom-Brijegu-igrali-u-dresovima-Crna-legija/433239.

6. Croatia has long had a problem with World War II revisionism that mirrors the same problem in Serbia, seeping into almost every sector of society (see Pérouse 2019). In some cases, this has manifested in outright censorship of educational lessons about the Holocaust, as in 2017, when the headmaster of Šibenik's Technical School removed some of the panels from a traveling international exhibition about Anne Frank because they discussed the Ustasha. There was little response from the government to this incident, despite the choice of exhibition organizers to pack up and leave instead of submitting to this censorship (see Ilic and Robinson 2017).

7. Interestingly, the phenomenon of foreign fighting during the Bosnian War tends to be associated only with Muslim mujahidin. Still, there were also Russian fighters in the country supporting Serb forces and European fighters supporting Croat forces (Popovic 2021).

8. The International Criminal Tribunal for the former Yugoslavia (ICTY) has characterized only the mass killing of Bosniaks in Srebrenica in 1995 as genocide. The 2004 Appeals Chamber's ruling in the case of Radislav Krstić was the first ICTY judgment to classify crimes in Srebrenica as genocide. In total, the ICTY found fifteen people guilty of genocide in and around Srebrenica, while the State Court of BiH has found twenty-five people guilty of these crimes. Information on cases and judgments is available on the websites of the ICTY: https://www.icty.org/en/cases; and the State Court of BiH: https://sudbih.gov.ba.

9. Notably, some analysts contend that foreign fighters who deployed to Ukraine may pose a threat when and if they return to BiH, yet they have been mainly ignored by researchers and policymakers (see Karcic 2020).

8

Exporting Radicalization and Strengthening Resilience: Tunisia and Kosovo

Simeon Evstatiev, Andreas Lind Kroknes, and Francesco Strazzari

Tunisia and Kosovo are countries of origin of a significant number of radicalized individuals who have joined the ranks of jihadist insurgencies in the Middle East, such as the Islamic State in Iraq and Syria (ISIS) and al-Qaeda-affiliated groups. Therefore, although Tunisia and, to a lesser degree, Kosovo have experienced the occurrence of violent extremism (VE), they are often indicated as examples of an externalization of the problem (Fahmi and Meddeb 2015; Consigli 2018). In repressing and persecuting radicalized individuals while showing a certain degree of externally assisted institutional solidity, these two countries have created an environment conducive to these individuals' departure. The return of foreign terrorist fighters (FTFs) after the territorial defeat of ISIS in the Middle East and, in turn, the demise of the self-proclaimed Caliphate has opened a whole range of challenges, such as the lack of social, economic, or psychological support for them and mechanisms to handle their eventual reappearance in what are still enabling environments. Against a backdrop marked by tumultuous histories of the war in Kosovo and authoritarian rule in Tunisia, optimism rose for both nations in recent decades as they seemingly stood on the precipice of significant change. However, as time progressed, the hopeful narrative of democracy remained applicable solely to Kosovo, highlighting a noteworthy divergence in Kosovo's and Tunisia's trajectories. Yet, despite the underlying structural and contingent differences that make proper comparison difficult, in this chapter we maintain that observing and contrasting patterns of radicalization and, more broadly, jihadist militants and counterterror responses in Tunisia and Kosovo is fruitful. It yields new insights that problematize "hydraulic" representations of social order—that is, views that violent extremism is a force to be channeled—and that better explicate the phenomenon of "exporting jihad." Therefore, we examine the empirical evidence to understand how the emigration and the return of radicalized individuals are linked to domestic political stability.

Focusing on Tunisia and Kosovo, we do not neglect the larger contexts of the Middle East and North Africa (MENA) region and the Western Balkans, where Kosovo is part of the Albanian-speaking populations in countries like Albania and the Republic of North Macedonia. In the modern Balkans, unlike in the Arab world, religion—not only Islam—is intertwined with national belongings, an essential part of even nonbelievers' identity (Evstatiev 2019). In the 1990s, the Yugoslav succession wars added violent connotations, portraying the region as distinct from Europe and affiliating it with the Middle East through Islam's transnational community—the *umma* (Sadriu 2019). We amplify the cases of Tunisia and Kosovo as indicative of regional and international developments in "exporting jihad" to reveal some commonalities and differences between the Western Balkans and the MENA, seeking to grasp cases of occurrence and nonoccurrence of VE as a result of social resilience.

This chapter's analysis of Tunisia and Kosovo is based on interdisciplinary collaborative research, including fieldwork in specific localities in both countries. It unfolds through our examination of cases of VE occurrence in Tunisia and Kosovo, in which we address the drivers and historical, social, and political contexts shaping these enabling environments. We discuss the role of external actors, particularly the European Union (EU) and the United States of America, before focusing more closely on the issue of FTFs and closing off with our conclusions.

Tunisia, Kosovo, and Violent Extremism

Tunisia in the Maghrebi Context

Violent extremism is certainly a significant issue in Tunisia. A dozen years after the 2011 revolution, we must debunk two parallel myths: the idea of Tunisian democracy gaining traction through a linear transition in which violent political extremism did not play a crucial role; and the idea that, faced with no chance of success in the domestic arena, Tunisian jihadism simply "found its way" abroad, under the guise of thousands of Tunisian nationals who joined the legions of foreign terrorist fighters. The following paragraphs provide details to dispel these two notions.

Set within a regional context deeply marked by transitions derailed into resurgent forms of authoritarianism, militarization, and civil wars, for some years, Tunisia stood out as an exception. It was acclaimed as a model of national compromise and resilient democracy. At the same time, observers noted that, as a proportion of its overall population,

Tunisia contributed the highest number of foreign terrorist fighters in the MENA region.

Over time, things have become more complex. There is ample evidence of the critical role Tunisian citizens played in terror attacks, including attacks in Europe. Yet, the "outward diversion hypothesis" rests on a simplistic "hydraulic" assumption (i.e., VE as a force to be channeled) concerning the nature of political order and social relations. This hypothesis should be relaxed, considering the unfolding of *voice* (citizens expressing their discontent and grievances in an effort to improve conditions) and *exit* (citizens opting to leave or disengage) and the political interactions during transition years (Hirschman 1970).

The elected President Kais Saied seized de facto control in mid-2021, divesting the authority of democratic institutions and actors, including Parliament, the political parties—most notably the Islamist party Ennahda—and the trade unions. Counterterrorism laws are now being exploited and used as a tool of political repression and to overtly criminalize the democratic opposition, thus effectively turning counterterrorism into a means of governance.

Tunisia was shaken by major terrorist attacks in the years 2013–2015, and its security forces have continued to be targeted by violent extremist groups.[1] In particular, the homicides of socialist leader Mohamed Brahmi and unionist leader Choukri Belaid marked the first apparent interventions of jihadi violence in Tunisia's policy arena. The murders put Islamist leaders on high alert and possibly contributed to their adopting a pragmatic line in search of a constitutional consensus to stabilize a transition where the party could affirm itself. This was a somewhat momentous choice, given how events unfolded in other countries where political parties affiliated with the Muslim Brotherhood were making their way through elections.

By then, religious extremism had long been waxing in Tunisia, just as much as everyday manifestations of violent intimidation (e.g., against women's associations) (Salem 2021). By targeting and killing dozens of foreign tourists, the terror attacks at the Bardo Museum in March 2015 and three months later at Sousse beach were heavy blows to the Tunisian economy. The next phase was mainly focused on Mount Chambi, near Kasserine, where an al-Qaeda-affiliated group started a violent insurgency, which was met with a series of military counterinsurgency operations. Parallel to this, in March 2016, ISIS-affiliated jihadists crossed into the border city of Ben Guerdane from Libya in a foiled attempt to seize the city, leaving many casualties.

As of the writing of this book, it can be claimed that jihadism as an insurgency has been defeated in Tunisia. Both the border with Libya and Mount Chambi are seeing declining levels of violence. More broadly, one can safely say that jihadi violence in North Africa has failed to advance. Yet this state of affairs could not be taken for granted in the mid-2010s and stands in stark contrast with the propagation of jihadist movements active across the Sahara Desert and the Sahel Belt (ICG 2021).

Kosovo and the Albanians

The foreign fighters' phenomenon in the Western Balkans dates to the Yugoslav Wars in the 1990s, when jihadis from Middle Eastern countries supported the Muslim fighters in the region, particularly in Bosnia and Kosovo.[2] Islamic relief organizations from or supported by the Gulf states, especially Saudi Arabia, proliferated and set up branches across the Balkans. They funded mosques and educational facilities that disseminated a "new" interpretation of Islam and granted scholarships for Muslims to study in the Middle East. In the Balkans, ubiquitous were the perceptions of a "traditional" as opposed to an "alien" Islam imported from the Arab world, in which "Arab" Islam was described by a plethora of terms with negative connotations such as *Wahhabism*, *Salafism*, *Islamism*, and *radical Islam* (Evstatiev 2022, 75–78). Over the years, several *para-jamaats*, or parallel "underground" mosque communities, have been established in all these countries, attracting disillusioned youth.[3] The areas around the *para-jamaats* became gathering places for radical indoctrination and the recruitment of FTFs because they were beyond the purview of formal Islamic institutions recognized by the states. The recent focus on Islamist extremism in the Western Balkans thus came mostly with the spread of global Salafism clashing with the locally practiced Hanafi tradition of Islam (Azinović 2018).

The issue of extremism became particularly pressing after the outbreak of the recent war in Syria, as violence occurred—mostly following the export of FTFs to the theaters of Salafi insurgency in the Middle East. More than 1,070 persons from the Western Balkans made their way to Syria and Iraq and joined the ranks of primarily Islamic State (IS) and al-Qaeda affiliates (Azinović 2018, 3–6; Shtuni 2019, 18). The Western Balkans is currently Europe's region with the highest number of returned FTFs. The return of jihadis to their Balkan homelands was perceived as a direct threat to national security, and by 2015, foreign fighting was criminalized in virtually all countries in the region (Shtuni 2019; Azinović and Bećirević 2017). Although enabling environments where extremism is shaped are usually associated with drivers such as economic depression, rising unemployment, and low and declining levels of education, the Western Balkans indicate that these factors are not necessarily the primary driving force and their relative weight should be considered context-specific.

In Kosovo, religious extremism has been shaped in an enabling environment entailing violence along ethnic and political lines. Kosovo is the country in the MENA region with the highest number of FTFs and jihadi mobilization in Europe (Azinović 2018). The jihadi groups were not welcomed by the political and military structures of the Kosovo Liberation Army (KLA), which followed national ideologies and sought to avoid the influence of religion. The generations educated in a nationalist spirit were not susceptible to radical Islamic movements and propaganda. However, the educational system, ruined by the Kosovo War of 1998–1999 opened the door to the spread of Islamist ideologies. Societal disorientation amid a weak economy and political vacuum made Kosovo fertile ground for the resurgence of religion (Demjaha and Peci 2016). As in Bosnia and Sandžak, the "new" Islam was imported to Kosovo from Saudi Arabia and other Middle Eastern countries. According to some estimates, faith-based aid agencies from Middle Eastern and Gulf countries invested around $800 million in Kosovo, mainly in rural areas (Azinović 2018).

Kosovo declared independence in 2008, with the Serbs governing ten out of thirty-eight municipalities and certain government ministries. Kosovo's Strategy for the Prevention of Violent Extremism and Radicalization Leading to Terrorism 2015–2020 puts the threat of "national radical extremist groups of Albanian and Serbian origin" on par with the threat posed by Islamic extremism (Republic of Kosovo 2015). The four municipalities in the northern part of the country bordering Serbia (Leposavic, Zubin Potok, North Mitrovica, and Zvecan) lack effective control by the central government, and extremist and organized crime groups continue to obstruct the basic rule of law in this area. The city of Mitrovica, divided since 1999 between an Albanian south and a Serbian north, and especially the Ibar Bridge connecting the two areas, has become a focal point of numerous protests since 1999.[4] Almost 80 percent of violent extremist threats were political, and nearly 70 percent of unexecuted threats were religious (Kursani 2018a, 10).

Over the past several years, approximately a dozen protests organized in Kosovo have turned violent. In March 2015, for example, Albanians from Kosovo were suspected of performing violent acts in the Republic of North Macedonia. During operations carried out by the North Macedonian police in the city of Kumanovo, eight policemen and ten members of armed groups were killed, and thirty-seven people were indicted, most of whom came from Kosovo (Radio Free Europe 2017). In another operation of the North Macedonian police, carried out in 2010 in Tetovo, six people were killed, including some from Kosovo (Voice of America 2010). More recently, after the defeat of ISIS in the Middle East, nationalist-motivated riots and social-based violent protests are on the rise in Kosovo. Those believed to be at the highest risk of engaging in violence are found to be educated individuals who have failed to achieve an occupational position commensurate with their level of education (Kursani and Krakowski 2021).

International Assistance and the Extremist Challenge

Tunisia

The Tunisian Islamic landscape has evolved considerably since the 2011 uprising, becoming more complex, as mentioned earlier. This complexity goes beyond secularization to involve the contention and renunciation of political violence as a revolutionary and transformative tool (Merone, Sigillò, and De Faci 2018). Hence, the polarization and fragmentation of the Islamic landscape can be seen as a result of dynamics of political contention, opportunities and closures provided therein, and resource mobilization.

Salafism in Tunisia can be divided into two major currents (Torelli, Merone, and Cavatorta 2012; Marks 2013). *Salafiyya 'ilmiyya* ("scientific Salafism") is a quietist current that rejects the use of violence while preaching a purist interpretation of Islam. The second, jihadi Salafis, grew significantly after the 2011 revolution (Merone and Cavatorta 2013). Despite their heterogeneity, Salafis are perceived by secular liberal elites as a homogeneous group and a major threat to the Tunisian social order (Cavatorta 2015). It should probably be remembered how Habib Bourguiba, the first Tunisian president, pursued a secular, modernist, and socialist governing model in which religion was considered primarily a private affair. He closed several mosques, prohibited the wearing of the veil in public institutions, and undermined the power and authority of *ulama* (religious scholars) vis-à-vis politics. Zine al-Abidine Ben Ali, who ruled Tunisia between 1987 and 2011, followed the same ideological and political path. Yet, with some opening to religious influence during periods of crisis, characterized by acute competition among elites, stricter rules on Islamists were imposed during the end of the 1990s.

By 2012, the ideological spectrum of the Islamic landscape had crystallized into four main trends: Islamists akin to the Muslim Brothers (represented by Ennahda), Salafi political parties (the most prominent being Jabhat al-Islah—the Reform Front), religious associations of various ideological affiliations, and revolutionary jihadi Salafis (mainly Ansar al-Shari'a). After the 2013 political assassinations, the jihadi Salafi group Ansar al-Shari'a was banned, and Salafi associations suspected to have links with terrorist groups were shut down. The post-2011 political equilibrium hinged on the inclusion of the majoritarian party Ennahda in the institutional field as a legitimate political force and the redefinition of Tunisian religious space. Mosques and several religious associations were brought under the state's control. In reaction to the attacks at the Bardo Museum in Tunis and the resort in Soussa, the government officially announced a new campaign of securitization under the label of the "war against terrorism," aimed at curtailing all the "extremisms" present in the country.

Overall, Tunisian authorities have often been quick to label these attacks and assassinations as more or less direct expressions of terrorism. At the same time, however, they have also proved eager to seek international assistance on how best to respond to such challenges. These two circumstances have generated strong contradictions. Initially, strong securitized approaches emerged and prevailed at the meeting point of the supply and the demand of counterterrorism cooperation. International cooperation efforts usually targeted the Tunisian Ministry of Interior as a local counterpart, a choice that incidentally undermined the hopes for change that had animated the 2011 revolution. As a matter of fact, during the revolution, popular mobilization was very explicit in targeting the national police, portrayed as the quintessential expression of systematic regime abuse.

In a very critical moment for the survival of democracy in Tunisia, EU member states collaborated with Tunisian authorities to design counterterrorism tools and EU support for the Tunisian security sector and, crucially, to target Tunisia's counterterrorism law enforcement apparatus. At the same time, the rise of irregular migration flows from Tunisia to Europe and the fear that they would increase the EU's vulnerability to terrorism led the EU to increasingly focus security cooperation on land and sea borders. The EU and its member states, such as Italy and Germany, have been intensifying their support for the Tunisian Coast Guard by supplying training, equipment, border surveillance technologies, and Germany's Integrated Border Management system. Although Tunisia views the EU as a key security partner, it harbors concerns that militarizing border regions might fuel grievances and exacerbate the discontent of marginalized communities in enabling environments, where the features conducive to the journey into VE exist. The growing emphasis of EU cooperation with Tunisia on countering irregular migration raises concern among Tunisian stakeholders, at least in public rhetoric, who see it as prioritizing the EU agenda to the detriment of local ownership. The clampdown on irregular cross-border flows exhibits a limited context sensitivity: extra-legal economies are crucial to the resilience of borderland communities and help reduce the vulnerability to VE (Meddeb 2020).

In recent years, the (perceived) reduction of terrorist threats in Tunisia has softened the sense of emergency. Consequently, Tunisian authorities and their international partners have increasingly focused on longer-term approaches to combat VE. These include framings, concepts, programs, and tools inspired by preventing and countering violent extremism (P/CVE) approaches, which involve as Tunisian partners not only the ministries of security and defense but also those of social affairs, justice, and youth. The EU and the United Nations (UN) agencies support community policing projects, security sector reform (SSR), and an updated national counterterrorism strategy, aiming to inject a human rights–based and whole-of-society approach. Within this framework, a specific emphasis is laid on the judicialization of counterterrorism response, preventive measures, and inclusion of civil society, the private sector, and academia (Simoncini 2021). The EU is also sponsoring small-scale pilot projects in youth engagement for the social rehabilitation of individuals incarcerated for terrorism and, most crucially, reform of the Tunisian education sector.

Overall, we can observe an expansion of the counterterrorism agenda toward prevention. This shift is backed by a professionalization discourse that materializes through expanding capacity-building and train-and-equip formats targeting the police, usually through multilateral schemes. If Tunisia has so far rejected structured cooperation with some law enforcement agencies, such as FRONTEX (European Border and Coast Guard Agency), its security institutions are involved in regional programs by CEPOL (EU Agency for Law Enforcement Training—with whom Tunisia has recently signed a working agreement) and EUROPOL (EU Agency for Law Enforcement Cooperation). It is also active in cooperation on criminal justice as part of a consortium led by Eurojust.

These accounts show how most EU resources in Tunisia are invested in traditional security cooperation and counterterrorism, although the EU claims to attach considerable importance to P/CVE action and goals in Tunisia. On paper, P/CVE features alongside the EU's crosscutting priorities in the country, alongside gender mainstreaming and human rights. In practice, though, the EU appears to lack the conceptual and financial resources to bridge the intention–implementation gap. Moreover, although the EU's considerable investments in other more "social" domains, such as youth, education, and development, are considered supportive of the EU's P/CVE agenda, we cannot help but note the lack of a convincing theory of change and assessment tools to back up this claim. EU actions could benefit greatly from a broader engagement in the Tunisian religious field. Yet, the fragmentation of Tunisia's religious field makes it hard for program coordinators to identify valuable partners without fueling feelings of exclusion, stigmatization, and polarization in the population. This suggests that the EU should pay special attention to context and conflict sensitivity if it decides to increase its role in this domain; then it may play a constructive part in building and supporting local sources of resilience. But this must happen with a light footprint, which would minimize the risk of undermining and delegitimizing local actors of resilience.

Kosovo

The transnational type of radicalization and VE spread throughout the region, coupled with the "export of jihad," brought Islamist VE into focus for the EU and other external stakeholders. Their P/CVE approaches in the Western Balkans vary along the continuum of "hard" to "soft" measures.

Hard approaches focus on security and securitization, whereas soft approaches entail programs aimed at social cohesion. Several external stakeholders operating in the region have pursued distinct strategies, which has created a tapestry of competitive and partially overlapping approaches to both preventing and countering violent extremism. Most instrumental, next to the EU, has been the United States, working through entities such as the US Agency for International Development (USAID) and alongside the UN Development Programme (UNDP), Organization for Security and Co-operation in Europe (OSCE), and local nongovernmental and civil society organizations (NGOs/CSOs). In addition, external stakeholders active in the Western Balkans include institutions based in the Muslim-majority world, such as the Turkish Diyanet or the Hedaya, an international organization based in the United Arab Emirates.

The EU strategy for combating VE is spelled out in the March 15, 2017, EU Directive 541 of the European Parliament and Council of Europe (European Council 2017, 6–21). This directive builds on the 2005 EU Counter-Terrorism Strategy, which envisages countering radicalization by "promoting even more vigorously good governance, human rights, democracy as well as education and economic prosperity, and engaging in conflict resolution" (European Council 2005). In 2020, while pointing to the dangers posed by far right and far left forms of VE, the EU restated that Islamist movements, such as al-Qaeda and the IS, remain the main threat to the union (European Council 2020). Nevertheless, both the EU and other external stakeholders, notably the United States, seek to combine hard and soft approaches. Whereas the United States continues to prioritize hard measures, with a strong emphasis on law enforcement and developing military instruments to persecute terrorists, in contrast, the EU emphasizes softer approaches.

When it comes to influencing the P/CVE policies of Western Balkan states, the EU possesses a set of comparative advantages that are not available to governments in the MENA and the Sahel. The union's enlargement and integration process are instrumental as incentives for most Western Balkan countries to undertake various reforms, including implementation of preventive measures, enforcement of the rule of law, democratization, and transparency, which could positively address the key drivers of the emergence of VE. The region's proximity to the EU means its security directly impacts the union's stability.[5] Since 2018, all EU engagements in the region have been aligned with its overall strategy for the Western Balkans (European Commission 2018a). Compared to earlier regional strategies, this overall strategy puts more emphasis on counterterrorism and P/CVE.[6] To strengthen states' cooperation on P/CVE, the European Commission (2018b) and the Western Balkans governments signed "Joint Action Plan on Counter-Terrorism for the Western Balkans 2018–2020," which builds on the outcomes of a series of high-level counterterrorism (CT) visits ("CT Dialogues") in 2017–2018 with the interior and justice ministers, police heads, intelligence agencies, CSOs, and umbrella structures such as national CVE coordination centers.[7] Complementing this joint initiative, between 2018 and 2020, the EU concluded separate bilateral "arrangements on antiterrorism cooperation" with the governments in the region.

Overall, unlike in the MENA region, where the EU pursues a "security first" approach (Skare et al. 2021b, 4), the union's P/CVE strategy in the Western Balkans has been predominantly soft, entailing measures targeting democratic and systemic reforms or community initiatives. In some "hot" areas, such as Kosovo, the EU approach also involves security-based programs prioritizing deradicalization in prisons and of released violent extremists.

In Kosovo, several lawsuits were filed against imams. The biggest case was that of Zeqirja Qazimi, an imam who lectured at the El Kudus Mosque in Gjilan who was sentenced to ten years in prison on charges of indoctrination and recruitment of FTFs (Leposhtica 2016). During interviews with relatives of FTFS in 2021, most respondents highlighted the decisive role of imams in three localities, from where some of those involved in the war in Syria and Iraq originated.[8] At the same time, the interviewees were divided regarding the role of the Islamic Community of Kosovo (BIK). Some believe that it has performed a deterrence role by identifying and counteracting extreme interpretations of Islam.[9] Others claim that BIK was reluctant to face these new extremist currents and interpretations while they were at their earliest stages of growth. Perhaps because it feared them.[10]

An issue of particular relevance to Kosovo and other Western Balkan countries is the use of communication platforms for online radicalization (Peci and Demjaha 2021a, b). In 2020, the Kosovo Police arrested a person who promoted participation in foreign wars through social media. There have been many cases in Kosovo where extremist individuals use the internet to spread extremist ideologies and recruit adherents (Shtuni 2016). Digital communication systems have also been vital in recruiting Kosovo's diaspora through the distribution of propaganda videos to indoctrinate audiences. Forty-eight of the 255 Kosovar FTFs, or nearly 20 percent, who joined different terrorist organizations in Syria and Iraq came from the diaspora (Perteshi 2020).

The Foreign Fighters Question

Tunisia

Religiously motivated extremism is deeply rooted in Tunisia. During the early 1980s, a small radical organization called Jamaat Al Jihad aimed to support all Muslims against hypocrisy and injustice. Historically speaking, and much like Morocco, in comparison to Algeria and Libya in the 1980s and 1990s, Tunisia did not produce FTFs on a massive scale. The first cases of domestic VE took place in the late 1980s, in the wake of the ban on the Islamist party Ennahda. Violent contestation in Tunisia remained limited, far from the scale and intensity it reached in Algeria in the early 1990s or Libya between 1995 and 1998. Some young Tunisians answered the ever more pervasive and pressing calls to "protect Muslims" and left to join jihad battalions in Afghanistan, Chechnya, and Bosnia and Herzegovina. Most of them gathered around Tarek Maaroufi and Seifallah Ben Hassine, who were Tunisian émigrés who became active outside of Tunisia itself. By the year 2000, the al-Qaeda-affiliated Tunisian Islamic Fighting Group (TIFG) stood out as the main Tunisian jihadi group. Under the Ben Ali regime, surveillance and repression were such that Tunisian jihadists were forced to fight abroad. An exception was the so-called Suleiman Group, a group of Tunisian jihadists linked to al-Qaeda in the Islamic Maghreb (AQIM), which failed to provoke an Islamist uprising from December 2006 to January 2007. In 2003, Tunisia's involvement in global jihad was minimal until the US-led invasion of Iraq. In 2006, a document, later known as the Sinjar Report, containing a list from al-Qaeda in Iraq, revealed that out of 570 Arab FTFs who went to Iraq in the 2000s, only 3 percent were Tunisians. Most of the fighters came from Saudi Arabia and Libya (Bergen et al. 2008).

A closer look at the numbers indicates their significance. It can be claimed that 1.7 percent of FTFs killed in Iraq between 2003 and 2005 were Tunisians, and out of the fighters held in Camp Bucca in 2008, 3.8 percent were Tunisian (Bergen et al. 2008; Zelin 2020). The Sinjar Report points out the fact that 41 percent of the fighters who entered Iraq were marked as volunteers for suicide bombing, showing their strong commitment to both the movement and its ideology.[11] A lawyer who defended arrested jihadists claims that as many as six hundred Tunisians were detained between 2005 and 2007 while attempting to join jihadist resistance in Iraq (Zelin 2020). Still, the numbers of Tunisian FTFs were insignificant and were perceived as such.

It was only after the Arab Spring that this perception changed as a result of thousands of young men leaving to join the jihad in Syria and Iraq via Turkey or Libya. In addition, the local insurgency led by the AQIM-affiliated Okba Ibn Nafaa Brigade (OIN-B) in Western Tunisia garnered attention, while a smaller Daesh affiliate called Jund Al Khilafa in Tunisia (JAK-T) emerged too (Ben Dhaou 2021). But by the beginning of the 2020s, with domestic armed insurgencies severely weakened, the main issue concerned the revenants (i.e., foreign fighter returnees), with some eight hundred cases still pending in Tunisian courts.

A key to understanding radicalization in Tunisia was the creation in 2011 of the organization Ansar al-Shari'a in Tunisia (AST). Seifallah Ben

Hassine (aka Abu Ayyad) is a former Tunisian "Afghan" (TIFG) who, along with some two thousand prisoners reportedly with some jihadist record, was released from jail in 2011 shortly after the fall of Ben Ali. According to a former associate, Abu Ayyad had been strongly influenced by the ideas of a radical preacher, London-based Abu Qatada al-Filistini. With two other imams, Abu Ayoub and Al Khatib al-Idrissi, Abu Ayyad founded AST in the context of a security vacuum that followed the revolution.

As Ayari (2017) explains, Abu Ayyad intended to unify all the radical currents in the country, much like the Islamic Salvation Front (FIS) in Algeria in the 1990s. By helping poor, marginalized people from populated areas, AST aimed at indoctrinating and mobilizing the people for its Islamic radical project. AST grew at the intersection of two radical schools of thought: radical jihadi Salafism and Maqdisism.[12] AST meant to mobilize the people for the jihad without actually crossing the threshold of violence: following al-Maqdisi's teaching, AST portrayed Tunisia as a land of preaching (Da'wa) rather than a land of violent jihad. By so doing, AST became a referent for the post-2011 revolutionary fever of large segments of the Tunisian youth, which did not agree with the Islamist party Ennahda's decision to endorse democracy.

Ennahda itself has often been blamed for the rise of AST because it did not act decisively against it during the first phase of transition (2011–2013) and instead allowed the AST network to develop all over Tunisia. It was only after the attack against the US embassy in September 2012 and the political assassinations in 2013 that the Tunisian state decided to crack down on AST. However, by that time, thousands of Tunisian youths had already joined the areas of conflict in Syria, Iraq, or Libya.

Ayari (2017) reveals the typical profile of youths arrested and incarcerated for terrorist involvement as predominantly young adult males under the age of thirty-five. Between 2013 and 2016, out of four hundred people prosecuted for terrorism, a surprising 40 percent had a university diploma or a university level of education. Although the jihadists came from various socioeconomic groups all over Tunisia, a noticeable proportion were from the Governorate of Tunis and southwestern region of Tunisia. It is estimated that more than 36 percent of Tunisian jihadists came from the semiurban populated areas (*zone peri-urbaine*) of Tunis (Sterman and Rosenblatt 2018).

The youth in marginal areas, neglected by state intervention and often suffering from police repression and unemployment, became vulnerable to radicalization and recruitment. They had little or no religious knowledge. Thus, by clearing and abandoning the religious field during his rule, Ben Ali had removed a crucial source of local resilience in the enabling environment of rural Tunisia, rendering the youth in those areas open to radical ideas and VE. It is also significant that many of these young men had some form of criminal record: joining the jihad offered them a redemption narrative and status. The collapse of Ben Ali and the ensuing political fluidity, the free-for-all postrevolutionary situation, paved the way for AST in these semiurban areas. AST provided help and economic support for the local poor population. The fact that the young people did not recognize themselves in the Tunisian state, which was identified as the (defeated) police, facilitated this process of brainwashing. AST provided youths with jobs, food, and money, thus becoming an alternative to the state. Using propaganda and mobilization, AST organized big rallies and demonstrations in semiurban areas. The absence of "the family cell," which would have otherwise protected the youth, made the radicalization process easier. Young adults' lack of education in the context of conservatism and poverty, amplified by their rejection of the state, created a permissive and enabling environment. Furthermore, the utilization of modern technologies simplified the process of mobilization and radicalization. AST developed its website and Facebook page, which were accessible to the marginalized youth of Tunis's suburbia.

At this point, AST set up "preaching tents," or *Khayamat al-Douawiya*, for the youth. In those tents, AST would address these young people with an extremely efficient and strong religious and political discourse to psychologically empower. Leaders of AST would claim: "You are today's leaders" and "You are the ones who will revive the Islamic Sharia." AST recruiters attempted to respond to and tap into youths' social-economic grievances and discomfort through the "preaching tents," which amounted to a nearly one-to-one strategy of recruitment and indoctrination.[13]

Note that not all in AST were in favor of jihadi violence. As Georges Fahmi and Hamza Meddeb (2015) explain, although AST was ideologically linked to al-Qaeda, it was neither politically nor operationally connected to that organization.[14] Also, some members, such as Abu Iyadh, advocated for Tunisia to be a land of predication and did not see AST as an organization to lead the jihad in Tunisia, but others advocated for the use of violence. Among them were Boubaker al-Hakim, who went on to become one of the most important ISIS leaders in Syria, and Ahmed Rouissi, a prominent ISIS fighter in Libya.

The first wave of foreign fighters' departures occurred as early as 2011, when AST had just been created. At that point, Ennahda supported anti-Asad fighters in Syria and thus played an essential role in mobilizing Tunisian youth. The recruitment for the jihad was not done openly or in public but rather more discreetly at the intersection of various local networks, including AST, Ennahda, and other organizations claiming to be for charity and moderation while in reality radicalizing and recruiting young people and sending them abroad.[15] Overall, the mobilization for jihad resulted from favorable socioeconomic conditions or strong idealism matching puritanical ideas and opportunities created by these networks. The recruiters typically played heavily on the emotions of the youths, showing civilian massacres to convince them to cross the line and veer into jihadism, not simply religious radicalism.

By mid-2013, after violent attacks and assassinations, the government, dominated by the Ennahda party, finally decided to crack down on AST. Thus, the authorities barred the organization from organizing its congress in May 2013 and accused it of being directly responsible for the attacks. The AST reaction happened directly in the suburb of Hay Ettadhamen, where its supporters mobilized massively, which led to confrontations with law enforcement. This was the moment when the first violent riots against the Tunisian government occurred, which ended the permissive environment that had allowed the organization to recruit and radicalize young Tunisians. The second and maybe largest wave of departure to Syria and Iraq occurred after 2013, while the AST leadership went into exile and joined either al-Qaeda or ISIS. Faced with state repression by a government run by an Islamist party, many decided to leave, causing an upsurge of FTFs voluntarily joining ISIS.

Thus, as Hatem Chakroun argued in a 2017 interview, poor socioeconomic conditions in the context of an absent or hostile state played an important role in the semiurban centers, of which Hay Ettadhamen was a good example.[16] However, in the semirural areas, other factors played roles. Mobilization and radicalization took a distinct path in rural versus semirural areas because of somewhat different drivers: in rural areas the cultural element was crucial; in urban centers the material element was important. In semirural areas, modernity and modernization often clashed with traditionalism. In these contexts, political secularization was not necessarily well received by many Tunisian conservatives because it was perceived as pushing the country away from its Islamic identity.

Ennahda, which represents one of the most evident cases of an Islamist party undergoing a process of moderation as a result of external pressures and social changes, and Ansar al-Shari'a, which underwent a failed process of institutionalization between 2011 and 2013 before being neutralized in 2013, are both telling examples. Thus, while social and economic problems played an important role in mobilization, other important factors, primarily defense of the community defined in either religious terms (*Umma*) or Arab nationalist terms (Pan-Arabism), also played key roles. In Tunisia, the post-2011 Arab Spring revolutionary situation weakened the state. It paved the way for a major upsurge of VE, with Tunisia the country from which the largest number of FTFs originated while AQIM and IS were deployed in the country itself. Another essential obstacle in the propagation of VE in Tunisia has been the role of CSOs as agents of resilience. The crackdown on violent extremists who gravitated to jihadi Salafi groups and the reorder of mosque activities under the frame of state authority made clear the need to address the issue of VE.

Kosovo

According to the Kosovo Police Department, at least 356 Kosovars have traveled to Syria and Iraq (256 male adults, 51 females, and 49 children), making Kosovo the country with the highest per capita share of FTFs in Syria (Gazeta Express 2020). Still, several researchers estimate that the actual number of Kosovar FTFs in Syria and Iraq may have been as many as 1,000 (Krasniqi 2020, 157). Most of these fighters were males between the ages of twenty-one and twenty-five; more than a third of the FTFs originated from five municipalities in Kosovo: Hani i Elezit, Kaçanik, Mitrovica, Gjilan, and Viti, where 14 percent of the country's population lives (Demjaha and Peci 2016). Indicative of the transnational character of jihadism, 30 percent of the people who went to Syria and Iraq were from the diaspora.

After 2014, an estimated 120 Kosovars returned (Krasniqi 2020, 157), and Kosovo stepped up its CVE activities, with investigations and arrests of persons suspected of being involved in recruitment activities for terrorist organizations such as ISIS and the al-Qaeda affiliate Al-Nusra Front. Some individuals were arrested on suspicion of planning terrorist acts or for being part of terrorist organizations. Several terrorist attacks had been planned and attempted, both inside Kosovo and abroad, but were thwarted by police and intelligence agencies (Govori, 2016).

A second wave of repatriations followed in April 2019, when Kosovo brought home from Syria another 110 of its citizens, including 74 children, 32 women, and 4 men. The total number of adult returnees has reportedly reached about 250 (Ahmeti, Dahsyla, and Murtezaj 2021; Gazeta Express 2020; Krasniqi 2020).

Kosovo has been praised for its ability to deradicalize and reintegrate returnees (Deutsche Welle 2019). However, if, for the time being, the immediate threat from FTFs and returnees has been eliminated, there is still a latent threat from Islamist fundamentalism (Kursani 2018b). Two future threats have been highlighted: imprisoned FTFs and religious preachers who are serving sentences on terrorism charges, and future returnees from Syria and Iraq (Kursani 2018b).

In an analysis of FTFs in Kosovo, about 64 percent came from average or above-average economic circumstances, and only about 36 percent lived in poor conditions (Shtuni 2016, 7). It is interesting that, of the five municipalities exporting the most foreign fighters, none is ranked among the regions with the lowest scores in Kosovo on the 2014 Human Development Index (HDI) (Lücke 2014). Extreme poverty and low levels of education in Kosovo are highest in other municipalities, such as Skenderaj,

Kastriot, and Malisheve, from which a smaller number of FTFs originate (Shtuni 2016). Therefore, no correlation can be observed between income or educational level and VE.

Some radicalized citizens of Kosovo were introduced to radical Islam and extremist ideologies in public schools in EU countries. For example, Bujar Behrami, a Kosovar born in Belgium, became radicalized after attending Islamic religious classes taught by a Chechen teacher who later became a well-known extremist imam. Behrami's family moved to Germany to disengage him from extremist network, but he continued spreading propaganda embracing Islamist extremism online and was involved in planning and financing terrorist acts. In 2018, he was arrested in Germany and extradited to Kosovo, where he was sentenced for planning terrorist acts.

In Kosovo, radicalization in schools also remains an issue. An OECD Programme for International Student Assessment (PISA) report (OECD 2018) shows that Kosovar pupils are not educated to read and think critically. In contrast, the Ministry of Education data demonstrate that less than 10 percent of schoolteachers are trained in media literacy or how to cope with extremism among younger generations (Ahmeti, Dahsyla, and Murtezaj 2021). This reveals that Kosovar pupils might be vulnerable to being deceived by the recruitment propaganda of extremist groups.

Jihadi extremists in the Western Balkans are not acting in isolation. They are well connected with those who share their views in the region, the Gulf, the Middle East, and elsewhere. Many individuals who joined militants in Syria and Iraq had previously stayed in Bosnian villages (e.g., Gornja Maoča, Ovše, Bočinja), where strict Salafis live, wherefore these villages have been dubbed "jihadist hotbeds" (Qehaja 2016). It is reported that leaders and individuals from these settlements were well connected with several extremist groups operating in masjids (mosques) in Vienna. The Austrian capital became a center for indoctrination and recruitment of FTFs, as well as for collecting money from the diaspora and funneling Saudi funds to the Western Balkans. Austrian authorities conducted several law enforcement operations, including arrests of preachers and members of these masjids, until many of the groups had been suppressed. Among the most prominent and radical group leaders were individuals from Sandžak, which neighbors Kosovo: Mirsad Omerovic, Adem Demirovic, and Nedzad Balkan. Each was arrested and prosecuted for recruiting, organizing departures of people to Syria, and financing VE and terrorism (Kešmer 2020). They had direct ties with ISIS and Al-Nusra as well as with extremists in Bosnia and Serbia. According to Austrian authorities, Omerovic maintained a direct line of communication with ISIS leader Abu Bakr al-Baghdadi (Counter Extremism Project n.d.).

In neighboring Albania, VE was fueled by individuals' deepened sense of belonging to the global Islamic Community, which led a great number of

FTFs to join jihadist groups. Narratives of victimization evoked emotional responses and strengthened ties to the perceived oppressed community (Wright-Neville and Smith 2009). They likened the Syrian conflict to the Spanish Civil War, portraying Assad as a modern Franco, to recruit fighters (Dyrmishi et al. 2021). The emotional pull of the *umma* was also exploited, appealing to Muslims' anxieties and aspirations to rebuild the Caliphate (Fernandez 2015).

In Kosovo, local-global connections and transnational dynamics are crucial drivers of radicalization and VE (Demjaha and Peci 2016). Transnational Islamic movements, migration dynamics and diaspora networks, pilgrimage, and cultural and educational links have catalyzed such trends. The local-global connections in Kosovo must be seen through two lenses: transnational cooperation in the diffusion of extremist interpretations of Islam, on the one hand, and the proselytization of more conservative and radical religious interpretations, on the other (Kursani 2018a). A further distinction may be made between international and regional connections regarding their ideological goals. The transnational cooperation in the diffusion of violent extremist interpretation involves nonstate actors—predominantly a handful of Albanian-speaking individuals from North Macedonia (and some from Kosovo), who spent time in the MENA region during the late 1990s and early 2000s and whose ideological motives are driven by the call to jihad in conflicts abroad. Such individuals often explicitly called for the use of violence and participation in foreign conflicts (Kursani 2018a).

The Kosovo Islamic Council (BIK) follows the Hanafi school of Sunni Islam and positions itself as the only Islamic authority in Kosovo. However, several radical religious figures in Kosovo do not accept the legitimacy of the BIK and try to undermine this institution by following radical imams and the Salafi interpretation of Islam adopted by groups such as ISIS. These interpretations, calling for the establishment of an Islamic state based on Islamic law (sharia) and jihad as its appeal, are perceived by local analysts as inherently contradicting Albanian ethnonational identity. According to analysts, this type of transnational loyalty to the global *umma* and conflict with the official BIK disturb the traditional Albanian interreligious harmony based on tolerance of religious customs (Peci and Demjaha 2021b).

Demographic data show that Kosovan recruits originate predominantly from the country's two most populous municipalities: Pristina (35 persons) and Prizren (26 persons) (Peci and Demjaha 2021a). However, the rate of mobilization per capita is highest in the five municipalities mentioned earlier: Hani i Elezit, Kaçanik, Mitrovica, Gjilan, and Viti, which together account for only 14 percent of the country's total population (Shtuni 2016). Our research indicates that the high mobilization rates result from targeted and effective radicalization, recruitment, and mobilization efforts by extremist networks that have operated in that particular geographic space across borders for more than a decade.[17] After 2014, ISIS changed its strategy from concentrating attacks in a single area to instead organizing attacks in countries where adherents to its ideology are located.

With increased communication via the internet and a changed ISIS strategy, there is a high risk of attacks in Kosovo and the region. In 2021, five people, radicalized primarily online, were arrested for planning attacks in Kosovo (Sejdiu 2021). What is it that stops decisive moments such as the appeal of ISIS from erupting into violence in such enabling environments as Kosovo? And what makes local communities resilient? Cragin (2014, 337) reasonably suggests that it is impossible to understand pathways to radicalization or to design policies to preempt them without a complementary knowledge of why individuals resist the influence of VE.

Social Resilience

Tunisia

Maybe the most important demonstration of how resilient Tunisia—and especially Tunisian youth and society—has proven to be vis-à-vis the call of VE is the aforementioned battle that took place in December 2016 in Ben Guerdane. A medium-sized city at the frontier between Tunisia and Libya, Ben Guerdane is part of the Medenine governorate and has historically suffered from the lack of coordinated state actions there, such as economic investment and delivery of basic services. Marginalization, especially since the fall of Ben Ali, was widely felt by inhabitants in the city. Since then, the city saw a rise in the popularity of Ennahda, and the border increasingly became an income-generation source. The end of the Ghaddafi regime and the rise of civil war in the neighboring country unleashed violent power competition between new and old actors in the smuggling business. During the 1990s and 2000s, jobs generated by the "border economy" progressively overshadowed private or public employment. This area of Tunisia also presents a very conservative social outlook compared to that in more advantaged areas of the North (i.e., Tunis, Sfax, Sousse). The fear of spillover of violence from Libya fueled people's feelings of insecurity, most notably in connection to the restrictions on cross-border activities imposed by Tunis.

Increasingly, the public space in Ben Guerdane has become dominated by protest movements calling for a state-supported development project and the immediate reopening of the border for business. Since 2014, strikes, roadblocks, sit-ins, and protests, particularly involving youth in precarious employment situations and unemployed persons, have shaped collective action in the city. But the cross-border economy also allowed the circulation of networks linked to VE. Violent jihadi Salafis have started to play more critical roles in cross-border smuggling, especially after the closure of the frontier. Such networks and their ramifications among local families in Ben Guerdane proved crucial in staging the 2016 attack by the Islamic State from neighboring Zuara in Libya.

Unlike the attacks at the Bardo Museum or in Sousse, this was a violent extremist attack aimed at overthrowing authorities in the city and capturing the city. The assailants from Libya and their local allies in Ben Guerdane simultaneously attacked the army barracks, the headquarters of the National Guard, and the city's main police station. Although there were casualties among the police and Customs officials, the anti-terrorist unit mobilized and eventually managed to repulse the attack.

The attack was an attempt by violent extremists to use their rage against authorities, politicians, and the state to start a mass revolt in the city. However, Ben Guerdane's inhabitants showed outstanding resilience by rallying with the state security forces upon their deployment. They resisted or even sabotaged the propaganda of the Islamic State that asked Ben Guerdane's people to join the revolt, ignored messages on loudspeakers, and even refused to be intimidated. Additionally, they provided intelligence and information so the army could find violent extremists.

Nonoccurrence of VE in Tunisia was also seen in the areas of Sfax and Sousse. These cities have historically benefited from larger state investments and might qualify as the wealthiest regions in Tunisia, which makes them much less of an enabling environment. Yet, the sprawling city of Tunis can be seen as an environment that fosters VE because of its large size, geographical features, and significant inequality. In more remote areas such as Ben Guerdane, the lack of government presence, relative underdevelopment, and active cross-border trade can all contribute to the growth of VE.

Still, the foiled attack on Ben Guerdane at the Tunisia–Libya border proves to be an important case of nonoccurrence. Despite the deep infiltration of VE networks in the city, not to mention the city's booming smuggling economy, most of the population not only avoided joining VE networks while these were staging an armed attack but also actively resisted them. Families and social networks proved to be veritable sources of resistance to VE, although vulnerable to be exploited or manipulated by VE actors, as the Ben Guerdane case demonstrates. Despite the relative estrangement from the central government, local authorities, or even state symbols and the discontent in peripheral areas of the country, protests and contestation demonstrate citizens' deep attachment to the Tunisian state. They are meant to be instruments to engage institutions in peaceful manners. On the other hand, attempts to overthrow the state and feed a violent extremist attack against state representatives are met with ambiguity or are vastly rejected. In particular, the Ben Guerdane case demonstrates how everyday forms of resistance and small-scale subversion can coexist with regime opposition and regime contestation, showing the strength of civic values and the resilience of Ben Guerdane's inhabitants to extremist discourses (Simoncini 2021).

Tunisia shows that amid all the confusion and chaos of an unfulfilled transition, most people remain deeply attached to their state if they can engage meaningfully with it through legitimate institutions. If this is the case, attempts to overthrow the state using violence based on an extremist ideology will be resisted by most of the population.

Kosovo

Some explanations for Kosovo's social resilience focus on the diversity of the religious sphere (Kurzman 2011); logistical and financial barriers to violence; strong ideas against violence; family influence; and the efficiency argument related to cost-benefit (Fahmi 2017). Our study indicates that two types of factors have strengthened communities' resilience to VE: (1) resilience factors during the radicalization wave (2011–2014), and (2) resilience factors after the radicalization wave (from 2015 onward). The first category includes religious counternarratives, social cohesion, and civic values as the main factors that helped communities resist radicalization during the peak propaganda wave. The second category involves the hard approach by state institutions and the soft response by international donors and CSOs. Seeking to understand the nonoccurrence of violence and resilience to violence and extremism in the Middle East in the example of Egypt's Muslim Brotherhood, Georges Fahmi (2020, 7) outlined four main factors: legitimacy, social trust, institutional rules, and external pressure. In the Balkans, our fieldwork-based research foregrounded three major factors of resilience and nonoccurrence of violence: (1) local communities exhibiting social cohesion and civic values; (2) the role of imams and individuals of authority; and (3) preventive measures (Evstatiev and Mishkova 2022, 3–4).

Besides the local predominantly Hanafi Muslim traditions, half a century of communist rule in Eastern Europe instilled a sense of secularism in Balkan Muslim communities that gave rise to a local Muslim culture palpably different in its interpretations and practices from its more conservative counterparts in the Arabian Peninsula and elsewhere in the MENA. Hence, many refer to Muslims in the Balkans as "progressive Muslims" or "cultural Muslims" (Akyol 2019). These specific features of mainstream Muslim communal life in the Balkans draw on inherited prevailing traditions of religious and interethnic tolerance.

An important factor of resilience on the community level in Kosovo is the inherited religious tolerance, which also embraces interethnic communication. In the aftermath of the Kosovo War, people went out in the streets requesting a return to their homes in the north, which then escalated into protests.[18] Gradually, tensions calmed in an environment where imams and priests demonstrated respect for each other using the communal religious celebrations to build religious harmony (Koha.net 2021). The Islamic Community, the leading religious institution of Muslims, played an awareness-raising and preventive role.[19] It sends out imams to provide lectures in state correction institutions that contributes to the rehabilitation and resocialization of convicts and helps prevent the radicalization of other prisoners (Indeksonline.net 2018).

Communities with stronger social cohesion are less conducive to the occurrence of violence because social connections within and between communities help mitigate the risk factors associated with VE (Ellis and Abdi 2017). Mainstream Muslim institutions can play a crucial role in Kosovo (Evstatiev and Mishkova 2022, 8). Imams and other individuals of authority also play important roles in the nonoccurrence of VE and in strengthening resilience. As explained by a Muslim official in the area of Maliq in neighboring Albania, radicals exploit certain sensitive topics, and through these forms of "scouting," they manage to polarize people.[20] In Kosovo, major radicalization drivers were neutralized in areas such as Podujeva and Prizren, because imams refused to accept groups that promoted such ideas. Muslim officials from the Islamic Community in North Macedonia also stressed the efforts their institution exerted in combating religious radicalism. Although this institution did not predefine the texts to be read at sermons in the mosques, it closely monitored sermon content, and the religious leaders criticized the radical ethos of "those who had returned from studies in the Middle East and with whom one cannot talk in a normal way."[21]

After 2014, the hard measures have limited violent extremist activity to propaganda because violent extremists are now more easily spotted and risk facing criminal proceedings for recruitment activities. This has influenced their modus operandi by making it harder for them to organize in groups. In Kosovo, the hard approaches to P/CVE receive and often depend on strong support from the US government. Foreign actors, including the EU, mainly support the soft measures. Nonstate actors, such as international NGOs and CSOs, have engaged in P/CVE by setting up referral mechanisms, capacity-building initiatives, awareness-raising campaigns, and grassroots projects to build stronger community resilience. Moreover, training programs are still in great demand in Kosovo. Our study brings to the fore the importance of the interrelations between the three factors: hard and soft preventive measures combined with the decisive role of the local community and individuals of authority in bolstering resilience (Evstatiev and Mishkova 2022, 10).

Conclusion

During our observation period, the two cases navigated crucially different trajectories: Kosovo consolidated as and has remained a democracy, while at the same time, Tunisia, heralded as the Arab Spring's success story, has regressed on its democratic journey into autocracy through a gradual coup. This marked a critical shift away from a contended power landscape in Tunisia to one where the democratic mechanisms and the option of contesting power are markedly constrained, with implications for voice and exit dynamics. Along the divergent paths of Kosovo's democratic consolidation and Tunisia's backsliding, the focus shifts to understanding the multifaceted nature of community resilience and the localized response to VE through examination of these contrasting political environments.

Resilience is systemic in that it does not depend on one single factor but rather on the interconnection of factors and the role actors play in shaping them. Overall, local resilience to VE in Kosovo and the Western Balkans is determined by the community's social cohesion and civic values; the efficiency of the preventive measures and interventions undertaken by state institutions, religious authorities, and community actors; and the community's attitude toward these measures. As the cases of Tunisia and Kosovo indicate, nonoccurrence and resilience are highly context-specific. Concentrating the preventive efforts in areas where there has been an occurrence of violence threatens to oversaturate certain communities while it ignores the needs of communities that are commonly acknowledged as resilient.

Salafism, which underlies the recent jihadi appeal, is, despite its global call, intimately context-specific and tied to drivers present in each enabling environment. It has different appeal in the Muslim-majority societies of the Middle East, where Islamic identity is already established and concerns mainly theology, and in Europe, where it is more closely tied with identity (Hegghammer 2021, 26). First, jihadi Salafism spread most widely in places where the quest for a revived Islamic identity blended with severe social disruptions, such as the Bosnian and Kosovo Wars. Second, despite its global appeal and transnational channels, Salafism in the Balkans has become increasingly "localized" as radicalized individuals are reaccommodated into local "traditional Islam" and its official institutional representation. Thus, local Muslims who had previously "globalized" through Salafism and its jihadi branch undergo a process of "relocalization" by finding a modus vivendi with the "traditional" Hanafi school of Sunni Islam—a tendency already noticed in Tunisia and the Middle East (Drevon and Haenni 2021, 27).

This (re)localization is related to hybridizing Islam, which also affects Islamism. As a result of external (securitization) and internal (the local Muslim communities and its institutions) pressures, Salafis in the Balkans, including Bulgaria, have adopted a strategy of merging into the locally embedded Hanafi tradition. Sociologically, Salafis are becoming less exclusive, more flexible, and adaptable to the national context. Doctrinally, the outcome is a hybrid combination of a Salafi creed and Hanafi practices—a new phenomenon of "Salafi-Hanafism" (Evstatiev 2023). Hybridized Islamism leaves less room for political Islam and shifts the stress from activism to a more inclusivist approach to religion, society, and communal life.

The reshuffling resembles what some recent studies designate as "Salafi-Malikism" in Tunisia, where the adaptation to the local Maliki context allows Salafis to preserve their teaching and preaching activities within the securitization wave (Merone, Blanc, and Sigillò 2021). Others observe hybridized forms of Islamism and nationalism by which Salafis and movements influenced by the Muslim Brotherhood adopt "Islami-nationalist stances" (Gade and Palani 2022, 222). In the Balkans, including Kosovo, these developments assume a "Hanafization" of Salafism (Kursani 2018c). The paradox in this competition for autochthony amid social and existential uncertainty (Bøås and Dunn 2013a, 20), from which Salafism provides a way out, is that Salafism seeks to doctrinally assimilate Hanafism, getting, in the same time, locally legitimized through an adaptive hybridization with Hanafi discourses and practices. This major shift in Islamist pathways signals a new stage of hybridization and adaptability.

Notes

1. See Inkyfada's map of attacks: https://inkyfada.com/fr/2014/06/15/carte-terrorisme/.
2. Interview with an official from the Anti-Terrorism Unit in Kosovo, Pristina, 2021.
3. From Arabic *jama'a* (assembly)—either the entire community of believers or a certain community or local assembly around a religious leader or a mosque. *Para jammaats* are groups of Salafi Muslims proliferated in the Western Balkans following the Bosnian War (1992–1995).
4. The interviewed (2021) Nexhmedin Spahiu, a university professor from Mitrovica, and Nerimane Ferizin, a civil society activist in Mitrovica, hold that the impossibility for Albanians to return to their homes in the northern part of the city is the main reason for the recurrent protests.
5. Interview with EU official, October 26, 2020; interview with EU official, November 2, 2020.
6. Interview with EU official, November 2, 2020.
7. Interview with EU official, October 26, 2020.
8. Interviews with relatives of and people involved in the wars in Syria and Iraq, November 3–9, 2021.
9. Interview with a citizen in Polac, November 3, 2021.

10. Interviews with citizens and relatives in Bukovik, Capar, Polac, as well as Shipol in Mitrovica, November 5–9, 2021.

11. Bergen et al. (2008, 56).

12. Derived from the ideas of the radical Jordanian preacher Muhammed al-Maqdisi.

13. PREVEX interview of the head of an NGO consultant and specialist in radicalism in Tunisia, October 2021.

14. See, for example, Wolf (2013) about the factors leading to this rally organized by AST in May 2012 led by Abu Iyadh.

15. PREVEX interview with an expert on those issues, November 2021.

16. PREVEX interview with Hatem Ben Chakroun, researcher at the Observatoire Tunisian de la Transition Democratique, Tunis, Tunisia, October 2021.

17. Interview with Luan Keka, Head of the Anti-Terror Unit of Kosovo Police, November 2, 2021.

18. Interview with Professor Nexhmedin Spahiu, Mitrovica, November 2021.

19. Islamic Community of Kosovo. See https://bislame.net/intvstvoa/.

20. Interview with Muslim official in Maliq, August 31, 2021.

21. Interview with local representatives of the Islamic Religious Community, Tetovo, August 25, 2021.

9

Regime Survival and Mobilization: Iraq, Mali, and Syria

Colin Powers, Luca Raineri, and Stéphane Lacroix

Empirical evidence suggests that state weakness is a factor contributing to the rise of or resilience to jihadist insurgencies. Countries such as Afghanistan, Algeria, Iraq, Somalia, Libya, Syria, Yemen, Mali, and Burkina Faso all experienced a major regime break characterized by violent change, disruption, collapse, or armed contestation before or during the emergence of jihadist agitation. Accordingly, scholarship focusing on the drivers of jihadism's proliferation (for instance, in the Middle East: Saloukh 2016; in Africa: Hansen 2019) tends to stress the salience of weak states, whose inability to assert sovereign prerogatives across geographic and functional planes invites jihadists to stake their claim. The causal relation between state weakness and insurgency extends beyond the specific case of jihadism; it is affirmed in the literature at the onset of civil wars in general (Kalyvas 2009).

The oft-noticed nexus between state weakness and a society's proneness to jihadist insurgencies has prompted researchers to seek the mechanisms that may metabolize the linkage. Many of those pursuing this line of inquiry have identified social cleavages, particularly sectarian ones, as a mechanism of potential import. Though diverse in form, sectarianism can be conceptualized as a system of sociopolitical organization that emphasizes nonstate identities and exhibits a tendency toward reified nativism, narratives of victimization, supremacist views, and outgroup othering. Sectarianism may help explain insurgencies in two ways. First, the presence of sectarian currents within a society—itself a function of history—renders the building of state capacity and the consolidation of a civic national identity fraught. This, in turn, enhances the probability of a regime break occurring and widens the opportunity structure for an insurgent challenge. Second, in the eventuality of a regime break, sectarianism constitutes a uniquely potent vehicle for taking advantage of the security dilemma that comes in the wake of polarizing communities and positioning sect-based affiliation as the optimal choice for those seeking safety (Posen 1993). We may, therefore, posit that sectarianism fosters an enabling environment for jihadist groups to take root and thrive.

At the same time, contemporary jihadism is at least partially defined by its transnational membership and global frame of reference. Because of its cosmopolitan nature, it must demonstrate plasticity and a willingness to deploy borrowed semiotics to anchor in a given place. Absent a strategic narrative through which its violent entrepreneurs may interpret, aggregate, rescale, and ultimately commandeer the parochial grievances of a population or subpopulation (Schmid 2014), jihadism can hardly mobilize a challenge to the prevailing order (Andersen and Sandberg 2020). In many contexts, sectarianism offers the needed strategic narrative. A means of *glocalization,* putting sectarianism to work, allows jihadism's transnational Sunnism to be grafted onto primordial fault lines and for its millenarianism to accommodate local communities' contingent interests and resentments. By facilitating the recruitment of adherents and furnishing a device for calcifying societal divisions, the mobilization of sectarianism might, therefore, be viewed as a valuable hypothesis to explain why and how violent extremism occurs in enabling environments.

Hypotheses of a sectarianism-jihadism relation, however, require greater testing and refinement. Certainly, large-n studies like those conducted by Svensson and Nilsson (2022) can establish that jihadism mobilizes most frequently in the presence of ethnicity-based cleavages and most violently in the presence of religious ones. Yet correlation does not amount to causation. Noting the variable inversion bias that was spotted by scholars of civil war many decades ago (Fearon and Laitin 2003), one needs to stress that if most jihadist mobilizations and insurgencies indeed occur where sectarian cleavages are observed, there are nevertheless a great many places where sectarian cleavages persist in the absence of jihadist insurgency. Such correlations, in other words, explain very little about the circumstance in which sectarian preconditions do not give way to jihadist insurgencies—to wit, the nonoccurrence of violent extremism that is at the heart of this edited volume—or the circumstance in which sectarianism might have an expressly negative effect on jihadism. Concerning the latter, we need only recall examples of state authorities nurturing sectarianism to instrumentalize communal self-defense groups against jihadist interlopers or examples in which jihadists' embrace of sectarianism provoked anti-jihadist resistance and resilience in large segments of society. In these cases, rather than facilitating jihadism, certain features of sectarianism seem to have limited its grip.

Cognizant of the cavity in our understanding of the relations between sectarianism and enabling environments for violent extremist mobilization, in this chapter we engage the problem of sectarianism and its impact on the occurrence and nonoccurrence of jihadist insurgencies and counterinsurgencies through a comparative analysis focused on Mali, Iraq, and Syria. Case selection was determined by the observation of key phenomena—sectarianism, jihadist mobilizations, and counterinsurgencies—which potentially renders heuristic cases for the three featured (George and Bennett 2005). Because the diversity of independent and dependent variables across our cases advises against undertaking a structured analysis of the Millsian variety, a loose approach to comparison is deemed more appropriate to host the thick description and causal process tracing, which can enrich and imbricate one another in complex and unpredictable ways. Ultimately, the resulting medley facilitates grounded theorization to induce tentative, middle-level propositions. We center our concerns on the causal mechanism of sectarianism vis-à-vis cases of occurrence or nonoccurrence of violent extremist mobilization, finally, because it allows our analysis to move between generalizability and specificity. On the one hand, adopting this focus brings jihadism into conversation with categories already in use for studying asymmetric conflicts. On the other, it permits this conversation to proceed without losing jihadism's specific ideological scope.

Accordingly, the analysis of each case herein singled out rests on discussing a considerable amount of qualitative evidence. As part of the Preventing Violent Extremism in the Balkans and the MENA (PREVEX) Project, we performed immersive fieldwork for data collection to map causal pathways across time; develop acquaintances with local actors, norms, and meanings; and gain access to key informants in target communities characterized by occurrence and nonoccurrence of violent extremism. Through open-ended interviews, we posed questions to various relevant principals regarding their participation in and observations of decisive moments in the (non)mobilization of jihadist insurgencies. Principals include tribal, religious, and social leaders; traditional chiefs; members of nonviolent Islamist movements subjected to internal fracturing as a result of state repression; jihadist sympathizers; and prospective jihadist recruits. To gain traction on counterinsurgency dynamics, national and international officers in Mali (predominantly in and from the region of Mopti), Iraq, and Syria were also engaged during several rounds of fieldwork between mid-2021 and late 2022. A recursive approach to the field has contributed to building local networks and relationships of trust, corroborating findings, detecting trends across time, and ensuring the safety of research protocols.

In terms of organization, each case study begins by locating the factors underpinning the local form of relevant jihadist insurgencies and interrogating the relations between states, societal fractures, and jihadist appeals. We also study the relevant counterinsurgencies and explain their relative impacts by taking a holistic view that places the state's interventions within an environment defined by social cleavages and a jihadist alternative. Investigating violent extremism from two ends, our analyses parse when and why sectarianism can amount to a resource for jihadist mobilization, counterinsurgency, or regime survival, and thereby should be considered, or not, as a defining factor of violent extremism's enabling environments.

Social Cleavages and Jihadism: A Literature Review

Theorization of social cleavages and their consequence for jihadist insurgencies has greatly advanced in recent years (for instance, Sedgwick 2007; Phillips 2015; Hinnebusch 2016; Collombier and Roy 2017). Roy (2017a) contends that the polarization of tribes along generational and clan-based lines, alongside the globalization of the smuggling economy, has increased the attractiveness of jihadism for disenfranchised social groups, especially youths. Lia (2021) seconds this argument, adding that intertribe rivalries and kinship networks' nonhierarchical, loosely organized nature also enhance the vulnerability to jihadist frames, narratives, and practices. This is because, in seeking purchase within a particular context, jihadist entrepreneurs have proven capable of transfusing their struggle into cleavages that are already salient (Thurston 2020). The so-called Boko Haram group in Nigeria provides a standard illustration of this: by expressing its aims in terms compatible with local grievance (Krause 2020), scholars have shown the group deftly exploited preexisting socioethnic polarization (Agbiboa 2013) and ethnonational irredentism (Pieri and Zenn 2017) in building its presence. In addition, in circumstances where social cleavages are complemented by high levels of competition among nonstate actors, researchers have induced that the available resources through affiliation with transnational jihadism may lead local groups to pursue such an association (Collombier et al 2018). Some have also posited that decision-making on the association can derive purely from communications-related concerns, such as branding oneself connected with an entity of international renown (Bøås and Dunn 2013b).

Other scholars, however, contend that social cleavages, tribal and sectarian ones included, need not furnish an enabling environment for jihadist groups to take root and mobilize support. On the basis of their decade-long study of insurgency and counterinsurgency in Chechnya, Aliyev and Souleimanov (2022) highlight that the socially embedded obligation of blood revenge present in "honorific" societies like tribal networks constitutes a natural firewall against jihadism because of the latter's tendency toward violent excess. Similarly, Taha (2017)posits that the customs of matrilineality, gender progressivism, and religious tolerance among Libya's Tuaregs have served to inoculate local communities against the risk of radicalization, thereby hindering the spread of jihadism within an exceedingly fractured social environment. In Mali, however, note that the same Tuaregs have exhibited a more pragmatic attitude that does not exclude building ties with jihadists. In their case, interests trump norms as local rivalries and quotidian concerns like personal vendettas and aspirations to power govern choices on engagement with jihadism (Skretting 2021).

If the works hitherto discussed help clarify how social cleavages like sectarianism do or do not facilitate transnational jihadism as it lays down local roots, other works elucidate why these roots often fail to run deep. Sheikh (2022) attributes this to the explosive and tension-ridden process that is the bundling of a "conflict constellation"—that is, the active and reciprocal exchanges through which local and transnational fights (and fighters) amalgamate. Hafez (2018) points to the extreme doctrines and ideological priorities that bind jihadist cadres to their cause and posits that this renders such actors less adaptive and less amenable to accommodating their messaging and praxes to local environs. Researchers of the Sahel, meanwhile, find that for tactical as much as normative reasons, jihadism's local emergence may provoke vigorous opposition among designated outgroups (Cold-Ravnkilde and Ba 2022; Poudiougou 2022). Just as this expression of violent extremism can radicalize communities where it embeds, so can it animate a militant reaction devoted to its destruction.

In this framework, states frequently mobilize counterinsurgency campaigns that hinge on the recruitment of auxiliaries (Jentzch, Kalyvas, and Schubiger 2015). Be they paramilitaries, militias, or communal brigades of self-defense, these para-state armed actors benefit from diverse sponsorship, from the state to local oligarchs and foreign governments of different stripes and persuasions. They tend to be especially active in contexts with fragmented social fabric. Militarily speaking, para-state militias contribute to intelligence collection, the conduct of operations, and security provision in reclaimed lands. Politically speaking, their deployment affords state authorities a degree of plausible deniability for their (indirect) violence. They have also been shown to provoke insurgencies into retraining their focus away from the incumbent power and onto the civilian populations perceived to be harboring the auxiliaries (Clayton and Thomson 2014). In some cases, paramilitary auxiliaries may help delegitimize an insurgency. In other cases, however, because of their penchant for engaging in or facilitating communal score-settling, they can create conditions conducive to a jihadist resurgence (Raineri 2022).

Sectarianism and Jihadism in Mali, Iraq, and Syria

The heuristic case studies of Mali, Iraq, and Syria attempt to set into the conversation and complicate three of the threads that can be extracted from this wide-spanning literature: (1) that sectarian divides provide enabling environments for jihadism to take root, strategically sell its narrative, and mobilize recruits; (2) that sectarianism undercuts the spread of jihadism by way of its normative incompatibility, intense othering dynamics, and propensity toward provoking counterinsurgency mobilization and, as such, causes the nonoccurrence (or at least limited spread) of violent extremism; and (3) that the leveraging of sectarianism shores up incumbent regimes facing violent contention.

Mali

From its epicenter in Mali, jihadism has been expanding steadily in the Sahel over the past decade. According to the 2023 edition of the Global Terrorism Index, Mali and neighboring Burkina Faso rank among the five countries most impacted by terrorism worldwide (IEP 2023).

Although most of Mali's jihadists are now mobilized locally, including both rank and file and leaders, the genealogy of the movement needs to be traced back to North Africa. Beginning in the late 1990s, jihadists from Algeria, facing mounting repression and the drying of their social fields of leverage (Reno 2011), sought refuge and opportunities across the country's Saharan borders. The remote borderlands of North Mali proved especially welcoming. Initially, scholars explained this by emphasizing the Malian state's limited capacity to monitor its peripheries and counter jihadist proliferation, thereby aligning with the Pentagon's "ungoverned space" thesis (Lacher 2008). As the years passed, however, researchers would instead identify the lack of political resolve by Malian authorities—whose security perceptions were then shaped more by sectarian concerns than any bother with transnational terrorism—as the factor of perhaps decisive salience: it was the fear of a latent insurgency by Tuareg rebels in the north of the country that led Bamako's authorities to frame jihadist groups in the region through ethnic lenses and to see the settling of "Arab" jihadists on Malian land less as a threat to state security than as an opportunity to counterbalance the Tuaregs' hegemony and irredentism (Guichaoua and Pellerin 2017).

The tacit blessing that the then-Malian regime afforded to the jihadists would eventually prove ill-advised. Though the jihadists avoided directly threatening state interests during the early years of their stay, they also did little to antagonize the Tuaregs. On the contrary, through their discourses and practices, the jihadists explicitly sought to transcend sectarian divides, whether of ethnic or racial origin, stressing instead the universal appeal of their call to the entire *Umma* (Chelin 2018). As a result, many prominent Tuareg insurgents, including former ethnonationalist leaders, came to associate with jihadism to one degree or another, opportunistically harnessing the movement's symbolic and material resources to reframe their struggle against the alleged corruption of the Malian state.

In 2011, the collapse of the Gaddafi regime in Libya and the ensuing spillover of Tuareg fighters across the Sahara-Sahel region brought three geopolitical imaginaries previously coexisting in—and competing for—northern Mali into tension: (1) the postcolonial state order centered in Bamako; (2) the secessionist project of the North led by Tuareg irredentism; and (3) an emergent jihadist insurgency combining ethnonationalist and transnational elements (Raineri and Strazzari 2015). The first imaginary—Malian nationalism—quickly gave way as the advances of the rebels prompted a coup d'état, which plunged the state into chaos. The second, meanwhile, would itself backfire, allowing the third to rise to prominence in its wake: the Tuaregs' sectarian appeals and abuses in attempting to mold a homogeneous constituency for their aspired state project provided jihadists with a valuable opportunity to posture as protectors, chastise the impious corruption of tribal leaders and legacies, and make inroads among the local population. Having managed to marginalize the Tuareg irredentists, fight off the hardliners, and co-opt others, and having presented their alternative polity as one where universal religious prescription would supersede ethnic cleavages and tribal norms, it would be the jihadists that could proclaim a (short-lived, it should be said) caliphate in mid-2012.

As should be apparent, though it may be true that the early rooting of jihadism in northern Mali correlates with state collapse, our analysis reveals a more complicated picture. In the final instance, it was in a negative sense that sectarianism provided fertile ground for jihadist mobilization during the years in question: by claiming to fight against sectarian divides rather than by appealing to one side of those divides, did jihadists succeed in building power?

The following years saw a different dynamic emerge. In 2013, a French-led military intervention swiftly managed to evict jihadist groups from the main towns in northern Mali. Defeated yet not destroyed, jihadists scattered and reformed in rural areas, making it harder to track them. From their hideouts in the bush, jihadists adopted a new strategy, in keeping with al-Qaeda's global orientation (and possibly with a nomadic warfare tradition): they prepared for a long war of attrition, initially directed against soft targets and supply lines through hit-and-run attacks, to erode the enemy's capacity—and, in the long term, resolve—to fight back.

This new approach required building friendly ties with the local communities. Accordingly, beginning in 2014, we could say that jihadist groups across the Sahel moved to tactics centered on "winning people's hearts and minds." They did so by organizing some rudimentary yet effective schemes to deliver criminal justice, social mobility, and protection in their nested areas, constituting a hybrid kind of political order (Bøås and Strazzari 2020). Moreover, their rhetoric explicitly challenged the legitimacy of traditional ethnic cleavages and leadership (Sangaré 2016). Illustrating this, in 2017, a constellation of jihadist formations and splinter groups, many of which had featured implicit ethnic allegiances, merged under an umbrella organization—Jama'at Nasr al-Islam wal Muslimin (JNIM)—which at least nominally rejected those ethnic divides. As many interviewees from central Mali communities point out, JNIM's strategic narrative consistently emphasized religious compliance and global struggles while downplaying the salience of communal cleavages.

Naturally, the proliferation of jihadism across the region and the buildup of a sizable jihadist coalition prompted the rearticulation of the counterterrorist *dispositif*. France agreed to complement its light-footprint intervention based on air dominance and special forces strikes with enhanced coordination with auxiliaries on the ground. The problematic situation faced by the Malian Armed Forces (FAMa) led to the decision to work with local allies from nonstate, ethnic-based armed groups, many of whom were from Tuareg self-defense militias. The Malian government, unable to assert its authority, seconded and expanded this strategy. Malian officers not only tolerated the rise of self-defense militias from different ethnic groups—mainly Dogon, Arabs, and Songhay—but also politically sponsored, economically bankrolled, and militarily armed these groups (UNSC 2020; Benjaminsen and Ba 2021; Raineri and Strazzari 2022).

Ultimately, this complex counterinsurgency strategy backfired. The ethnic-based armed groups enrolled in the transnational counterterrorism *dispositif* frequently used the symbolic and material resources acquired to settle scores against local rivals. Razzias, abuses, and mass reprisals against ethnic groups perceived to be collectively complicit, if not outright members of terrorist organizations, had a detrimental effect. Not only did these actions cement ethnic cleavages and exacerbate social polarizations, but, more importantly, they also elicited an urgent demand for protection by the groups targeted in the name of counterterrorism. Jihadists seized the opportunity to step in, posturing as protection providers and depicting the ethnic-based abuses as part of a transnational conspiracy tying together foreign infidels, corrupted national governments, and their local armed puppets.

The scholarship on "radicalization" has extensively demonstrated that this mechanism—whereby abuses perpetrated by state and para-state forces prompt demand for protection that jihadists address—is one of the most solid drivers of jihadist mobilization in the Sahel at large, if not in Africa altogether (UNDP 2023; ICG 2020; Raineri 2022). Homing in on this mechanism can also contribute to explaining how the jihadist threat in the region turned from one organized around small cells hidden and secluded from the rest of the society into a large-scale insurgency deeply entangled in societal divides.

Our review of the dynamics of jihadist rooting, proliferation, and mobilization in central Mali—which certainly does not claim to be exhaustive—provides a useful heuristic perspective vis-à-vis our problematic highlighting that sectarianism is dialectically linked to jihadist insurgencies and counterinsurgencies in at least two ways. First, even though sectarian divides—ethnic cleavages, tribal hierarchies, racial biases—indeed permeated Malian society even before the country became a hotbed of jihadism, their political salience was greatly amplified as a result of the dynamics of insurgency and counterinsurgency. In that sense, and in keeping with social constructivist claims on sectarianism and conflict, sectarian cleavages are perhaps less the cause than the outcome of conflict dynamics, midwives through violent othering practices. Second, although the emphasis on sectarian rivalries and communal polarization has contributed to triggering the mechanism of jihadist mobilization and insurgency in Mali, it has, by the same token, limited the spread of jihadist allegiances to certain social groups while pushing others to, by and large, join counterinsurgency efforts. Sectarianism, in other words, appears to be at the root of both the poison of jihadism and its antidote, and hence both a factor of vulnerability and of resilience in a diverse and multicultural society like Mali's.

Interestingly, jihadist groups in Mali and the Sahel seem aware of this, though they have adopted different responses to face the challenge of sectarianism. Groups linked to al-Qaeda, like JNIM, have consistently tried to downplay sectarian and ethnic divides, molding their call in universalist terms and purporting their fight as one against profane tribal legacies. By contrast, jihadist groups linked to the Islamic State, which have been expanding in the borderlands of Mali, Burkina Faso, and Niger, have tapped into existing social cleavages, perpetrating ethnic-based retaliations and massacres and sometimes posturing as a mere self-defense militia formed out of communal rather than ideological identities (Lyammouri 2021).

Last, we should observe that the government of Mali has actively contributed to fomenting sectarianism, both as a cheap counterinsurgency strategy and as a deceptive rationalization of jihadism, which obscures its radical ideological scope and glosses over the failures of the Malian state. The inherent tensions between this strategy and the growing appeals to the national(ist) fiber of "the Malian people" run the risk of jeopardizing the sustainability of the counterinsurgency doctrine and the regime's survival. Since the military takeover of state institutions in mid-2021, Mali has experienced an escalation of violence against civilians at the hands of state forces and their Wagner Group–dispatched military aides. Individuals face a growing risk of being accused of colluding with jihadists merely because of their ethnic or geographic origin. As a result, the increasing militarism and nationalism of Malian authorities are paradoxically fueling sectarian divides in the country's periphery, and the fragmentation of the state that ensues appears to be shaping a social environment further allowing violent extremism to take root and thrive (Nasr 2022).

Iraq

Salafist jihadism made its initial incursion into Iraq amid the fallout from the second American invasion of 2003. Led at the outset by the Jordanian Abu Musab al-Zarqawi and organized under the banner of al-Qaeda in Iraq (AQ-I), the movement operated from hubs in the Sunni triangle of the country's West, where its presence was blessed or consented to at the outset by the majority of the tribal federations. The causes underlying the welcome offered by AQ-I during the early days of its existence correspond closely to those emphasized in the literature.

To begin with, conditions on the ground in the province of al-Anbar were especially inviting to anti-system challengers. Though governments dating back to 1921 consistently worked to cultivate a unified sense of national Iraqi identity, the version of unity they promoted and institutionalized had always been one premised on conformity and coercion (Haddad 2017). This deprived the Iraqi state of popular buttresses and civic credibility. Decisions made upon the ascent of Saddam Hussein subsequently functioned to compromise the outlook for civic nationalism further: Although the bureaucracy of the Baathist single party instantiated a nondiscriminating system of rights and benefits, from the start, Hussein also deployed patrimonial practices in the realm of security that privileged Sunni communities, particularly those from al-Anbar, Salahedin, Diyala, and Nineveh (Hinnebusch 2016; Haddad 2017). With the decline of Pan-Arabism in the late 1970s and the rupture of the Iranian Revolution in 1979, his Sunni-privileging sectarianization of the state—and the attendant emergence of Shia communalism—only grew more pronounced. This culminated in the Iraqi state's wholesale repression of Shia populations in 1991, a move provoked by a handful of Shia Islamist movements joining the uprisings of that year. Sectarian cleavages widened thereafter as Hussein reconsolidated his power on Arab Sunni foundations (Long 2004) and "retribalized" the state, the latter a response to fiscal crisis, a desperate search for ideological legitimacy, and a pivot that benefited hitherto marginal Arab Sunni shaikhs in western Iraq (Jabar 2000).

Ironically, Hussein's privileging of Iraq's Arab Sunni constituency in the latter stages of his rule ultimately left these communities more vulnerable to the coming Salafist-jihadist appeal. In the first instance, this was because the deepening of Sunni Arabs' imbrication within the state meant Sunni Arabs would be the biggest losers when the Coalition Provisional Authority, directed by the United States, introduced de-Baathification measures in 2003. The fact that the identity of Iraq's Arab Sunni minority had always been discreetly coconstitutive of the identity of the Iraqi state (Haddad 2017, 123–135)—a reality Hussein unveiled more than created—also proved salient: after all, large segments of the communities were genuinely vested in the conceptual and symbolic frames of the pre-2003 status quo and, as a privileged category, had never been compelled to build their own independent, faith-centric institutions. This was the case when the American occupation upturned the status quo—and when a Shia-led state took shape shortly after that; they had few institutional means for channeling the uncertainty, fear, and loss being experienced. This opened the door, ideationally and otherwise, to a Salafist-jihadist movement that offered answers to the dislocation felt, that pledged to direct a response to the Shias being elevated into a new *staatsvolk,* and that could provide jobs for the thousands of soldiers and intelligence officers unemployed by Paul Bremer's diktat. The coalescence of multiple temporalities (see Braudel and Wallerstein 2009), then, the coming together of history's long durée and its contingent post-2003 turns, furnished the enabling environment and necessary preconditions for Salafist jihadism to gain traction in parts of Iraq.

Conducive as conditions were for Salafist jihadism in al-Anbar and farther afield, the character of the *appeal* offered by AQ-I limited the movement's capacity to seize the chance before it. In these regards, the individual shortcomings of Abu Musab al-Zarqawi are very much pertinent: the extremism of his beliefs and practices was such as to earn the reprobation of Ayman al-Zawahiri himself (Gartenstein-Ross 2015). Zarqawi also saw to it that AQ-I aggressively monopolized the smuggling trade along the Syrian border—much to the frustration of the Albu Mahal tribe—while his terror campaign prevented firms and communities in al-Anbar from benefiting from the large reconstruction contracts being doled out by Baghdad (Benraad 2011). The upshot of Zarqawi's feckless constituency management was that anti-al-Qaeda vigilante violence began popping up across Iraq's westernmost province starting in 2004. This reaction, in turn, created an opportunity for those directing the fledgling counterinsurgency. With capable strategists like Colonel Greg Reilly in the lead, the United States swiftly took advantage (Whiteside and Elallame 2020). They did so by first persuading Iraq's elected leadership to partner with the Tribal Revolutionaries, as the vigilantes became known, and by integrating them within the state apparatus. Baghdad obliged in the autumn of 2006, agreeing to arm, train, and pay the tribesmen and to enlist them as the Ministry of Interior's official police force in Ramadi, Hit, al-Qaim, Haditha, and Fallujah

(Gartenstein-Ross 2015). Come the following summer, whether due to the force of the Revolutionaries' example or the reconstruction fund money that flowed into al-Anbar following the Revolutionaries' joining of the anti-insurgency, Sunni tribes throughout Iraq were also making themselves available to the American army. Capitalizing on this chance, the United States enlisted most of them as auxiliaries (Clayton and Thomson 2014). This second contingent, initially called the Concerned Local Citizens, though later rebranded the Sons of Iraq, went on to play an essential role in debilitating AQ-I's operational capacity.

If a spent force by 2008, a similar contest over local politics allowed Salafist jihadism to regroup and relaunch its offensive just a few years later. On this occasion, Baghdad and Washington played into the insurgents' hands. The withdrawal of American troops from urban areas between 2009 and 2011 opened a security vacuum that the Iraqi state was unable to fill. This afforded the remnants of Zarqawi's organization room to breathe when they were close to suffocation. The government of Nouri al-Maliki next furnished AQ-I with an aggrieved population to reconcile with. First, al-Maliki stripped those Tribal Revolutionaries who had helped secure al-Anbar of their military rank before proceeding to reduce their pay, withdraw their weapons permits, and arrest many of their number on accusations of terrorism. Second, he returned to pledges to provide the Sons of Iraq with public sector jobs. Third, he met the protest movement that rose across al-Anbar in 2013 in response to his government's apparent failings with a mix of neglect and repression (Gartenstein-Ross 2015). Fourth, he moved against current and former leaders from the Iraqi Islamic Party, the largest Sunni-oriented partisan organization, and to more generally consolidate a modality of "electoral authoritarianism" that was to the stark disadvantage of Sunni nationals.[1] Fifth and perhaps most consequentially, *after* AQ-I reformed and managed to capture Fallujah in a lightning advance in 2014, al-Maliki chose to lock down the Sunni triangle and thereby prevent civilians from fleeing (Lia 2021).

The ball back in their court, AQ-I—its leadership ranks nationalized and filled predominantly by intelligence officers as of 2010 (Dowad 2017)—exploited every one of al-Maliki's blunders. Having closely scrutinized their past failures, the movement commissioned its cadres to infiltrate and conduct anthropological research on the tribes of al-Anbar (Whiteside and Elallame 2020). The knowledge gained informed what became known as the "Fallujah Memorandum," a tactical guide for AQ-I as it set about regime rebuilding. While steered by the tenets of this strategy and by the steadier hand of Abu Omar al-Baghdadi (killed in 2010), AQ-I demonstrated impressive aptitude not only in appealing to those alienated by Baghdad but also in targeting fractures within and between tribal federations—fractures that were not insignificant in size, it should be said (Benraad 2011; Gartenstein-Ross 2015). They co-opted more marginal members within those federations and then leveraged the co-opted to commandeer the tribes and manage local administration. Partnered with a brutal assassination campaign targeting the individuals and clans that had been most prominently involved in the US/Baghdad-led counterinsurgency of the 2000s (Gartenstein-Ross 2015), AQ-I cleared the West of institutional rivals and built a resilient organizational presence able to take hold and govern the territory. With their patronage system lubricated with petro rents following the capture of oilfields in the Northwest in 2014 and the denizens of their lands cowed by appropriate fear, their Islamic State attained more robustness than anything achieved during al-Zarqawi's tenure.

The counterinsurgency that Baghdad eventually mobilized to uproot the Islamic State is likely to prove of great consequence for Iraq's future. Instead of empowering an opposition from within—a less than great prospect given the Islamic State's intelligence capabilities and liquidation of dissidents—al-Maliki's government opted to rely on a popular Shia mobilization. Organized under the banner of the Hashd al-Shaabi, the constellation of paramilitary forces summoned through this mobilization and then dispatched to take on the Islamic State alongside the government's official security forces did show themselves to be additive and essential to victory. At the same time, their emergence functioned to bolster the power of the Shia right wing, weaken the state's claim to secularism, and compromise the outlook for civic nationalism even further. Where militarily successful, then, the politics of al-Maliki's counterinsurgency underwhelmed. As a consequence, it is improbable that the door to Salafist jihadism in Iraq has been closed for good.

Taking into view a history unfolding across more than twenty years, it becomes clear that jihadism in Iraq is a function of two interacting variables: (1) Environments rendered enabling or not by way of the state's mediation of sectarian cleavages, and (2) the contingent character of jihadist politics.

Syria

Jihadism had only a minor presence in Syria before 2011. Up until this point, the country had been under the helm of the Baath regime led by members of the al-Assad family (Hafez al-Assad from 1970 to 2000, and his son Bashar al-Assad since 2000), whose various security agencies exerted heavy control over society. To the extent jihadism was observable, it was an exported phenomenon: in the wake of the 2003 invasion of Iraq, the regime allowed foreign jihadis to travel through the country to join the fight in Iraq (Lister 2015).

In the spring of 2011, the regime faced a popular uprising inspired by the revolutions in Tunisia and Egypt. It was in the southern city of Deraa where the spark of widespread popular mobilization caught after instances of shocking police brutality against schoolchildren came to light. After that, large protests took place, inspiring similar actions nationwide. The initial protests united people from varying social classes and sects to bring down a repressive regime. No religious slogans were used. The ability of the movement at these stages to transcend sectarian cleavages was remarkable (Bartolomei 2018). Syria is a country with a majority of Sunnis (around 70 percent), along with two significant minorities (Alawis and Christians, each numbering around 10 percent) and some smaller minorities (Druzes, Ismailis, etc.). Since the formation of the modern state in 1920 under the auspices of the French colonial mandatory power, sectarianism has been a significant feature of Syrian politics. Many of the military officers who seized power in 1963 in the name of the Baath party belonged to sectarian minorities. And Hafez al-Assad, who eventually imposed his dominance over the group and became Syria's president in 1970, was an Alawi.

Despite the fact that Assad's regime proclaimed an adherence to Arab nationalist ideals, sectarianism quickly became a central tool of governance. Seeking people he could trust, Assad appointed Alawis to the most sensitive positions within the coercive apparatus of the state. By doing this, he would create an organic bond between his regime and the Alawi community he belonged to (Seurat 2012).

Even though far from all Alawis benefited from the system, the group was now widely seen as politically favored, binding its members together against the rest of the population, who envied—or feared—them. Given the fact that Alawis had, until the early twentieth century, been a disenfranchised rural minority group in Syrian society, their gains decades later represented a significant achievement worth defending. None of this was verbalized. The regime insisted on appointing members of the other sects to visible positions in the state apparatus, although those positions held little sway in Syria's securitocratic system.

The reforms of economic liberalization adopted since the last years of Hafez al-Assad's reign offered the regime an opportunity to co-opt some of the urban Sunni and Christian elites: they could now compensate for their political exclusion by getting involved in the economy and thereby have a stake in the system (Hinnebusch 1997). Still, they continued to resent the Alawi dominance over the country's affairs. The biggest losers in that bargain were the rural Sunnis, who combined political exclusion with economic marginalization. Unsurprisingly, this social group would become the backbone of the 2011 uprising (Deraa was a rural Sunni city).

Just as sectarianism had been a tool of governance, faced with the uprising of 2011, the Assad regime acted to transform it into a tool of crisis management. The regime knew a transsectarian political revolution could defeat it—but if it could activate sectarian support, it would prevail. From early on, the regime denounced protesters as Sunni extremists and jihadis (Phillips 2015). And to give credibility to that narrative, the regime released from prison some of the most prominent jihadi leaders who had been detained throughout the 2000s (Lister 2015). Within a few months, the brutal repression of protests led to a growing militarization of the uprising, with army defectors—mostly Sunnis—forming a group called the Free Syrian Army. Islamist splinter groups started forming around the same time, some led by jihadi leaders who had been released from prison. In 2012, a new group called Jabhat al-Nusra was established: its battle-hardened tactics and its use of terrorist attacks made it stand out among the opposition. It also more openly used sectarian rhetoric to denounce the Syrian regime's Alawi core. This fits so well with Bashar al-Assad's playbook that some observers initially discarded the group as a hand of the Syrian regime. A year later, in 2013, the story of the group's formation was revealed: it had been created by members of al-Qaeda in Iraq (which had rebranded itself as the Islamic State in Iraq) who had crossed the border, hence its comparatively large resources, the presence of veterans in its ranks, and its unscrupulous use of sectarian language—transported from the Iraqi battlefield, where it had been prevalent during the conflict of the 2000s.

In the wake of the rise of Jabhat al-Nusra, sectarian rhetoric became more common among the armed opposition, especially within the Sunni Islamist groups. In 2013, Jabhat al-Nusra fragmented into two separate groups: the Islamic State in Iraq and Syria (ISIS) and Jabhat al-Nusra (in keeping with the initial name), which now rejected the leadership of the Iraqi organization. ISIS would quickly come to dominate, though, fighting other opposition groups to take control of large chunks of Syria's territory. Its uncompromising jihadi rhetoric, with its framing of the Syrian conflict in purely religious terms, would also push sectarianism to new heights (McCants 2015).

That growing sectarianism had several consequences. The first was to activate the bond between the regime and the Alawis, who were now easily convinced that, whatever they might personally think about the regime, their survival as a community now depended on the regime's resilience. To compensate for military defections, the bulk of which had come from Sunnis, the regime recruited heavily in the Alawi community, also encouraging its members to form paramilitary militias known as Shabbiha. The second consequence of growing sectarianism, this time concerning the opposition, also led the other minority groups—with a few notable exceptions—to dissociate themselves from the uprising and join ranks with the regime. The initial transsectarian nature of the uprising was thus fading away (Mazur 2020).

To be sure, there were local contexts that complexified and sometimes contradicted the general narrative outlined here. Both the Kurds and the Druzes saw the opportunity of the uprising and its subsequent militarization to increase their political autonomy by playing both the regime's and the opposition's card, depending on the moment. The Kurdish Democratic Union Party (PYD) would eventually manage to carve a piece of Syrian territory for itself, where it developed its structures of government in what is now called Rojava.

Now more than ten years after the beginning of the conflict, the Syrian regime has managed to survive. Sectarianism was critical to its initial survival, though certainly not the only reason. The Syrian case also tells us about the limits of sectarianism as a political strategy. In 2015, there was a noticeable sentiment of fatigue among Syrian Alawis. Also, dissent resurfaced in the Alawi community, with competing factions expressing anger at the regime's management of the uprising while pushing forward their interests (Schneider 2016). If there had been one moment when the regime could have fallen, it was then. Yet, in September 2015, Russia decided to intervene on the regime's side. With such a powerful backer, the pro-Assad side regained strength—and, more importantly, unity. The regime would prevail over ruins—but it would prevail.

As for ISIS, which had emerged as Syria's foremost jihadi group in 2014, it was eventually toppled after having managed to hold up to a third of the country for about three years. Behind its fall was an international military coalition led by the United States. Locally, the coalition partnered with the Kurdish PYD (a local branch of Turkey's PKK), which saw this as an opportunity to win favors with the West to protect the territory they had gained. Again, willingly or unwillingly, the coalition was playing on sectarianism—this time ethnic rather than religious. This resulted in the deep distrust of many among the Arab tribes who now lived under Kurdish control despite the PYD's (largely unfulfilled) promises of inclusive policies. The result, many specialists claim, could be a resurgence of ISIS in the not-too-distant future (Haenni and Quesnay 2022).

Conclusion

As this chapter's case studies have emphasized, the environments that enable violent extremism are functions of parochial and global history. Endowments from the distal and recent past, the present-day opportunity structures for jihadists in Mali, Iraq, and Syria were laid in processes of state formation and in the contingencies of decisive moments—specifically, in choices concerning governing sectarian cleavages. As our inquiries have also shown, contests between insurgency and counterinsurgency are determined through the dialectical interplay of jihadist and state politics.

Based on these findings, it is possible to suggest the following theoretical claim: the occurrence or nonoccurrence of violent extremism and the resilience of local communities to violent extremism are primarily influenced by politics, including identity politics. The ability of a state to counter a jihadist challenger depends on what the state offers to the communities where the insurgents are based. The offer in question must contain material, ideational, and identitarian terms. The last of these items should not be neglected. Questions of *who* the state is to be for—who it is to incorporate within its symbolic and legal personhood—are of decisive importance. At the same time, for individuals and for larger social formations forced to navigate the quagmire of civil war, whether the state can win the fight, protect its citizens, and create material possibilities that trump those presented by the status quo are of undiminishable salience. The state's dexterity in local identity politics is ultimately decisive. Counterterrorism interventions may succeed or fail on the basis of military effectiveness but also on the basis of their ability to shift the decision matrices of high-leverage principals and institutions within relevant communities and their ability to affect the incentives, interests, and identitarian attachments of a critical mass of the population.

Notes

1. The Iraqi Islamic Party included major public supporters of the Tribal Revolutionaries such as Rafi el-Essawi, who was al-Maliki's minister of finance when he saw his bodyguards arrested at the prime minister's request.

10

Traditional Authority and Local Community Resilience: Bosnia and Herzegovina, Iraq, and Syria

Kjetil Selvik, Dlawer Ala'Aldeen, Ahmad Mhidi, Diana Mishkova, and Kamaran Palani

In a global context where violent extremists exploit the vulnerabilities of weak and divided states to extend their reach across different regions, specific communities have demonstrated notable resilience in comparison to others. Despite the presence of enabling environments, violent extremism does not take root (EU Research 2023). This observation has sparked the interest of policymakers and scholars in understanding the role of local agents of resilience. In particular, there is a keen focus on uncovering the potential contributions of traditional community leaders in fostering these favorable outcomes. It is assumed that conventional authorities can play a constructive role in preventing the rise of violent extremism by leveraging their moral weight, influence, and community connections. In this chapter, we compare empirical evidence from the Western Balkans, Iraqi Kurdistan, and northeastern Syria to evaluate to what extent this assumption holds. Then, we discuss the conditions under which interventions from traditional authorities are likely to be effective.

Focusing on community leaders makes sense because communities are the locus of most violent extremist activity. Extremist groups exploit local grievances and divisions to establish a presence in communities, making it essential to address these issues at the grassroots level (Van Metre and Scherer 2023). However, traditional authorities' presence is no panacea because they cannot always protect communities effectively. Understanding why they fail in some contexts is essential. It is also important to acknowledge that community leaders can contribute to the problem if they lack inclusivity, practice corruption, or misuse their authority in other ways. Research suggests that the main factor generating violent extremism is the systematic exclusion of young people from power (Mercy Corps 2022b).

The Jihadi Assault and Traditional Authorities' Ability to Strike Back

The struggle to contain violent extremism is, in part, a contest over authority in Islam and in society in which traditional community leaders have come under attack from proponents of jihadism coupled with Salafism. We define *jihadism* as the belief that "armed confrontation with political rivals is a theologically legitimate and instrumentally efficient method for sociopolitical change" (Ashour 2011, 379), and Salafism as the idea that believers should "exclusively and meticulously adhere to the example of the *salaf* [the first generations of Muslims] while rejecting all other sources of influence" (Wagemakers 2016, 1). Salafi-jihadi groups such as al-Qaeda and the Islamic State in Iraq and Syria (ISIS) represent a revolt against conventional religious interpretations, established forms of social organization, and people of authority in both the Muslim and the Western world. Their doctrines, recruitment patterns, and ruling practices pose multiple challenges to community leaders.

Starting with doctrine, the Salafi-jihadi project is based on the ideological judgment that the current sociopolitical order is "un-Islamic" and that fighting it is a religious obligation. Its warriors denounce not only the states and societies of "infidels" but also the Muslim communities and leaders they believe have "fallen from Islam." Jihadis differ in how radically they practice excommunication (*takfir*), which ranges from targeting "tyrannical" Muslim rulers to targeting society as a whole (Stenersen 2020). But all are instinctively opposed to the wielders of power in this "pagan" world. Above all, they decry religious leaders who collaborate with and thereby legitimize nonreligious states. Jihadi ideologues encourage religious interpretation (*ijtihad*) independently of the *ulama*, evoking the individual's direct relationship with God (Lahoud 2010). This individualization of *ijtihad* undermines religious hierarchies and leads to spiraling clashes among competing groups and actors over issues such as who is considered a true Muslim and who is not.

In its sociological dimension, the global jihad phenomenon bears the signs of a youth revolt. In Roy's (2008, 2017b) assessment, it is a youth movement aiming for the authority of elders. Salafi-jihadist organizations recruit individuals who feel alienated by and have a grudge against the societies they live in. They offer rootless youth a sense of purpose and belonging through adherence to an ideological community, which aims to turn the tables on the mainstream (Byman 2013; Postel 2013). Writing about Europe, Khosrokhavar (2021) argues that the crisis of Muslim families lies beneath this movement. In his view, youngsters protest their fathers' (fallen) status by stating that they recognize no other authority than God.

The generational conflict and revolt against community leaders are also evident in situations where Salafi-jihadi groups gain control over territories and build the embryos of state structures. As Lia (2017) notes, the ruling class in jihadi proto-states is almost exclusively composed of young men. There is precious little room for traditional religious authorities, clan leaders, and heads of tribes in the higher echelons of power. In Lia's words, "the traditional holders of power in patriarchal societies—elderly men and tribal shaykhs—are relegated to the role of bystanders, subjects, or propaganda mascots" (5). This upending of traditional authority structures is in part a consequence of Salafi-jihadi ideology emphasizing the equality of believers before God and the rejection of kinship-based structures (Maher 2016). However, it also results from sociological shifts within the tribe propelled by the Salafi-jihadi organizations' ruling tactics. Jihadi groups frequently infiltrate tribes to establish a foothold in the territories they conquer. In doing so, they ally themselves with new and younger leaders within the tribe who use Salafi-jihadi ideology to wrest power from the older generation (Collombier and Roy 2017, 10–12).

The ability of traditional leaders to repel these attacks and become an effective shield against violent extremism depends on their authority, which, again, is influenced by developments in society and the state.[1] Traditional authority rests on a belief in the sacredness of tradition; legitimacy is claimed on the basis of the sanctity of order and the powers of control handed down from the past (Matheson 1987, 207). Conforming to this reasoning, traditional leaders counterattack jihadists, decrying their break with long-established customs, conventions, and norms. They refute their trustworthiness by dismissing them as "self-styled preachers." The challenge religious leaders face is that Salafism is grounded in its claim to tradition and orthodoxy. Salafists charge that current practices of Islam are perverted and that believers must return to the example of the first generation of Muslims (*al-salaf al-salih*). Thus, a battle has broken out over whose interpretations of Islam align with tradition or whose tradition is correct.

To prevail in this narrative battle, traditional leaders must stand firmly in their communities. Such good standing can, in part, emanate from their personal qualities and behavior, but, just as importantly, it is contingent on the state of society itself. In situations where traditional forms of social organization are upended, the authority of traditional leaders is naturally diminished. If society is falling apart, traditional authorities will lose ground as well. The point is that the extent to which traditional leaders can stem the spread of Salafi-jihadi ideas is influenced by the underlying social structure—and whether it helps sustain their claims to authority or not. This further means that the role of the state is a crucial factor. A state may help preserve the traditional order or undercut it through its policies. It may ally with or turn against community leaders. Where the state grows ties with traditional community leaders, the state's legitimacy (or lack thereof) also affects the standing of traditional authorities. Finally, a state may cease to work and leave power vacuums in society that violent extremists fill.

These observations imply that scholarly investigations of traditional leaders' role in preventing violent extremism must be grounded in careful assessments of the social and political contexts in which these leaders operate. What helps contain the propagation of Salafi-jihadi thought and organizations in one place may have a different effect in another. In the remainder of this chapter, we compare the role of traditional leaders in preventing violent extremism in the Western Balkans, Iraqi Kurdistan, and northeastern Syria and discuss explanations for the differences we observe between these contexts.

Religious Leaders and the Occurrence or Nonoccurrence of Violent Extremism in the Western Balkans

From Ottoman times, Muslims in the Balkans have traditionally practiced the Hanafi interpretation of Islam, which remains the prevalent religious orientation among Sunni Muslims in the region. Notably, the majority of citizens in these countries, regardless of their religious affiliations, view themselves as part of secular societies. The recent rise of Islamist extremism in the Western Balkans, particularly in Albania, Bosnia and Herzegovina, Kosovo, North Macedonia, and Serbia, has been accompanied by the spread of Salafism. In countries where national and religious identities are deeply intertwined and ethnoreligious nationalism prevails, radical ethnonationalism and Islamist extremism either feed off each other or evolve as separate and opposing forms of ideological and social radicalization, depending on the specific context. Consequently, the phenomenon of foreign terrorist fighters (FTFs) as a form of supra- and transnational Islamist extremism is nurtured and conditioned, both psychologically and socially, by often politically exploited ethnoreligious grievances. Conversely, Islam in the region has often been instrumentalized and manipulated in the service of local ethnonationalist political objectives.

During and after the Yugoslav Wars of the 1990s, Islamist relief organizations and nongovernmental organizations (NGOs), primarily from or supported by the Gulf states, particularly Saudi Arabia, established branch offices across the region. Often operating under the guise of humanitarian aid, they funded mosques and educational facilities disseminating the conservative Salafi interpretation of Islam and provided scholarships for Muslims to study in the Middle East (Bešlin and Ignjatijević 2017). Over the years, especially following the wars in Bosnia (1992–

1995) and Kosovo (1998–1999), several *para-jamaats*, or parallel "underground" mosque communities of Salafi Muslims, were established in all these countries and attracted disillusioned youth in some areas. Operating beyond the reach of official Islamic institutions recognized by the states, these *para-jamaats* became hubs for radical indoctrination and the recruitment of potential foreign fighters.

The first instances of the FTF phenomenon were also a result of the Yugoslav Wars. FTFs from Middle Eastern countries supported or joined Muslim fighters in the region, particularly in Bosnia and Herzegovina and Kosovo. The emergence of ISIS once again fueled extremism in the region, with approximately a thousand citizens from Western Balkan countries joining militant jihadi groups in the Middle East and participating in conflicts in Iraq and Syria. The return of some of these individuals to their homelands was generally seen as posing a direct threat to national security and led to the introduction of laws criminalizing foreign fighting in all these countries by 2015 (Shtuni 2019; Azinović and Bećirević 2017). The threat of violent Islamist extremism has significantly diminished in recent years, primarily because of the weakening of pull factors.

Against this backdrop, it is instructive to comprehend the role played by traditional religious leaders and institutions in furthering or preventing violent extremism in the Western Balkan countries.

An important finding of this analysis is that mainstream Muslim communities in the Western Balkans associate the resurgence of Islam and political Islam, as well as related phenomena such as radical Islamic fundamentalism, jihadism, and Salafi Wahhabism, with the transnational mobilization, penetration, and adaptation of "alien" Islamic doctrines. This finding was confirmed during the fieldwork of the Preventing Violent Extremism in the Balkans and the MENA (PREVEX) Western Balkan teams in the summer of 2022. These doctrines, primarily imported from the Arab Middle East, denounce local Muslim tradition as "deviant" as a result of the folk elements added over time to the original, "pristine" normative core. Referred to as "Arab" Islam by its detractors, this interpretation claims to spearhead a return to Islam's doctrinal roots and to strengthen a sense of belonging to the global *umma*—the "imagined community" of Sunni Islam.[2] In contrast, many local Muslims tend to perceive these Middle Eastern influences as foreign and a "distortion" of the Islam they traditionally practice in the Balkan context. As a Bosnian Islamic Community official and professor on the Islamic Faculty in Bihać put it,

> Salafi activities run counter to our culture and the Bosnian Muslim interpretation of Islam. Even those who went to Syria, it is known exactly what kind of congregations they attended and who led them, and none of those congregations belong to the [official] Islamic Community.[3]

Traditional (Hanafi) Islam has long been institutionalized in the form of state-authorized Islamic Communities in the respective Western Balkan countries. It is considered a vital facet of Balkan Muslims' ethnic identity and culture. In Bosnia and Herzegovina and Kosovo, where the infiltration of proselytizing Salafists was most intense, Islamic Community officials have made sustained efforts to counter the spread of radical religious doctrines that were formally unknown to the local populations. The curricula in religious colleges and madrassas in Bosnia and Herzegovina were amended to include modules on preventing radicalization. The Islamic Community (IC) there organizes conferences on coexistence and tolerance. It cooperates with various international organizations to host seminars to raise awareness about the dangers of radicalization and violent extremism. At the height of global attention on Salafism, when FTF departures to Syria and Iraq from Bosnia and Herzegovina peaked in 2014, the Islamic Community established an office to coordinate its cooperation with NGOs, which helped it better monitor the network of NGOs with a Salafi orientation.[4] Despite the formal separation between state and religion, the Islamic Community of Kosovo demanded resolute government intervention in preventing the opening of new mosques and masjids operating outside its jurisdiction, where extremist imams preached (Jakupi and Kraja 2018).[5] In contrast, the parallel existence and action of two official religious institutions in Serbia—the Islamic Community in Serbia (ICiS) based in Novi Pazar, the center of the Muslim-majority-dominated region of Sandžak; and the Islamic Community of Serbia (ICoS) based in Belgrade—has been seen as creating a vacuum suitable for exploitation by alternative religious groups and hampering efforts to tackle radicalization (Petrović and Stakić 2018).

In all Western Balkan countries under examination, the role of individual mainstream imams and religious instructors from the official Islamic Communities is found to be significant in achieving community resilience to violent extremism. This role primarily involves providing religious counternarratives to radical interpretations of Islam and strengthening social cohesion within the *jamaat*, making it difficult for radicals to infiltrate. Our fieldwork in countries less affected by manifestations of violent extremism, such as Albania, indicates that the work of imams there has mainly been oriented toward preventing Salafi preachers and radicalized individuals from gaining access to mosques under their jurisdiction and raising awareness of the violent extremism (VE) phenomenon through regular and, in some cases, daily informative sessions. In countries more exposed to the risks of violent extremism, such as Bosnia and Herzegovina, cultivating resilience requires more comprehensive and imaginative approaches. Given that Salafists have shown particular agility on social media, with better outreach to youths, the Islamic Community in Bosnia and Herzegovina saw the need to activate its media platforms. At the

Islamic Pedagogical Faculty at the University of Bihać, the IC established a media department to meet the demand of young people "for something that is fast, flexible, alive, for real, live authorities who are ready for discussion and willing to stay up all night in online conversations with them."[6] Though the Islamic Community currently has only a handful of young representatives active on social media, several recent graduates of the Islamic Faculty in Bihać have begun contributing to progressive media platforms, where imams from all over Bosnia and Herzegovina collaborate to produce modern and dynamic religious content accessible to Muslim youths.[7] Plans are also in place to begin social media training for young imams in the Islamic Community to prepare them for engaging online in countering extremist narratives.

In Kosovo, imams and community representatives have also been found crucial for building community resilience. Data from both the Kosovo Police Anti-Terror Unit and our fieldwork indicate that major radicalization drivers were neutralized in areas such as Podujeva and Prizren because imams refused to let in groups that promoted such ideas. Kosovar imams belonging to the official Islamic Community and lecturers in its educational bodies strongly and openly oppose radical narratives and activities, even at the risk of verbal or physical attacks. However, like elsewhere in the region, the Islamic Community of Kosovo cannot control sermons and materials broadcast on the internet by imams who were expelled by the community or who are active in other countries.

The region of Sandžak in Serbia presents an interesting case in this respect. Several influential imams, such as Mufti Muamer Zukorlić, Sead Islamović, and Bekir Makić, who were previously active in spreading Salafism and even suspected of recruiting foreign fighters, have played a crucial role in alleviating their communities. They are now openly distancing themselves from political and militant interpretations of Islam and directing their activities toward humanitarian community aid, such as during the Covid-19 pandemic, and solving local community problems.[8] Various interpretations exist regarding this change of heart. Some emphasize external factors, such as political and religious reforms in Saudi Arabia or pressure from the United States and other countries. In contrast, others attribute it to persecution by security services inside and outside Serbia. Still others hold that these imams realized that they had to change their approach to avoid doing more harm than good to Muslims.

All in all, while we believe that resilience is systemic and depends on the interconnection of factors, it can be argued that in the Western Balkan context, two elements have played a paramount role in preventing violent extremism. The first is the prevalence of what has often been designated as "moderate Islam" among Muslims, leading the local population to reject intrusive and violent interpretations of Islam brought by Salafi jihadis.

Our fieldwork across the region suggests that the existence of sufficiently stable local traditions of tolerance and their reproduction in the cultural memory have a strong preventive effect on processes of radicalization. We may indeed argue that in the Western Balkan context, traditional Muslim identity, safeguarded by relatively stable states, acts as the primary brake on the adoption of radical versions of Islam. The second crucial element is the indispensable role of religious officials, such as muftis or imams, in creating close-knit communities, where radical elements are quickly identified, and in preventing, countering, and raising awareness about violent extremism. As a rule, and often with support from the state, imams in Albania, Sandžak, North Macedonia, Kosovo, and Bosnia and Herzegovina, who espouse the Hanafi strain of Sunni Islam, restrict access to radical recruiters in their mosques and make it difficult for recruiters to connect with believers in other ways. In some cases, such as Sandžak and Bosnia and Herzegovina, imams and individuals of authority over Salafi groups have played an essential role in radicalized individuals' relocation and integration into the moderate local community or the *jamaats* belonging to the official Islamic Community.

The Role of Religious Authorities in Countering Violent Extremism in the Kurdistan Region of Iraq

Between 2011 and 2017, more than five hundred Kurds joined violent extremist organizations in Syria and Iraq. With the emergence of ISIS in 2014 and the concern that hundreds of young Kurds might join its ranks, the Kurdistan Region of Iraq (KRI) adopted a policy to support traditional and new religious scholars and leaders in countering violent extremist campaigns. This included a quietist Salafist movement and efforts by several conventional and new Kurdish Islamic intellectuals and authorities to strengthen the relationship between religion and Kurdish nationalism. There exists a fundamental divergence between quietist Salafism and traditional religious nationalism, and their empowerment may lead to conflicting religious practices. However, these two ideologies share a joint alignment with the interests of the Kurdish ruling authorities.

There are eight religious communities in Kurdistan, all of which are regulated by law within the Ministry of Endowments and Religious Affairs of the Kurdistan Regional Government.[9] These communities carry out their activities within a directorate called Religious Coexistence. Most Iraqi Kurds are Sunni Muslims and broadly follow the Shafi'i school (Van Bruinessen 1992, 23). However, the traditional and dominant religious type in the KRI is also influenced by Sufi tribal and conservative practices.

Since the establishment of the Kurdistan government in 1992, the authorities have sought to integrate traditional religious authorities into government and state-like institutions. Gradually, traditional religious authorities have come under the control of the Kurdish political authorities. Traditional religious authorities are now represented by imams and scholars who are dominant within the Islamic Scholars' Union of Kurdistan and the Ministry of Endowments and its associated institutions.[10]

With the ISIS threat looming in 2014, Kurdistan introduced several countermeasures. A significant change within the Ministry of Endowments and Religious Affairs was the unifying and centralizing of Friday sermons. The ministry aims to counter hate speech, prevent extremism, and promote tolerance. Before 2014, Friday sermons and the process of becoming an imam were not subject to systematic regulation and centralized procedures. After 2014, the ministry organized both Friday sermons and the requirements to become an imam. The ministry ensures that the sermons are aligned with two key policy priorities: (1) KRI national interests, and (2) coexistence and tolerance among the various ethnoreligious communities. Many preachers were banned or warned from delivering Friday sermons for charges related to disrespecting ethnoreligious minorities in Kurdistan.

One of the primary policies of the ministry is to transition the role of imams from being sacred and unique figures in society to that of government employees with both rights and duties. The ministry has made progress in this area but still needs to improve because some imams defy the ministry and use different platforms, such as social media, an exceedingly difficult space for the ministry to regulate. Here, it is essential to mention that the Ministry of Endowments and other religious institutions in Kurdistan are under the influence of Kurdistan's two leading parties, the Kurdistan Democratic Party (KDP) and the Patriotic Union of Kurdistan (PUK). Some imams and preachers view the ministry and other Islamic institutions as part of KDP's and PUK's broader governing and power structure. Moreover, the challenge lies in the idea that the excessive centralization and regulation of religious institutions, including mosques, will engender a legitimacy problem for these centers, because trust (real or perceived) in government institutions is low (Palani 2021, 233).

Over the last decade, specifically since the rise of ISIS in 2014, a new generation of Kurdish Islamic intellectuals has contributed to the effort to renegotiate the relationship between religion and Kurdish statehood. These intellectuals are inspired by Kurdish identity, culture, and nationalism and seek to reformulate Islam in consideration of the Kurdish national struggle for independence (Gade and Palani 2022; Mustafa 2020). They have close relations with the traditional Kurdish religious institutions and authorities. The leading proponents of this Kurdish Islam are Abdulrahman Saddiq,[11] Tahsin Hama Gharib,[12] Abubakir Karwani,[13] and Mohammad Sharif.[14]

Many Kurds have an opinion about the distinction of Kurdistan religious practice and religious understanding, arguing that Kurdish Islam differs from "Arab Islam." The most prominent feature of religious nationalism in Kurdistan is the attempt to erect clear discursive boundaries between a supposedly "radical" Arab Islam and a presumably "moderate" Kurdish Islam in Iraq. It is pretty standard for the supporters of Kurdish Islam to define it as more focused on spiritual aspects (*batiniyya*) (Gharib 2013). One of the main aims of the politicians' Kurdish Islam discourse is to prevent violent extremism and promote coexistence between the various religious and ethnic components of Kurdistan (Mamakani 2016). In this context, Kurdish Islam's narrative appealed to the authorities and is seen as the antidote to violent extremism. According to supporters of Kurdish Islam, the relationship between religion and authority is based on partnership, not separation (Gharib 2013).

Salafism is a branch of Islamism with a growing popular appeal, as quietist Salafism has been on a steady rise in Kurdistan for many years. The most famous scholar is Dr. Abdul Latif Salafi, a shaikh in Sulaymaniyah. Abdul Latif is an example of a scholar who focuses on proselytizing through lessons and sermons while refraining from politics or from establishing a political party, thus leaving it to the authorities in place (Ahmed 2017). He preaches support for the Kurdish rulers because they are Muslims, and the alternative would be worse and more chaotic. He often refers to violence and instability in Yemen, Syria, and the region. Abdul Latif's movement is the most widespread Salafi current in Kurdistan.

Salafist figures have existed in Kurdistan for decades, but Salafism as a visible movement with clear and systematic discourses is a recent phenomenon. Salafis benefit from a good relationship with the authorities because it has allowed them to proselytize and establish institutes across Kurdistan. Abdul Latif was an important government ally in the struggle against ISIS (NRT 2016; Jalal and Ahram 2021; Rudaw 2014). The jihadi threat at the time also came from within, as Kurdistan faced the challenge of homegrown radicalization. Salafis believe that they had a significant role in preventing radicalization and extremism among Kurdish youths during the rise and rule of ISIS (2014–2017). Abdul Latif supported the military operations against ISIS: "Without our rejection of Daesh, thousands of young Kurds would have joined Daesh" (Mahmod 2018

Abdul Latif preaches the Salafi version of Islam in the Bahasht Mosque in Sulaymaniyah. Bahasht has become one of the most crowded mosques in Kurdistan, where hundreds of youths attend regularly. Women also attend the Friday sermons and wear Salafi-style niqab, which is uncommon among the residents in the region. In addition, Abdul Latif owns a popular TV station, Amozhgary, as well as a Quran memorization center and, recently, an Academy in Sulaymaniyah. The Amozhgary Academy seeks to provide education about Islam to children and youths in different districts and towns of Sulaymaniyah. Abdul Latif's opponents claim that his movement is supported by the Kurdish authorities (KDP and PUK) to weaken the Islamist parties in parliament.[15] They see his movement benefiting the government because he tells followers not to protest but to be more careful and patient and protect the stability and the status quo.

Although Salafis played an influential role in preventing young Kurds from joining ISIS and other extremist groups, many carry negative views especially of non-Muslim groups in Kurdistan, such as the Yezidis. Their growing role might undermine existing tolerance and coexistence in the region. Moreover, the KRI's security institutions are distrustful of Salafis, maintaining that these groups have the potential to radicalize youth and thus showing that the KRI's support for Salafis is conditional and limited. The authorities have provided this conditional support to Salafis and religious nationalists to both prevent support for extremist organizations and ideology and weaken the Islamist opposition parties. However, there is growing concern that the continuation of policies that may be designed to marginalize and fragment the Islamist organization threaten coexistence and social peace in the KRI and pave the way for future extremism.

Tribal Leaders' Ineffectiveness in Preventing Violent Extremism in the Eastern Countryside of Deir ez-Zor

Tribal figures have historically played a prominent role in the sociopolitical landscape of Deir ez-Zor and eastern Syria. Beginning in the mid-nineteenth century, this role underwent a series of transformations due to interventions by the central state. The tribes were forced to abandon their nomadic lifestyles, own land, and pay taxes. Nevertheless, the tribe remained significant, with the tribal leader serving as a symbol expected to unify and lead during times of crisis.[16] The central authorities continued to recognize tribal leaders as symbolic figures with powers to mediate in the event of intratribal conflicts (al-Mnadi not dated, 11) or conflicts with the state. Although traditional leaders maintained their social status, they were gradually forced to compete with others who could fulfill the same role, such as mayors, wealthy businessmen, Baath Party officials, and tribesmen with ties to state security (Khattab 2017).

From the time Hafez al-Assad took power in 1970, Deir ez-Zor, which today has a population of approximately 1.6 million, remained one of the most neglected and poorest provinces in Syria (El Laithy and Abu-Ismail 2005). Its population was one of the least educated, and economic desperation triggered massive waves of migration out of the province, especially in the 1990s. Despite the province's considerable oil and gas reserves, residents saw comparatively few investments in public services, infrastructure, or the local economy. The region's poverty and historic neglect contributed to high levels of popular support for the Syrian uprising that began in the spring of 2011.

The Syrian uprising shattered the broadly accepted notion that a tribal leader maintains authority over his tribesmen and determines the tribe's political orientation. Although the Syrian regime went to great lengths to push tribal leaders to influence their tribesmen in its favor, these efforts were largely futile (Mashhour 2017, 28). Some stood behind the regime, while others stayed neutral. However, the positions tribesmen adopted toward the uprising rarely mirrored those of the traditional leadership. Many who joined the demonstrations were outraged at the tribal leaders' failure to exhibit relevance and agency. At a time of severe political upheaval, tribal leaders were largely absent from public life, even as violence escalated against protesters and armed groups were established under the banner of the Free Syrian Army (FSA) to oppose the regime.

Most tribal leaders also refrained from taking sides or engaging in the events that unfolded after the regime's withdrawal from northeastern Syria in late 2012 and appeared to virtually resign from public affairs. Their low profile was not surprising, considering that the FSA and many tribal commoners viewed tribal leaders as regime affiliates.

Following the collapse of the regime in Deir ez-Zor, FSA and opposition-affiliated groups failed to address the security and governance challenges generated by the political vacuum. As a result, opportunists began to seize control of oil and gas wells, most located in tribal territories belonging to the Ageidat, east of the Euphrates, in an area referred to as the eastern countryside (Ayn Al-Madina Magazine 2015, 6).

A new power structure emerged among tribesmen based on the wealth and power associated with controlling oil resources and revenues. By early 2013, the majority of oil and gas wells were controlled by tribal groups, whether by a small armed group operating in the name of the FSA or by a family or group of families in a village that agreed to take turns benefiting from the wells. The seizure of oil wells—and the tremendous amount of wealth amassed by a few along tribal lines—revealed the continued strength of tribal ties but reinforced a localization of these identities (Khaddour and Mazur 2017, 11). It also triggered intertribal competition and bloody conflicts that fragmented the tribes. These micro-tribal identities came at the expense of a broader tribal identity and led to a wider sidelining of the traditional leadership.

Jihadist groups began injecting themselves into Deir ez-Zor's local conflicts in early 2013, starting with the rise of the al-Qaeda-affiliated Jabhat al-Nusra. The village of Ash Shail offered a natural base for the group's operations because many of the Buchamel tribesmen there had ties to al-Qaeda in Iraq (Awad 2018, 10). Nusra used its alliance with the Buchamel to mobilize support, gain protection, and secure access to a share in oil resources and revenues. The coalition offered the Buchamel power and influence but also put Ash Shail at odds with several neighbors. Internal grievances split Jabhat al-Nusra. In April 2013, the influential Bkair commander, Amir al-Rafdan, who headed a group of Bkair tribesmen and controlled the Conoco gas plant, broke away from Al-Nusra to join ISIS after disputes with influential Buchamel in the ranks of Al-Nusra. Rafdan shifted control of the gas plant to ISIS (Ayn Al-Madina Magazine 2015, 11). At the time, ISIS did not have a robust military presence, and therefore, Rafdan could not withstand attacks from Al-Nusra and the Buchamel, so he called the Bkair tribal elders and dignitaries to a meeting in the village of Hussain in September 2013 to garner tribal support (Mashhour 2017, 50). To the surprise of the invitees, most of whom were unaware of Rafdan's intentions, the prominent Iraqi ISIS leader Abu Ossama was at Rafdan's side and asked for Bkair leaders to support ISIS to counter the Buchamel's monopoly over resources, promising oil and an end to the economic hardship from which Bkair tribesmen had long suffered.

Abdelaziz al-Hummada, a prominent Bkair leader, left the meeting as soon as Rafdan's intent was defined and asked his tribesmen to steer clear of the conflicts. He warned that joining Rafdan and ISIS to ally against Al-Nusra and the Buchamel would bring nothing but destruction. al-Hummada tried to reach out to other notables and armed leaders from the Bkair to prevent Rafdan from deploying the tribe in support of ISIS.[17] He also visited Ash Shail and held meetings with several Buchamel notables in an attempt to separate the tribes, both of which belong to the Ageidat tribal federation, from the conflict between Al-Nusra and ISIS.

However, al-Hummada's requests were disregarded. Many Bkair were discontent and criticized their leader for paying no heed to the abuses of the Buchamel and Al-Nusra. By the beginning of 2014, not only had al-Hummada failed to convince his tribesmen of the risks of joining ISIS, but also his tribe no longer guaranteed his safety, and he was forced to leave Deir ez-Zor as ISIS closed in on his home region. Many Bkair saw Rafdan's promised benefits as too good to turn down. Rafdan continued to mobilize support from Bkair tribesmen by framing the Al-Nusra–ISIS conflict in tribal terms, using the Al-Nusra siege on Busayrah in March 2014, which prompted massive clashes between the Buchamel and Bkair, to seal Bkair support for ISIS. Exploiting and investing in the tribal dynamics, ISIS took complete control of Deir ez-Zor by mid-2014. Long after the defeat of ISIS, some Bkair tribesmen continued to insist that al-Hummada lacked credibility as a tribal leader because his calls to resist ISIS were not in the Bkair's interest.[18]

Since entering Deir ez-Zor in late 2017 to confront ISIS, the Kurdish-dominated Syrian Democratic Forces (SDF) and later the Autonomous Administration for Northern and Eastern Syria (AA) made repeated attempts to mobilize Deir ez-Zor's tribes to pursue its political project and counter ISIS, including appealing to the traditional leadership. The SDF established the Deir ez-Zor Military Council and later the Deir ez-Zor Civil Council. Local tribal dynamics largely determined a tribe's participation in the Military Council, similar to past alliances formed with Al-Nusra and ISIS. By early 2018, most areas east of the Euphrates were liberated from ISIS.

Despite its territorial defeat in Baguz in the spring of 2019 and concerted efforts by the International Coalition and SDF to close the chapter of ISIS rule in eastern Syria, the jihadi group continued to maintain a significant presence and influence in Deir ez-Zor's eastern countryside. Turmoil and insecurity from ISIS cell activity began to affect some areas, prompting the SDF to conduct security raids that often resulted in the death of civilians and arbitrary arrests. A cycle of ISIS attacks and security raids left communities trapped and cut off from the stabilization efforts underway elsewhere in northeastern Syria. As living conditions deteriorated, locals in these villages expressed severe frustration with the SDF and AA, blaming the authorities for their economic and security woes. ISIS expanded by creating and exploiting governance vacuums, spreading fear, and fueling local rejection of the SDF and AA. In many parts of the eastern countryside, nascent institutions collapsed altogether (Haenni and Quesnay 2020, 14). The authorities' presence dwindled to soldiers operating checkpoints and security patrols entering villages to conduct anti-ISIS operations. The SDF and AA continued to engage tribal leaders, believing tribesmen would fall in line, but their engagement did not reflect positively in countering ISIS and stabilizing the region.

In August 2020, several tribal figures were assassinated in the eastern countryside, with Shaikh Motashar al-Hifl being the most prominent among them. A member of the leading family of the Ageidat tribal federation, Motashar was targeted in his car, together with his nephew Shaikh Ibrahim al-Hifl, the acting general leader of the Ageidat, who survived the attack. Motashar's assassination triggered severe unrest in the eastern countryside (Abu Nabut 2020). After the assassination, Ibrahim al-Hifl called for the formation of a political project that would help the tribal federation escape from the security crisis. He invited Ageidat tribesmen to a conference that was attended by hundreds of people, including representatives of tribes from more than a half dozen villages in the eastern countryside (Al-Ali 2020). Al-Hifl did not address the threat of ISIS directly but urged unity and called for inviting the International Coalition to partner with tribes to address the insecurity plaguing the region. His efforts failed almost immediately, once again reflecting the marginal influence of the region's traditional leadership and the fragmentation of tribes. Al-Hifl himself commented that the Ageidat disappointed him because they were not willing to listen to the tribal leadership.[19]

Conclusion

In sum, our three cases leave a mixed picture of traditional authorities' ability to curb the spike in violent extremism represented by ISIS. Whereas religious leaders made essential contributions to upholding stability in the Western Balkans, tribal leaders were unable to prevent jihadism from taking root in Deir ez-Zor. The achievements in Iraqi Kurdistan ranked somewhere in the middle, but of note is that the region produced a relatively limited number of recruits for ISIS, considering its geographical proximity to the epicenter of the "caliphate."

To explain these differences, we must look at the broader political context. As described in the analytical framework, the authority of traditional leaders is affected by developments in society and the state. Syria has experienced extreme volatility on both levels, which is reflected in tribal leaders' faltering position. The micro-tribal identities that emerged amid revolt and state collapse have undermined the influence that the traditional leadership once enjoyed. The Syrian uprising constituted a turning point for the tribes in Deir ez-Zor, with conflict, displacement, multiple loyalties, and disputes over resources leading to divisions in which traditional leaders lost their functional and symbolic roles. Tribal divisions were also instrumentalized by jihadist groups, which pitted rival tribesmen against each other. Today, weak governance, a deteriorating economic situation, and chaos and abuses in many tribal areas continue to provide fertile ground for violent extremism. ISIS remains active and continues to capitalize on the tribal feuds that persist to maintain its presence.

In the Western Balkans, kinship-based structures like those in Syria and Iraq that fragment society and open opportunities for intervention by Salafi jihadists are absent, comparatively curtailing the scope of action of extremist groups. Outside social media, extremists in the Western Balkans can vie for control mainly by infiltrating the traditional religious communities, where they clash directly with the imams, who generally command the respect of their communities and, themselves, have vested interests in countering such interference. The largely accepted legitimacy and institutionalization of the official religious communities also narrow the space for intergenerational conflict. The state typically aligns with traditional leaders, and the communities then seek the state's support.

A similar, albeit more precarious, partnership between the state and community leaders is observed in Iraqi Kurdistan. The KRI has made conscious efforts to prop up certain actors' authority. The strategy is to combine nationalism with traditional "Kurdish" Islam, which is construed as being inherently peaceful. The KRI has also lent its support to Salafi preachers who are loyal to the political authorities. Some worry that this policy may inadvertently lay the ground for more conservative and potentially radical religious practices in the long term. A further concern is that the government's legitimacy deficit might weaken the authority of the actors it pushes forward to prevent the spread of violent extremism. As much as state support can help sustain the ascendancy of community leaders, it becomes a liability if the state is perceived to be corrupt.

When considering the local sources of resilience against violent extremism, a holistic view is therefore essential. Traditional leaders can serve as agents of resilience only when certain conditions are present. Our findings point to the contingent nature of traditional authority: it is not a force that works ex nihilo but rather a potential power that takes shape through interaction with the environment. In situations where social structures collapse under the long-term weight of a dysfunctional state, relying on "tradition" as a rescue is futile. Policymakers should take note of this conclusion and avoid supporting community leaders in a knee-jerk position.

Although traditional authorities contribute agency to the prevention of violent extremism and provide policymakers with someone to work with, there is a risk of reifying community leaders as "the solution." People in positions of authority may operate in ways that effectively hinder social mobility for youths. They may also lack genuine authority in the sense that commoners dispute their powers. The challenge represented by the Salafi-jihadi trend is precisely this, as explained. To deepen our understanding of community leaders' capacity to withstand such assaults, more research from concrete localities is needed.

Notes

1. *Authority* is defined as socially approved domination implying the "acceptance by subordinates of the right of those above them to give them orders or directives" (Giddens and Griffiths 2006, 581).
2. On the ubiquitous Balkan perceptions of a "traditional" as opposed to "non-traditional" Islam, see Evstatiev (2022).
3. Interview with an Islamic Community official in Bihać, July 25, 2021.
4. Interview with an Islamic Community employee in Bihać, July 27, 2021.
5. A masjid is essentially a mosque without the minaret, but it can be more informal, whereas mosques are only part of the official Islamic Community network.
6. Interview with a professor at the Islamic Faculty in Bihać, July 25, 2021.
7. See https://islamedu.ba.

8. See ((82) Muamer Zukorlić - YouTube, n.d.; Akademska inicijativa Forum 10, 2017; Islamović, n.d.). See https://www.youtube.com/results?search_query=muamer+zukorli%C4%87, https://www.forum10.org.rs/, and S Islamovic (n.d) Facebook, https://facebook.com/profile.php?id=100067706756991&ref=page_internal.

9. The religious communities in Kurdistan are Islam, Christianity, Yezidis, Baha'is, Sabian Mandeans, Jews, Zoroastrians, and Kakais.

10. The Islamic Scholars' Union of Kurdistan was established in 1970 during the Kurdish national liberation movement. It has close relations with the KRI authorities.

11. Saddiq is an Islamic intellectual and former member of the Kurdistan Islamic Union, also a former Minister of Environment (2003–2004). In 2021, he was appointed Head of KRG's Environment Conservation and Improvement Board.

12. Gharib is a university professor in law and politics at the University of Human Development in Sulaymaniyah. He was among the first to theorize Kurdish religious nationalism of the 2000s.

13. Karwani is a senior member of the Islamic Union and a former KRG minister.

14. Dr. Sharif is an Islamic figure and intellectual who founded the Islamic Thought Forum in Kurdistan.

15. The Islamic Movement, Justice Group, and the Islamic Union of Kurdistan.

16. Interview with a tribal leader in eastern Deir ez-Zor, July 2022.

17. Interview with Hummada, Turkey, June 2017.

18. Interviews with tribesmen from Bkair, eastern Deir ez-Zor, June 2022.

19. Interview with Hifil, eastern Deir ez-Zor, August 2020.

11

External Donors and the Marketing of P/CVE: Niger, Tunisia, and Syria

Laura Berlingozzi, Silvia Carenzi, and Daniela Musina

Twenty years after September 11 and the subsequent launch of the war on terror (WoT), the counterterrorism agenda has shown its limitations. To achieve better results, traditional hard enemy-centric military approaches have been coupled with "softer" population-centric approaches, namely, preventing and countering violent extremism (P/CVE). External donors, including the European Union (EU), have devoted enormous funding to the P/CVE agenda in so-called fragile countries.

The European Union's cooperation with African and Middle Eastern countries to prevent and counter violent extremism has received increased scholarly attention following several terrorist attacks in Europe in the last decade (Bøås et al. 2021; Raineri et al. 2020). The EU's emphasis on promoting so-called good governance, democracy, and human rights to prevent violent extremism has gone hand in hand with a growing path toward prioritizing a "security first" approach (Skare 2022).

In these contexts, the legacy of colonialism has endured over time. Postcolonial states inherited strong traditional leadership and well-trained militaries, along with limited public health and education facilities in some cases (Wilén 2023) or unequal access to public services and social justice in others. Although these legacies have caused harm, they should not be misconstrued as perpetual victimhood or a lack of agency among national political elites. These elites have developed strategic competencies and have employed "extraversion" mechanisms (Bayart and Ellis 2000) to mobilize resources based on their unequal relationships with external partners.

In this chapter, we delve into the evolution of these interrelated dynamics: on one side, how a range of donors have sustained efforts and shaped narratives in the P/CVE spheres, and on the other, how states have sought to adapt their narratives by portraying themselves as trustworthy partners and proactive upholders of P/CVE and counterterrorism policies to attract economic and military assistance. To do so, we adopt a comparative approach among three case studies across different regions in the broader Mediterranean—namely, Niger in West Africa, Tunisia in North Africa, and Syria in the Middle East. These cases show various levels of authoritarian restoration, repression, and democratic backsliding. Similarly, they hold distinct positions vis-à-vis Western countries and international partners. Yet, they display several similarities in their discourses and practices of extraversion in P/CVE and counterterrorism.

For instance, in line with Preventing Violent Extremism in the Balkans and the MENA (PREVEX) project analysis, all three cases have known occurrences of violent extremism that was driven by common factors such as youth unemployment and socioeconomic marginalization that have been exacerbated by environmental challenges, population growth, and lack of state-delivered services, which contribute to heightened competition for resources, creating a fertile ground for extremist ideologies (Bøås et al. 2021). The resulting identity-based cleavages and perceived inequalities provide opportunities for violent entrepreneurs to exploit grievances. On the basis of PREVEX findings, we identify how the scattered and fragmented EU activities fall short of developing a holistic, multiscalar, and multithematic P/CVE model (Ben-Nun and Engel 2022b).

In the chapter, we employ qualitative text and discourse analysis to examine patterns of actors' positionality vis-à-vis external actors and how these interactions shape and co-construct their identities. Specifically, the concept of extraversion is utilized to understand how actors compensate for their difficulties in power autonomization by strategically mobilizing resources on the basis of their unequal relationships with external partners, and it offers a valuable framework for understanding the dynamics of political power in postcolonial states. We shed light on the complex interactions and power dynamics between national and external actors in shaping political outcomes—stressing how political elites actively participate in the *mise en dépendence* of their societies. Additionally, this approach provides insights into how identity construction is shaped by external influences, such as donor and sponsor countries, and how actors navigate these influences to accrue power and legitimacy.

The findings of the analysis reveal that ruling elites in Niger, Tunisia, and Syria have sought to capitalize on fears of extremism and portray themselves in their discourse as key actors in the domains of P/CVE and counterterrorism. Nevertheless, the cross-case findings show a noteworthy disparity (Niger, Tunisia) or a complete divergence (Syria) between the external image projected by these countries and their actual behavior. P/CVE policies are often used as political tools by governments to gain international support and bolster domestic consensus rather than to genuinely address violent extremism. It is important to understand the interplay between external and internal political dynamics and how counterterrorism strategies can negatively interact across governance levels.

First we operationalize the concept of extraversion; second, delve into each case study; and finally, draw conclusions and make policy recommendations based on a comparative cross-country analysis.

P/CVE: A Field for Political Extraversion

The concept of extraversion, as it was theorized by Bayart (2010, 20), refers to the capacity of states and state elites to capitalize in one way or another on their position of dependence on the world system and to "mobilize resources derived from their unequal relationship with the external environment." According to this perspective, dependency and outward orientation are crucial to the configuration of internal politics as state elites mobilize external resources to produce power centralization and manage internal populations (Bayart and Ellis 2000). The concept of extraversion is also valuable for framing contemporary processes of transformation of postcolonial states, including security-related processes, such as the P/CVE sphere. Just as other intervention concepts and constructs (such as "good governance" and "reform conditionality") mediate the adoption of these agendas, P/CVE is a field of intervention that also determines the entanglement of these contexts in the world system (Bayart 2010).

The manifestations of extraversion processes exhibit variability across different contexts. Whereas it involves providing exclusive resource access to loyal social groups or classes in certain situations, in others, it relies more on manipulating factional and social struggles. These dynamics contribute to reducing states' dependence on and accountability to internal resources for governance (De Waal 2009). Indeed, even though they are all former colonies or protectorates, Niger, Tunisia, and Syria present different levels of economic dependency and market integration; have diverse historical, socioeconomic bases; and are more or less reliant on internal resource extraction or production. Global asymmetries of wealth and power and histories of subjection do not necessarily imply passiveness and do not exclude performative roles by dependent countries. From a *long durée* perspective, strategies of extraversion date to precolonial and then colonial times but represent a useful heuristic tool to understand the postcolonial state confronted with unprecedented levels of heterogeneity in aid and resource provision by a plethora of donors.

Even though the concept of extraversion has been applied to economic, humanitarian, and developmental aid, it is less utilized in the field of security.

This is surprising given the global prioritization of security politics, which, continuing from colonial times and especially since the WoT, intertwines with financial and developmental agendas and reflects the "security-development nexus" mantra (Beall, Goodfellow, and Putzel 2006). In particular, today, transnational P/CVE agendas provide massive opportunities for ruling elites or strategically positioned (non)state actors to capitalize on them.

Besides opening channels for material provisions to militaries and police for both reactive and preemptive scopes, P/CVE agendas also offer maneuvering ground at the symbolic and discursive levels, to an extent, where governments and other recipients can play on ideas and perceptions linked to reputation, efficacy, and exceptionalism, as the three case studies presented in this chapter illustrate. Extraversion, in this sense, resorts to manipulation of perceptions, where states have the power to play "belief games" (Fisher 2014) by leveraging racially biased perceptions of Africa and the Middle East as incubators of our century's most dangerous "terrorist" threats.

Since 2001, P/CVE has emerged as the new frontier for risk- and threat-based extraversion, as illustrated by the designation of "terror zones" in Africa and the Middle East during the WoT. State elites, recognizing the benefits, have actively supported these designations. The Algerian positioning vis-à-vis the "crisis" in Mali as a regional bulwark against the spillover effects is emblematic (Keenan 2013; see also Keen and Andersson 2018). Not only images of strength but also those of alleged "fragility" are bargained to secure external support, and these often coexist with contradictory but equally pervasive "good reformer" discourses (Fisher 2014). In an era where capacity-building and other technical paradigms characterize the new ascendant parable of interventionism and, arguably, of war and warlike action, extraversion as an orientation to external resources but also sources of authority and legitimacy seems to illuminate connections between inequality and coercive political centralization and transnational P/CVE agendas in postcolonial settings.

Niger: Between Adaptive Strategies and Bargaining Power

The influence of global jihadist franchises is significantly increasing, making sub-Saharan Africa an emerging epicenter of global jihadism (IEP 2022). Niger, situated in the central Sahel region, faces numerous challenges, including illicit migration, drug trafficking, intercommunal and interethnic rivalries, depletion of natural resources, and the presence of various armed groups that have expanded since the early 2000s (Thurston 2020). In the northwestern and southeastern regions, jihadi governance has largely replaced state control, with groups like the Islamic State Sahel

Province (ISSP) and Islamic State West Africa Province (ISWAP) operating in these areas (Bøås and Strazzari 2020).

To tackle these issues, over the last decade, the European Union's involvement in Niger has intensified in recognition of its importance as a critical country in the Sahel—a region deemed a "strategic priority for the EU and its member states." The EU's strategy for the Sahel is based on an integrated approach that focuses on the security-development nexus to strengthen "a solid and long-standing partnership . . . that can facilitate the adoption of common positions to address common challenges." In the EU policy discourse, the Sahel region is frequently depicted as grappling with complex situations involving mutually exacerbating vulnerabilities, fragilities, and insecurity (Council of the EU 2021). This portrayal reinforces the existence of an internal-external security nexus (Blockmans et al. 2020).

Niger's economic fragility is highlighted by its low ranking on the UN Development Programme's Human Development Index (HDI): it is currently 189th out of 191 countries (UNDP 2021). Areas with social and economic marginalization, various insecurities, religious or ideological indoctrination, strong state security responses, fragile masculinities, and long-standing grievances are more likely to foster violent extremism (Bøås et al. 2021). To combat this fragility, Niger has established an Inter-ministerial Committee to monitor and improve its HDI ranking and developmental status. Additionally, external partners like the EU have committed to a stabilization agenda to strengthen Niger's state capacity, particularly in the security sector (Marsh et al. 2020). Thus, beyond development aid, Niger obtains other benefits from cooperating with the EU, which includes the externalization of both migration-management and security-building costs (Colomba-Petteng 2019), whereby security and migration operate as "bargaining chips." Niger serves as a key transit country for migrants en route to North Africa and Europe and thus holds a significant position as the EU's first border in West Africa (Idrissa 2021). The mutual dependence between Niger and the EU has deepened since the onset of the 2015 "migration crisis" in Europe (Collet and Ahad 2017). Although the EU has emerged as the primary donor to Niger, Niamey has become increasingly indispensable to the EU's efforts in the areas of migration and security.

The EU's broader intervention in Niger, particularly in the field of P/CVE, is part of the EU Strategy for Security and Development in the Sahel, which views the relationship between the Sahel and the EU as mutually beneficial (EEAS 2011) and aims for a stable Sahel to fully realize economic opportunities through a win-win partnership (Council of the EU 2021). As scholars from the PREVEX project outlined, the EU has encouraged, assisted, and guided Nigerien authorities in adopting various strategies related to security and development. These include Niger's Security and Development Strategy, Internal Security Strategy, Sustainable

Development and Inclusive Growth Strategy, and National Border Policy and Comprehensive National Migration Policy (Raineri et al. 2020). However, if the European Union conceptualizes its intervention in terms of mutual benefit, it is essential to consider how the Nigerien government perceives these developments.

Historically, Niger has been considered unstable because of four coups (in 1974, 1996, 1999, and 2010) since its independence from France in 1960. However, 2011 marked a significant shift in its political trajectory and EU-Sahel relations. In March 2011, the EU adopted its first strategy for the Sahel, which addressed irregular migration and terrorism and coincided with Mahamadou Issoufou becoming president of Niger. President Issoufou sought EU support for Niger's security sector, and this led to the establishment of the EU civilian mission EUCAP Sahel Niger in 2012, which aims to strengthen Niger's security by enhancing law enforcement capacities, providing technical assistance to the justice system, and improving border management to address irregular migration. The creation of EUCAP Sahel Niger resulted from mutual interests: Niger sought help in combating terrorism and handling migration issues, and the EU aimed to increase its regional engagement. President Issoufou emphasized international cooperation to prevent weapons smuggling via migrant routes (Frowd 2018) and used EU resources to bolster Niger's strategic goals and cultivate an image of stability (Ibrahim 2014).

During Mahamadou Issoufou's presidency in Niger, Prime Minister Brigi Rafini significantly advanced Niger's development objectives by leveraging his extensive knowledge of European institutions and his consensus-building skills. As an alumnus of both the Nigerien and French National School of Administration (ENA), Rafini crucially deployed his expertise in international aid to secure funding for development initiatives. He served as prime minister for a decade, which overlapped with Issoufou's two terms, and they collaborated to attract European investments and expand security and defense partnerships. A key component of their strategy involved expanding Niger's diplomatic reach to leverage external resources and expertise.

Following the approval of EUCAP Sahel Niger, European embassies were quickly established by the United Kingdom, the Netherlands, and Italy, with Germany and Belgium also expressing interest in strengthening relations with Niger. During Issoufou's presidency, Niger developed a Strategy for the Security and Development of the Sahelo-Saharan Zones (Cabinet of the Prime Minister 2012) that closely mirrored the European strategy. This alignment highlighted the congruence of EU and Nigerien objectives and indicated the government's preference for adopting external models and procedures. Mohamed Bazoum, who assumed the presidency in April 2021 and was ousted in a coup d'état after two years in office, continued with this strategy. He effectively shaped the country's storyline to demonstrate Niger's ability to tackle a range of challenges and to align with the priorities of international donors. Amid the recent coups in neighboring countries, such as Mali (August 2020 and May 2021) and Burkina Faso (January and September 2022), Niger's 2021 elections were portrayed as the "first peaceful transfer of power in Niger's history" (Al Jazeera 2022). This narrative positioned Niger as a model of democracy in the Sahel, contrasting with the region's shift toward authoritarianism.

Despite the ongoing threat of jihadist insurgencies in the region, Niger has been portrayed as the *only* stable partner, which reinforces its image as a stronghold in regional security (Jeune Afrique 2022). In this context, Niger has increased its efforts and taken on an unprecedented expansive role in regional security dynamics. At the same time, while the Malian junta leader Assimi Goïta revoked defense agreements with France, President Bazoum invited foreign armies to redeploy in Niger (France 24 2022), and in particular the French counterterrorism mission Barkhane.

In July 2022, the European Union approved the disbursement of 25 million euros from the European Peace Facility to support the Nigerien Armed Forces in protecting Niger's territorial integrity, sovereignty, and civilians from terrorist threats (Council of the EU 2022). The EU plans to establish a technician training center and to construct a forward operating base in the Tillabéri region. Some scholars argue that this military aid has caused Nigerien elites to shift their reliance from development aid to military assistance (Bøås and Strazzari 2020).

The Niger-EU partnership saw significant developments, including a request by President Bazoum and Foreign Affairs Minister Ibrahim Yacoubou in November 2022 to deploy an EU Common Security and Defence Policy (CSDP) military partnership mission in Niger. Consequently, the EU established the EU Military Partnership Mission, launched in February 2023, with an initial three-year duration. The mission aims to enhance the military capacity of the Niger Armed Forces to combat terrorism. Additionally, for the first time, the EU agreed to provide lethal equipment through the European Peace Facility (Borrell 2023), marking a significant shift from its traditional "normative" stance.

In the EU discourse, resilience-based participatory engagements are more effective in preventing and countering violent extremism than top-down approaches focused on hard security. However, in practice, the EU tends to prioritize security concerns. As the EU seeks to distinguish its approach from that of other international actors, such as those inspired by the WoT, a combination of criminal justice–inspired policies and militaristic undertones is apparent. The EU's approach to the Sahel region's P/CVE policies, programs, and actions combines significant political prioritization with limited practical tools (Raineri et al. 2020).

Despite the EU's efforts to adhere to normative commitments, the lack of clear definitions and policy templates presents challenges. To address the limitations of hard-security approaches, the EU emphasizes trust building with local communities, in consideration of historical abuses by security forces, and sponsors disarmament, demobilization, and reintegration (DDR) programs. These activities aim to build stability and strengthen social cohesion and resilience to violent extremism. However, respondents to a PREVEX survey noted that most EU-sponsored P/CVE initiatives at the local level are implemented by local nongovernmental organizations (NGOs) that focus on conflict analysis, intercommunity dialogue, early-warning-signs recognition, and violent extremism and radicalization prevention. PREVEX data indicate difficulties in implementing comprehensive, participatory, and inclusive strategies, reveal a significant gap between intentions and actual implementation, and highlight the need for a more coordinated framework to achieve robust outcomes in strengthening resilience and creating nonoccurrence environments (Bøås et al. 2021).

By successfully projecting an image of stability, Niger has established itself as a key player in P/CVE in the region. This positioning enables Niger to secure a dominant role and reap various benefits. Despite this, the effectiveness of Niger's P/CVE policies, including the EU Military Partnership Mission, EUCAP Sahel Niger, and DDR programs, remains uncertain, particularly after the July 2023 coup d´état and the renegotiation of international partnerships with entities like the European Union. Nevertheless, before the coup, Niger had become a trusted and crucial partner for the EU in the Sahel.

Trajectories of P/CVE Extraversion in Tunisia: Playing on Imaginaries of Exceptionalism

Tunisia can be considered an emblematic case of extraversion, considering its extensive integration into P/CVE global and regional cooperation programs and its strategic position at the crossroads of the Mediterranean Middle East. If we suppose that action in the name of anti-terrorism has been a constant under both Bourguiba's and Ben Ali's regimes, and often correlated with modernization measures or state control of the religious sphere (Mabrouk 2012), it is only after September 11 and with the onset of the WoT that a veritable transnationally linked counterterrorist agenda took hold and was brought to the forefront of politics (Simoncini 2024).

For Zine al-Abidine Ben Ali, the global emergence of a counterterrorist agenda represented an opportunity to tighten even more the state's grip on the religious milieux and political Islamism (Lahlou and Fahmi 2020). In 2002, the attack on the synagogue on the southern Tunisian island of

Djerba served as a plea for the adoption of the 2003 anti-terrorist law: "Relating to the Support of International Efforts to Combat Terrorism and the Repression of Money Laundering." This law aligned the Tunisian regime's action with international efforts in the framework of the WoT. However, the international community, and Western partners in particular, reacted to the attacks with underestimation and reassurance in order to preserve foreign direct investment flows and the image of Djerba, and of Tunisia in general, as a popular tourist destination.

In the meantime, the repressive machine was strengthened internally, as the vast evidence of abuses committed under the 2003 law demonstrates. This two-pronged strategy of extraversion consists, on the one hand, of riding the wave of discourses of stability and responsibility to secure external political support and foreign capital, especially since the *infitah* of the 1980s, and on the other, of crafting disproportionate responses to violent extremism at home. Such a stance has characterized Tunisian leadership and ruling elites at least since Ben Ali's era and has capitalized on long-standing exceptionalist (and Orientalist) views of Tunisia—which in turn feeds on rhetoric of modernization—as the "good student" (*le bon élève*) well placed in the path of development and bulwark in the fight against transnational crime and terrorism (Hibou 2006; see also Camau 2018 and Geisser and Allal 2018). On the P/CVE front, this trend is exacerbated, especially in the way certain internationally fueled discourses of effectiveness and efficacy are mobilized to expand a P/CVE regulatory infrastructure while adapting it to international standards.

The aftermath of 2011 has meant, besides undeniable elements of change more broadly, the rapid intensification of funds, tools, and channels of cooperation in Tunisia on all fronts, particularly that of security.

If we were to suppose that the 2003 anti-terrorist law was ostensibly entrenched in stability measures and reactive state-led responses, the 2015 Organic Law No. 26 (as amended in 2019) "Dealing with Combating Terrorism and Preventing Money-Laundering" maintains this dimension while adding a more markedly preventive and preemptive one and expanding the incrimination potential over terrorist intents and related money-laundering activities (Bras 2016). The law comes after a period of intense political crisis caused by, among other things, the 2013 series of political assassinations, for which the radical Islamist group Ansar al-Sharia in Tunisia (AST) has been accused of masterminding. It was immediately adopted after the Bardo Museum and Sousse attacks (perpetuated, respectively, in March and June 2015). Concurrently, the issue of Tunisian returning fighters (*al-'ā'idūna*) emerged vigorously, especially after the territorial defeat of the Islamic State in Iraq and Syria (ISIS) and the increase in return mobility.

In 2016, in the aftermath of the ISIS attacks on Ben Guerdane, the *Nidā' Tūnus*-led Tunisian government announced the adoption of a

"National Strategy for Countering Extremism and Terrorism," which was the result of a top-down process directly supervised by the president-led Conseil de Sécurité Nationale in close collaboration with international partners and donors (Santini and Cimini 2019). The strategy claims to advance a multidimensional approach built around four main axes: prevention, protection, pursuit, and response. The same axes are to be found in the European counterterrorism strategy of 2005 and in some national strategies of member countries with a history of countering violent extremism, such as Spain. It is not merely a matter of legal and institutional isomorphism. Still, it calls into question the will of the Tunisian ruling elites to develop their national strategy while adapting it to transnational models, languages, and paradigms of action.

Likewise, the constant mobilization of "gray literature" terminology in the security and defense domains (such as that of the Livres Blancs) points to the same trend of appropriating the technical jargon proper to keep cooperation channels open. These are not rhetorical efforts but have heavy practical and political implications. The imaginary and image projection of Tunisia transnationally has a central role in the production of politics and its relation to the practices of material culture (Schouten 2012 quoting Bayart). When we consider concrete extroverted practices, we see that pledged state-led efforts in preventing violent extremism (PVE) are completely focused on law-based, intelligence-led preemptive actions and freezing financial assets. They conform to transnational security cooperation agendas and do not engage with the more comprehensive civil-led actions that tackle the causes of radicalization. Civil-led prevention efforts that include provisions for education, awareness raising, enhancement of social cohesion, and mitigation in marginalized contexts or prisons are, in practice, thwarted by state-responsive or preemptive action.[1]

Many across the spectrum of academia and practitioners believe that top-down counterterrorism and "securitarian" approaches should leave more room for civil society–led PVE action.[2] The point is that even bottom-up processes are subject in one way or another to the brokerage of state institutions and the Ministry of Interior (MoI) at the forefront. The most striking example are the community policing programs implemented by the UN Development Programme (UNDP) enjoying the support of a range of external donors. These programs are inspired by so-called human security and social cohesion paradigms and, as such, intersect with P/CVE scopes. They have benefited the MoI as a fruitful channel for upgrading and reequipping local police infrastructure, while their core objectives of comprehensive violence prevention, including both institutional and extremist violence as well as violence against women, are widely considered as failed ones—and yet boasted as successful by the Tunisian security institutions and the donors' community alike.

Extraversion strategies depend on the fabrication of images for external consumption (Gallagher 2015), projections of something false that fits external racially biased and xenophobic preconceptions about the threats coming from Africa and Islam majoritarian contexts. The relative but palpable general decline of jihadi political violence across Tunisia and the wider North Africa and Sahel region has not, indeed, been followed by a scaling down of the security response action (ICG 2021). Neither has the alarm over returning fighters cooled down despite the lack of substantive recurrence of radicalization and extremist violence among them (Lounnas and Ayari 2023). Capitalizing on this "threat-based extraversion" (Pastore and Roman 2020) and increasingly stretching it to migration policies, successive Tunisia ruling elites have secured constant support for the state, particularly for coercive state institutions.

The MoI, in particular, has been successful in its bargaining over specific programs and policies, and has done so not even covertly. The EU-sponsored security sector reform (SSR) program (EU PARSS) is a case in point: Pillar 2 (border control enforcement) and especially Pillar 3 (improving intelligence on counterterrorism and "in the field of financing new forms of crime and money laundering") have made some progress, according to their promoters, while more normative-driven components of the program (Pillar 1: reform and accountability) are primarily considered deadlocked. These types of interventions based on professionalization-as-reform logic seem purposely neglectful of the historically established intelligence system that became extremely professional under Ben Ali and that have since colonial times ensured the survival of the regimes that have followed (Safi 2020).

The stretch of P/CVE agendas to other crime domains (often called the crime-terror nexus) considerably expands this system's pervasiveness. A trend made hypervisible by the opening of new cooperation channels, especially in the form of law enforcement cooperation (including with EU law enforcement agencies such as CEPOL and EUROPOL), is increasingly established as a precondition for obtaining funding and material support.[3] The progressive entrenchment of the Tunisian security apparatus in transnational P/CVE agendas has been a constant in the governments of the post-2011 phase. So-called troika governments, including the then majoritarian political force Ennahda, tried to prove to their constituencies that they had the credentials to manage security challenges in a desperate quest to break away from allegations of "culpable benevolence towards radical Islamism" (Bras 2016, 14). The "technocratic" government of Mehdi Jomaa (2014–2015) and successive Nidā' Tūnus-led ones (that of Habib Essid, 2015–2016, and Youssef Chahed, 2016–2020) placed an even higher priority on P/CVE cooperation. Beyond the extraversion effects visible in the negotiation of regulations and policies, therefore, and within a so-called legal framework of action, concrete extralegal measures illustrate the link with transnational practices and rationales and their repressive abuse, for example, profiling measures (*fichage*), and in particular the extensive and indiscriminate use of the S17 fiche as a mobility ban for all suspected terrorists. Equally emblematic is the extensive recourse to attacking the *takfiri*, that is, those who allegedly use accusations of unbelief (*takfir*) to label and politically isolate entire environments that are depicted as inherently violent—a stance that has been praised as an effective prevention model in international cooperation settings (see, for instance, documents put out by EuroMed Justice in 2018 [Badar et al. 2018]).

The current political conjuncture, which started with President Kais Saied's July 25, 2021, self-coup, has further made hypervisible the distortions of anti-terrorist discourses and regulations. Their tendency to extraversion and political (ab)use to target opponents designated as "saboteurs of the national security order" is evidenced by the wave of arrests ordered by the anti-terrorist security pole.[4]

State Violence (Un)disguised: The Syrian Regime's Appropriation of Counterterrorism and P/CVE Discourses

Syria is a peculiar case study that illustrates the web of contradictions inherent in the weaponization of countering extremism and counterterrorism. Ruled by the authoritarian regime of Bashar al-Assad, the country has suffered from a lack of civil liberties and suppression of genuine political opposition. Like Tunisia, it witnessed a wave of mobilizations in 2011, albeit with a different trajectory: heavy repression on behalf of the state apparatus ensued, which gave way to an escalation of violence and full-fledged armed conflict—with the intervention of external actors.

Historically speaking, Syria's relations with Western countries have been strained. As early as 1979, the United States designated Syria as a state sponsor of terrorism (US Department of State 2019). Relations between Syria and the EU have ebbed and flowed, with attempts to enhance political dialogue (EEAS 2014). Still, after 2011, following massive use of violence and human rights violations, Assad's Syria became a pariah in the international community—at least until recently. In contrast, the Syrian regime has typically relied on its alliance with Russia, which in September 2015 militarily intervened to support Assad.

In this case, a state that has characteristically projected an "anti-Western" image has reappropriated West-driven WoT frames in its image-building domestically and vis-à-vis external powers (Lee 2024). As noted by Calculli (2016, 230), the WoT embodies a "disfigured form of just war theory," whereby in the name of (competing) "wars on terror" different states pursue even opposite agendas. Another paradoxical effect of the WoT logic is that—despite nominal declarations—Western countries, including EU countries, became captive of a "terror-centered understanding of Syria" that has skewed their policies (Orsini 2016). Analysis of selected state-linked media releases shows that, after 2011, the Syrian regime has increasingly sought to portray itself as a bulwark against terrorism, domestically and externally—while it is part and parcel of the cycle of political violence and has instrumentally deployed the labels of "terrorism" and "extremism."[5]

The "centrality of violence" has been a hallmark of the Assad family's rule in Syria (Ismail 2018, 131), with both Hafez al-Assad (who came to power in 1971) and his son, Bashar (president since 2000). The Syrian regime has always had a convoluted relationship with religious movement(s), with oscillations and changes over time (cf. Khatib 2011). It had frequently agitated the specters of Islamism, Wahhabism, and external plots, even long before the WoT was launched—most notably, when it brutally crushed an Islamist insurgency in the late 1970s and early 1980s that culminated in the massacre of Hama. The 2011 popular uprising affected how Assad manipulated the country's image externally and domestically. After the rebellion, the regime capitalized on the rise of the self-styled Islamic State to cast itself as a guarantor of stability in the face of terrorism and to delegitimize the widespread opposition. The label of "extremism" was weaponized domestically as well: by equating dissent with supposed extremism and terrorism, the Assad regime sought to justify the state's use of brutal force.

Most notably, a counterterrorism law was approved in June 2012, de facto replacing the state of emergency lifted in 2011. In the same year, a law establishing a Counterterrorism Court and a further decree on terrorism were introduced. The June 2012 law's definition of terrorism was so broad that peaceful dissent and activism related to human rights could be very easily framed as terrorism (Tahrir Institute for Middle East Policy 2019). Egregious violations of human rights, such as arbitrary detention, torture, enforced disappearances, and death sentences, took place in this framework. As the Violations Documentation Center in Syria (2015) noted, the Counterterrorism Court served as "a tool for war crimes." In parallel, after 2011, the regime increasingly resorted to religious discourse to legitimize its authority and chastise political dissent (Aldoughli 2020). It sought to exert complete and direct control over the religious sphere (Pierret and Alrefaai 2021). Its novel discourse "strongly blurred the distinction between the state and religion" (Aldoughli 2021, 17), conflating patriotism and supposedly correct religious belief (Aldoughli 2020) and framing dissidents as an existential threat to the nation—also in religious terms, as bearers of a "wrong" form of Islam.

Although in the literature, P/CVE practices and discourses are occasionally presented as an alternative to violent and military practices, according to some authors, they may often go hand in hand (Heydemann 2014, 2), as the very P/CVE practices are deeply embedded in the WoT logic. In the case of Assad's Syria, proximity and continuity exist between state violence, what the state labels as "counterterrorism," and initiatives adopting typical P/CVE language. As for the latter, three examples are worth mentioning. First, the religious establishment developed what is known as "jurisprudence of the crisis" (*fiqh al-azma*)—an encyclopedia published by the Ministry of Awqaf ("religious endowments") in 2014 and aimed at correcting "false interpretations of Islam" (Aldoughli 2020, 17). Second, a "youth religious team" was created in 2016 under the auspices of the Minister of Awqaf (Pierret and Alrefaai 2021). This regime-sponsored voluntary team, headed by 'Abdallah al-Sayyed (son of the minister of Awqaf), was expected to mobilize a new generation of religious scholars—that, according to al-Sayyed, are trained and tasked with developing a "moderate religious discourse" in relation to extremism and fanaticism (Syrian Ministry of Awqaf, YouTube 2016). Third, the International Islamic Sham Center to Confront Terrorism and Extremism was launched in 2019. Affiliated with the Ministry of Awqaf and composed of different departments (including a national institute for the qualification of imams and preachers), it is described by state media as promoting "the method of the moderate Levant's religious scholars" (Syrian Arab News Agency 2019).

Despite the ostensibly polished rhetoric deployed to characterize such initiatives, there is more to it than meets the eye. For instance, the youth religious team served as a "patronage network that members join in search of political and security benefits," in a way similar to Assad's Baath Party (Pierret and Alrefaai 2021). The emphasis of such initiatives on concepts such as "moderation" (Kundnani 2009) or efforts to "reform religion" (Hafez 2021, 53–54) phrases that are very typically associated with P/CVE—is instrumental. Indeed, in the Syrian context and in authoritarian settings more generally, concepts such as religious moderation easily become synonymous with political subservience to incumbent authorities; P/CVE practices can become a cloak for different enterprises and formulas to mobilize support and seek internal legitimacy.

The instrumentalization of the counterterrorism narrative is also evident at the international level, as shown by interviews that Assad gave to Russian and Western media. Assad's discourse easily resonates with the Kremlin, its main sponsor at the international level, because it advocates prioritization of stability over chaos (Takvorian 2022). Assad's discourse depicts Putin's Russia as a protector of "stability in this region" (Ministry of Foreign Affairs and Expatriates 2013a). Assad's interview with Russian media in September 2015 (at the time of Moscow's intervention) embraces a heavily security-centered discourse that calls for fighting and defeating terrorism beyond the so-called Islamic State and prioritizing security and military aspects at that stage of the war (Ministry of Foreign Affairs and Expatriates 2015b). In a mirrorlike fashion, the Russian chief of staff at the time (misleadingly) framed the military intervention in Syria as a form of support to Assad's forces facing the Islamic State (IS). Yet, the intervention was (and still is) aimed at propping up the Assad regime in the face of rebel forces—whom the Kremlin's narrative conflated with "terrorists," reproducing Assad's discourse (Williams and Souza 2016, 23). In an international interview a few years later, at a time when some regional countries (e.g., Bahrain and the United Arab Emirates) started normalizing with the Syrian regime, Assad once again deployed the WoT narrative, praising the role of Russia and describing its military intervention as a "defense of the Russian people, because terrorism and its ideology do not know borders" (Ministry of Foreign Affairs and Expatriates 2019).

In contrast, the messages the regime addresses to countries outside its traditional fold of allies—especially Western countries—are more complex and ambivalent; nonetheless, the WoT rhetoric is still dominant. The interviews include ubiquitous mentions of the September 11 World Trade Center attacks (and references to attacks perpetrated by IS supporters in general, cf. Ministry of Foreign Affairs and Expatriates 2015a) in an attempt to link them with the 2011 uprising. In an interview given in 2013—at a time when the regime used chemical weapons against civilians in Eastern Ghouta, and the United States was considering military action—Assad contended that a US strike "would constitute a support to al-Qa'ida and the same people who killed Americans on 9/11." Exploiting fear of jihadism, Assad frequently makes use of the "authoritarian stability" trope, stating that US military action would have entailed "instability" and "spread of terrorism" in the region in a way that "would directly affect the West" (Ministry of Foreign Affairs and Expatriates 2013b). His narrative casts the stability of Syria as a prerequisite for the stability of the region (Ministry of Foreign Affairs and Expatriates 2013a) and the stability of the region as essential for the stability of the entire world (Ministry of Foreign Affairs and Expatriates 2013b). Assad also tends to externalize the threat: he portrays internal dissent as the result of an externally directed plot backed by Western governments and their allies; nonetheless, he still urges the formation of an "international coalition to fight terrorism" and claims that he is open to collaboration with any country, provided that those countries "change their policies" and show genuine "willingness to fight terrorism" (Ministry of Foreign Affairs and Expatriates 2015b). On their side, Western governments have displayed plenty of ambiguities, too. Although they claim to oppose the Assad regime and call for political transition, they often seem to have fallen for this very terrorism-driven understanding of events in Syria. As Martini (2020, 732) observes, international actors have struggled to respond adequately to Assad's weaponization of the WoT discourse precisely because it closely resonates with the "international conceptualization of terrorism."

Conclusion

The cases under scrutiny are paradigmatic examples of the limitations and contradictions of current approaches to P/CVE and of how different ruling elites weaponize and opportunistically resort to security-centered discourses and practices to accrue material and symbolic resources. All three cases under consideration ended up weaponizing the trope of the "extremist threat" (whether real, exaggerated, or manufactured) to attract external support at the economic, military, and diplomatic levels and legitimize themselves internally and externally as bulwarks against "extremism."

The case of Niger demonstrates how the country's political elite adeptly balanced their response to internal needs while concurrently shaping external perceptions and controlling the flow of external resources to advance their agendas. Niger's partnership with the EU in development and security has aligned strategies and bolstered its image as a reliable partner. This alignment has made Niamey a key EU ally in the Sahel, central to counterterrorism and P/CVE efforts, which enables the country to enhance its position and gain benefits. Interestingly enough, these extroverted dynamics also contributed to the military coup d'état in July 2023, the subsequent banishment of the former colonial ally, France, and the souring of relations with the European Union.

As for Tunisia, local elites' practices of extraversion have traditionally consisted of a double-cross strategy aimed at enhancing the external image of Tunisia as a stable, reliable partner, on one hand, while, on the other, capitalizing on the co-constructed perceptions and imaginaries of Africa and the Middle East as sources of transnational security threats. Like Niger and Syria, politics of extraversion are primarily played at the symbolic and discursive level, but in the Tunisian case, they considerably materialized through the (re)centralization of the state's coercive power, well epitomized by the role of the MoI and its use of anti-terrorist legal and extralegal dispositions.

Finally, Syria is a sui generis case compared to Niger and Tunisia, diverging in many respects. Despite its strained relations with Western countries, the Syrian ruling elite has frequently redeployed WoT discursive frames to delegitimize popular dissent and opposition to its rule. In his interviews with foreign media, Assad resorts to a double-pronged discourse: while condemning Western countries and their allies for their purported "interferences," he also tries to appeal to them by agitating the specter of extremism. Both domestically and externally, he has sought to present himself as a bulwark against extremism; however, beneath the cloak of what is instrumentally branded as extremism lie extensive war crimes, repression, and human rights abuses perpetrated by the regime.

The case studies under consideration are not exceptions but indicative of more general patterns in the broader Mediterranean region and beyond. In countries across the globe, P/CVE and counterterrorism discourses and practices are increasingly becoming political tools in the hands of ruling elites to be exploited to attract external support and legitimize their positions. The weaponization of the P/CVE discourse leads state authorities to overlook violence, which perpetuates cycles of political violence. More in general, P/CVE approaches tend to be blinded by their (over)emphasis on nonstate violence, yet "asserting the security agenda of wealthy nations ahead of local priorities is likely to end badly," as noted by Attree (2017).

In line with previous PREVEX findings, our analysis also highlights how the promotion of EU values in Muslim countries clashes with the harsh realities of autocratic despotic regimes and has led the EU to adopt a "principled pragmatism" approach (Ben-Nun and Engel 2022b). Consequently, efforts to prevent violent extremism have focused more on security cooperation with authoritarian governments rather than on addressing the broader societal factors that contribute to extremism (Ben-Nun and Engel 2022b). The EU's struggle to bridge the cultural gap has resulted in a lowest common denominator approach that translates into partial measures aligned with principled pragmatism on the EU side and an extroverted approach from Tunisian, Nigerian, and Syrian elites.

PREVEX findings show that more attention should be devoted to centering local contexts—shifting from security-centered top-down approaches to localized participatory engagements that foster community trust-building mechanisms. Second, efforts should be made to bridge the intention-implementation gap by providing practical tools, expertise, and resources to effectively translate political prioritization into action while also developing clear definitions and policy templates that guide the implementation of P/CVE strategies—and abandoning the WoT legacies. Third, critical assessment of external interventions should be improved: scrutinizing the impacts of external interventions, particularly in authoritarian contexts, can help avoid inadvertently supporting oppressive regimes. Finally, it is essential to ensure that P/CVE efforts prioritize human rights, the rule of law, and inclusive governance.

Notes

1. Interviews with P/CVE practitioners in Tunis, March 2022–December 2023.

2. Ibid.

3. Interview with international cooperation representatives from the Ministry of Interior, Tunis, October 2022.

4. Kais Saied speech, a video from the presidency's official Facebook page, published in February 2023: https://www.facebook.com/KaisSaiedTN/.

5. For an in-depth study of how Assad has gradually embraced the WoT rhetoric over the last two decades, see Lee 2024.

12

P/CVE Policies of Europe and the United States

Dylan Macchiarini Crosson, Pernille Rieker, Tatjana Stankovic, Steven Blockmans, and Elsa Lilja Gunnarsdottir

Although concerns over great power conflict may prevail today, addressing terrorism and violent extremism has driven the foreign policy debate in the collective West for the better part of two decades since September 11.[1] The United States and its closest allies in Western Europe have set the international political agenda, identifying terrorism and violent extremism as primary threats to their respective national security interests. In the European Union (EU), these concerns most prominently emerged in the 2003 European Security Strategy (ESS). The ESS identified the first critical threats as terrorism and "violent religious extremism" originating in the EU's neighborhood as a result of weak institutions, conflict, and state failure. The ESS further asserted that the EU, with its policy tools, is "particularly well equipped to respond to such multi-faceted situations" (Council of the EU 2003).

Although the nature of their respective political regimes differs, and they are, therefore, not fully comparable international actors, the United States and the EU share common concerns about global challenges posed by terrorism and violent extremism. Already highlighted as a primary concern by the 1996 National Security Strategy (White House 1996, 2011), the September 11 terrorist attacks moved terrorism further up the list of US security priorities and have shaped the US policy agenda over consecutive presidential administrations since. The Boston Marathon bombings, the war in Syria, and the rise of the Islamic State in Iraq and Syria (ISIS or Daesh) occupied significant political attention in the 2000s and 2010s. In 2005, the United States also began to speak of a new concept of operations that would transition away from a military-based "Global War on Terrorism" to a more comprehensive, long-term "Struggle

Against Violent Extremism" that made use of diplomatic, economic, and political tools as well (Fox 2005).

The assessment that countering terrorism and preventing and countering violent extremism (CT-P/CVE) requires a comprehensive approach that includes enhancing state capacity, supporting responsive institutions, and promoting peace aligns with policy-oriented literature. Existing literature concurs that addressing structural drivers of violent extremism is crucial but often pits security considerations against those related to democratic governance, human rights, and peacebuilding (Allan et al. 2015). As a result, scholars have questioned whether EU and US approaches to the multifaceted challenge of violent extremism and terrorism are genuinely holistic, addressing structural grievances to build resilience, or if they lean toward a more limited (i.e., specific) security-centered and treatment-oriented CT-P/CVE approach that neglects the EU's core values of promoting peace, democratic governance, and the protection of human rights to the detriment of the EU's stated CT-P/CVE objectives (Keohane 2008).

More specifically, some have argued that the EU's external CT-P/CVE-*specific* policies, particularly in its neighborhood, excessively emphasize security concerns (e.g., border management, security sector reform, military capacity building) to "treat" the problem of violent extremism. This approach may come at the expense of promoting democratic norms and good governance, leading to substantial conflict-sensitivity risks and harm (Skare 2022). Therefore, in this chapter we aim to unpack the EU's approach and, to ground it better contextually, offer a comparative benchmark (the US approach) to assess whether security considerations outweigh all others or this argument loses validity when considering the full spectrum of EU (and US) activities. These activities may not be defined as CT-P/CVE-*specific*, yet are indirectly CT-P/CVE-*relevant* in addressing the structural fragilities and enabling factors that drive the occurrence of terrorism and violent extremism.

Although the multilevel and multiactor nature of EU decisionmaking involving various institutions (e.g., European Commission, European External Action Service) and member states makes it difficult to discern straightforward answers, first we deconstruct the question by reviewing general concepts discerned from research on CT-P/CVE policy, then trace the EU's approach to CT-P/CVE (focusing on the EU, not EU member states) and analyze key CT-P/CVE policy documents and funding. We replicate this analysis for the United States and finally distill key elements of (comparative) analysis.[2]

The analysis in this chapter is based on a multimethod approach: it combines quantitative text-as-data analysis with a qualitative analysis of official documents, a quantitative analysis of funding, and a review of the existing literature.[3] The analysis of the EU's approach is complemented by a synthesis of findings from semistructured interviews, public events, and stakeholder dialogues conducted in 2021 and 2023.[4] The analysis of the US approach in practice is based on secondary sources. Because findings here have not been corroborated with interviews or policy outcomes (i.e., whether the policy was mirrored by practice), the approach must be interpreted as a snapshot of US policies and funding that offers a reference for analyzing the EU's approach rather than a methodological comparison.

General Concepts of CT-P/CVE Policy

Findings from previous research, also presented in other chapters of this volume, indicate several structural drivers of violent extremism (VE) that persist over time and across various regions (Ben-Nun and Engel 2021). These include social factors such as disenfranchisement, horizontal inequalities, and marginalization based on age, ethnicity, religion, social status, employment type, lifestyle (e.g., sedentary vs. nomadic), and geographic origin. In the existing literature, low trust in institutions, political malperformance, political polarization, repressive governance, and the absence of inclusive decisionmaking can be political drivers of violent extremism. In the legal domain, patchy administrative capacities and uneven application of the law resulting from criminal, informal, and extralegal dynamics can also serve as structural causes of VE. Coupled with a culture of impunity and lack of redress mechanisms, these factors may reinforce perceptions of injustice (Mishkova et al. 2021; Bøås et al. 2021; Skare et al. 2021a).

This research also aimed to identify what drives nonoccurrence or resistance to VE. In the social sphere, gender equality, high social costs of radicalization, social cohesion, and individual educational and economic opportunities all help mitigate the risk of VE. Legitimate counternarratives are essential for rebalancing the religious and ideological ecosystem and cultivating resilience to radicalization. Accessible and robust channels of dialogue between decisionmakers and rule-takers, such as civil society organizations (CSOs), trade unions, political parties, independent media, and social movements, play a crucial role in promoting inclusivity and offsetting clientelism that may favor certain groups over others. Equitable law enforcement and decent prison systems contribute to nonoccurrence in the legal domain, while strong intelligence capacities and information sharing help address radicalization early and effectively (Mishkova et al. 2021).

As such, CT-P/CVE initiatives may both address structural drivers of violent extremism and counter the individual and group-based incentives leading radicalized individuals to engage in violent extremist activities. CT-P/CVE initiatives may, therefore, encompass both CT/CVE-*specific* objectives and those considered *relevant* to CT/CVE although not explicitly developed for this purpose. Furthermore, some strategies focus on short-term interventions to counter immediate threats of terrorism, whereas others target long-term structural drivers. Policymakers may deem imminent threats of a terrorist attack to require a different response than the types of action needed to prevent violent extremism and counter-radicalization in the long term. The EU has developed guidelines for staff working on these topics in third countries, including a hierarchy of interventions that differentiate related responses but require different tools, methods, and implementing agencies: a distinction that can be observed in Figure 12.1.

Key Elements of EU CT-P/CVE Policy

The EU has incorporated many of these concepts in its CT-P/CVE policies, recognizing the need for a multifaceted approach to CT-P/CVE for the first time in its 2003 European Security Strategy. Its identified policy solution was counterterrorism, achieved by mixing "intelligence, police, judicial, military and other means." Although the EU did not concretely identify how those tools might be deployed in the EU's external action, the 2005 EU Counter-Terrorism Strategy (Council of the EU 2005) reflected the added concern over violent extremist activities and terrorist attacks on EU territory carried out by radicalized actors claiming links to al-Qaeda (Blockmans et al. 2020). The strategy identified four key action streams

Figure 12.1 A Hierarchy of Interventions (Policy Implementation) for CT-P/CVE

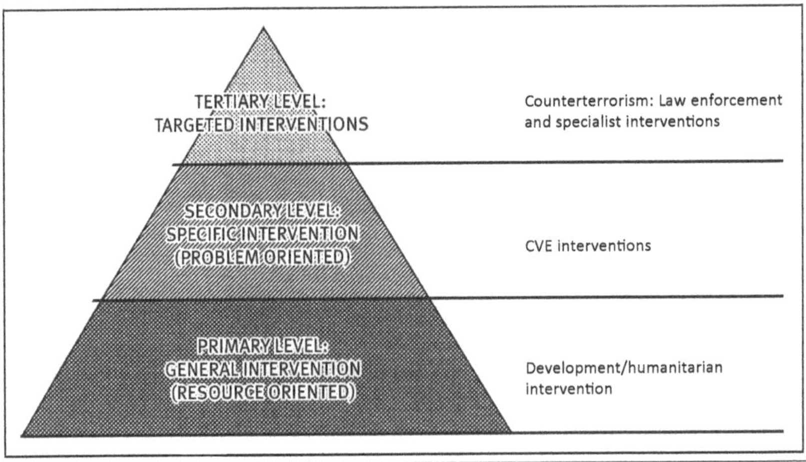

```
                    TERTIARY LEVEL:              Counterterrorism: Law enforcement
                  TARGETED INTERVENTIONS          and specialist interventions
                ─────────────────────────
                  SECONDARY LEVEL:
                  SPECIFIC INTERVENTION           CVE interventions
                  (PROBLEM ORIENTED)
              ─────────────────────────────
                  PRIMARY LEVEL:
                  GENERAL INTERVENTION            Development/humanitarian
                  (RESOURCE ORIENTED)             intervention
```

Note: European Commission 2014.

for countering terrorism: prevent, pursue, protect, and respond. However, the strategy sought to address threats inside EU borders rather than outside threats, which consequently favored policies pertaining to border management and justice and home affairs rather than P/CVE in the EU's external action (Keohane 2008).

The policy responses to the violent implosion of Syria and Libya, the rise of Daesh, ISIS-affiliated terrorist attacks on EU territory in 2015 and 2016, the 2015 refugee/migration crisis, the multi-crisis plaguing the Sahel, and the subsequent 2016 EU Global Strategy (EUGS) did little to quell the scholarly democracy *versus* security debate introduced in the mid-2000s after the ESS (EEAS 2016). Because of these changes in the EU's strategic environment, the EUGS focused on the concept of "principled pragmatism," indicating that the stability of neighboring countries is a core interest of the EU and should be supported by enhancing their resilience to factors of instability. The call to action resulting from the EUGS is clear: "Security at home depends on peace and stability beyond the EU's borders." To do so, the EU stated that its approach should combine the competencies of the EU and its member states: development aid, diplomacy, crisis response actions, and civilian and military missions and operations, among others.

The EU's approach stresses cooperation with third countries and international organizations and a reinforced focus on strengthening local resilience on crosscutting issues such as foreign terrorist fighters, organized crime, recent technologies and digital platforms, critical infrastructure, evidence collection, engagement of youth and women, humanitarian needs, and capacity building. This was recognized in the 2005 CT strategy, later reiterated in the EU's 2014 Strategy for Combating Radicalization and Recruitment to Terrorism (Council of the EU 2005, 2014). It has also recently been revisited in the June 2022 "Council Conclusions on Addressing the External Dimension of a Constantly Evolving Terrorist and Violent Extremist Threat" (Council of the EU 2022), which aims to deepen engagement with local communities, CSOs, and the private sector to enhance resilience to terrorism.

Most recently, the 2022 Strategic Compass for Security and Defense lists violent extremism and terrorism as factors undermining EU security, both near its borders and beyond, and as significant aspects of the EU's strategic environment. In it, terrorism and violent extremism appear to be pertinent challenges in the Middle East and North Africa (MENA) region and the Sahel as well as policy areas of potential cooperation with the Association of Southeast Asian Nations (ASEAN). Collaboration with partners in the Western Balkans on counterterrorism is also emphasized. Although the document does not explicitly mention violent extremism concerning this region, it does stress the importance of "strengthening the resilience of partners" in the Western Balkans, making it P/CVE-*relevant*.

EU CT-P/CVE in Words and Funding

Although it is difficult to identify precisely which EU funding may be considered CT-P/CVE-*relevant* or -*specific* and to distinguish between CT and P/CVE, we have gleaned much with an in-depth reading of crucial documents that outline the EU's understanding of the optimal CT-P/CVE policy mix (see "Key Elements of EU CT-P/CVE Policy" earlier in this chapter). However, a fuller understanding of the EU's policies emerges from a quantitative text analysis of EU strategies and (European) Council Conclusions. These documents are important because they indicate the position of the EU on a particular issue or event at the highest political levels, set the general political directions and priorities, and suggest guidelines for the EU's response.

We used text-as-data methods to try to understand whether, how, and to what extent the EU CT-P/CVE approach varies across the Western Balkans, the Sahel, the Middle East, and North Africa. We examined how the EU professes to approach the issues of radicalization, terrorism, and violent extremism in five policy areas (widely defined): political, socioeconomic, security, diplomatic, and peacebuilding. We analyzed 13 general, policy-specific, and regional foreign policy strategies, 144 European Council Conclusions, and 69 out of 1,324 readable Conclusions of the Council of the EU (5.2 percent) that deal explicitly with security, terrorism, (violent) extremism, and radicalization. We explored whether and how often language linked to these five policy areas (operationalized as strings of case-insensitive regular expressions) appears in close proximity to the regions in question. As shown in Figure 12.2, we focused on the period from January 2003 (see the ESS) to June 2022 (end of the research project).

We proceeded to investigate (1) which of the EU policy instruments are related to the region in question, and (2) whether EU strategies for preventing terrorism and violent extremism vary between the three regions. In Table 12.1, we give an overview of the policies that discussed preventing terrorism and violent extremism in a particular region. The results (Table 12.1 and Figures 12.2–12.5) show that the EU primarily relies on diplomatic rhetoric to address terrorism and violent extremism–related security challenges, followed by phrasing in the socioeconomic and security domains.

When combining strategic documents such as the ESS and EUGS with regional strategies and Council Conclusions, differences emerge by region. Diplomatic and security-related rhetoric is most prevalent in the Western Balkans, and socioeconomic terminology and diplomatic language are used in the Middle East. Document analysis on North Africa and the Sahel demonstrates the most significant balance of terminology, albeit with a similarly heavy diplomatic focus. Political governance, conflict prevention, and peacebuilding rhetoric are lacking across the three regions.

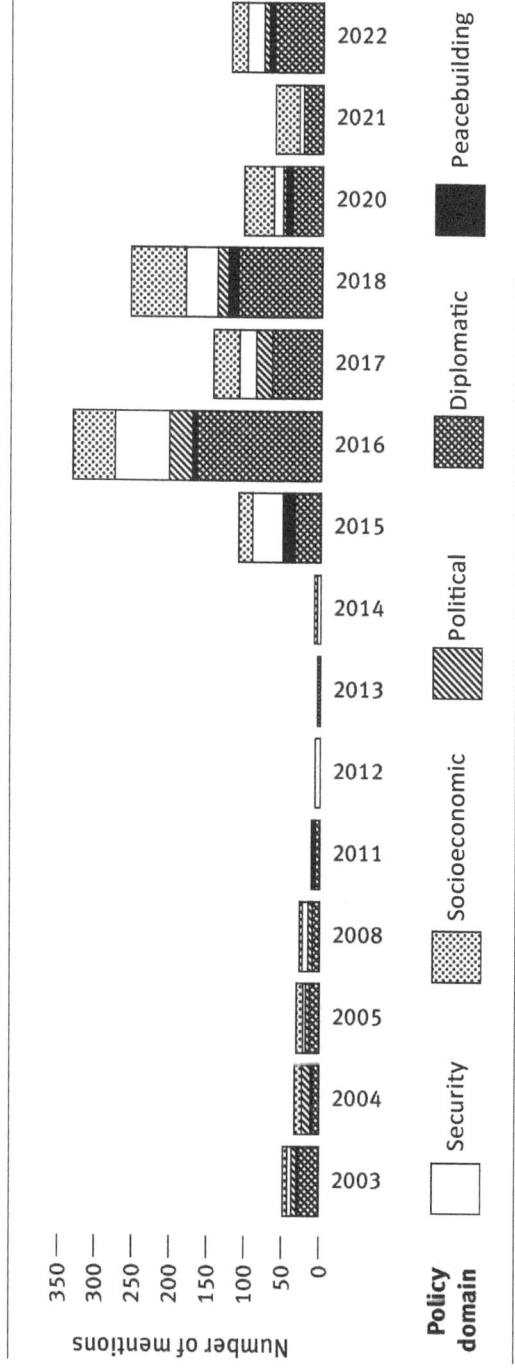

Figure 12.2

Table 12.1 The Combined Frequency of Mentions of the Five Policy Areas in Relevant EU Strategies and Policy Documents Between 2003 and 2022

Region	Political	Socioeconomic	Security	Diplomatic	Peacebuilding	Total
Western Balkans	40 / 10%	64 / 16%	93 / 24%	182 / 47%	11 / 3%	390
North Africa and the Sahel	34 / 7%	108 / 23%	98 / 21%	210 / 44%	27 / 6%	477
Middle East	72 / 12%	195 / 31%	72 / 12%	257 / 41%	29 / 5%	625
Total	146 / 10%	367 / 25%	263 / 18%	649 / 43%	67 / 4%	1492

Source: Authors' compilation based on own text analysis.

In general, political attention to terrorism and violent extremism increased thirty-fold between 2014 and 2016. It was primarily dedicated to the Middle East, specifically ISIS (Figure 12.3). In fact, as opposed to waning attention after 2003, the EU's renewed attention on radicalization, terrorism, and violent extremism after 2015 persisted, perhaps proof of a broader effort by EU member states to approach the challenge through EU structures.

There is an emerging prevalence of socioeconomic-oriented language in these key strategic and policy documents, thereby supporting the view that the EU makes a bona fide CT-P/CVE-relevant effort to tackle structural grievances that may be at the root of violent extremism, as is described at the primary level of the CT-P/CVE pyramid (Figure 12.1). On the other hand, as indicated in broad strokes by funding (non)priorities, the most notable finding is that language on democratic decisionmaking, governance, rule of law, human rights, conflict prevention, and peacebuilding is lacking in these strategy and policy documents.

These CT-P/CVE policy documents fit the vision laid out by the broader 2016 EU Global Strategy, which emphasizes the need to link internal EU CT-P/CVE policies with the EU's external action. The EU aimed to foster a "whole of government" approach to external action by creating an umbrella funding tool, the 2021 Neighbourhood, Development, and International Cooperation Instrument (NDICI) for a Global Europe. With this, it aimed to break down previous funding siloes and simplify its geographic and thematic programs to better respond to security-development nexus challenges and enhance the timely deployment of EU funding for pressing foreign policy needs (Debuysere and Blockmans 2019). Under the NDICI funding stream of the EU's current Multiannual Financial Framework run-

Figure 12.3 Middle East in EU Policy Documents

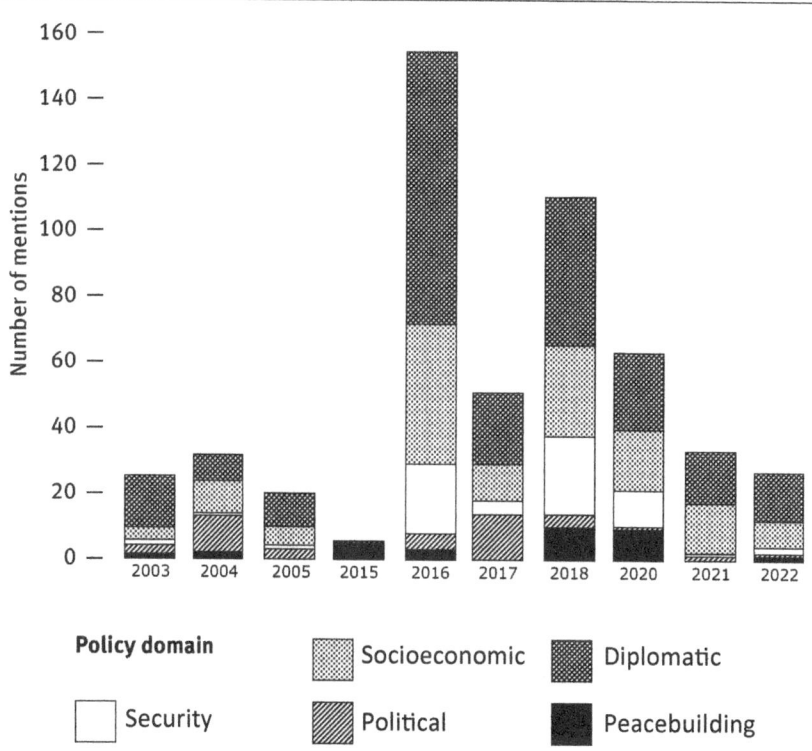

ning from 2021 to 2027, CT-P/CVE programs are funded through the geographic/thematic pillars of NDICI and, notably, are considered part and parcel of its development policy—where the EU can allocate significant financial resources.

The primary thematic program is "Peace, Stability and Conflict Prevention"; however, CT-P/CVE-relevant development-oriented funding can also be channeled through the NDICI's geographic pillars, and CT-P/CVE-specific actions may be funded through the Global Challenges and Rapid Response programs. Although we are unable to estimate the amount dedicated to the EU's CT-P/CVE-relevant engagements, about EUR 220 million is specifically dedicated to CT-P/CVE under the Peace, Stability, and Conflict Prevention stream (0.3 percent of NDICI's total allocation; see Figure 12.6). Significant resources are dedicated to the Middle East, North Africa, and the Sahel under the geographic portfolios, some of which may be CT-P/CVE-*relevant* interventions alongside those under the Global Challenges and Rapid Response pillars managed by the Commission's Service for Foreign Policy

Figure 12.4 North Africa and the Sahel in EU Policy Documents

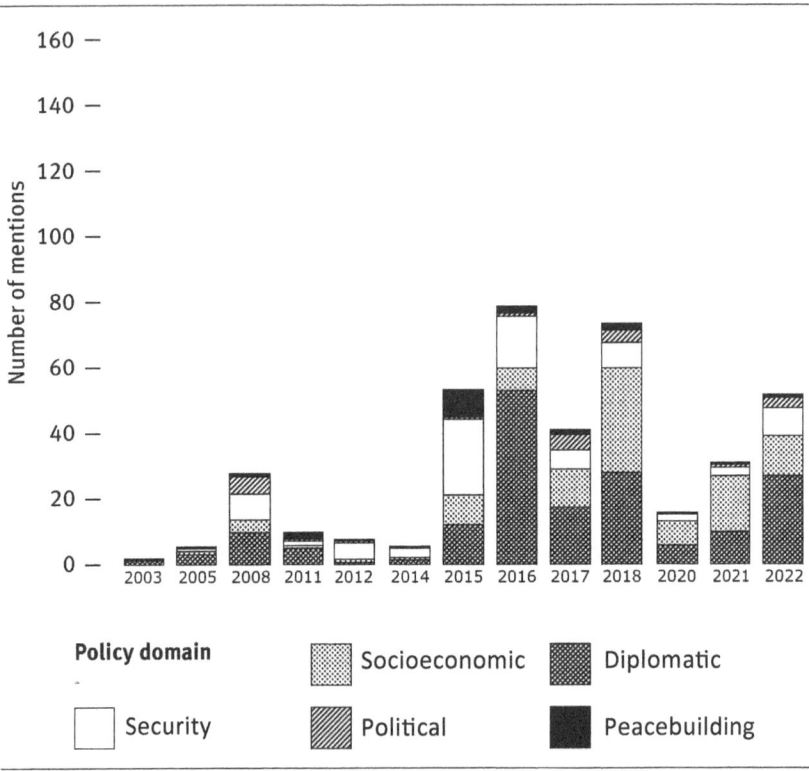

Instruments (Skare 2022). A further EUR 14.2 billion has been allocated to the Western Balkan countries and Turkey under the Instrument for Pre-Accession Assistance from 2021 to 2027 for rule of law, fundamental rights, and democracy (15 percent); good governance, EU acquis alignment, good neighborly relations, and strategic communications (17 percent); the green agenda and sustainable connectivity (42 percent); competitiveness and inclusive growth (22 percent); and cross-border cooperation (4 percent). Many of the areas touched here may be considered CT-P/CVE-relevant, too. Overall, the socioeconomic focus in EU documents is clearly mirrored by its funding.

Key Elements of the US CT-P/CVE Approach

Outlining the main characteristics of the approach the United States has taken to CT-P/CVE over the past twenty years can contextually ground the analysis of the EU's approach and provide a starting point for comparison.

Figure 12.5 Western Balkans in EU Policy Documents

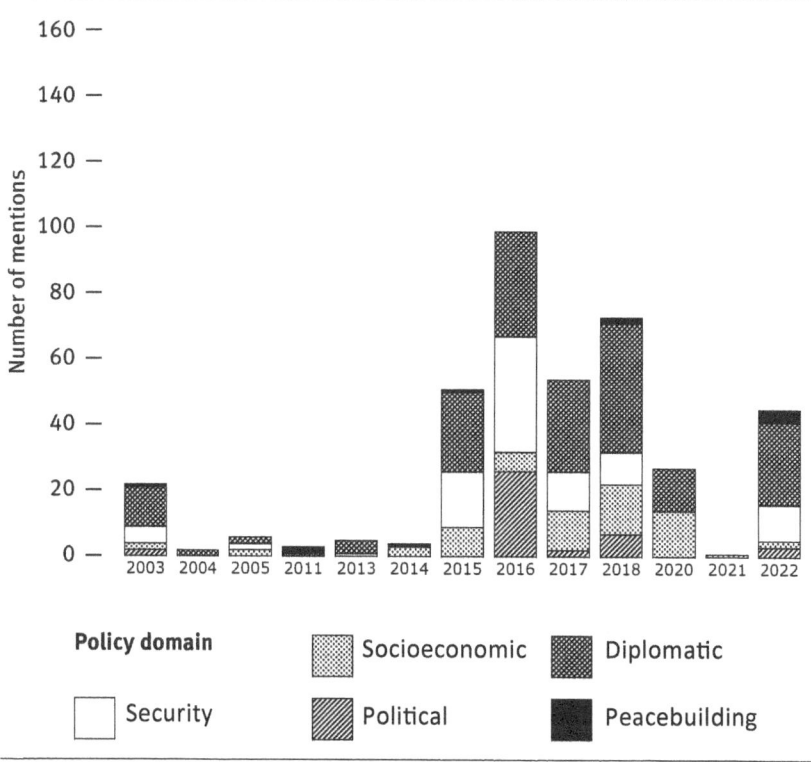

Like the EU, in the 2010s the United States began to acknowledge that a kinetic, security-based approach to CT and P/CVE had its limits. Whereas in tactical terms, the United States had been successful in thwarting attacks and eliminating terrorists since 2001, far more people were radicalized and were engaging in violent extremist activities than ten years prior, with a more fragmented and diversified picture of violent extremist groups operating globally. The White House's 2011 National Strategy for Counterterrorism and the US Agency for International Development's (USAID) first-ever government policy, "The Development Response to Violent Extremism and Insurgency," shed light on the need to target identified drivers ("push and pull factors"), such as grievances relating to socioeconomic marginalization, endemic corruption and elite impunity, and poor governance, in a coordinated, interagency fashion using military, civilian, diplomatic, development, communications, and business-related tools (Jenkins 2021; USAID 2011).

With the alleged defeat of ISIS, the 2018 National Defense Strategy under Donald Trump marked a shift in priorities. The strategy stated that

Figure 12.6 Breakdown of the 2021–2027 NDICI Multinational Financial Framework

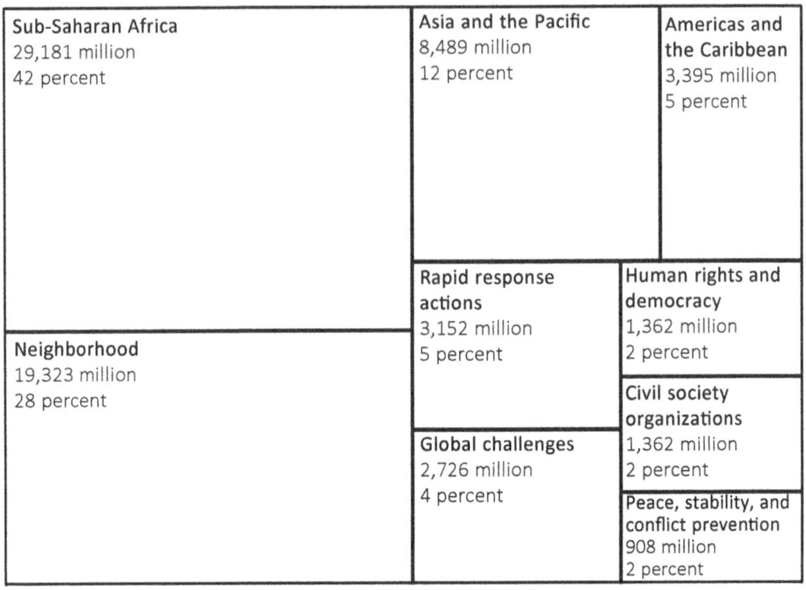

Sub-Saharan Africa 29,181 million 42 percent	Asia and the Pacific 8,489 million 12 percent	Americas and the Caribbean 3,395 million 5 percent
Neighborhood 19,323 million 28 percent	Rapid response actions 3,152 million 5 percent	Human rights and democracy 1,362 million 2 percent
		Civil society organizations 1,362 million 2 percent
	Global challenges 2,726 million 4 percent	Peace, stability, and conflict prevention 908 million 2 percent

Source: Authors' compilation via the NDICI regulation.
Note: In 2018 prices (EUR) and as a share of the NDICI portfolio.

"inter-state strategic competition" was the primary concern for US national security in reference to China and Russia as well as regional threats from states like North Korea and Iran (Levitt 2021, 4). In 2019, in continuity with policy shifts under the second Obama administration, Mark Mitchell, then acting US Assistant Secretary of Defense for Special Operations and Low-Intensity Conflict, acknowledged that "to achieve enduring results, we must ensure that our successes on the battlefield are complemented by well-resourced post-conflict stabilization efforts." He also acknowledged the United States' shortcomings in establishing a "prevention architecture to thwart terrorist radicalization and recruitment" (Levitt 2021, 21–24; Bast 2018).

Taking the Trump administration's approach one step further, the Biden administration prioritized diplomacy, international and local partnerships, and civilian-led capacity building as critical tools for CT-P/CVE. Washington sought to enable partners by providing intelligence and logistical support while only taking the lead in counterterrorism if terrorism posed a more critical threat to the United States or its vital interests abroad. At the same time, the Biden administration committed to programs on civilian capacity building, multilateral diplomacy, conflict prevention and stabilization, anti-corruption, and intelligence forecasting while continuing to fund tactical efforts as necessary (Levitt 2021, 5). Greater emphasis was put on law enforcement and the rule of law to limit terrorist radicalization and recruitment (Landberg 2021, 56). The Biden administration has also called for more significant investment in tools to avert threats before they become imminent. These adjustments help free funds for other foreign policy priorities and focus efforts on domestic terrorism and homegrown terrorists following the January 6, 2021, storming of the Capitol building. By enhancing its strategic focus elsewhere (e.g., the Indo-Pacific theater), the United States has since had to pursue CT-P/CVE on a tighter budget (Jenkins 2021, 67).

USAID's 2020 updated policy on P/CVE through development assistance acknowledges that the challenges posed by violent extremism have evolved, and the ability of violent extremist organizations to use violence has increased (USAID 2020, 4). Over the past decade, USAID and other donors have realized that strengthening and systematically influencing local institutions and communities has a more significant impact on radicalization and recruitment to violence than programs that aim to address specific drivers (USAID 2020, 4). The policy seeks to foster greater "self-reliance," with a vision of "ending the need for foreign assistance" by building capacity and commitment in partner countries across civil society, communities, individuals, the private sector, and governing institutions to enable them to eventually solve development challenges autonomously (USAID 2019). The goal is strengthening local institutions and whole-of-society ownership by working alongside partners. For example, USAID provides education, life skills, and other services to youth from marginalized communities where extremist recruitment cells are active and the authority of legitimate institutions is weak (USAID 2020, 6). The importance of engaging with and empowering local actors is emphasized in the 2020 strategy: "Government institutions, civil society, customary authorities, religious leaders, women's groups, youth organizations, the private sector, and communities must lead their own CVE efforts." USAID identifies resilience as key to whether and how radicalization or recruitment to violence occurs (USAID 2020, 11).

According to Ilkka Salmi, the EU counterterrorism coordinator (2021–2026), the Biden administration's shift from military action to civilian counterterrorism tools aligns the US approach with that of the EU (Salmi 2021, 17). Salmi adds that, although EU member states (particularly France, which has taken a leading role in military operations in the Sahel) have often supported American use of force to fight terrorist groups worldwide, a preventive, CT-P/CVE-*relevant* approach focusing on development and law enforcement is the preferred course of action as opposed to responding to imminent threats (frequently under strategies that the US labels as counterterrorism).

Addressing structural causes and drivers appears to be emphasized more broadly now. Dissecting the strategies, activities, and funding of US agencies reveals evidence suggesting that the United States sought to address the challenge in a CT-P/CVE-relevant rather than exclusively CT-P/CVE-specific manner before 2018, too.

US CT-P/CVE in Words and Funding

To unpack the US approach as a benchmark for comparison, we also analyzed national security and counterterrorism strategy documents from the US Department of State, USAID policy documents on preventing violent extremism (PVE), and their joint regional strategies. Since September 11, US CT-P/CVE efforts have focused on the Middle East, beginning with the Bush administration's efforts to dismantle al-Qaeda, starting with the "war on terror" in Afghanistan in 2001. To better understand the US approach to North Africa, the Sahel, and the Western Balkans, we added Country Reports on Terrorism (CRTs), Integrated Country Strategies (ICSs), and USAID development policies and funding documents to our database.

As in the analysis of the EU's approach, we used text-as-data methods to investigate variations in the US CT-P/CVE approach across regions. We examined how key documents approach the issues of radicalization, terrorism, and violent extremism in rhetoric associated with five policy areas: political, socioeconomic, security, diplomatic, and peacebuilding. To accomplish this, we reviewed 53 documents, including 25 general, policy-specific, and regional strategies and 28 ICSs. We focused on September 2002 to December 2022, beginning with the 2002 National Security Strategy adopted in the aftermath of September 11. Furthermore, because CRTs are annual global publications, we parsed the text to focus on the parts related to the three specific regions and their associated countries, resulting in a corpus of 221 documents.

We explored whether and how often language linked to five policy areas appears in designated policy instruments related to the regions. We investigated whether US strategies for CT/PVE vary among the three regions. In Table 12.2, we give an overview of the policies discussed about preventing terrorism and violent extremism in a particular region. The results (Table 12.2 and Figures 12.7–12.10) show that the US primarily relies on diplomatic rhetoric to discuss terrorism and violent extremism–related security challenges, followed by wording in the security and socioeconomic domains. There was a noticeable decrease in the emphasis on security-related rhetoric during the Trump and Biden administrations, with an increase in the share of wording related to socioeconomic, political, and

Table 12.2 The Combined Frequency of Mentions of the Five Policy Areas in Relevant US Strategies and Policy Documents Between 2002 and 2022

Region	Political	Socioeconomic	Security	Diplomatic	Peacebuilding	Total
Western Balkans	48 / 5%	203 / 20%	440 / 44%	295 / 29%	23 / 2%	1,009
North Africa and the Sahel	198 / 8%	559 / 24%	684 / 29%	884 / 38%	18 / 1%	2,343
Middle East	157 / 10%	412 / 27%	280 / 19%	629 / 42%	23 / 2%	1,501
Total	403 / 8.3%	1174 / 24.1%	1,404 / 28.9%	1,808 / 37.2%	64 / 1.3%	4,853

Source: Authors' compilation based on own text analysis.

diplomatic tools for CT-P/CVE. As in the EU documents, the language of good governance, conflict prevention, and peacebuilding is notably lacking in US policy documents.

Differences emerge when combining strategic documents such as general, regional, and Integrated Country Strategies with Country Reports on Terrorism. Diplomatic language is used concerning the Middle East, North Africa, and the Sahel, whereas security-related rhetoric and diplomacy are most prevalent in the Western Balkans. Security terminology remains significant in other regions, albeit less in the Middle East, which emphasizes socioeconomic measures. Regarding political attention, since 2021 the rise in policy documents regarding the Sahel has been sharp. The region has been prioritized as a result of concerns about the spread of extremist violence resulting from an enabling environment characterized by underlying development and governance issues; the prevalence of fragility, insecurity, and political conflict; and preexisting cycles of violence (USAID 2021).

An overview of CT-P/CVE funding also supports this view that US priorities have shifted and that the approach has become more comprehensive. According to a 2018 report by the Stimson Center, the United States spends around $175 billion (USD) per year on counterterrorism efforts, a reduction from the $260 billion that was spent annually in the immediate aftermath of September 11 (Levitt, Mulligan, and Costa 2021, 17; Stimson Study Group on Counterterrorism Spending 2018). Looking beyond CT-P/CVE-specific funding, CT-P/CVE-relevant funding offers a more holistic picture of the US approach. Strategies for and spending on programs related to CVE in the

Figure 12.7 CT-P/CVE Discourse by Policy Area in US Policy Documents

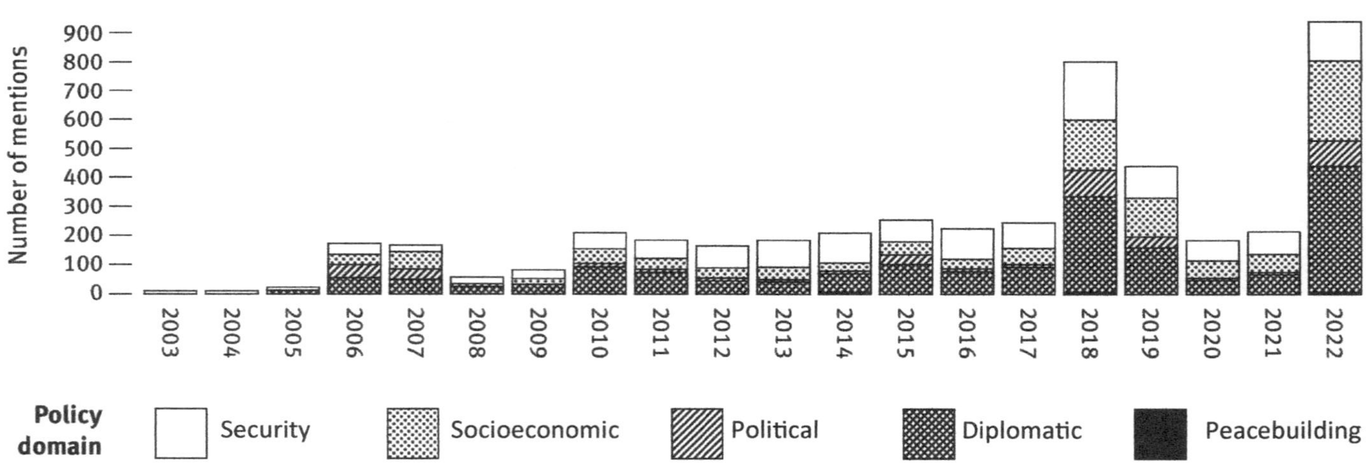

Figure 12.8 Middle East in US Policy Documents

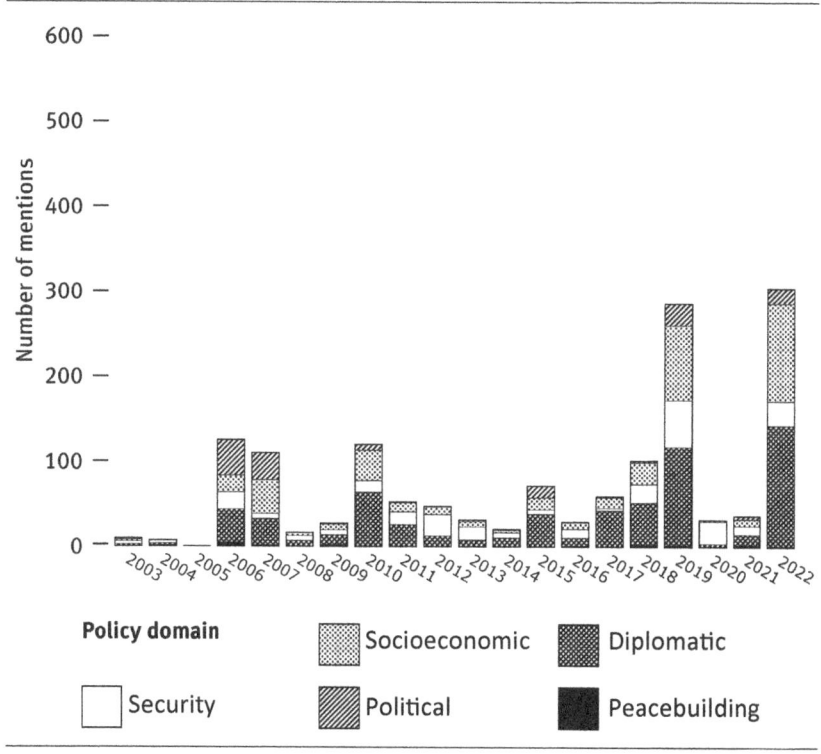

long run often come from separate agencies, budgets, and funding sources compared to those that are counterterrorism-specific (tackling the pressing security symptoms of violent extremism), which are usually connected to the Departments of Defense or Homeland Security. USAID is an independent government agency primarily responsible for civilian foreign aid and development assistance. Because it accounts for more than half of all US foreign assistance, USAID spending, primarily on peace and security-related development actions, can offer a good indication of how the United States structures allocations for CT-P/CVE-relevant engagement abroad and demonstrates how the more kinetic, military-focused approach is being retooled through a development lens.

By scrutinizing US foreign assistance disbursements in the prepandemic era between 2014–2020, we can reveal that the MENA region and South and Central Asia were the largest aid recipients. Significant portions of the aid resources are earmarked to the policy domain of peace and security. The second largest domain of focus in these regions was civilian programs

Figure 12.9 North Africa and the Sahel in US Policy Documents

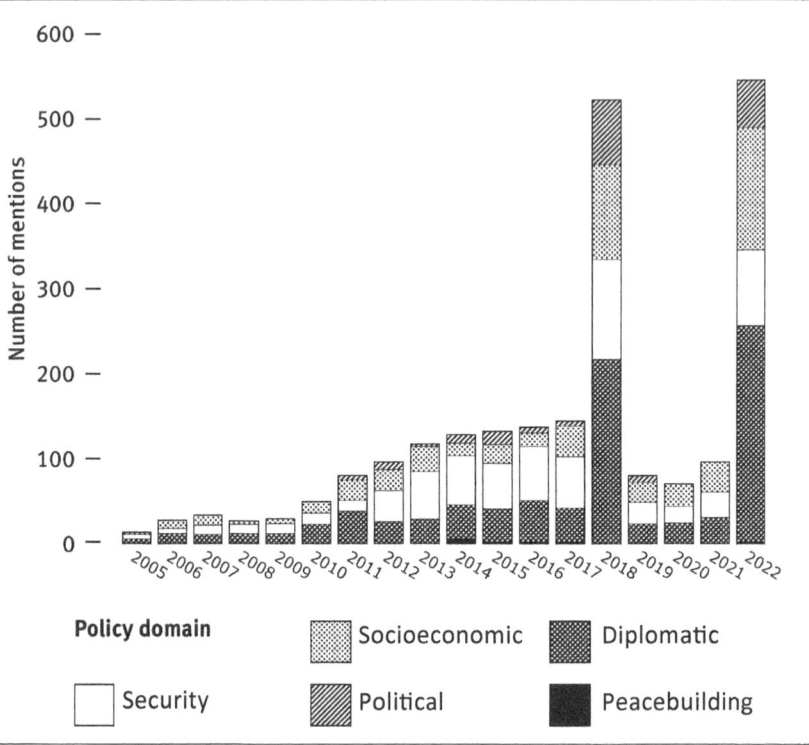

such as humanitarian assistance and governance-promoting initiatives. In comparison, in Sub-Saharan Africa (SSA), the policy domains of health and humanitarian assistance made up a substantial share of aid disbursements. SSA ranked as the third-largest recipient of US foreign aid, followed by the Western Hemisphere, Europe, and East Asia and Oceania. Aid programs that addresses better governance and human rights share, more or less, equal amount of aid with peace and security in the Western Hemisphere and in Europe, respectively.

The shifting funding priorities and the use of various approaches reflect the US-targeted efforts to address CT-P/CVE-*relevant* structural drivers (see Figure 12.7). From looking at USAID policy documents, we can discern that the United States has dedicated significant resources to kinetic responses to CT-P/CVE in Afghanistan, Iraq, and Syria. At the same time, and increasingly over the past ten years, the United States has adopted a long-term approach to violent extremism centered on addressing drivers and empowering local partners.

Figure 12.10 Western Balkans in US Policy Documents

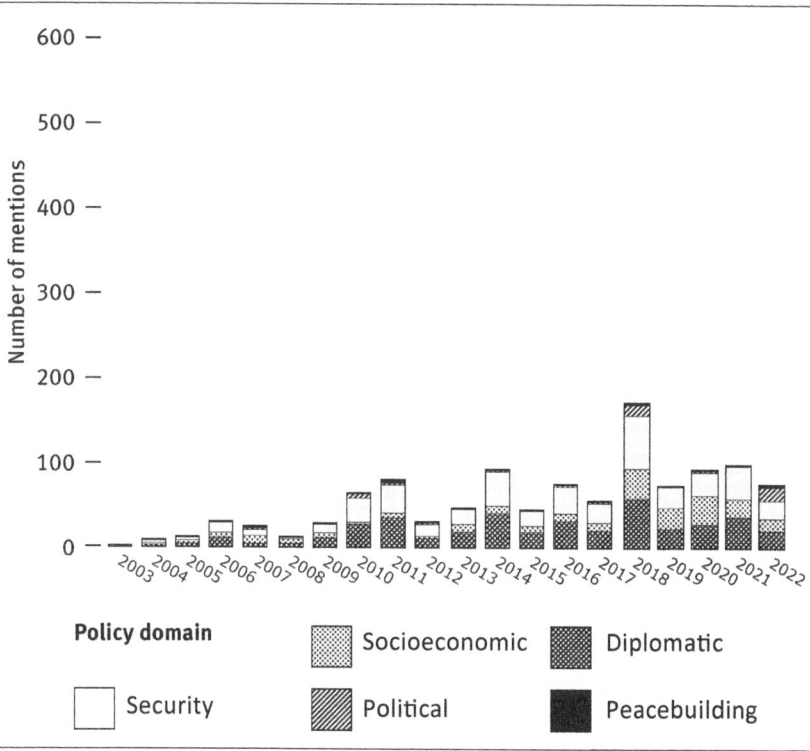

EU and US CT-P/CVE Approaches in Practice

The EU Approach in Practice

The text analysis and the overview of both the EU and US funding priorities demonstrate that there is considerable overlap between the areas identified as crucial for CT-P/CVE-*relevant* intervention by academic literature and the type of language used by EU and US policy documents and the funding. Considering the aforementioned CT-P/CVE pyramid (Figure 12.1), the current focus of both EU and US intervention is at the primary, developmental, resource-oriented level (in the socioeconomic domain), a *conditio sine qua non* for any CT-P/CVE activities. Whereas this has been the case for the EU since the beginning, there has been a gradual shift in the US approach since it became evident that the more security-oriented approach had not produced its intended outcome: a reduction in VE activities worldwide.

On the basis of the evidence, we can see that the EU and the United States struggle to address good governance, democracy, human rights, and peace. The EU dedicates only 14 percent of space in CT-P/CVE policy documents to the language of governance and peace across the Western Balkans, North Africa, Middle East, and the Sahel, and only 3.25 percent of its funding to human rights, democracy, peace, stability, and conflict prevention. We conducted semistructured interviews with EU officials to further unpack the puzzle and synthesize common threads in the EU's CT-P/CVE approach. Triangulating context, policy guidance, and funding with the views of EU policymakers helps complete the picture of the EU's external approach to CT-P/CVE.

Previous research identified shortfalls in the EU's CT-P/CVE-*specific* approach. In the Sahel, for example, this research indicated that the language of "principled pragmatism" has resulted in an emphasis on security cooperation with (authoritarian) governments, which disregards good governance (Bøås et al. 2021). The focus on drivers of violent extremism in the Middle East and North Africa, rather than factors of resilience and drivers of nonoccurrence, has led the EU to focus on border management and security challenges rather than promoting social cohesion, encouraging moderate voices, fighting hate speech, supporting good governance, and building stakeholder capacities (Skare 2021). On the other hand, research suggests that the EU's policy toward the Western Balkans has been framed differently, with a greater focus on community-level rather than security-related initiatives to build resilience, an approach likely tailored to consider these countries' EU membership perspectives (Mishkova et al. 2021). Previous research indicates that, to achieve their objective successfully, CT-P/CVE-*specific* policies must avoid emphasizing security concerns and strengthen their focus on good governance, community resilience, and social justice (Ben-Nun and Engel 2022).

As such, several adjustments to the EU's action have been identified in previous research. First, the EU concentrates its efforts on communities that are considered at risk. This may lead to negligence toward communities considered resilient and foster grievances in those communities not receiving political attention or funding (Mishkova et al. 2021). In some cases, groups identified as disproportionately at risk of radicalization are marginalized at the intracommunity level, thereby creating a vicious cycle requiring additional efforts to provide channels for dialogue and socialization (Mishkova et al. 2021). Second, the EU's engagement should build upon its important youth component and seek to identify (religious) community leaders as another entry point for engagement, because these medium-level leaders are essential for meaningful consultation as well as channeling needs (e.g., better public service delivery, enhanced economic opportunity, access to education) toward higher decisionmaking levels.

In a series of interviews with policymakers in the European Commission and European External Action Service (EEAS), as well as with officers in EU delegations on the ground, we tried to glean common elements of the EU's CT-P/CVE policy in practice, which challenges were faced and mitigating strategies adopted, and provide country-specific examples where relevant. After all, it is difficult to compare and contrast the EU's approach in each region because of differing interests, threat perceptions, and levels of engagement and the dynamic nature of policymaking. In our effort to understand the EU's approach to intervention, we examined whether its efforts in countering terrorism and preventing violent extremism could withstand external scrutiny in terms of balancing democracy and security. This is done by addressing the developmental resource-related grievances that can lead to radicalization and by adhering to the principle of "do no harm" in its development and diplomatic endeavors. If, as our conceptual and evidence base suggests, we should expand our scope of analysis to include CT-P/CVE-*relevant* activities rather than only those that are CT-P/CVE-*specific*, we find that the EU adopts a holistic approach to the socioeconomic development of partner countries with positive spillover for its CT-P/CVE objectives while simultaneously struggling to address good governance, democracy, human rights, and peace. Interviews conducted with EU policymakers indicate that this should be attributed to the fact that CT-P/CVE is but one element of a broader diplomatic balancing act with third countries.

According to some, "key [third country] partners have little interest in giving up their privileges by promoting democracy, strengthening civil society, or implementing improved governance" (Skare 2022). Our interviews revealed that when there is ample space for upstream action, the EU's CT-P/CVE engagements are formulated in context-responsive ways to best consider local needs, cultural specificities, and varying incentives for radicalization. Counter to a straightforward democracy *versus* security narrative in some literature, interviews with officials corroborate the main findings of the text analysis: a broad array of considerations, including socioeconomic development, factor into the EU's design of CT-P/CVE activities, both *relevant* and *specific*. They highlighted that because strategy implementation occurs on the basis of needs jointly identified with third-country authorities, the EU primarily implements what it can in a CT-P/CVE-*relevant* way, with a prevention focus on the socioeconomic domain rather than through CT-P/CVE-*specific* measures. When designing CT-P/CVE engagements, a partnership is necessary. For example, security sector reform cannot occur without engaging with a country's security forces, and educational programming cannot be done without cooperating with a third country's education ministry, and so on.

Cooperation with third countries is also a prerequisite for context-sensitive policies at the subnational level. As such, EU engagement with

CT-P/CVE relevance (considered as such by the practitioners) often takes shape at the local level, allowing for more in-depth engagement, albeit limited in geographic scope. Context is of utmost importance: insurgencies, such as those in the Sahel, require different forms of engagement than repression-driven grievances in authoritarian regimes in the Middle East or organized crime-funded ethnonationalist extremism in the Western Balkans. In line with what peacebuilding academics and practitioners have advocated for (European Commission 2014), the EU uses comprehensive context and conflict analysis to identify areas where social grievances may be exploited by terrorist and violent extremist organizations to radicalize and mobilize certain groups to ensure their engagement is conflict-sensitive. It also respects the principle of "do no harm" (European Parliament and Council of the EU 2021a, b). In the Sahel and North Africa, for instance, policies are often focused on criminal justice, that is, law enforcement cooperation and the effectiveness of the judicial system (Key Stakeholder Dialogue 1). In the Western Balkans, the approach changes to promoting civilian capacity building, such as in public administration, given prospective EU membership (Mishkova et al. 2021).

The ability to partner also depends on other contextual factors outside the EU's immediate control. For example, the broader the reach of extremist activities within a country, the harder it becomes for the EU to engage in P/CVE actions and the greater the urgency to adapt to a changed security environment through more security-oriented crisis management activities. At times, it is not politically desirable within the EU to interact with national authorities if they are considered to be grossly violating human rights. This is the case with northern Syria, where engagement with national and Turkish authorities raises political eyebrows.

Moreover, national or local authorities may inhibit any EU engagement because of their desire to reset the terms of engagement with the EU, possibly under the influence of other external actors or because that engagement could present itself as a risk for those regimes' authoritarian control. For instance, EU engagement in the Sahel is severely constrained by those countries' perceptions of the EU and its member states. In Mali, military authorities have constrained the scope of action of CSOs, some of which are EU implementing partners. Indeed, some of the most challenging environments for the EU are in countries that depend on actors such as China and Russia in the economic and political-security spheres (respectively) or that have strong ideological ties, particularly to Wahhabism. In the case of the Western Balkans, both the EU and national authorities struggle to broadly address the challenges posed by violent extremism because of the general implications this would have for those countries' progress on EU accession. The EU's engagement passes from being context-responsive to becoming context-constrained because the primary conditions for longer-term engagement are lacking. The result is an attempt to concretely address particular security challenges that are limited in scope.

The EU also faces difficulties in deconstructing the language of extremism, combating disinformation, and implementing effective strategic communications. These challenges are further exacerbated by those related to designing and implementing communications and awareness-raising campaigns that provide robust and credible alternatives to radical narratives inherent to reactionary schools of Islamic thought or far right extremist propaganda. Practitioners refer to the challenge of successfully sustaining a valid counternarrative in the face of accusations that the EU endorses double standards.

To mitigate these constraints, EU practitioners reveal a tendency to reflect on how their engagement could best be tailored in a conflict-sensitive way. In Libya, for example, this has included reinforcing de-mining, supporting the establishment of fact-checking platforms, promoting social dialogue to address hate speech, and providing channels for vocational training to former combatants. In Mali, the EU responded to worsening violence by supporting efforts to integrate state security forces to include northern Tuareg in their ranks as a way to build ties with local communities during stabilization operations—activities that have been severely constrained, if not discontinued, since the second half of 2022. Another mitigating strategy is for the EU to rely on significant diplomatic engagement with national and local authorities. In Tunisia, for example, close cooperation with authorities allows the EU to engage with former detainees.

A common thread throughout conversations was that to address these challenges, facilitate effective implementation, and successfully communicate positive results, the EU's CT-P/CVE activities must also be implemented in cooperation with locally embedded, trusted, and knowledgeable CSOs. In turn, local CSOs provide the EU with additional and valuable intelligence to better frame and target CT-P/CVE engagements. Authorities can limit CSO engagement to the CT-P/CVE-*relevant* realm because civil society empowerment runs counter to their interest in maintaining political control (Skare 2022; European Commission 2014). Also, identifying and empowering trusted interlocutors perceived as legitimate by local communities is a challenge in and of itself. Moreover, EU officials state that adopting a CT-P/CVE-*specific* focus identifying the mitigation of radicalization and extremism as concrete objectives may achieve the opposite effect: decreasing buy-in to those activities from local populations that have become "labeled" as vulnerable to violent extremism.

As such, actions with CT-P/CVE-*specific* objectives may be billed more broadly to enhance their acceptability and extend their reach. If politically acceptable, this occurs through the lens of security sector reform or capacity building. Otherwise, the focus begins to overlap with broader

CT-P/CVE-*relevant* activities targeting economic opportunity and growth or social cohesion. In Tunisia, for example, an implementing partner with strong links with civil society, national ministries, and former detainees has been supported by the EU in efforts to match former detainees with companies to offer gainful employment and break the cycle of violence.

Security is an element considered by EU practitioners in their engagement, which is by no means inward looking and which attempts to support local communities. If anything, EU CT-P/CVE attempts to address various policy areas—education, public service delivery, security sector, et cetera—recognized as necessary to addressing structural drivers of CT-P/CVE. Contrary to observations in the literature, EU policymakers are cognizant of the risks of using language related to terrorism and violent extremism, including in the security sphere. One possibility is that this may alienate the EU's diplomatic counterparts in third countries; another is that it may lead those countries to use the language of violent extremism to justify repressive policies (Skare 2022).

Also, building on recommendations from the peacebuilding community (European Commission 2014), interviews with practitioners revealed the EU's attention to the gender dimension. Policy formulation takes gender sensitivity seriously and benefits from targeting women because of their role in framing family and social norms, such as caretaking and education. Yet, several conversations highlighted that local traditional beliefs about gender roles could challenge efforts to enhance female empowerment, a crosscutting consideration in religiously conservative societies.

The choices EU officials face to address constraints at the local level are often highly political and involve critical discussions about governance. However, their ability to address those political topics is diplomatically limited, which is also due to limited human and financial resources. The result is that the EU implements a broad array of programs that may be construed as CT-P/CVE-*relevant* while lacking the good governance, democracy, human rights, and peacebuilding focus they might require. The cumulated effect of needing to partner with third countries, respond to local needs, speak the same "language" as local communities in strategic communications, ensure the conflict sensitivity of the EU's approach, balance against the intervention of other third countries, and enhance local buy-in means that the EU's CT-P/CVE engagement often settles for the lowest-common-denominator solution. Attention toward socioeconomic development then emerges rather than toward activities to promote good governance, human rights, and peacebuilding.

As is apparent, the EU's CT-P/CVE approach is not just context considerate but teeters on being context-constrained, so the key elements receive less attention and become atomized across the EU's CT-P/CVE action in specific contexts. Although the EU lacks a systematic focus on good governance and social justice, it cannot be said that the EU's priority is to emphasize security-related elements of its external action at the expense of efforts to promote good governance in third countries, which would unintentionally undermine its CT-P/CVE policies.

The US Approach in Practice

Thematically, USAID has identified *local resilience* as key to whether and how radicalization or recruitment into extremist violence occurs (USAID 2020, 6–11). On the ground, this has translated into funding for and partnerships with local leaders. For example, in Niger, USAID has worked with civil society leaders to create the Nalewa Mada network, aimed at enhancing resilience against Boko Haram and the so-called Islamic State–West Africa Province. The network includes more than three hundred religious, traditional, youth, and women leaders in thirty villages. Further, USAID has acknowledged that the exclusion of women has led to communal instability and fueled violent extremism. As a result, USAID concentrates funding on promoting women's participation in peace and security processes, for example, through the SHE WINS (Supporting Her Empowerment: Women's Inclusion for New Security) initiative that aims to provide grants and technical assistance to CSOs across Africa, the Middle East, and North Africa led by women (Mendoza and Zurka 2021). As a further testament to efforts toward bolstering local resilience by empowering local actors, USAID allocates funding to reinforce community resilience and support local voices that provide alternative storylines to those pushed by violent extremist groups (Mendoza and Zurka 2021).

Western Balkan countries do not feature prominently in US CT-P/CVE strategies, yet examples can be found in Country Reports on Terrorism. These suggest that the return of foreign fighters is a main concern, along with weak institutions, organized crime, and corruption. For example, in Albania, US agencies have worked closely with the State Police Counterterrorism Unit (CTU) to align government training and equipment requirements with US expertise and resources. While this seems to indicate a security-driven approach, by looking into funding disbursements in both amount and priorities, we see the United States dedicates much attention to issues that may be P/CVE-*relevant*. Additionally, working with local law enforcement complies with the logic of addressing structural issues such as strengthening regional institutions and the rule of law. In overall US foreign assistance disbursements to Albania for 2021, the top sector to receive aid was "conflict, peace and security," closely followed by "government and civil society," with governance ($12 million) also receiving some funding.

Despite ambitions, the goal of fostering local resilience does not always match realities on the ground. In 2018, the United States adopted the Stabilization Assistance Framework to reinforce donors' ambition to coordinate bottom-up, context-specific, and locally informed efforts to build on preexisting capacities in fragile states such as Iraq, Libya, and Mali. However, in the case of Syria, the political-military realities of the war progressively undermined the intended effects of such programs. Moreover, as time passed, local political assistance diverged progressively from US high-level policy decisions (Brown 2018).

Conclusion

Reviewing general concepts discerned from previous research, analyzing key policy documents, tracing the rhetoric and funding, and conducting interviews with key policymakers in the EU institutions has moved the needle in research on the EU and US CT-P/CVE approaches. Transcending the democracy versus security scholarly debate, this chapter emphasizes how the EU and the United States—in their words and deeds—pay significant attention to third countries' development needs, which often lie at the root of radicalization to violent extremism and terrorism. Whereas this has been part of the EU approach since the beginning, the United States has gradually become more holistic, increasingly addressing the structural fragilities and enabling factors that drive its occurrence more comprehensively.

By doing so, both the EU and US CT-P/CVE policies stand against criticism of undue emphasis on security concerns, an approach that, if implemented, would undermine the success of their CT-P/CVE activities. In comparing the EU and US cases, our research acknowledges that *specific* CT-P/CVE policies and responses have failed to address the full spectrum of VE's structural issues, drivers, and push/pull factors. Looking into development policy, funding, and practice does, however, demonstrate awareness and efforts to adopt a more holistic, CT-P/CVE-*relevant* response by addressing structural issues, developmental needs, and target drivers across regions. Though it is difficult to assess whether these efforts intend to target radicalization and violent extremism, interviews with EU officials point to why they may avoid explicitly labeling policies as CT-P/CVE.

Despite attempts to make their policies context-sensitive, garner local ownership of projects, and enhance gender responsiveness, the main challenge for both actors is a lack of systematic focus on good governance and social justice in external CT-P/CVE approaches. It is vital to consider radicalization processes as ongoing social phenomena that take place in a space where several actors vie for material and ideational resources. Therefore, they require careful assessment and multiscalar prioritization, including at the regional and transnational levels (Raineri and Strazzari, this volume).

Notes

1. We would like to acknowledge the valuable contributions of Leonardo De Agostini and Linus Vermeulen to the research underpinning this chapter. We also thank Morten Bøås and Kari Osland for their detailed comments and feedback. Last, we thank EU officials for their availability for interviews and candor in discussions about key research findings.

2. We use a methodology familiar to readers of M. Furness and S. Gänzle (2016).

3. We collected and analyzed relevant strategy and policy documents from 2002 to 2022 using text-as-data methods. These documents provided insights into the EU and the US positions on counterterrorism/violent extremism and their regional and country-specific priorities. As such, they serve as the basis for a systematic comparison between the CT-P/CVE approaches of the EU and United States. Using text-as-data methods, we investigated the variations in the US CT-P/CVE approach across the Western Balkans, the Sahel, Middle East, and North Africa. We examined how they approached the issues of radicalization, terrorism, and violent extremism in five policy areas (widely defined): political, socioeconomic, security, diplomatic, and peacebuilding. Please contact coauthor Tatjana Stankovic for a list of strategic documents and a methodological overview of the text analysis.

4. Please contact coauthor Dylan Macchiarini Crosson for more information about the interviews, public events, and key stakeholder dialogues that formed part of the empirical basis for this chapter.

13

Implications for Policy and Future Research

Ulf Engel, Gilad Ben-Nun, Morten Bøås, and Kari Osland

The conceptual innovation at the core of this volume is the focus on the nonoccurrence of violent extremism in what we call enabling environments. The Balkans, the Middle East, and North Africa—the world regions where we and our partners conducted research—are characterized by precarious living conditions, potentially making them fertile ground for radical ideas. And yet, despite genuine grievances and legitimate grounds for anger, most people living in these regions are not radicalized and do not embrace ideas that lead to acts of violent extremism. To increase our understanding of local community resilience toward violent extremism, we probed the nonoccurrence of violent extremism in enabling environments. And we asked why some communities are more likely to experience violent extremism than others.

Given the heterogeneous spatiality and sociology of the Balkans, the Middle East, and North Africa, with their unique historical, social, and cultural characteristics, the methodology employed in this volume had to be sensitive to the limits but also the opportunities for cross-cultural comparison. This ruled out straightforward political science, most-similar/most-different systems designs, and other forms of conceptual Eurocentrism. Instead, we opted for a global studies approach that emphasizes the topic's historicity and the researcher's positionality (see Engel and Gelot 2021). At the epistemological level, we have tried to do justice to this challenge by focusing on a careful empirical bottom-up analysis to identify local context conditions and avoid hasty generalizations. Second, we developed a new ontology by introducing the notion of an enabling environment. This lens allowed us to relate empirical observations in seemingly noncomparable world regions and to connect them to other analytical categories that were consciously context-sensitive (such as "violent extremism"). Third, where possible, we focused on the transregional entanglements that connect our case studies—for instance, the role of diaspora communities, certain expressions of Islam (e.g., Hanbali-Wahabi Islam), or foreign fighter returnees.

To deal with the inherent limits of cross-cultural comparison and a possible Eurocentric bias, we conducted our research in close collaboration with local stakeholders and mixed research teams in every country where we did fieldwork. Reflecting our positionalities has been a permanent, reiterative process. We hope the findings presented in the various chapters do justice to the politics and cosmologies of the actors we have researched. In this last chapter, we offer a comparative synthesis, and on that basis, we discuss the implications of our conclusions regarding policy and future research.

Three Comparative Lessons

Seen through the wide optical prism of the case studies and the methodological approach explained earlier, several key lessons emerge. The first and perhaps most salient lesson concerns the issue of trust in governance, over, above, and beyond whether a particular society adheres to democracy in the more Western understandings implied by this term. In their approach to tackling extremism, Western actors have all too often resorted to a thematic focus centered on the conduct of elections, often without paying sufficient attention to structural parameters of social cohesion and societal resilience toward extremism as it manifests through more traditionally embedded long-standing local governance structures. As seen in Tunisia, elections, once held in high regard, seem meaningless in retrospect once the entire political edifice upon which they rest suffers an almost complete "governmental cardiac arrest." In contrast, places such as Jordan and Morocco, which back in the day were rebutted for their partial electoral politics, emerge as relative bastions of stability and, indeed, of increased measures of democracy over the *longue durée*. Structural stability, social cohesion, and measures of public trust should be put much more at the center of Western policies than the mere measure of whether or not elections have been held and the allegedly abstract measure of the extent elections are or are not representative of so-called public opinion.

The second generic lesson from our work concerns economic conditions that intertwine with violent extremism. Across the board and almost without exception, notwithstanding the radically divergent social and regional environments within which our case studies were situated, dire economic conditions virtually always trumped ideological or doctrinal motivations to engage in violent extremism. From Kosovo to Mali and Niger, and from Tunisia to Iraq, economic drivers and especially youth unemployment were, more often than not, at the heart of people's drive toward extremism. And vice versa: in countries such as Morocco, where a focus on strong economic development via major structural investment into broad infrastructure projects ensues, violent extremism could be mitigated. While many Arab countries' GDP per capita ran lower in 2021 than a decade earlier in 2011, at the beginning of the popular uprisings, Morocco and Jordan were two of the few countries that saw their GDP per capita grow steadily through this decade. Correspondingly, it is little wonder that Egypt has embarked on similar major infrastructure investments, to tackle economic woes, while reasoning that these run to the heart of its violent extremism challenges. Much of the same can be said of the economic hardships of Western Balkan countries, with a possible relationship between the mitigation of violent conditions and the prospects of European Union (EU) accession, and its apparent economic benefits. Since September 11, all too often, Western powers have resorted to seeing violent extremism primarily through a narrower security-related lens. It is high time to bring back the focus on economic conditions, because they relate to long-term governance and social cohesion perspectives at center stage.

The last general lesson is probably the most straightforward and has to do with Western military interventions, especially within Islamic countries. From Iraq to Afghanistan, Mali, and the Sahel and the North Atlantic Treaty Organization (NATO) bombing and Western-forced regime change in Libya, it is by now exceedingly clear that such military interventions by Western powers only breed further calls for violent extremism yet achieve virtually no result in mitigating it. The last failure in this regard is the interventions by France, the United Nations (UN), and the European Union in the Sahel. The demands of host countries that France (e.g., Mali, Niger, and Burkina Faso) and the UN (e.g., Mali) leave have been written off way too easily as examples of "democratic backsliding" and Russian interference. However, if this is a case of democratic backsliding, there should have been a previous process of democratic progress. For those who have lived through the ten years of international intervention (2013–2023), it is difficult to see this. The only thing they have got from the elections that took place in this period and the interventions by France, the UN, and the EU is more violence, jihadi insurgents that come steadily closer to capital areas, and the right to vote for a political class that are only good at mismanagement and corruption. There are some painful lessons that the international community should draw from its ten years of massive involvement in the Sahel (see Osland and Erstad 2020; Bøås 2025). The question is whether this will be done in the honest manner that it should be.

Implications for Policy

Violent extremism is more than religious extremism that draws on radical Islamic theology. It can also be ethnonational and have an extremist right-wing agenda, as the cases of Bosnia and Serbia (see Chapter 7) have shown. However, it also cannot be denied that during the last decades, a significant challenge has been how to deal with Islamic violent extremism. How to work with Muslim-majority societies is, therefore, a key issue. Cooperation with religious authorities, most notably with high Muslim councils, is essential both for the success of violence-mitigating activities and, more broadly, for the attainment of social buy-in. That said, non-Muslim interlocutors dealing with Muslim-majority societies should pay heed and, by and large, avoid entering the doctrinal spheres of Islam and engaging in theological change efforts. The standing of legitimately recognized Muslim bodies should be enhanced and empowered to act against violent extremism. Yet, neither the European Union nor the United States have the intricate knowledge needed to delve into efforts at theological Islamic change.

With that said, and even under conditions where violence occurs, policies should avoid an all-out securitization of everything Islamic. Most traditionalists are not Salafists, and even most Salafists are certainly not terrorists. Understanding the nuances of religious consultation and focusing on work with community elders can facilitate extremism mitigation efforts.

This volume shows that when we navigate the murky waters of violent extremism, what is revealed is a complex socioeconomic mosaic that reaches far beyond ideology. Addressing the root causes may, therefore, hold the key to preventing and countering violent extremism. As we already have stated, the intense focus on the manifestations of violent extremism and the persons behind them also, unfortunately, contributed to the creation of a blind zone. Not only the leaders of groups like al-Qaeda and the Islamic State but also their rank-and-file fighters and followers around the globe were considered die-hard violent extremist militants. People were so fully radicalized into the world of violent extremism that a violent extremist agenda had come to engulf their entire persona.

There is no doubt that radicalized leaders and cadres exist. However, not necessarily all of those involved are radicalized. For those who do become radicalized, the journey into violent extremism tends to start elsewhere than with religion or ideology. The journey into extremism is not disconnected from their ordinary lives but a pathway to provide an alternative social order to improve life chances. It is, therefore, the turn to extremist worldviews that we need to understand.

What this means is that becoming part of an armed movement that commonly is defined as a terrorist group may have less to do with an all-consuming conviction to the ideology of extremism but rather could instead be a pragmatic pose that is context determined.

This has important policy implications. If somebody has gone through a process of radicalization and ends up as a being of pure conviction, it makes sense to focus on programs of deradicalization as the pathway out of extremism. However, if the journey into extremism is much more determined by a person's context, the circumstances of their situation, foregrounding deradicalization may have little effect and could even lead to unintended results if the person is labeled a danger to society. Focusing on the material dynamics that made a person turn to extremism may yield better and more sustainable results. Therefore, policies and programming that take seriously the material grievances that provoke extremism are crucial.

Likewise, much ado has been made about the anti-state and anti-modernity agenda of contemporary violent extremist movements. However, if many of those who embarked on the journey to extremism did so not out of religious conviction or ideological motivation, we have good reason to believe that what they crave isn't a return to a medieval state. Instead, they may search for modernity and a state that works *for* them and not as they have experienced modernity, which is not for them, and a state that works *against* them. Policies and programming that take the lived experiences of these people into consideration, therefore, have a much better chance of yielding positive results than those that see radicalization as a closed door of conviction. If we want to bring people back from the world of violent extremism, we need to seriously examine why they took this path in the first place.

Future Research

This volume's conceptual work and the comparisons presented in the case studies indicate a need for further research in several areas. The conventional approach would be to compartmentalize the research within the confines of bounded disciplinary fields, for instance, (1) international relations, international studies, and global studies; (2) peace and security studies, critical security studies, and (3) area studies. However, our work has demonstrated the added value of transcending disciplinary boundaries and bringing together people from different disciplinary backgrounds and academic training in different parts of the world. The workflow may not always have been the most straightforward, but repeated rounds of critical reviews of how we implemented our research agendas and interpreting the results collectively helped develop the innovative perspectives presented in this volume.

The comparative method we used invites further comparisons and determining which comparison design is most promising. Bringing in other actors (such as regional organizations, interregional organizations, private sector organizations, and civil society networks) to research in different cultural and religious settings (e.g., Southeast Asia) and in more world regions (e.g., the Horn of Africa, Latin America) would undoubtedly add to the overall understanding of the occurrence and nonoccurrence of violent extremism in enabling environments.

Among the loose ends or promising avenues of inquiry is the question of transnational and transregional entanglements. These include connections between local places and diaspora spaces, the sociology of migration of violent extremists, and the role of external agents in manipulating and polarizing public discourse and undermining governance. The latter includes actors traditionally considered "out of region" (think, Russia) but also neighbors or forces in the vicinity of conflict landscapes (e.g., Iran, but also Turkey, Saudi Arabia, the United Arab Emirates, and Qatar). This question is closely linked to the political economy of violent extremism. As important as it is to reconstruct the way that violent extremists are financing themselves or are being financed, there also is a potential to investigate the political economy of the nonoccurrence of violent extremism.

Some chapter authors have identified concrete questions that merit further investigation. On the concept of social cohesion, future research needs to examine non-Western cosmologies and their practical relevance in daily life, or lack thereof. This could help recalibrate indices and barometers and make comparisons even more fruitful. In this respect, gendered perspectives and consideration of intersectionality can be strengthened. In addition, research into cultures of remembrance, art, and popular culture will contribute to a better understanding of the local dynamics associated with the occurrence and nonoccurrence of violent conflicts. More emphasis should be put on fine-tuning the definition of resilience vis-à-vis other fields of research (e.g., resilience in the context of transnational organized crime is defined and measured differently from what is proposed in this volume). More systematic comparisons of cases and contexts can be undertaken. More knowledge needs to be created on community leaders' capacity to withstand extremist pressure. On the topic of religion, at least two questions can be posed: Is there a nexus between the decline of Islamist extremism and the rise of extremist ethnonationalism? Is there causality between the Sharifian composition of the kingdoms of Morocco and Jordan and their apparent relative political stability?

Finally, an academic evaluation of nonmilitary interventions in conflicts in general, and structural conflict prevention in particular, is urgently needed to establish lessons learned and best practices to help make these interventions more sustainable in theory and practice. The empirical evidence discussed in this volume suggests a close relationship between locally owned preventive actions and the nonoccurrence of violent extremism. However, further robust empirical research is needed to contextualize and understand best practices for how international, regional, national, and local actors can interact to prevent violent extremism, especially at a time when "violent extremism in the Sahel currently induces local and regional disorder while violent extremists gain support as purveyors of order and from global positions proclaiming to supply it" (Cissé and Vigh, Chapter 3 in this volume). This requires comprehending how to bridge the gap between local knowledge and (often) regional action, making external interventions more fine-grained, and developing a sense of how to collaborate. Furthermore, this research direction would include observing the cultural transfers between neighboring zones of nonoccurrence and better networking these zones with each other.

We firmly believe that only with such future research can the policy implications discussed previously be critically monitored and constructively assisted. This volume represents an important building block for this debate but can only be a start.

Acronyms

AA	Autonomous Administration for Northern and Eastern Syria
AIS	Armée Islamique du salut
AQ-I	Al-Qaeda in Iraq
AQIM	Al-Qaeda in the Islamic Maghreb
ARBBiH	Army of the Republic of Bosnia and Herzegovina
AST	Ansar al-Sharia in Tunisia
ATG	Armed terrorist group
AU	African Union
BiH	Bosnia and Herzegovina
BIK	Islamic Community of Kosovo
BMZ	Federal Ministry for Economic Cooperation and Development (Germany)
CEPOL	European Union Agency for Law Enforcement Training
CNDH	National Council on Human Rights
CRTs	Country Reports on Terrorism
CSDP	Common Security and Defence Policy
CSOs	Civil society organizations
CT	Counterterrorism
CT-P/CVE	Counterterrorism and preventing and countering violent extremism
CTU	State Police Counterterrorism Unit
CVE	Countering violent extremism
DDR	Disarmament, demobilization, and reintegration
EEAS	European External Action Service
ENA	French National School of Administration
ESS	European Security Strategy

EU	European Union
EUCAP Sahel Niger	European Union Capacity Building Mission in Niger
EUGS	European Union Global Strategy
EUROPOL	European Union Agency for Police Cooperation
FAMA	Malian Armed Forces
FIS	Front Islamique du salut
FRONTEX	European Border and Coast Guard Agency
FSA	Free Syrian Army
FTFs	Foreign terrorist fighters
GATIA	Groupe d'Autodéfense Tuareg Imghad et Alliés
GDP	Gross domestic product
GIA	Groupe Islamique Armé
GLD	Groupes de Legitime Defense
GSPC	Group for Predication and Combat
HDI	Human Development Index
HDZ	Croatian Democratic Union
HDZ BiH	Croatian Democratic Union Bosnia and Herzegovina
HNS	Croat National Assembly
HSRC	Human Sciences Research Council
IAF	Islamic Action Front
IC	Islamic Community
ICG	International Crisis Group
ICiS	Islamic Community in Serbia
ICoS	Islamic Community of Serbia
ICSs	Integrated Country Strategies
IJR	Institute for Justice and Reconciliation
INDH	National Initiative on Human Development
IS	Islamic State
ISGS	Islamic State of Greater Sahara
ISIL	Islamic State in the Levant
ISIS	Islamic State in Iraq and Syria
ISSP	Islamic State Sahel Province
ISWAP	Islamic State West Africa Province
JAK-T	Jund Al Khilafa in Tunisia
JNIM	Jama'at Nasr al-Islam wal Muslimin
KDP	Kurdistan Democratic Party
KLA	Kosovo Liberation Army
KRI	Kurdistan Region of Iraq
LIDD	Islamic League for Predication and Djihad
MB	Muslim Brotherhood
MENA	Middle East and North Africa
MoI	Ministry of Interior

NATO	North Atlantic Treaty Organization
NDH	Independent State of Croatia
NDICI	Neighbourhood, Development and International Cooperation Instrument for a Global Europe
NGO	Nongovernmental organization
NSP	National Socialist Party
NUPI	Norwegian Institute of International Affairs
NURC	National Unity and Reconciliation Commission
OECD	Organisation for Economic Co-operation and Development
OIN-B	Okba Ibn Nafaa Brigade
OSCE	Organization for Security and Co-operation in Europe
P/CVE	preventing and countering violent extremism
PISA	Programme for International Student Assessment
PJD	Party of Justice and Development
PKK	Kurdistan Workers' Party
PLO	Palestine Liberation Organization
PREVEX	Preventing Violent Extremism in the Balkans and the MENA
PSD	Public Security Directorate
PUK	Patriotic Union of Kurdistan
PVE	Preventing violent extremism
PYD	Democratic Union Party
RFTFs	Rehabilitation and reintegration of returning foreign terrorist fighters
RS	Republika Srpska
SARB	South African Reconciliation Barometer
SASAS	South African Social Attitudes Survey
SCI	Social Cohesion Index
SCORE	Social Cohesion and Reconciliation
SCR	Social Cohesion Radar
SDF	Syrian Democratic Forces
SeeD	Centre for Sustainable Peace and Democratic Development
SHE WINS	Supporting Her Empowerment: Women's Inclusion for New Security
SNS	Serbian Progressive Party
SRS	Serbian Radical Party
SSR	Security sector reform
TIFG	Tunisian Islamic Fighting Group
UN	United Nations
UNDP	United Nations Development Programme
UNDP ACT	United Nations Development Programme's Action for Cooperation and Trust
UNMIK	United Nations Interim Administration Mission in Kosovo

US	United States
USAID	United States Agency for International Development
USD	United States dollar
V-Dem	Varieties of Democracy
VDP	Volunteers for Homeland Defense
VE	Violent extremism
VET	Violent extremist terrorism
WoS	Web of Science
WoT	War on terror

References

Abbas, Tahir (2020). "Far Right and Islamist Radicalization in an Age of Austerity: A Review of Sociological Trends and Implications for Policy." *ICCT Policy Brief*, January 2020.

Abdelhalim, Muhammad (1973). *The Muslim Brotherhood: Events that Made History Part 3: 1953–1971*. Alexandria: Dar Al Daawa.

Abou-Tabickh, Lilian (2022). "How Significant Is the Term 'Condition' (*ḥāl*) to Understanding Ibn Khaldūn's Historical and Political Thought? Al-aṣabiyya as an 'Essential Condition' of Human Association." *Journal of North African Studies*, 27(4), 761–785.

Abu Nabut, M. (2020). "Tension Arises Between Tribes of Deir ez-Zor and the SDF" [in Arabic]. Al-Jazeera.

Abu Rumman, Mohammad, ed. (2021). *After the Caliphate: Ideology, Propaganda, Organization, and Global Jihad. Will ISIS Make a Comeback?* Friedrich-Ebert-Stiftung Jordan and Iraq Office, https://library.fes.de/pdf-files/bueros/amman/18915-20220214.pdf.

Acket, Sylvain, Monique Bersenberger, Paul Dickes, and Francesco Sarracino (2011). "Measuring and Validating Social Cohesion: A Bottom-Up Approach." Paper presented at the International Conference on Social Cohesion and Development, OECD Development Centre, Paris, January 20–21, 2011.

Agbiboa, Daniel E. (2013). "Why Boko Haram Exists: The Relative Deprivation Perspective." *African Conflict and Peacebuilding Review*, 3(1), 144–157.

Agnew, John (1994). "The Territorial Trap: The Geographical Assumptions of International Relations Theory." *Review of International Political Economy*, 1(1), 53–80.

Ahmed, Ali (2017). "When the Salafis in Kurdistan Will Become a Party" [in Kurdish]. YouTube video, 1:15, September 11, 2017, https://www.youtube.com/watch?v=wvajQYBzAkg.

Ahmeti, Adelina (2021). "Dosja e Prokurorisë: Grupi terrorist që planifikonte sulme në Kosovë i lidhur me ISIS." Kallxo.com, October 12, 2021. https://kallxo.com/lajm/dosja-e-prokurorise-grupi-terrorist-qe-planifikonte-sulme-ne-kosove-i-lidhur-me-isis/.

Ahmeti, Adelina, Egzon Dahsyla, and Xheneta Murtezaj (2021). "Mijëra mësues në Kosovë, vetëm rreth 3 mijë morën trajnime për trajtim të fëmijëve të rikthyer." Kallxo.com, October 20, 2021. https://kallxo.com/gjate/mijera-mesues-ne-kosove-vetem-rreth-3-mije-moren-trajnime-per-trajtim-te-femijeve-te-rikthyer/.

Akademska inicijativa Forum 10 (2017). *Debata: Radikalizam i ekstremizam—uzroci, posledice i buduci izazovi*. YouTube video, 1:51:33, February 14, 2017, https://www.youtube.com/watch?v=vrb8aMncMZk.

Akyol, Riada A. (2019). "Want to Cultivate a Liberal European Islam? Look to Bosnia." *The Atlantic*, January 13, 2019.

Al Jazeera (2022). "Mohamed Bazoum: Is Niger France's New Key Partner in the Sahel?" https://www.aljazeera.com/program/talk-to-al-jazeera/2022/3/10/mohamed-bazoum-is-niger-frances-new-key-partner-in-the-sahel.

Ala'Aldeen, Dlawer, Kamaran Mohammed, and Khogir Wirya (2022). *Violent Extremism in Mosul and the Kurdistan Region: Context, Drivers, and Public Perception*. Erbil: MERI.

Al-Ali, Yusuf (2020). "Between Tribes and the SDF—Will Deir ez-Zor Ignite a Clash in Syria?" Al-Estiklal, August 17, 2020, https://www.alestiklal.net/ar/view/5659/dep-news-1597425584.

Al-Anani, Khalil (2015). "Upended Path: The Rise and Fall of Egypt's Muslim Brotherhood." *Middle East Journal*, 69(4), 527–543.

Al Bawsala (2023). Marsad Budget, Budget MoI and MoD for 2023. https://budget.marsad.tn/ar/budget/organization/list/.

Aldoughli, Rahaf (2020). "Departing 'Secularism': Boundary Appropriation and Extension of the Syrian State in the Religious Domain." *British Journal of Middle Eastern Studies*, 49(2), 360–385.

——— (2021). "Securitization as a Tool of Regime Survival: The Deployment of Religious Rhetoric in Bashar al-Asad's Speeches." *Middle East Journal*, 75(1), 9–32.

al-Mnadi, R., *Tribal Judiciary*. Haramoon for Studies. (no year)

Aliyev, Huseyn, and Emil Souleimanov (2022). "Fighting Against Jihad? Blood Revenge and Anti-insurgency Mobilization in Jihadist Civil Wars." *Studies in Conflict and Terrorism*, published online December 6, 2022.

Allan, Harriet, Andrew Glazzard, Sasha Jesperson, Sneha Reddy-Tumu, and Emily Winterbotham (2015). "Drivers of Violent Extremism: Hypotheses and Literature Review." Royal United Services Institute, https://gsdrc.org/document-library/drivers-of-violent-extremism-hypotheses-and-literature-review/.

Alshech, Eli (2014). "The Doctrinal Crisis Within the Salafi-Jihadi Ranks and the Emergence of Neo-Takfirism: A Historical and Doctrinal Analysis." *Islamic Law and Society*, 21, 419–452.

Amin, Samir (1988). *Eurocentrism*. London: Zed Books.

Amit, Sajid, and Abdulla Al Kafy (2022). "A Systematic Literature Review on Preventing Violent Extremism." *Journal of Adolescence*, 94(8), 1068.

Andersen, Jan, and Sveinung Sandberg (2020). "Islamic State Propaganda: Between Social Movement Framing and Subcultural Provocation." *Terrorism and Political Violence*, 32(7), 1506–1526.

Anderson, Mary B., and Marshall Wallace (2013). *Opting Out of War: Strategies to Prevent Violent Conflict*. Boulder: Lynne Rienner.

Arij (2018). "Made in Prison: Third Generation of Jihadists in Egyptian Prisons." https://arij.net/made_in_prison_en/.

Ashour, Omar (2009). *The De-Radicalization of Jihadists: Transforming Armed Islamist Movements*. London: Routledge.

——— (2011). "Post-Jihadism: Libya and the Global Transformations of Armed Islamist Movements." *Terrorism and Political Violence*, 23(3), 377–397.

"Assassination of King Abdullah." *The Guardian*, July 21, 1951.
Association for Democratic Initiatives, Sarajevo (2021). "Civil Society Reacts to Fatmir Alispahić Verdict: Hate Speech Is Not Freedom of Speech." November 24, 2021, https://adi.org.ba/en/2021/11/24/civil-society-reacts-to-fatmir-alispahic-verdict-hate-speech-is-not-freedom-of-speech/.
Atieh, Adel, Gilad Ben-Nun, Gasser El Shahad, Rana Taha, and Steve Tulliu (2005). *Peace in the Middle East: P2P and the Israeli Palestinian Conflict.* Geneva: United Nations Institute for Disarmament Research.
Atlayar (2023). "Le Maroc démantèle une cellule terroriste liée à Daesh." https://atalayar.com/fr/content/le-maroc-d%C3%A9mant%C3%A8le-une-cellule-terroriste-li%C3%A9e-%C3%A0-daesh.
Attree, Larry (2017). "Shouldn't YOU be Countering Violent Extremism?" Saferworld, https://www.saferworld.org.uk/long-reads/shouldnat-you-be-countering-violent-extremism.
Atwan, Abdel (2007). *L'histoire secrète d'Al Qaida*. Paris: Éditions Acropole.
Awad, Ziad (2018). *Deir Al-Zor After Islamic State: Between Kurdish Self Administration and a Return of the Syrian Regime.* Fiesole: EUI.
Ayari, Michaël (2017). *Revue analytique: Les facteurs favorisant l'extrémisme violent dans la Tunisie des années 2010*. Tunis: Programme des Nations Unies pour le Développement.
Ayn Al-Madina Magazine (2015). "Oil of Deir Ezzor from Revolution to ISIS." https://aynalmadina.com/details/The%20Oil%20of%20Deir%20Ezzor%20From%20the%20Revolution%20to%20ISIS/2933/en.
Ayyash, Abdelrahman (2019). "Strong Organization, Weak Ideology: Muslim Brotherhood Trajectories in Egyptian Prisons Since 2013." Arab Reform Initiative, https://www.arab-reform.
Azinovic, Vlado (2018a). *Understanding Violent Extremism in the Western Balkans*. London: British Council.
——— (2018b). "Understanding Violent Extremism in the Western Balkans: Regional Report." *Extremism Research Forum* (Western Balkans), June 2018, 1–16. https://www.britishcouncil.me/sites/default/files/erf_report_western_balkans_2018.pdf.
Azinović, Vlado, and Edina Bećirević (2017). *A Waiting Game: Assessing and Responding to the Threat from Returning Foreign Fighters in the Western Balkans.* Sarajevo: Regional Cooperation Council.
Ba, Boubacar, and Morten Bøås (2017). *Mali: A Political Economy Analysis.* Oslo: NUPI (Report commissioned by the Norwegian Ministry of Foreign Affairs).
Badar, Mohamed Elewa, Dan Suter, David Mayor Fernandez, and Giel Franssen (2018). *Legal and Gaps Analysis Report, Scope of Terrorist Offences/Action Plans for the Prevention of Violent Extremism,* edited by Virgil Ivan-Cucu. EuroMed Justice, June 2018. https://euromedjustice.eu/wp-content/uploads/publications/7_lga_counter-terrorism_en.pdf.
Bąkowski, Piotr (2022). *Preventing Radicalization in the European Union: How EU Policy Has Evolved. In-Depth Analysis.* Brussels: European Parliamentary Research Service, European Union.
Bank, Leslie (2021). "Culture, Covid and Social Cohesion in Rural Southern Africa." *African Arguments*, March 16, 2021.
Barber, Tony (2023). "Serbia Is a Poor Fit for EU Enlargement Plans." *Financial Times*, November 11, 2023.
Barrett, Christopher, Kate Ghezzi-Kopel, John Hoddinott, Nima Homani, Elisabeth Tennant, Joanne Upton, and Tong Wu (2020). "A Scoping Review of the Development Resilience Literature: Theory, Methods and Evidence." Charles H.

Dyson School of Applied Economics and Management working paper. Ithaca, NY: Cornell University.

Bartolomei, Enrico (2018). "Sectarianism and the Battle of Narratives in the Context of the Syrian Uprising." In *The Syrian Uprising: Domestic Origins and Early Trajectory,* edited by Raymond Hinnebusch and Omar Imady, 223–241. London: Routledge.

Barzegar, Abbas, Shawn Powers, and Naghem El Karhili (2016). *Civic Approaches to Confronting Violent Extremism: Sector Recommendations and Best Practices.* Institute for Strategic Dialogue.

Bast, Sarah (2018). "Counterterrorism in an Era of More Limited Resources." Center for Strategic and International Studies, May 18, 2018, https://www.csis.org/analysis/counterterrorism-era-more-limited-resources.

Bátora, Jozef, Matej Navrátil, Kari Osland, and Mateja Peter (2018). *EU and International Actors in Kosovo: Competing Institutional Logics, Constructive Ambiguity and Competing Priorities.* Oslo: EUNPACK.

Bayart, Jean Francois (1978). "Clientelism, Elections and Systems of Inequality and Domination in Cameroun: A Reconsideration of the Notion of Political and Social Control." In *Elections Without Choice,* edited by Guy Hermet, Richard Rose, and Alain Renquie, 66–87. London: Macmillan.

——— (2010). *The State in Africa: The Politics of the Belly.* Cambridge: Polity Press.

Bayart, Jean Francois, and Stephen Ellis (2000). "Africa in the World: A History of Extraversion." *African Affairs,* 99(395), 217–267.

Beall, Jo, Thomas Goodfellow, and James Putzel (2006). "Introductory Article: On the Discourse of Terrorism, Security, and Development." *Journal of International Development,* 18(1), 51–67.

Beaujouan, Juline, Veronique Dudouet, Maja Halilovic-Pastuovic, Johanna-Maria Hülzer, Marie Kortam, and Amjed Rasheed, eds. (2024). *Vulnerability and Resilience to Violent Extremism: An Actor-Centric Approach.* London: Routledge.

Beauvais, Caroline, and Jane Jenson (2002). "Social Cohesion: Updating the State of the Research." CPRN Discussion Paper No. F22. Ottawa, ON: Canadian Policy Research Networks.

Bechev, Dimitar (2019). "Russia's Strategic Interests and Tools of Influence in the Western Balkans." *New Atlanticist,* December 20, 2019.

Bećirević, Edina (2016). *Salafism vs. Moderate Islam: A Rhetorical Fight for the Hearts and Minds of Bosnian Muslims.* Sarajevo: Atlantic Initiative.

——— (2018). "Bosnia and Herzegovina Report." *Extremism Research Forum Policy Report,* April 2018. London: British Council.

Ben Dhaou, Fatma (2021). "Tunisie: Okba Ibn Nafaa, une Katiba à l'ombre d'AQMI." *Analyse Afrique.*

Benjaminsen, Tor Arve, and Boubacar Ba (2009). "Farmer-Herder Conflicts, Pastoral Marginalisation and Corruption: A Case Study from the Inland Niger Delta of Mali." *Geographical Journal,* 175(1), 71–81.

——— (2018). "Why Do Pastoralists in Mali Join Jihadist Groups? A Political Ecological Explanation." *Journal of Peasant Studies,* 46(1), 1–20.

——— (2021). "Fulani-Dogon Killings in Mali: Farmer-Herder Conflicts as Insurgency and Counterinsurgency." *African Security,* 14(1), 4–26.

——— (2024). "A Moral Economy of Pastoralists? Understanding the Jihadist Insurgency in Mali." *Political Geography,* 113, 1–10.

Ben-Nun, Gilad, and Ulf Engel (2021). "Comparing the EU and Other Stakeholders' Prevention Strategy Towards Violent Extremism in the Balkans and the Broader MENA Region." PREVEX Policy Brief D8.1. Oslo: PREVEX, https://www.prevex-balkan-mena.eu/wp-content/uploads/2022/01/D8.1-final.pdf.

——— (2022a). "A Comparison of 'Enabling Environments,' Drivers and Occurrence/Non-occurrence of Violent Extremism in the Balkans and the MENA Region." PREVEX Working Paper D8.3. Oslo: PREVEX. https://www.prevex-balkan-mena.eu/wp-content/uploads/2022/08/D8.2-1.pdf.
——— (2022b). "Summarising the Lessons Learned from Assessing the EU's Measures to Prevent Violent Extremism in a Comparative Perspective." PREVEX Policy Brief D8.3. Oslo: PREVEX. https://www.prevex-balkan-mena.eu/lessons-learned-from-assessing-the-eus-measures-to-prevent-violent-extremism-in-a-comparative-perspective/.
Benraad, Myriam (2011). "Iraq's Tribal 'Sahwa': Its Rise and Fall." *Middle East Policy*, 28(1), 121–131.
Bergen, Peter, Joseph Felter, Vahid Brown, and Jacob Shapiro (2008). *Bombers, Bank Accounts and Bleedout: Al-Qa'da's Road in and out of Iraq*, edited by Brian Fishman. Harmony Report No. 5, 36. West Point, NY: Combating Terrorism Center at West Point.
Berger-Schmitt, Regina (2002). "Considering Social Cohesion in Quality-of-Life Assessments: Concepts and Measurement." *Social Indicators Research*, 58(3), 403–428.
Bergh, Sylvia (2013). "Governance Reforms in Morocco: Beyond Electoral Authoritarianism?" In *Governance in the Middle East and North Africa: A Handbook*, edited by Abbas Kadhim, 435–451. London: Routledge.
Bernard, Paul (1999). *Social Cohesion: A Critique*. CPRN Discussion Paper No. F09. Ottawa, ON: Canadian Policy Research Networks.
Bertelsmann Stiftung (2013). *Social Cohesion Radar: Measuring Common Ground. An International Comparison of Social Cohesion*. Gütersloh: Bertelsmann Stiftung.
——— (2018). *What Holds Asian Societies Together? Insights from the Social Cohesion Radar*. Gütersloh: Bertelsmann Stiftung.
Beslin, Jelena and Marija Ignjatijevic (2017). "Balkan Foreign Fighters: From Syria to Ukraine." European Union Institute for Security Studies (EUISS) Brief Issue 20, June 2017. https://www.iss.europa.eu/content/balkan-foreign-fighters-syria-ukraine
Bešlin, Milivoj (2021). "Svetosavlje bez Svetog Save." *Akuzativ*, https://akuzativ.com/teme/921-svetosavlje-bez-svetog-save.
Bhamra, Ran, Samir Dani, and Kevin Burnard (2011). "Resilience: The Concept, a Literature Review and Future Directions." *International Journal of Production Research*, 49(18), 5375–5393.
Bianchi, Robert (1989). *Unruly Corporatism: Associational Life in Twentieth-Century Egypt*. New York: Oxford University Press.
Bieber, Florian (2002). "Nationalist Mobilisation and Stories of Serb Suffering: The Kosovo Myth from 600th Anniversary to the Present." *Rethinking History*, 6(1), 95–110.
Bisson, Loïc, Ine Cottyn, Kars de Bruijne, and Fransje Molenaar (2021). *Between Hope and Despair: Pastoralist Adaptation in Burkina Faso*. The Hague. Clingendael Institute.
Björkdahl, Annika (2018). "Republika Srpska: Imaginary, Performance and Spatialization." *Political Geography*, 66, 34–43.
Blaut, James M. (2000). *Eight Eurocentric Historians*. New York: Guilford Press.
Blockmans, Steven, Loes Debuysere, Georges Fahmi, Magnus Langset, Pernille Rieker, and Oliver Roy (2020). "EU's Policies and Instruments for PVE." PREVEX Working Paper D4.1. Oslo: PREVEX. https://www.prevex-balkan-mena.eu/eu-prevention-strategies/.
Blum, Constanze, and Ulf Engel (2023). "Introduction. Populism and Social Cohesion in Southern Africa and Beyond: Towards a Research Agenda." *Comparativ*, 33(4), 449–459.

Blum, Constanze, Ulf Engel, and Chirstian van der Westhuizen, eds. (forthcoming). *The Routledge Handbook on Social Cohesion in Africa*. London: Routledge.

Bøås, Morten (2015). "Crime, Coping, and Resistance in the Mali-Sahel periphery." *African Security*, 8(4), 299–319.

——— (2017). "Mali: Islam, Arms and Money." In *Africa's Insurgents: Navigating an Evolving Landscape*, edited by Morten Bøås and Kevin C. Dunn, 135–155. Boulder, CO: Lynne Rienner.

——— (2024). "Violent Extremism: The Journey in and the Pathway Out." *OpenAccessGovernment*, https://www.openaccessgovernment.org/article/violent-extremism-the-journey-in-and-the-pathway-out/173727/.

——— (2025). *Sahel—the Perfect Storm*. London: Hurst.

Bøås, Morten, Abdoul Wakhab Cissé, and Laouali Mahamane (2020). "Explaining Violence in Tillabéri: Insurgent Appropriation of Local Grievances?" *International Spectator*, 55(4), 118–132.

Bøås, Morten, and Kevin C. Dunn (2013a). *Politics of Origin in Africa: Autochthony, Citizenship and Conflict*. London: Zed Books.

——— (2013b). "Understanding African Guerrillas." In *Routledge Handbook of African Security*, edited by James J. Hentz, 84–95. London: Routledge.

———, eds. (2017). *Africa's Insurgents: Navigating an Evolving Landscape*. Boulder, CO: Lynne Rienner.

Bøås, Morten, and Kathleen M. Jennings (2005). "Insecurity and Development: The Rhetoric of the Failed State." *European Journal of Development Research*, 17(3), 385–395.

Bøås, Morten, Kari M. Osland, and Henriette U. Erstad (2019). "Islamic Insurgents in the MENA Region: Global Threat or Regional Menace?" Working Paper No. 884. Oslo: NUPI.

Bøås, Morten, Kari Osland, Alessio Iocchi, Viljar Haavik, Abdoul Cissé, Luca Raineri, Laouali Mahamane, Djalill Lounnas, and Akram Benmrahar (2021). "Enabling Environments, Drivers and Occurrence/Non-occurrence of Violent Extremism in North Africa and the Sahel." PREVEX Report D6.2. Oslo: PREVEX. https://www.prevex-balkan-mena.eu/wp-content/uploads/2023/01/D6.2-2-1.pdf.

Bøås, Morten, and Francesco Strazzari (2020). "Governance, Fragility and Insurgency in the Sahel: A Hybrid Political Order in the Making." *International Spectator*, 55(4), 1–17.

Bøås, Morten and Natasja Rupesinghe (2021). "Local Factors Contributing to Violent Extremism in Central Mali." NUPI-UNDP.

Borum, Randy (2004). *Psychology of Terrorism*. Tampa: University of South Florida.

Borum, Randy (2011). "Radicalization into Violent Extremism II: A Review of Conceptual Models and Empirical Research." *Journal of Strategic Security*, 4(4), 37–82.

Borrell, Josep (2023). "Schuman Security and Defence Forum: Keynote Speech by High Representative/Vice-President Josep Borrell." European Union External Service, March 21, 2023, https://www.eeas.europa.eu/eeas/schuman-security-and-defence-forum-keynote-speech-high-representativevice-president-josep_en.

Bourdieu, Pierre (1977). *Outline of a Theory of Practice*. Cambridge: Cambridge University Press.

Bras, Jean-Philippe (2016). "Tunisie: L'élaboration de la loi antiterroriste de 2015 ou les paradoxes de la démocratie sécuritaire." *L'année du Maghreb*, 15, 309–323.

Braudel, Fernand, and Immanuel Wallerstein (2009). "History and the Social Sciences: The Long Duree." *Review-Fernand Braudel Center*, 32(2), 171–203.

Breen, Clairissa (2019). "Exploring Terrorism Through Criminological Theories." *International Journal of Business and Social Science*, 10(7), 195–211.

Brown, Carl, ed. (1996). *Imperial Legacy: The Ottoman Imprint on the Balkans and the Middle East*. New York: Columbia University Press.

Brown, Frances (2018). *Dilemmas of Stabilization Assistance: The Case of Syria*. Washington, DC: Carnegie Endowment for International Peace.

Bruneau, Thomas (2015). "Impediments to Fighting the Islamic State: Private Contractors and US Strategies." *Journal of Strategies Studies*, 39(1), 120–141.

Bryant, Rebecca, ed. (2016). *Post-Ottoman Co-existence: Sharing Space in the Shadow of Conflict*. Berlin: Berghahn.

Buljubašić, Mirza (2022). *Violent Right-Wing Extremism in the Western Balkans: An Overview of Country-Specific Challenges for P/CVE*. Luxembourg: Publications Office of the European Union, Radicalization Awareness Network.

Burchi, Francesco, and Gabriela Zapata-Román (2022). *Inequality and Social Cohesion in Africa: Theoretical Insights and an Exploratory Empirical Investigation*. Bonn: German Institute of Development and Sustainability.

Burns, John, Kate Lefko-Everett, and Lindokuhle Njozela (2018). *From Definition to Measurement: Constructing a Social Cohesion Index for South Africa*. Paris: Agence Française de Développement.

Busher, Joel, Leena Malkki, and Sarah V. Marsden, eds. (2024). *The Routledge Handbook on Radicalization and Countering Radicalization*. London: Routledge.

Byman, Daniel (2013). "Fighting Salafi-Jihadist Insurgencies: How Much Does Religion Really Matter?" *Studies in Conflict and Terrorism*, 36(5), 353–371.

——— (2015). *Al-Qaeda, the Islamic State, and the Global Jihadist Movement*. Oxford: Oxford University Press.

Cabinet of the Prime Minister (2012). Stratégie de Développement et de Sécurité dans les Zones Sahélo—Sahariennes du Niger, Secretariat Executif de la SDS Sahel, Niamey. https://www.ipinst.org/images/pdfs/sds_version_francaise.pdf.

Calculli, Marina (2016). "Middle East Security: Conflict and Securitization of Identities." In *International Relations of the Middle East*, edited by Louise Fawcett, 218–235. Oxford: Oxford University Press.

Camau, Michel (2018). *L'exception tunisienne. Variations sur un mythe*. Paris: Khartala éditions.

Cammack, Diana, Dinah McLeod, and Alina R. Menocal (2006). *Donors and the Fragile States Agenda: A Survey of Current Thinking and Practice*. London: Overseas Development Institute.

Carmichael, Cathie (2012). "546 Brothers, Strangers and Enemies: Ethno-nationalism and the Demise of Communist Yugoslavia." In *The Oxford Handbook of Postwar European History*, edited by Dan Stone, 546–560. Oxford: Oxford University Press.

Carpenter, Ami C. (2006). "Resilience to Violent Conflict: Adaptive Strategies in Fragile States" (white paper). Baltimore: University of Maryland and United States Agency for International Development.

Cavatorta, Francesco (2015). "Salafism, Liberalism, and Democratic Learning in Tunisia." *Journal of North African Studies*, 20(5), 770–783.

Center for Insights in Survey Research (2022). *2022 Western Balkans Regional Survey*. International Republic Institute. https://www.iri.org/resources/2022-western-balkans-regional-survey-january-february-2022/.

Chabal, Patric, and Jean-Pierre Daloz (2005). *Culture Troubles: Politics and the Interpretation of Meaning*. London: Hurst.

Chan, Joseph, Ho-Pong To, and Elaine Chan (2006). "Reconsidering Social Cohesion: Developing a Definition and Analytical Framework for Empirical Research." *Social Indicators Research*, 75(2), 273–302.

Chelin, Richard (2018). "From the Islamic State of Algeria to the Economic Caliphate of the Sahel: The Transformation of Al Qaeda in the Islamic Maghreb." *Terrorism and Political Violence, 32*(6), 1186–1205.

Cissé, Abdoul Wakhab (2021). "Le Sahel et nous." *Afkar/idées, 63*, 14–16.

Claisse, Alain (1987). "Makhzen Traditions and Administrative Channels." In *The Political Economy of Morocco*, edited by William Zartman, 34–58. New York: Praeger.

Clapp, Alexander (2017). "Bosnia's Sordid Independence." *National Interest*, August 16, 2017.

Clayton Govinda, and Andrew Thomson (2014). "The Enemy of My Enemy Is My Friend… the Dynamics of Self-Defense Forces in Irregular War: The Case of the Sons of Iraq." *Studies in Conflict, and Terrorism, 37*(11), 920–935.

COAR (Centre for Operational Analysis and Research) (2022). *Social Cohesion in Support of Deradicalization and the Prevention of Violent Extremism: Programming Entry Points in North-East Syria*. Limassol: COAR.

Cold-Ravnkilde, Signe Marie, and Boubacar Ba (2022). "Jihadist Ideological Conflict and Local Governance in Mali." *Studies in Conflict, and Terrorism*, April 21, 2022, 1–16.

Collett, Elisabeth, and Aliyyah Ahad (2017). *EU Migration Partnerships: A Work in Progress*. Washington, DC: Migration Policy Institute.

Collier, Paul, and Anke Hoeffler (2004). "Greed and Grievance in Civil War." *Oxford Economic Papers, 56*(4), 563–595.

Collombier, Virginie, and Olivier Roy, eds. (2017). *Tribes and Global Jihadism*. Oxford: Oxford University Press.

Collombier, Virginie, Maria-Louise Clausen, Hiba Hassan, Helle Malmvig & Jan Pêt Khorto (2018). "Armed Conflicts and the Erosion of the State: The Cases of Iraq, Libya, Yemen and Syria." MENARA Working Papers No. 22, November 2018. https://d1wqtxts1xzle7.cloudfront.net/82876281/MENARA_Working_20paper_22 _18-libre.pdf?1648567077=&response-content-disposition=inline%3B +filename%3DArmed_conflicts_and_the_erosion_of_the_s.pdf&Expires=1724926 705&Signature=b4nQ7x-ZNhyB4V-Wp-WtM~tE4TeH67nn2xh~hqUj7lnkctwZtB- hDxNj4MV4J5nVEyjxxQ9bW1CLy-yQZCKCveFAIliJfle6WQMA8TPY2 vgk69qVx8DfIF0rWfJ7fMtXeujfBdhDFeR3ADnaC0INiuyMZ4JPcmYoCcO5Dccv djxYGUuPhaW382s5aScNbxl7RMg31e6ZgWPpFLX2cFZ6ubX2ki3PYd6hxrPS- bhrcYazxMhh2JG~hujVCKY6vd64no1bfN-NlncuLFkbcIUPqfjEn1ZI1t1DsGdp65 OkaVNG3dFexs29igwLxttXkrrhiu6KB~COghHSSXvcHINmt7Zg__&Key-Pair -Id=APKAJLOHF5GGSLRBV4ZA.

Colomba-Petteng, Léonard (2019). *The Common Foreign and Security Policy Under Test in Niger*. Brussels: Foundation Robert Schuman.

Consigli, Jenna (2018). "Countering Radicalization Efforts in the Middle East and North Africa." In *De-Radicalization in the Mediterranean: Comparing Challenges and Approaches*, edited by Vidino, Lorenzo. Milan: ISPI.

Coolsaet, Rik (2016). *All Radicalisation Is Local: The Genesis and Drawbacks of an Elusive Concept*. Egmont Paper No. 84. Brussels: Egmont.

Council of the EU (European Union) (2003). *A Secure Europe in a Better World: European Security Strategy*. EUR-Lex, December 12, 2003. https://eur-lex .europa.eu/legal-content/EN/TXT/?uri=LEGISSUM:r00004.

——— (2005). "The European Union Counter-Terrorism Strategy." No. 14469/4/05 REV4, 30/11/05, November 30, 2005. Brussels: European Union/Council of the European Union. https://data.consilium.europa.eu/doc/document/ST%2014469 %202005%20REV%204/EN/pdf.

——— (2011). "Report on the EU Counter-Terrorism Policy: Main Achievements and Future Challenges." Motion for a European Parliament Resolution

20/06/11. Brussels: European Union/Council of the European Union. http://www.europarl.europa.eu/sides/getDoc.do?type=REPORT&reference=A7-2011-0286&language=EN.

——— (2014). *Revised EU Strategy for Combating Radicalization and Recruitment to Terrorism*. Council of the European Union, May 19, 2014. https://data.consilium.europa.eu/doc/document/ST-9956-2014-INIT/en/pdf.

——— (2015). "Council Conclusions on Counterterrorism: Outcome of Proceedings." Press release 10384/17, Council of the European Union, September 2, 2015. http://data.consilium.europa.eu/doc/document/ST-6048-2015-INIT/en/pdf.

——— (2017). "EU External Action on Counter-Terrorism: Council Adopts Conclusions." Press release 351/17, June 19, 2017. www.consilium.europa.eu/en/press/press-releases/2017/06/19/conclusions-counterterrorism/.

——— (2019). "Council Conclusions on the Sahel." Council of the European Union, May 13, 2019. https://data.consilium.europa.eu/doc/document/ST-9103-2019-INIT/en/pdf.

——— (2020). "Council Conclusions on EU External Action on Preventing and Countering Terrorism and Violent Extremism." Council of the European Union, June 16, 2020. https://data.consilium.europa.eu/doc/document/ST-8868-2020-INIT/en/pdf.

——— (2021). "The European Union's Integrated Strategy in the Sahel." Council of the European Union, April 16, 2021. https://data.consilium.europa.eu/doc/document/ST-7723-2021-INIT/en/pdf.

——— (2022). "Council Conclusions on Addressing the External Dimension of a Constantly Evolving Terrorist and Violent Extremist Threat." *Official Journal of the European Union*, June 30, 2022. https://eur-lex.europa.eu/legal-content/EN/TXT/PDF/?uri=CELEX:52022XG0630(01)&qid=1681169450016.

Council on Foreign Relations (2023). "Violent Extremism in the Sahel." Center for Preventive Action, Global Conflict Tracker, August 10, 2023.

Counter Extremism Project (n.d.a). "Great Replacement Theory." https://www.counterextremism.com/content/great-replacement-theory.

——— (n.d.b). "Mirsad Omerovic." https://www.counterextremism.com/extremists/mirsad-omerovic.

Cox, Fletcher, and Timothy Sisk, eds. (2017). *Peacebuilding in Deeply Divided Societies: Toward Social Cohesion?* Cham: Palgrave Macmillan.

Cragin, Kim (2014). "Resisting Violent Extremism: A Conceptual Model for Nonradicalization." *Terrorism and Political Violence*, 26(2), 337–353.

Croissant, Aurel, and Peter Walkenhorst, eds. (2021). *Social Cohesion in Asia: Historical Origins, Contemporary Shapes and Future Dynamics*. London: Routledge.

Crosson, Dylan (2017). "Counterterrorism in the EU's External Relations." *Journal of European Integration*, 39(5), 609–624.

Crosson, Dylan, Tatjana Stankovic, Pernille Rieker, and Steven Blockmans (2023). "To Stakeholders with Policy Recommendations." PREVEX Policy Brief D4.5. Oslo: PREVEX. https://www.prevex-balkan-mena.eu/wp-content/uploads/2023/06/D4.5-Policy-brief-final-1.pdf.

Dann, Uriel (1991). *King Hussein and the Challenge of Arab Radicalism: Jordan 1955–1967*. Oxford: Oxford University Press.

Darif, Mohamed (2010). *Monarchie Marocaine et Acteurs Religieux*. Paris: Afrique Orient.

Davi, Mai'a (2017). "Counterterrorism in the EU's External Relations." *Journal of European Integration*, 39(5), 609–624.

De Waal, Alex (2009). "Vernacular Politics in Africa." *African Arguments*.

Debuysere, Loes, and Steven Blockmans (2019). *A Jumbo Financial Instrument for EU External Action?* Bertelsmann Stiftung, https://www.bertelsmann-stiftung

.de/en/publications/publication/did/a-jumbo-financial-instrument-for-eu-external-action#detail-content-6209-5.

Delfolie, David (2012). "Malaysian Extraversion Towards the Muslim World: Ideological Positioning for a Mirror Effect." *Journal of Current Southeast Asian Affairs*, *31*(4), 3–29.

Della Porta, Donatella (1995). *Social Movements, Political Violence and the State*. Cambridge: Cambridge University Press.

Demjaha, Agon, and Lulzim Peci (2016). "What Happened to Kosovo Albanians: The Impact of Religion on the Ethnic Identity in the State Building-Period." Policy Paper No. 1/16, June 2016. http://www.kipred.org/repository/docs/What_happened_to_Kosovo_Albanians_740443.pdf.

Demuynck, Méryl, and Mathis Böhm (2023). "Unravelling the Niger Coup and Its Implications for Violent Extremism in the Sahel." International Centre for Counter-Terrorism, August 4, 2023. https://www.icct.nl/publication/unravelling-niger-coup-and-its-implications-violent-extremism-sahel.

Deutsche Welle (2019). "Islamic State Returnees in Kosovo Guided Back into Society." Info Migrants, October 3, 2019.

Dervisbegovic, Nedim (2020). "Bosnia Authorities Argue over Risk of Covid-19 Autopsies." *Balkan Insight*, April 9, 2020.

Dervisbegovic, Nedim, and Danijel Kovacevic (2020). "Catholic Church in Bosnia to Hold Controversial WWII Mass." *Balkan Insight*, May 8, 2020.

Doboš, Bohumil, Martin Riegl, and Stig Jarle Hansen (2019). "Territoriality of Radical Islam: Comparative Analysis of Jihadist Groups' Approach to Territory." *Small Wars and Insurgencies*, *30*(3), 543–562.

Domi, Tanya, and Ivana Stradner (2021). "Bosnia Is Heading Toward Another Meltdown: EU and US Neglect Is Allowing Russia to Fan Ethnic Flames." American Enterprise Institute, June 1, 2021.

Đorđević, Nikola (2021). "Just How Much Influence Does Russia Have in Bosnia and Herzegovina?" *Emerging Europe*, January 26, 2021.

Dowad, Hosham (2015). *The Sunni Tribes in Iraq: Between Local Power, the International Coalition, and the Islamic State*. Oslo: Norwegian Peacebuilding Resource Centre.

Dragolov, Georgi, Zsofia Ignacz, Jan Lorenz, Jan Delhey, Klaus Boehnke, and Kai Unzicker (2016). *Social Cohesion in the Western World: What Holds Societies Together: Insights from the Social Cohesion Radar*. Heidelberg: Springer.

Drevon, Jerome, and Patrick Haenni (2021). "How Global Jihad Relocalises and Where It Leads: The Case of HTS, the Former AQ Franchise in Syria." EUI RSC Working Paper 2021/08. European University Institute. https://hdl.handle.net/1814/69795.

Dunai, Marton, and Max Seddon (2021). "Bosnia Divided over Ban on Genocide Denial as EU Fights for Influence." *Financial Times*, October 3, 2021.

Durkheim, Émile (1893). *De la division du travail social: étude sur l'organisation des sociétés supérieures*. Paris: Félix Alcan.

——— (1897). *Le suicide: Étude de sociologie*. Paris: Félix Alcan.

Dušanić, Srđan (2020). *Mladi i ekstremizam. Institut za razvoj mladih i zajednice*.

Duyvesteyn, Isabelle, and Bram Peeters (2015). *Fickle Foreign Fighters? A Cross-Case Analysis of Seven Muslim Foreign Fighter Mobilizations (1980–2015)*. The Hague: International Centre for Counterterrorism.

Dyrmishi, Arjan, Mandrit Kamolli, Mirsada Hallunaj, and Anila Shehi (Dollani) (2021). *Exploring the Development of a Strategic Communication on P/CVE in Albania: A Research Based Approach*. Center for the Study of Democracy and

Governance, February 2021. http://csdgalbania.org/wp-content/uploads/2021/05/Exploration-of-P-CVE-strategic-communication.pdf.

Dzhekova, Rositsa, Nadya Stoynova, Anton Kojhouharov, Mila Mancheva, Dia Anagnostou, and Emil Tsenkov (2016). *Understanding Radicalisation: Review of Literature.* Sofia: Centre for the Study of Democracy.

EEAS (European External Action Service) (2011). *Strategy for Security and Development in the Sahel.* Brussels: EEAS.

——— (2014). *The European Union and Syria.* Brussels: EEAS.

——— (2016). *Shared Vision, Common Action: A Stronger Europe. A Global Strategy for the European Union's Foreign and Security Policy.* Brussels: High Representative of the Union for Foreign Affairs and Security Policy/Vice-President of the European Commission. http://eeas.europa.eu/archives/docs/top_stories/pdf/eugs_review_web.pdf.

Ejdus, Filip, and Predrag Jureković, eds. (2016). *Violent Extremism in the Western Balkans.* Vienna: Republic of Austria, Federal Ministry of Defence and Sports.

El Laithy, Heba, and Khalid Abu-Ismail (2005). *Poverty in Syria: 1996–2004. Diagnosis and Pro-Poor Policy Considerations.* Damacus: UN Development Programme.

Ellis, Heidi, and Saida Abdi (2017). "Building Community Resilience to Violent Extremism Through Genuine Partnerships." *American Psychologist,* 72(3), 289–300.

ENACT (2021). *Global Organized Crime Index 2021.* Pretoria: Institute for Security Studies and Interpol.

Engel, Ulf, and Linnéa Gelot (2021). "Navigating APSA Research from a Global Studies Perspective." In *Researching the Inner Life of the African Peace and Security Architecture. APSA Inside-Out,* edited by Katharina Döring, Ulf Engel, Linnéa Gelot, and Jens Herpolsheimer, 247–268. Leiden: Brill.

Engel, Ulf, and Matthias Middell (2020). "Gesellschaftlicher zusammenhalt und populismus: überlegungen zur varianz in zeit und raum." In *Gesellschaftlicher Zusammenhalt. Ein interdisziplinärer Dialog,* edited by Nicole Deitelhoff, Olaf Groh-Samberg, and Matthias Middell, 88–108. Frankfurt/Main: Campus.

EU Research (2023). "How Can Violent Extremism Be Prevented?" *EU Research,* September 5, 2023. https://doi.org/10.56181/ZHLY9628.

Euronews (2023). "Night Wolves and Praise for Putin Mark Milorad Dodik's Unconstitutional Fête." January 9, 2023.

European Commission (2014). *Operational Guidelines on the Preparation and Implementation of EU Financed Actions Specific to Countering Terrorism and Violent Extremism in Third Countries.* https://ctmorse.wpenginepowered.com/wp-content/uploads/2017/11/EU-CT-CVE-guidelines.pdf.

——— (2018a). "A Credible Enlargement Perspective for an Enhanced EU Engagement with the Western Balkans: Six New Flagship Initiatives to Support the Transformation of the Western Balkans." European Commission Publications Office. https://data.europa.eu/doi/10.2775/902991.

——— (2018b). "Signature of the Joint Action Plan on Counter-Terrorism for the Western Balkans." Available at: https://home-affairs.ec.europa.eu/system/files/2018-10/20181005_joint-action-plan-counter-terrorism-western-balkans.pdf.

——— (2019). *Document relatif à l'action pour le PARSS Tunisie, Annex.* Réf. Ares (2019)7307599, November 27, 2019. Brussels: European Commission.

——— (2020). *Communication from the Commission: A Counter-Terrorism Agenda for the EU: Anticipate, Prevent, Protect, Respond.* Brussels: European Commission.

——— (2021). *Serbia 2021 Report*. European Commission document SWD(2021) 288 final, October 19, 2021. https://www.ecoi.net/en/file/local/2073027/Serbia-Report-2021.pdf.

European Commission's Expert Group on Violent Radicalisation (2008). *Radicalisation Processes Leading to Acts of Terrorism: A Concise Report*. European Commission, May 15, 2008. https://www.clingendael.org/sites/default/files/pdfs/20080500_cscp_report_vries.pdf.

European Council (2005). "The European Union Counter-Terrorism Strategy." Doc. 14469/4/05, art. 11, November 30, 2005. https://data.consilium.europa.eu/doc/document/ST%2014469%202005%20REV%204/EN/pdf.

——— (2017). "Directive (EU) 2017/541 of the European Parliament and of the Council of 15 March 2017 on Combating Terrorism and Replacing Council Framework Decision 2002/475/JHA and Amending Council Decision 2005/671/JHA." *Official Journal of the European Union*, 88, 6–21.

——— (2020). "Preventing and Countering Terrorism and Violent Extremism: Council Adopts Conclusions on EU External Action." Press release, June 16, 2020. https://www.consilium.europa.eu/en/press/press-releases/2020/06/16/preventing-and-countering-terrorism-and-violent-extremism-council-adopts-conclusions-on-eu-external-action/.

——— (2022). "Council Decision (CFSP) 2022/1236 on an Assistance Measure Under the European Peace Facility to Support the Nigerien Armed Forces." July 28, 2022. https://www.europeansources.info/record/council-decision-cfsp-2022-339-on-an-assistance-measure-under-the-european-peace-facility-to-support-the-ukrainian-armed-forces/.

European Parliament and Council of the European Union (2017). "Directive (EU) 2017/541 on Combating Terrorism and Replacing Council Framework Decision 2002/475/JHA and Amending Council Decision 2005/671/JHA." *Official Journal of the European Union*, L88, 6–21.

——— (2021a). "Regulation 2021/947 Establishing the Neighbourhood, Development, and International Cooperation Instrument—Global Europe." EUR-Lex, June 9, 2021. https://eur-lex.europa.eu/legal-content/EN/TXT/?uri=CELEX%3A32021R0947.

——— (2021b). "Regulation (EU) 2021/1529 Establishing the Instrument for Pre-accession Assistance (IPA III)." *Official Journal of the European Union*, September 20, 2021. https://eur-lex.europa.eu/legal-content/EN/TXT/PDF/?uri=CELEX:32021R1529&from=EN.

Evstatiev, Simeon (2019). "Milletic Secularism in the Balkans: Christianity, Islam and Identity in Bulgaria." *Nationalities Papers*, 47(1), 87–103.

——— (2021). "Salafism as a Contested Concept." In *Knowledge, Authority and Change in Islamic Societies: Studies in Honor of Dale F. Eickelman*, edited by James Fromherz and Nadav Samin, 172–201. Leiden: Brill.

——— (2022). "Salafism Is Coming: 'Balkan' Versus 'Arab' Islam in Bulgaria Under Milletic Secularism." In *Islam, Christianity, and Secularism in Bulgaria and Eastern Europe: The Last Half Century*, edited by Simeon Evstatiev and Dale Eickelman, 74–111. Leiden: Brill.

——— (2023). "Hybridizing Islam in the Balkans: The Rise of Salafi-Hanafism in Bulgaria." In *Handbook of Political Islam in Europe*, edited by Thomas Jäger and Ralph Thiele, 375–395. Wiesbaden: Springer.

Evstatiev, Simeon, and Diana Mishkova (2022). "Summarizing Lessons Learnt on the EU's Measures to Prevent Violent Extremism in the Region." PREVEX Policy Brief D5.6. https://www.prevex-balkan-mena.eu/wp-content/uploads/2022/01/D5.6-Policy-Brief_WB.pdf.

Fahmi, Georges (2017). "Why Aren't More Muslim Brothers Turning to Violence?" Expert Comment 27/04/2017, London: Chatham House. https://www.me-policy.org/2017/04/27/why-arent-more-muslim-brothers-turning-to-violence/.

——— (2020). "Resilience Against Violent Radicalisation: Why Haven't More Islamists Taken Up Arms in Egypt Since 2013?" EUI RSCAS Working Paper 2020/17. European University Institute, Robert Schuman Centre for Advanced Studies. https://cadmus.eui.eu/handle/1814/66466.

Fahmi, Georges, and Hamza Meddeb (2015). *Market for Jihad: Radicalization in Tunisia*. Beirut: Carnegie Endowment for International Peace.

Falina, Maria (2007). "Svetosavlje: A Case Study in the Nationalization of Religion." *Schweitzerische Zeitschrift für Religions-und Kulturgeschichte, 101*, 505–527.

Fana, Valon (2021). "*Kosova kthen 11 shtetas nga zonat e konfliktit në Siri.*" Kallxo.com, July 17, 2021. https://kallxo.com/lajm/kosova-kthen-11-shtetas-nga-zonat-e-konfliktit-ne-siri/.

Farhadi, Adib (2022). "Post-9/11 Radicalization Theory and Its Impact on Violent Extremism." In *Handbook of Security Science*, edited by Anthony J. Masys, 123–148. New York: Springer.

Fathollah-Nejad, Ali (2018). "Iran: Fighting 'Terror' Publicly, Mourning the Dead Secretly." Al Jazeera, May 1, 2018.

Fearon, James, and David Laitin (2003). "Ethnicity, Insurgency, and Civil War." *American Political Science Review, 97*(1), 75–90.

Fernandez, Alberto (2015). "Here to Stay and Growing: Combating ISIS Propaganda Networks." US–Islamic World Forum Papers. Brookings Project on US Relations with the Islamic World. https://www.brookings.edu/wp-content/uploads/2016/06/IS-Propaganda_Web_English.pdf.

Fetiu, Arber, Diana Mishkova, Edina Bećirević, Evlogi Stanchev, Leonie Vrugtman, Predrag Petrović, Simeon Evstatiev, and Stoyan Doklev (2020). "Summarizing the EU and Other Stakeholders' Prevention Strategy Towards Violent Extremism in the region, the Balkans." PREVEX Policy Brief D5.1. https://www.prevex-balkan-mena.eu/wp-content/uploads/2021/01/D5.1-Policy-brief-the-Balkans-1.pdf.

Fiedler, Charlotte, and Christopher Rohles (2021). "Social Cohesion After Armed Conflict: A Literature Review." Discussion Paper No. 7/2021. German Development Institute. https://doi.org/10.23661/dp7.2021.v1.1.

Filiu, Jean-Pierre (2009). *Les neufs vies d'Al-Qaïda*. Paris: Édition Fayard.

Fisher, Jonathan (2014). "When It Pays to Be a 'Fragile State': Uganda's Use and Abuse of a Dubious Concept." *Third World Quarterly, 35*(2), 316–332.

Fisher-Onar, Nora (2022). "A New Paradigm in Political Religion? Global Right-Wing Populism as the Great Leveler." Berkley Forum, Georgetown University Berkley Center for Religion, Peace, and World Affairs, March 30, 2022. https://berkleycenter.georgetown.edu/responses/a-new-paradigm-in-political-religion-global-right-wing-populism-as-the-great-leveler.

Fitzduff, Mari (2002). *Beyond Violence: Conflict Resolution Process in Northern Ireland*. New York: United Nations University.

Fox, Robert (2005). "Gwot Is History. Now for Save: After the Global War on Terror Comes the Struggle Against Violent Extremism. Robert Fox Explains." *New Statesman*, August 8, 2005.

France 24 (2022). "Niger Becomes France's Partner of Last Resort After Mali Withdrawal." February 18, 2022.

Frowd, Philippe (2018). *Security at the Borders: Transnational Practices and Technologies in West Africa*. Cambridge: Cambridge University Press.

Furness, Mark, and Stefan Gänzle (2016). "The European Union's Development Policy: A Balancing Act Between 'a More Comprehensive Approach' and Creeping

Securitization." In *The Securitization of Foreign Aid*, edited by Stephen Brown and Jörn Grävingholt, 138–162. Basingstoke: Palgrave Macmillan.

Gade, Tine, and Kamaran Palani (2022). "The Hybridization of Religion and Nationalism in Iraqi Kurdistan: The Case of Kurdish Islam." *Third World Thematics*, 5(3–6), 221–241.

Gallagher, Julia (2015). "Theorising Image: A Relational Approach." In *Images of Africa: Creation, Negotiation and Subversion*, edited by Julia Gallagher and Valentin Y. Mudimbe, 1–20. Manchester: Manchester University Press.

Gartenstein-Ross, Daveed (2015). "The Role of Iraqi Tribes After the Islamic State's Ascendance." *Military Review*, July–August, 102–109.

Gaye, Boubacar (2020). *Extrémisme violent au Mali: Cartographie des initiatives existantes*. Bamako: ARGA.

Gazeta Express (2020). "97 Kosovare kanë mbetur në Siri: Pse Kosova s'po mundet t'i kthejë ata?" https://www.gazetaexpress.com/97-kosovare-kane-mbetur-ne-siri-pse-kosova-spo-mundet-ti-ktheje-ata/.

Geisser, Vincent, and Amin Allal (2018). *Tunisie. Une démocratisation au-dessus de tout soupçon*. Paris: Editions CNRS.

Genger, Peter (2022). "Ubuntu: The Political Paradigm Africa Should Endorse to Impact the Global Community." In *The Palgrave Handbook of Africa in the Changing Global Order*, edited by Samuel Oluruntoba, and Toyin Falola, 257–278. Cham: Palgrave Macmillan.

George, Alexander, and Andrew Bennett (2005). *Case Studies and Theory Development in the Social Sciences*. Boston: MIT Press.

Ghadbian, Najib (1997). *Democratization and the Islamist Challenge in the Arab World*. London: Routledge.

Gharib, Tarik (2013). *Kurdish Islam and Religious Reform* [in Kurdish]. Sulaymaniyah: Sima.

Giddens, Anthony, and Simon Griffiths (2006). *Sociology*. Oxford: Polity.

Global Community Engagement and Resilience Fund (GCERF) and Atlantic Initiative. (2015). *Rehabilitation and Reintegration of Returning Foreign Terrorist Fighters (RFTFs) and Their Families in the Western Balkans: Regional Needs Assessment*. https://www.gcerf.org/wp-content/uploads/2015/12/GCERF-RNA-Western-Balkans-final.pdf.

Global Initiative Against Transnational Organized Crime (2023). "Balkan Fighters Are Taking Up Arms in Ukraine." *Risk Bulletin*, no. 14, February 2023.

Goldsmith, Leon T. (2015). *Cycle of Fear: Syria's Alawites in War and Peace*. London: Hurst.

Google Ngram Viewer. https://books.google.com/.

Govori, Skender (2016). "Denohet Sllobodan Gavriq." Kallxo.com, June 29, 2016. https://kallxo.com/shkurt/denohet-sllobodan-gavriq/.

Grip, Lina, and Jennilina Kotajoki (2019). "Deradicalisation, Disengagement, Rehabilitation and Reintegration of Violent Extremists in Conflict-Affected Contexts: A Systematic Literature Review." *Conflict, Security, and Development*, 19(4), 371–402.

Guest, Alexander, Marian Machlouzarides, and Amie Scheerder (2020). *Resilient Citizenship in Bosnia and Herzegovina. Building Resilience Against Radicalisation, Civic Apathy and Intergroup Tension*. Sarajevo: Centre for Sustainable Peace and Democratic Development.

Guichaoua, Yvan, and Mathieu Pellerin (2017). "Faire la paix et construire l'État: Les relations entre pouvoir central et périphéries sahéliennes au Niger et au Mali." *Étude de l'IRSEM* 51/2017.

Haddad, Fanar (2017). "Shia-centric State-Building and Sunni Rejection in Post-2003 Iraq." In *Beyond Sunni and Shia: The Roots of Sectarianism in a Changing Middle East*, edited by Fredric Wehrey, 115–134. Oxford: Oxford University Press.

Haenni, Patrick, and Arthur Quesnay (2020). "Surviving the Aftermath of Islamic State: The Syrian Kurdish Movement's Resilience Strategy." EUI Middle East Directions (MED) Technical Report 2020/03.

——— (2022). "Coming Up Through the Cracks: The Islamic State's Resurgence in Syria and Iraq." EUI Policy Brief 2022/16.

Hafez, Farid (2021). "The Muslim War on Terror." In *The Terror Trap: The Impact of the War on Terror on Muslim Communities Since 9/11*, 49–55. Washington, DC: Coalition for Civil Freedoms, Bridge Initiative at Georgetown University, ICNA Council for Social Justice, CAGE, Center for Islam and Global Affairs, Muslim Justice League, and United Voices for America.

Hafez, Mohammed (2000). "Armed Islamist Movements and Political Violence in Algeria." *Middle East Journal*, 54(4), 572–591.

Hafez, Mohammed M (2011). "Takfir and Violence Against Muslims." In *Fault Lines in Global Jihad: Organizational, Strategic, and Ideological Fissures*, edited by Moghadam, Assaf and Brian Fishman. London: Routledge.

——— (2018). "Fratricidal Jihadists: Why Islamists Keep Losing Their Civil Wars." *Middle East Policy*, 25(2), 86–99.

Halilović, Majda, and Nejra Veljan (2021). *Exploring Ethno-Nationalist Extremism in Bosnia and Herzegovina*. Sarajevo: Atlantic Initiative.

Halilovic Pastuovic, Maja, Johanna-Maria Hülzer, and Gillian Wylie (2023). "Violent Extremism in the Western Balkans and MENA Region: Key Findings and Implications for Research." Theoretical synthesis paper. PAVE Project, January 16, 2023.

Halilovic Pastuovic, Maja, Gillian Wylie, Karin Göldner-Ebenthal, Johanna-Maria Hülzer, and Veronique Dudouet (2021). *Preventing and Addressing Violent Extremism: A Conceptual Framework.* PAVE Consortium.

Hamming, Tore (2022). *Jihadi Politics: The Global Jihadi Civil War 2014–2019.* London: Hurst.

Hansen, Stig Jarle (2019). *Horn, Sahel, and the Rift. Fault-Lines of the African Jihad.* London: Hurst.

——— (2021). "Forever Wars? Patterns of Diffusion and Consolidation of Jihadism in Africa." *Small Wars and Insurgencies*, 33(3), 409–436.

Harb, Charles (2017). *Developing a Social Cohesion Index for the Arab Region.* Amman: UN Development Programme, Regional Bureau for Arab States.

Harlan, Chico (2022). "Bosnia Is Still Finding Bodies from a Genocide Some Leaders Claim Never Happened." *Washington Post*, February 21, 2022.

Hassan, Mohamed (2020). *Cartographie des initiatives de prévention et de lutte contre l'extrémisme violent au Niger.* Bamako: ARGA.

Heath-Kelly, Charlotte (2017). "The Geography of Pre-criminal Space: Epidemiological Imaginations of Radicalisation Risk in the UK Prevent Strategy, 2007–2017." *Critical Studies on Terrorism*, 10(2), 297–319.

Hegghammer, Thomas (2007). "Violent Islamism in Saudi Arabia, 1979–2006: The Power and Perils of Pan-Islamic Nationalism." PhD thesis, Sciences Po, Paris.

——— (2010). "The Rise of Muslim Foreign Fighters: Islam and the Globalization of Jihadi." *International Security*, 35(3), 53–94.

——— (2021). "Radicalization, Salafism, and the Crisis of Jihadism." In *Salafism: Challenged by Radicalization? Violence Politics, and the Advent of Post-Salafism*, edited by Theo Blanc and Olivier Roy, 25–26. Florence: European University Institute.

Hegghammer, Thomas, and Petter Nesser (2015). "Assessing the Islamic State's Commitment to Attacking the West." *Perspectives on Terrorism*, 9(4), 14–30.

Helfont, Samuel (2014). "Saddam and the Islamists: The Ba'athist Regime's Instrumentalization of Religion in Foreign Affairs." *Middle East Journal*, 68(3), 352–366.

Heydemann, Steven (2014). "Countering Violent Extremism as a Field of Practice." *United States Institute of Peace Insights*, 1(1), 9–11.

Hibou, Beatrice (2006). *La force de l'obéissance: Economie politique de la répression en Tunisie*. Paris: Découverte.

Hinnebusch, Raymond (1997). "Syria: The Politics of Economic Liberalization." *Third World Quarterly*, 18(2), 249–265.

——— (2016). "The Sectarian Revolution in the Middle East." *Revolutions: Global Trends, and Regional Issues*, 4(1), 120–152.

Hirschman, Albert Otto (1970). *Exit, Voice, and Loyalty: Responses to Decline in Firms, Organizations, and States*. Harvard University Press.

Hobson, John (2012). *The Eurocentric Conception of World Politics: Western International Theory, 1760–2010*. Cambridge: Cambridge University Press.

Hooghe, Marc (2011). "Social Cohesion in Contemporary Societies: An Update of Theoretical Approaches." In *Social Cohesion: Contemporary Theoretical Perspectives on the Study of Social Cohesion and Social Capital*, edited by Marc Hooghe, 7–13. Brussels: Koninklijke Vlaamse academie van België voor wetenschappen en kunsten.

Horgan, John (2008). "From Profiles to Pathways and Roots to Routes: Perspectives from Psychology on Radicalization into Terrorism." *Annals of the American Academy of Political and Social Science*, 618(1), 80–94.

Human Rights Watch (2004). "Failure to Prevent." July 25, 2004. https://www.hrw.org/report/2004/07/25/failure-protect/anti-minority-violence-kosovo-march-2004.

Ibrahim, Ibrahim Yahaya (2014). "Managing the Sahelo-Saharan Islamic Insurgency in Mauritania." Sahel Research Group Working Paper No 3. University of Florida.

ICG (International Crisis Group) (2005). "Serbia's Sanjak: Still Forgotten." Report No. 162. April 8, 2005.

——— (2016). "Exploiting Disorder: al-Qaeda and Islamic State." Special Report No. 1. March 14, 2016.

——— (2020). "Reversing Central Mali's Descent into Communal Violence." Report No. 293. November 9, 202.

——— (2021). "Jihadism in Tunisia: A Receding Threat?" Briefing No. 83. June 4, 2021.

Idrissa, Rahmane (2021). "Europe-Africa Unequal Pacts: The Case of West African Migration." In *Revisiting EU-Africa Relations in a Changing World*, edited by Valeria Fargion and Mamoudou Gazibo, 104–155. Northampton: Edward Elgar Publishing.

Idrissa, Rahmane, and Anna Isambourg (2020). "Regaining the Balance: Violent Extremism and Community Relations on the Niger-Mali Border." *Recherche Internationales*, 117, 151–170.

IEP (Institute for Economics and Peace) (2020). *The Global Terrorism Index 2020: Measuring the Impact of Terrorism*. IEP, February 4, 2021. https://www.visionofhumanity.org/wp-content/uploads/2020/11/GTI-2020-web-1.pdf.

——— (2022). *Global Terrorism Index 2022: Measuring the Impact of Terrorism*. IEP. https://www.visionofhumanity.org/wp-content/uploads/2022/03/GTI-2022-web.pdf.

——— (2023). *Global Terrorism Index 2023: Measuring the Impact of Terrorism*. Sydney: IEP.

IJR (Institute for Justice and Reconciliation) (2017). "Towards a Social Cohesion Index for South Africa Using SARB Data." https://www.ijr.org.za/portfolio-items/towards-a-social-cohesion-index-for-south-africa-using-sarb-data/.
Ilic, Igor, and Matt Robinson (2017). "Croatian Leaders Tread Softly in Face of World War Two Revisionism." Reuters, February 10, 2017.
Indeksonline (2018). "Imam Lectures Will Have a Positive Impact." https://indeksonline.net/ligjeratat-e-imameve-ne-burgje-do-te-ndikojne-pozitivisht/.
Ingram, Haroro (2016). "Deciphering Siren Call of Militant Islamic Propaganda: Meaning, Credibility and Behavioral Change." International Center for Counter-Terrorism, September 1, 2016.
Institute for Democracy and Mediation (2021). "The Status of Violent Extremism in Albania: A National Assessment of Drivers, Forms and Threats." March 24, 2021.
Inusah, Husein (2022). "Who Is Afraid of Epistemic Relativism? Disentangling African Philosophy from the 'Universalist Entrapment.'" In *African Potentials: Bricolage, Incompleteness and Lifeness*, edited by Itaru Ohta, Francis Nyamnjoh, and Motji Matsuda, 29–51. Bamenda: Langaa.
Islamovic S ef. (n.d.) Facebook. Available at: https://www.facebook.com/profile.php?id=100069706756991&ref=page_internal.
Ismail, Salwa (2018). *The Rule of Violence: Subjectivity, Memory, and Government in Syria*. Cambridge: Cambridge University Press.
Jabar, Faleh (2000). "Shaykhs and Ideologues: Detribalization and Retribalization in Iraq, 1968–1998." *Middle East Report*, 215, 28–48.
Jakupi, Rudine and Garentina Kraja (2018). "Accounting for the Difference: Vulnerability and Resilience to Violent Extremism in Kosovo. Country Case Study 3." Berlin/Pristina: Berghof Foundation and Kosovar Centre for Security Studies (KCSS). https://berghof-foundation.org/library/accounting-for-the-difference-vulnerability-and-resilience-to-violent-extremism-in-kosovo.
Jalal, Pishtiwan, and Ariel Ahram (2021). "Salafism, Sectarianism, and National Identity in Iraqi Kurdistan." *Middle East Journal*, 75(3), 386–406.
Jamal, Amaney, and Michael Robbins (2022). "Why Democracy Stalled in the Middle East: Economic Despair and the Triumph of the China Model." *Foreign Affairs*, March/April.
Jegic, Denijel (2020). "Croatia Is a Crucible of Hyper-nationalism." Al Jazeera, March 6, 2020.
Jenkins, Brian M. (1975). *International Terrorism: A New Mode of Conflict*. London: Crescent Publications.
Jenkins, Robert (2021). "Thinking Through Non-kinetic Counterterrorism Tools." Strategy Session on Non-Kinetic Counterterrorism Tools. Washington Institute for Near East Policy, November 8, 2021. https://www.washingtoninstitute.org/media/5024.
Jensen, Steffen, and Henrik Vigh, eds. (2018). *Sporadically Radical: Ethnographies of Organised Violence and Militant Mobilisation*. Copenhagen: Museum Tusculanum Press.
Jenson, Jane (2010). *Defining and Measuring Social Cohesion*. London: Commonwealth Secretariat and UN Research Institute for Social Development.
Jentzch, Corinna, Stathis Kalyvas, and Livia Schubiger (2015). "Militias in Civil Wars." *Journal of Conflict Resolution*, 59(5), 755–769.
Jeune Afrique (2022). Niger, Mohamed Bazoum: quel chef de guerre pour un casse-tête sécuritaire? https://www.jeuneafrique.com/1329389/politique/niger-mohamed-bazoum-quel-chef-de-guerre-pour-un-casse-tete-securitaire/.
Joffe, George (2011). *Islamist Radicalization in North Africa*. London: Routledge.
Johnson, Daryl (2018). "Holy Hate: The Far Right's Radicalization of Religion." *Intelligence Report*, Spring.

Johnson-Hanks, Jennifer (2002). "On the Limits of Life Stages in Ethnography: Toward a Theory of Vital Conjunctures." *American Anthropologist*, *104*(3), 865–880.
Jumet, Kira (2019). "Review of Armies and Insurgencies in the Arab Spring." *Journal of Political and Military Sociology*, *46*(2), 392–394.
Kalyvas, Stathis (1999). "Wanton and Senseless? The Logic of Massacres in Algeria." *Rationality and Society*, *11*(3), 243–286.
Kalyvas, Stathis (2003). "The Ontology of Political Violence: Action and Identity in Civil Wars." *Perspectives on Politics*, *1*(3), 475–494.
——— (2006). *The Logic of Violence in Civil War*. Cambridge: Cambridge University Press.
——— (2009). "Civil Wars." In *The Oxford Handbook of Comparative Politics*, edited by Carles Boix and Susan Stokes, 416–434. Oxford: Oxford University Press.
Kaplan, Seth (2008). *Fixing Fragile States: A New Paradigm for Development*. Westport, CT: Praeger.
Karcic, Hikmet (2020). "The Balkan Connection: Foreign Fighters and the Far Right in Ukraine." *Newlines*, May 1, 2020.
Kaungu, Gideon (2021). "Reflections on the Role of Ubuntu as an Antidote to Afro-Phobia." *Journal of African Law*, *65*(S1), 153–170.
Keen, David, and Ruben Andersson (2018). "Double Games: Success, Failure and the Relocation of Risk in Fighting Terror, Drugs and Migration." *Political Geography*, *67*(5), 100–110.
Keenan, Jeremy (2013). *The Dying Sahara: US Imperialism and Terror in Africa*. London: Pluto Press.
Kelly, Luke (2019). "Overview of Research on Far-Right Extremism in the Western Balkans." K4D Helpdesk Report, June 4, 2019.
Kelmendi, Pëllumb, and Elton Skendaj (2022). "Protests in Postwar Societies: Grievances and Contentious Collective Action in Kosovo." *Nationalities Papers*, *51*(5), 1143–1163.
Keohane, Daniel (2008). "The Absent Friend: EU Foreign Policy and Counter-Terrorism." *Journal of Common Market Studies*, *46*(1), 125–146.
Kepel, Giles (2005). *The Roots of Radical Islam*. London: Saqi Books.
Kešmer, Meliha (2020). "Radikalne veze." Osoba iz zapadnog Balkana S Austrijom RSE. https://www.slobodnaevropa.org/a/radikalne-veze-osoba-iz-zapadnog-balkana-s-austrijom/30930268.html.
Khaddour, Kheder, and Kevin Mazur (2017). *Eastern Expectations: The Changing Dynamics in Syria's Tribal Regions*. Carnegie Middle East Center, February 28, 2017.
Khashoggi, Jamal (2014) . "Morocco and Jordan Are Successful Arab Spring Models." Al Arabiya News, September 1, 2014, updated May 20, 2020.
Khatib, Line (2011). *Islamic Revivalism in Syria: The Rise and Fall of Ba'thist Secularism*. London: Routledge.
Khattab, Abdualla (2017). "Ala'sheera Almonfa'la." *Ayn AlMadina Magazine*.
Khosrokhavar, Farhad (2021). *Jihadism in Europe: European Youth and the New Caliphate*. Oxford: Oxford University Press.
Kilcullen, David (2015). *Out of the Mountains: The Coming Age of the Urban Guerrilla*. London: Hurst.
KIPPRA (Kenya Institute for Public Policy Research and Analysis) (2014). *The Status of Social Cohesion in Kenya, 2013 Draft Report. Abridged Version*. Nairobi: KIPPRA, for the National Cohesion and Integration Commission.
Kisić, Izabela, ed. (2020). *Desni ekstremizam u Srbiji*. Beograd: Helsinški odbor za ljudska prava.
Koha.net (2021). "Ipeshkvi Dode Gjergji i uron Myftiut Ternava dhe besimtarëve muslimanë Bajramin." https://www.koha.net/arberi/231568/ipeshkvi-dode-gjergji-i-uron-myftiut-ternava-dhe-besimtareve-myslimane-bajramin/.

Kostić, Branislava, Vukašin Simonović, and Lana Hoeflinger (2019). *Civilno drustvo u province i suzbijanju nasilnog ekstremizma u Srbiji.* Novi Pazar: Kulturni centar DamaD.
Kovacevic, Danijel (2020). "Hungary's Medical Aid Reopens Bosnia's Wounds." *Balkan Insight*, April 16, 2020.
Krasniqi, Köle (2020). "The Latent Dangers of Islamist Extremism in [the] Western Balkan[s]." *Perspectives of Law and Public Administration*, 9(2), 155–159.
Krause, Dino (2020). "How Transnational Jihadist Groups Are Exploiting Local Conflict Dynamics in Western Africa." Danish Institute for International Studies, May 10, 2020.
Kuljić, Todor (2002). *Prevladavanje prošlosti–uzroci i pravci promene slike istorije krajem XX veka.* Beograd: Helsinški odbor za ljudska prava u Srbiji.
Kundnani, Arun (2009). *Spooked! How Not to Prevent Violent Extremism.* London: Institute of Race Relations.
——— (2012). "Radicalisation: The Journey of a Concept." *Race and Class*, 54(2), 3–25.
Kursani, Shpend (2018a). *Extremism Research Forum: Kosovo Report.* London: British Council.
——— (2018b). *Reintegration of Returnees: The Challenge of State and Community Response in Kosovo.* London: British Council.
——— (2018c). "Salafi Pluralism in National Contexts: The Secular State, Nation and Militant Islamism in Kosovo, Albania, and Macedonia." *Southeast European and Black Sea Studies*, 18(2), 301–317.
——— (2019). *Violent Extremism in the Western Balkans.* London: British Council.
Kursani, Shpend, and Krzystof Krakowski (2021). *Engagement in Foreign Wars, Nationalist Riots and Violent Protests: An Experimental Survey Study of Types and Expectations of Violence in Kosovo.* London: British Council.
Kurzman, Charles (2011). *The Missing Martyrs.* New York: Oxford University Press.
Labat, Séverine (1995). *Les islamistes algériens: Entre les urnes et le maquis.* Paris: Éditions du Seuil.
Lacher, Wolfram (2008). "Actually Existing Security: The Political Economy of the Saharan Threat." *Security Dialogue*, 39(4), 411–439.
Laclau, Ernesto (2005). *On Populist Reason.* Brooklyn, NY: Verso.
Lacroix, Stephane (2011). *Awakening Islam: The Politics of Religious Dissent in Contemporary Saudi Arabia.* Cambridge, MA: Harvard University Press.
Lahlou, Mehdi, and Georges Fahmi (2020). "Radicalisation and Resilience Case Study: Tunisia." UM5R, GREASE Project, European University Institute, September 2020. https://grease.eui.eu/wp-content/uploads/sites/8/2021/01/WP4-Report Tunisia.pdf.
Lahoud, Nelly (2010). *The Jihadis' Path to Self-Destruction.* London: Hurst.
Landberg, Chris (2021). Statement for the Record. *House Foreign Affairs Committee, Subcommittee on the Middle East, North Africa, and Global Terrorism, FY 2022 Budget Hearing*, November 17, 2021. https://docs.house.gov/meetings/FA/FA13/20211117/114259/HHRG-117-FA13-Wstate-LandbergC-20211117.pdf.
Langer, Arnim, Frances Stewart, Kristien Smedts, and Leila Demarest (2011). "Conceptualizing and Measuring Social Cohesion in Africa: Towards a Perceptions-Based Index." *Social Indicators Research*, 131, 321–343.
Lažetić, Marina (2021). *Migration, Extremism, and Dangerous Blame Games: Developments and Dynamics in Serbia.* Washington, DC: Resolve Network and United States Institute of Peace.
Lee, Stan (2024). "How Bashar al-Asad Learned to Stop Worrying and Love the War on Terror." *International Studies Quarterly*, 68(2).

Lefko-Everett, Kate (2017). *Towards a Measurement of Social Cohesion for Africa*. Addis Ababa: UN Development Programme.
Lefko-Everett, Kate, Rajem Govender, and Donald Foster, eds. (2016). *Rethinking Reconciliation: Evidence from South Africa*. Pretoria: HSRC Press.
Leininger, Julia, Francesco Burchi, Charlotte Fiedler, Karina Moss, Daneil Nowack, Armin von Schiller, Christoph Sommer, Christoph Strupat, and Sebastian Ziaja (2021). *Social Cohesion: A New Definition and a Proposal for Its Measurement in Africa*. Bonn: German Development Institute.
Leposhtica, Labinot (2016). "Zeqirja Qazimi Convicted." Kallxo.com, May 20, 2016. https://kallxo.com/shkurt/denohet-zeqirja-qazimi/.
Levitt, Matthew (2021). "Rethinking US Efforts on Counterterrorism: Toward a Sustainable Plan Two Decades After 9/11." *Journal of National Security Law and Policy*, *12*(2), 1–11.
Levitt, Matthew, Katrina Mulligan, and Christoper Costa (2021). *Rethinking US Counterterrorism Two Decades After 9/11*. Washington, DC: Washington Institute for Near East Policy.
Lia, Brynjar (2017). "The Jihādī Movement and Rebel Governance: A Reassertion of a Patriarchal Order?" *Die Welt des Islams, 57*(3–4), 458–479.
——— (2021). "The Islamic State's Tribal Policies in Syria and Iraq." *Third World Thematics*, *6*(1), 32–51.
Lister, Charles (2015). *The Syrian Jihad: Al-Qaeda, the Islamic State and the Evolution of an Insurgency*. London: Hurst.
Ljubomirovic, Aleksandar (2022). *The Concept of the Serbian World: A Copy of the Russian World or a Unique Idea for the Multidimensional Cohesion of the Serbian People?* Berlin: Free University Berlin.
Long, Jerry (2004). *Saddam's War of Words: Politics, Religion, and the Iraqi Invasion of Kuwait*. Austin: Texas University Press.
Lounnas, Djallil (2018). *Jihadist Groups in North Africa and the Sahel: Between Disintegration, Reconfiguration, and Resilience*. MENARA Working Paper No. 16, Brussels: MENARA Project.
Lounnas, Djallil, and Michaël Ayari (2023). "Repenser le lien entre djihadisme et délinquance. La trajectoire singulière de revenants tunisiens." *Sécurité globale*, *33*, 35–47.
Lücke, Matthias (2014). *Kosovo Human Development Report: Migration as a Force for Development*. Kosovo: United Nations Development Programme. https://hdr.undp.org/content/kosovo-2014-migration-force-development.
Luković, Danijela (2017). "Za ISIS ratuje 49 osoba iz Srbije." Blic, Beograd.
Lund, Christian (2006). "Twilight Institutions: Public Authority and Local Politics in Africa." *Development and Change, 37*(4), 685–705.
Luxmoore, Jonathan (2018). "Church Urges Fairer Conditions as Bosnia-Herzegovina Elections Near." *National Catholic Reporter*, August 30, 2018.
Lyammouri, Rida (2021). *Tillabéri Region, Niger: Concerning Cycle of Atrocities*. Rabat: Policy Centre for the New South.
Mabrouk, Mehdi (2012). "Tunisia: The Radicalization of Religious Policy." In *Islamist Radicalization in North Africa*, edited by Joffe, George. London: Routledge.
Macaluso, Agnese (2016). "From Countering to Preventing Radicalization Through Education: Limits and Opportunities." HIGJ Working Paper No. 18. The Hague: Hague Institute for Global Justice.
Maghraoui, Abdeslam (2017). "Morocco: The King's Islamists." In *The Islamists Are Coming: Who They Really Are*, edited by Robin Wright, 91–99. Herndon, VA: Woodrow Wilson Center Press.
Maghraoui, Driss (2009). "The Strengths and Limits of Religious Reforms in Morocco." *Mediterranean Politics*, *14*(2), 195–211.

Magid, Aaron (2016). "The King and the Islamists: Jordan Cracks Down on the Muslim Brotherhood." *Foreign Affairs,* May 3, 2016.
Maher, Shiraz (2016). *Salafi-Jihadism: The History of an Idea.* Oxford: Oxford University Press.
Mahmod, Ahmad Kaka (2018). *Interview with Dr. Abdul Latif.* Available at: https://www.youtube.com/watch?v=Mxmnb7NM5X8.
Malkawi, Khetam (2016). "Authorities Close More Muslim Brotherhood Offices, Others to Follow." *Jordan Times,* April 14, 2016.
Mamakani, Ehsan (2016). "KRG Official: Kurdish Islam, Not Extremism." K24, January 6, 2016. https://www.kurdistan24.net/en/story/1741-KRG-official:-Kurdish-Islam,-not-extremism.
Manal, Taha (2017). "Matriarchal and Tribal Identity, Community Resilience, and Vulnerability in South Libya." USIP Special Report 416. Washington, DC: United States Institute of Peace.
Marks, Monika (2013). "Youth Politics and Tunisian Salafism: Understanding the Jihadi Current." *Mediterranean Politics, 18*(1), 104–111.
Marsh, Nicholas, Øystein Rolandsen, Julian Karssen, and Marie Sandnes (2020). *Compounding Fragmentation: Security Force Assistance to Fragile States in the Sahel and Horn of Africa.* Oslo: PRIO.
Martin-Breen, Patrick, and Marty Anderies (2011). *Resilience: A Literature Review.* Brighton: Institute of Development Studies.
Martinez, Jose (2022). *States of Subsistence: The Politics of Bread in Contemporary Jordan.* Redwood, CA: Stanford University Press.
Martinez, Luis (1997). "Les enjeux des négociations entre l'AIS et l'armée." *Politique Etrangère,* Winter, 499–215.
——— (1998). *La Guerre Civile en Algérie.* Paris: Les Editions Khartala.
——— (2000). "L'après guerre civile: les étapes de la réconciliation nationale." *Hal Open Science.*
——— (2003). *Algérie: Les Nouveaux Défis.* Report for the Centre des Etudes de Relations Internationales (CERI). Paris: Science Po.
——— (2005). "Algerie: Les massacres dans la guerre civile." *Revue Internationale de Politique Comparée, 8,* 43–58.
Martini, Alice (2020). "The Syrian Wars of Words: International and Local Instrumentalizations' of the War on Terror." *Third World Quarterly, 41*(4), 725–743.
Mashhour, Faisal Dahmoush Al (2017). *Tribes' Members in Deir Ezzor: From Stability to Revolution: Dynamics of Conflict and Factors of Civil Peace.* Justice for Life, July 2017. https://jfl.ngo/wp-content/uploads/2017/09/TRIBES-MEMBERS-IN-DEIR-EZZOR.pdf.
Matheson, Craig (1987). "Weber and the Classification of Forms of Legitimacy." *British Journal of Sociology, 38*(2), 199–215.
Mazur, Kevin (2020). *Revolution in Syria: Identity, Networks and Repression.* Cambridge: Cambridge University Press.
McCants, William (2015). *The ISIS Apocalypse: The History, Strategy and Doomsday Vision of the Islamic State.* New York: St Martin's Press.
McCauley, Clark, and Sophia Moskalenko (2008). "Mechanisms of Political Radicalization: Pathways Toward Terrorism." *Terrorism and Political Violence, 20*(3), 415–433.
McLaughlin, Gilbert (2024). *Radicalization: A Conceptual Inquiry.* London: Routledge.
Meddeb, Hamza (2020). *The Volatile Tunisia-Libya Border: Between Tunisia's Security Policy and Libya's Militia Factions.* Washington, DC: Carnegie Endowment for International Peace. https://xcept-research.org/wp-content/uploads/2020/10/Meddeb_TunisiaLibya.pdf.

Mendoza, Caroline, and Katy Zurka (2021). "The Summit for Democracy: Advancing Gender Equity and Equality for Representative Societies." Office of Global Women's Issues, US Department of State, December 17, 2021. https://www.state.gov/dipnote-u-s-department-of-state-official-blog/the-summit-for-democracy-advancing-gender-equity-and-equality-for-representative-societies/.

Menkhaus, Ken (2014). "State Failure, State-Building, and Prospects for a Functional Failed State in Somalia." *Annals of the American Academy of Political and Social Science*, *656*(1), 154–172.

Mercy Corps (2022a). *Mobilizing Communities to Build Social Cohesion and Reduce Vulnerability to Violent Extremism: Evidence from a Peacebuilding Program in Niger*. Portland, OR: Mercy Corps.

——— (2022b). *Thought Leadership on Peace and Conflict*. Portland, OR: Mercy Corps.

Merone, Fabio, Theo Blanc, and Ester Sigillò (2021). "The Evolution of Tunisian Salafism After the Revolution: From *la maddhabiyya* to Salafi-Malikism." *International Journal of Middle East Studies*, *53*(3), 455–470.

Merone, Fabio, and Francesco Cavatorta (2013). "Salafist Movement and Sheikhism in the Tunisian Democratic Transitions." *Middle East Law and Governance*, *5*(3), 308–330.

Merone, Fabio, Ester Sigillò, and Damiano De Faci (2018). "Nahda and Tunisian Islamic Activism." In *New Oppositions in the Middle East*, edited by Dara Conduit and Shahram Akbarzadeh, 177–201. London: Springer.

Merton, Robert (1938). "Social Structure and Anomie." *American Sociological Review*, *3*(5), 672–682.

Middell, Matthias (2021). "Cross-Cultural Comparison in Times of Increasing Transregional Connectedness: Perspectives from Historical Sciences and Area Studies on Processes of Respatialization." *Forum: Qualitative Social Research*, *22*(2), art. 19.

Milekic, Sven (2019). "Revisionist Accounts of Croatia's Second World War History Is Worrying Development." Maynooth University, January 22, 2019. https://www.maynoothuniversity.ie/research/spotlight-research/revisionist-accounts-croatia-s-second-world-war-history-worrying-development-writes-sven-milekic-phd.

Ministry of Awqaf of Syria (2016). "A Detailed Report on the Launch of the Youth Religious Team Project at the Ministry of Awqaf." YouTube video, 36:34, January 8, 2016. https://www.youtube.com/watch?v=XPmv0Ohlk-k&t=1668s

Ministry of Foreign Affairs and Expatriates (2013a). "President al-Asad to Le Figaro Newspaper: The Stability of the Region Depends upon Syria's Stability. The Strong Is the One Who Prevents War, Not the One Who Ignites It." Syrian Arab Republic, September 3, 2013. http://mofaex.gov.sy/

——— (2013b). "President al-Asad to the US CBS Channel: Any Aggression on Syria Will Constitute a Direct Support to the Actors Affiliated to al-Qa'ida Including Jabhat al-Nusra and the Islamic State in Iraq and the Levant." Syrian Arab Republic, September 10, 2013. http://mofaex.gov.sy/.

——— (2015a). "President al-Asad to the Italian RAI Television: Da'ish Does Not Have a Breeding Ground Incubator in Syria." Syrian Arab Republic, November 11, 2015. http://mofaex.gov.sy/.

——— (2015b). "President al-Asad to Russian Media: The West Is Crying over Syrian Refugees on the One Hand; and on the Other Hand, It Is Pointing Its Machine Guns at Them Through Its Support of Terrorism." Syrian Arab Republic, September 16, 2015. http://mofaex.gov.sy/.

——— (2019). "President al-Asad in an Interview with the Channel RT International World: In Spite of All Aggressions, Most of the Syrian People Support Its Government." Syrian Arab Republic, November 11, 2019. http://mofaex.gov.sy/.

Mishkova, Diana, Simeon Evstatiev, Edina Bećirević, Stoyan Doklev, Kreshnik Gashi, Marija Ignjatijević, Sara Kelmendi, Predrag Petrović, Albulena Sadiku, Romario Shehu, Evlogi Stanchev, and Sejla Pehlivanovic (2021). *Enabling Environments, Drivers and Occurrence/Non-occurrence of Violent Extremism in the Balkans.* Oslo: PREVEX.

Moghaddam, Fathali M. (2005). "The Roots of Radicalization: Disagreement as a Pathway to Extremism." *American Psychologist, 60*(2), 161–169.

Mokeddem, Mohamed (2002). *Les Afghans algériens: De la Djamaa à la Qaeda.* Alger: Éditions ANEP.

Morocco World News (2023). "Morocco Faces Complicated Return of Former ISIS Fighters." https://www.moroccoworldnews.com/2021/07/343448/morocco-faces-complicated-return-of-former-isis-fighters.

Moustakas, Louis (2022). "A Bibliometric Analysis of Research on Social Cohesion from 1994–2020." *Publications, 10*(1). https://doi.org/10.3390/publications 10010005.

Moyo, Otrude N. (2021). *Africanity and Ubuntu as Decolonizing Discourse.* Cham: Palgrave Macmillan.

Mundy, Jacob (2013). "Wanton and Senseless Revisited: The Study of Warfare in Civil Conflicts and the Historiography of the Algerian Massacres." *African Studies Review, 56*(3), 25–55.

Mustafa, Mohammad S. (2020). *Nationalism and Islamism in the Kurdistan Region of Iraq: The Emergence of the Kurdistan Islamic Union.* London: Routledge.

Nasr, Wassim (2022). "How the Wagner Group Is Aggravating the Jihadi Threat in the Sahel." *CTC Sentinel, 15*(11), 21–30.

Ndlovu-Gatsheni, Sabelo (2020). "The Cognitive Empire, Politics of Knowledge and African Intellectual Productions: Reflections on Struggles for Epistemic Freedom and Resurgence of Decolonisation in the Twenty-First Century." *Third World Quarterly, 42*(5), 882–901.

Nesser, Petter, and Henrik Gråtrud (2019). "When Conflicts Do Not Overspill: The Case of Jordan." *Perspectives on Politics, 19*(2), 492–506.

Neumann, Peter (2006). "Europe's Jihadist Challenge." *Survival, 48*(2), 71–84.

New York Times (1991). "Jordanian Cancels Most Martial Law Rules." July 8, 1991.

Njozela, Lindokuhle, Ingrid Shaw, and Justine Burns (2017). "Towards Measuring Social Cohesion in South Africa: Lessons nor Nation Branding Developers." *Strategic Review for Southern Africa, 39*(1), 29–64.

Nnodim, Paul, and Austin Okigbo (2023). *Ubuntu. A Comparative Study of an African Concept of Justice.* Leuven: Leuven University Press.

NRT (2016). "How Do Kurdistan Salafis View Violence?" YouTube video, 49:15. https://www.youtube.com/watch?v=TUU5X60CsL4.

NURC (National Unity and Reconciliation Commission) (2008). *Social Cohesion in Rwanda: An Opinion Survey. Results 2005–2007.* Kigali: NURC.

OECD (Organisation for Economic Co-operation and Development) (2011). *Perspectives on Global Development 2012: Social Cohesion in a Shifting World.* Paris: OECD Publishing.

——— (2018). "Student Performance and Equity in Education." In *Government at a Glance 2021.* https://www.oecd-ilibrary.org/governance/government-at-a-glance-2021_08ea873f-en.

——— (2020). *Government at a Glance: Western Balkans.* Paris: OECD Publishing.

OHCHR (Office of the United Nations High Commissioner for Human Rights) (2008). *Fact Sheet No. 32: Terrorism and Counterterrorism.* Geneva: United Nations.

Olson, Mancur (2000). *Power and Prosperity: Outgrowing Communist and Capitalist Dictatorships.* New York: Basic Books.

Onditi, Francis, Katharina Mclarren, Gilad Ben-Nun, Yannis Stivachtis, and Pontian Okoth (2023). *The Palgrave Handbook of Diplomatic Thought and Practice in the Digital Age*. London: Palgrave.

Onsomu, Eldah, Nafula Nelima, Munga Boaz, and Kingoro Sellah (2017). *Social Cohesion Index for Kenya: A Methodological Note*. Nairobi: Kenya Institute for Public Policy Research and Analysis.

Ordioni, Natacha (2019). "Les mourchidates marocaines, emblèmes de l'empowerment religieux des femmes?" *Altérités et résistances à l'épreuve du genre en Méditerranée*, November 2019. Aix-en-Provence, France. https://hal.science/hal-03469843/document.

Orsini, Christina (2016). *Narratives of (Non)Intervention: Syria from the Humanitarian to the Terror Lens*. Sciences Po Kuwait Program (Student Paper Award). https://www.sciencespo.fr/kuwait-program/wp-content/uploads/2018/05/KSP_Paper_Award_Spring_2016_ORSINI_Cristina.pdf.

OSCE (Organization for Security and Co-operation in Europe) Mission in BiH (2018). *Two Schools Under One Roof: The Most Visible Example of Discrimination in Education in Bosnia and Herzegovina*. Vienna: OSCE.

Osland, Kari M., and Henriette U. Erstad (2020). "The Fragility Dilemma and Divergent Security Complexes in the Sahel." *International Spectator*, 55(4), 18–36.

Ostiguy, Pierre, and Benjamin Moffitt (2021). "Who Would Identify with an Empty Signifier? The Relational, Performative Approach to Populism." In *Populism in Global Perspective: A Performative and Discursive Approach*, edited by Pierra Ostiguy, Francisco Panizza, and Benjamin Moffitt, 47–72. London: Routledge.

Palani, Kamaran (2021). "Youth Radicalization in Kurdistan: The Government Response." In *Youth Identity, Politics and Change in Contemporary Kurdistan*, edited by Shivan Fazil and Bahar Baser, 223–237. London: Transnational Press.

Pastore, Ferruccio, and Emanuela Roman (2020). "Migration Policies and Threat-Based Extraversion: Analysing the Impact of European Externalisation Policies on African Polities." *Revue européenne des migrations internationales*, 36(1), 133–152.

Peci, Lulzim, and Agon Demjaha (2021a). "Drivers of Radicalisation and Violent Extremism in the Light of State Dynamics in MENA and the Balkans: Kosovo." In *Connekt Country Paper on Macro-Level Drivers*, edited by Damir Kapidžić. Barcelona: European Institute of the Mediterranean. https://h2020connekt.eu/wp-content/uploads/2021/09/Kosovo_CONNEKT_Macro_Drivers.pdf.

——— (2021b). "Kosovo: Macro-drivers of Radicalisation and Violent Extremism." In *Connekt Country Paper on Macro-Level Drivers*, edited by Damir Kapidžić, September 7, 2021. Barcelona: European Institute of the Mediterranean. https://h2020connekt.eu/publications/mapping-the-drivers-of-radicalisation-in-the-light-of-state-dynamics-in-kosovo/.

Perica, Vjekoslav (2015). "Power, Corruption, and Dissent: Varieties of Contemporary Croatian Political Catholicism." *Occasional Papers on Religion in Eastern Europe*, 35(4), art. 2.

Perl, Raphael (2005). "Anti-terror Strategy, the 9/11 Commission Report, and Terrorism Financing: Implications for US Policymakers." *Strategic Insights*, 4(1), 1–13.

Pérouse, Josselin (2019). "Croatia Has a Problem with Historical Revisionism, and HDZ Is to Blame." *My Country? Europe*, June 7, 2019. https://mycountryeurope.com/politics/croatia-historical-revisionism-hdz/.

Perteshi, Skender (2020). *Kosova Resilience Index. Violent Extremism in Kosova: What Community Resilience Can Teach Us?* Kosovar Centre for Security Studies.

Pešić, Vesna (1996). *Serbian Nationalism and the Origins of the Yugoslav Crisis*. Washington, DC: United States Institute of Peace.

Petrović, Predrag (2024). "Serbia: Government and the Scarecrow." In *Russia and the Far-Right: Insights from Ten European Countries*, edited by Kacper Rekawek, Barbara Molas, and Thomas Renard, 77–110. The Hague: ICCT Press.

Petrović, Predrag, and Srdjan Hercigonja (2022). *There Is No Democracy in Serbia, nor Is It Desirable*. Belgrade: BCSP and KCSS.

Petrović, Predrag, and Marija Ignjatijević (2022a). *Migrants Are Leaving, but Hatred Remains: The Anti-Migrant Extreme Right in Serbia*. Belgrade: Belgrade Centre for Security Policy.

——— (2022b). *Resilience to Violent Extremism in Serbia: The Case of Sanjak*. Belgrade: Belgrade Centre for Security Policy.

Petrović, Predrag, and Isidora Stakić (2018). *Western Balkans Extremism Research Forum: Serbia Report*. Belgrade: British Council.

Phillips, Chrstopher (2015). "Sectarianism and Conflict in Syria." *Third World Quarterly*, 36(2), 357–376.

Pieri, Zacharias, and Jacob Zenn (2017). "The Boko Haram Paradox: Ethnicity, Religion, and Historical Memory in Pursuit of a Caliphate." In *Understanding Boko Haram: Terrorism and Insurgency in Africa*, edited by J. Hentz and H. Solomon, 56–80. London: Routledge.

Pierret, Thomas, and Laila Alrefaai (2021). "Religious Governance in Syria Amid Territorial Fragmentation." In *Islamic Institutions in Arab States: Mapping the Dynamics of Control, Co-option, and Contention,* edited by Frederic Wehrey, 53–73. Washington, DC: Carnegie Endowment.

Pilkington, Hilary. ed. (2024). *Resisting Radicalization? Understanding Young People's Journeys Through Radicalizing Milieus*. New York: Berghahn.

Popovic, Milos (2021). "Pathways of Foreign Fighters." Leiden Security and Global Affairs (blog), March 29, 2021. https://www.leidensecurityandglobalaffairs.nl/articles/pathways-of-foreign-fighters.

Popović, Viktor Gunnarsson (2020). "Who Is Bosnian? Ethnic Division in Bosnia and Herzegovina and Its Implications for a National Identity." Undergraduate thesis. Swedish Defence University.

Posen, Barry (1993). "The Security Dilemma and Ethnic Conflict." *Survival*, 35(1), 27–47.

Postel, Thérèse (2013). "The Young and the Normless: Al Qaeda's Ideological Recruitment of Western Extremists." *Connections*, 12(4), 99–118.

Poudiougou, Ibrahima (2022). "Terra e guerra nel paese Dogon: la nascita di Dan Nan Ambassagou, tra autodifesa e antiterrorism." In *Jihad in Africa: Terrorismo e Controterrorismo in Sahel*, edited by Eduardo Baldaro and Luca Raineri, 201–220. Bologna: Il Mulino.

Prelec, Marko, and Ashish Pradhan (2021). *Grappling with Bosnia's Dual Crises*. Brussels: ICG.

Qehaja, Florian (2016). "Beyond Gornje Maoče and Ošve: Radicalization in the Western Balkans." In *Jihadist Hotbeds: Understanding Local Radicalization Processes*, edited by Arturo Varvelli, 75–92. Milano: ISPI.

Qutb, Sayyid (1987). *Maʿālim fī al-ṭarīq*. 11th ed. Cairo: Dār al-Shurūk.

Rabasa, Angel, Stacie Pettyjohn, Jeremy Ghez, and Christopher Boucek (2010). *Deradicalizing Islamist Extremists*. Santa Monica, CA: RAND Corporation.

Radio Free Europe (2017). "Convictions for the Kumanova Group Rendered." Video, 1:53. https://www.evropaelire.org/a/denimet-per-grupin-e-komunoves-/28831384.html.

Radio Free Europe (2020). "Sarajevo Mass for Pro-Nazi WWII Collaborators Draws Widespread Condemnation", Radio Free Europe, May 15, 2020. https://

www.rferl.org/a/sarajevo-mass-for-pro-nazi-wwii-collaborators-draws-widespread-condemnation/30614272.html.
——— (2023). "Bosnian Serbs' President Leads Victory Day March in Banja Luka." *Radio Free Europe*, May 10, 2023. https://www.rferl.org/a/bosnia-serbs-victory-day-dodik/32404248.html.
Raets, Sigrid (2017). "That We in Me: Considering Terrorist Desistance from a Social Identity Perspective." *Journal for Deradicalization*, 13, 1–28.
Raineri, Luca (2018a). "Human Smuggling Across Niger: State-Sponsored Protection Rackets and Contradictory Security Imperatives." *Journal of Modern African Studies*, 56(1), 63–86.
——— (2018b). *If Victims Become Perpetrators: Factors Contributing to Vulnerability and Resilience to Violent Extremism in the Central Sahel*. London: International Alert.
——— (2022). "Explaining the Rise of Jihadism in Africa: The Crucial Case of the Islamic State of the Greater Sahara." *Terrorism and Political Violence*, 34(8), 1632–1646.
Raineri, Luca, Abdoul Wakhab Cissé, Jack Kalpakian, Djallil Lounnas, and Francesco Strazzari (2020). "Summarizing the EU and Other Stakeholders' Prevention Strategy Towards Violent Extremism in the Maghreb and the Sahel." PREVEX Policy Brief D6.1. Oslo: PREVEX. https://www.prevex-balkan-mena.eu/wp-content/uploads/2020/12/PREVEX-D6.1-Policy-Brief-Maghreb-and-Sahel-FINAL.pdf.
Raineri, Luca, and Francesco Strazzari (2015). "State, Secession and Jihad: The Micropolitical Economy of Conflict in Northern Mali." *African Security*, 8(4), 249–271.
——— (2022). "Drug Smuggling and the Stability of Fragile States. The Diverging Trajectories of Mali and Niger." *Journal of Intervention and Statebuilding*, 16(2), 222–239.
Rajulton, Fernando, Zenaida Ravanera, and Roderic Beaujot (2007). "Measuring Social Cohesion: An Experiment Using the Canadian National Survey of Giving, Volunteering and Participation." *Social Indicators Research*, 80(3), 461–492.
Ramadan, Salih (2013). "al-Ahālī yu'linūn al-nafīr al-'ām ḍidd 'al-maḥẓūra' . . . wa qarār shaʻbī bi-tahjīr al-ikhwān min 'al-manṣūra.'" *al-Watan*, December 26, 2013. https://www.elwatannews.com/news/details/380065.
Rambo, Lewis R. (1993). *Understanding Religious Conversion*. New Haven, CT: Yale University Press.
Reno, William (2011). *Warfare in Independent Africa*. Cambridge: Cambridge University Press.
Republic of Kosovo (2015). *Strategy on Prevention of Violent Extremism and Radicalization Leading to Terrorism 2015–2020*. Pristina: Office of the Prime Minister.
Rezrazi, Mostafa, Kei Nakagawa, and Shoji Matsumoto (2016). *Morocco's War on Terrorism: The Case for Security Cooperation Today*. Tokyo: Gilgamesh.
Ristic, Marija, Sven Milekic, Maja Zivanovic and Denis Dzidic (2017). "Far-Right Balkan Groups Flourish on the Net." *Resonant Voice Initiative*, 5 May. Available at: https://resonantvoices.info/far-right-balkan-groups-flourish-on-the-net/806/.
Roy, Olivier (2008). *Al Qaeda in the West as a Youth Movement: The Power of a Narrative*. CEPS Policy Brief 168. Brussels: Centre for European Policy Studies.
——— (2017a). "Introduction." In *Tribes and Global Jihadism*, edited by Virginie Collombier and Olivier Roy, 1–13. Oxford: Oxford University Press.
——— (2017b). *Jihad and Death: The Global Appeal of Islamic State*. Oxford: Oxford University Press.
Rubin, Lawrence, Rohan Gunaratna, and Jolene Jerard (2011). *Terrorist Rehabilitation and Counter-Radicalization: New Approaches to Counterterrorism*. London: Routledge.

Rudaw (2014). "Salafis in Kurdistan Condemn Islamic State." Rudaw, August 17, 2014. https://www.rudaw.net/english/kurdistan/170820142.
Ruge, Majda (2020). "Hostage State: How to Free Bosnia from Dayton's Paralysing Grip." European Council on Foreign Relations, November 18, 2020. https://ecfr.eu/publication/how-europe-and-the-us-can-take-bosnia-beyond-dayton-25-years-later/.
——— (2022). "The Past and the Furious: How Russia's Revisionism Threatens Bosnia." European Council on Foreign Relations, September 13, 2022. https://ecfr.eu/publication/the-past-and-the-furious-how-russias-revisionism-threatens-bosnia/.
Rupesinghe, Natasja, and Morten Bøås (2019). *Local Drivers of Violent Extremism in Central Mali*. Addis Abeba: UN Development Programme.
Sadriu, Behar (2019). "Rebranding the War on Terror and Remaking Muslim Subjectivities." *East European Politics*, 35(4), 433–456.
Safi, Omar (2020). *The Intelligence State in Tunisia: Security and Mukhabarat (1881–1965)*. London: I. B. Tauris.
Sageman, Marc (2004). *Understanding Terror Networks*. Philadelphia: University of Pennsylvania Press.
Saïed, Kais (n.d.) Facebook. Available at: https://www.facebook.com/KaisSaiedTN/.
Salem, Hajer Ben Hadj (2021). "Complementary or Equal? The Rise of Moderate Islamism and the Undeclared War on Women Rights in Tunisia." In *Küreselleşen Dünyada Kadın ve Siyaset II*, 107–116. London: Transnational Press.
Salmi, Ilkka (2021). *A European Perspective on Counterterrorism*. Washington, DC: Washington Institute for Near East Policy.
Saloukh, Bassel (2016). "Overlapping Contests and Middle East International Relations: The Return of the Weak Arab State." Memo for International Relations and a New Middle East symposium. https://pomeps.org/wpcontent/uploads/2016/01/POMEPS_BriefBooklet28_Sectarianism_Web.pdf.
Sandor, Adam, and Aurélie Campana (2019). "Les groupes djihadistes au Mali, entre violence, recherche de légitimité et politiques locales." *Canadian Journal of African Studies*, 53(3), 415–430.
Sangaré, Boukary (2016). *Le centre du Mali: épicentre du djihadisme?* Note d'Analyse. Brussels: GRIP.
Santini, Ruth Hanau, and Giulia Cimini (2019). "Intended and Unintended Consequences of Security Assistance in Post-2011 Tunisia." *Contemporary Arab Affairs*, 12(1), 91–106.
Sardan, Jean-Pierre (2023). *L'enchevêtrement des Crises au Sahel*. Paris: Karthala.
Sartorius, Raphael (2022). "The Notion of 'Development' in Ubuntu." *Religion and Development*, 1(1), 95–115.
Schiefer, David, and Jolanda van der Noll (2017). "The Essentials of Social Cohesion: A Literature Review." *Social Indicators Research*, 132(2), 579–603.
Schmid, Alex (2013). *Radicalisation, De-Radicalisation, Counter-Radicalisation: A Conceptual Discussion and Literature Review*. ICCT Research Paper. The Hague: International Centre for Counter-terrorism.
——— (2014). *Al-Qaeda's Single Narrative' and Attempts to Develop Counter-Narratives*. ICCT Research Paper. The Hague: International Centre for Counter-terrorism.
Schneider, Tobias (2016). "The Decay of the Syrian Regime Is Much Worse Than You Think." War on the Rocks, August 31, 2016. https://warontherocks.com/2016/08/the-decay-of-the-syrian-regime-is-much-worse-than-you-think/.
Schouten, Peer (2012). "Theory Talk #47: Jean Francois Bayart on Globalization, Subjectification, and the Historicity of State Formation." *Theory Talks*. https://www.files.ethz.ch/isn/155108/Theory%20Talk47_Bayart.pdf.
Schwedler, Jillian (2022). *Protesting Jordan: Geographies of Power and Dissent*. Redwood City, CA: Stanford University Press.

SCORE (2022). "About SCORE." Centre for Sustainable Peace and Democratic Development. https://www.scoreforpeace.org/en/about.
Sedgwick, Martin (2007). "Jihad, Modernity, and Sectarianism." *Nova Religio*, *11*(2), 6–27.
SeeD (Centre for Sustainable Peace and Democratic Development) (2018). "A Global Innovation Hub for Evidence-Based Policy and Programme Design." Nicosia: Centre for Sustainable Peace and Democratic Development.
——— (2022a). Website. Centre for Sustainable Peace and Democratic Development. https://seedsofpeace.eu/.
——— (2022b). "Our Methodology." In *The Centre for Sustainable Peace and Democratic Development*. https://scr4.scoreforpeace.org/storage/pdfs/ORG_Methodology_Summary_FINAL.pdf.
Sejdiu, Erblina (2021). "Planifikonin sulme terroriste ndaj KFOR-it, diskotekave në Graçanicë dhe Kishës Ortodokse, dënohen me 25 vite burgim." Kallxo.com, September 4, 2019. https://kallxo.com/ligji/planifikonin-sulme-terroriste-ndaj-kfor-it-diskotekave-ne-gracanice-dhe-kishes-ortodokse-denohen-me-25-vite-burgim/.
Seurat, Michel (2012). *Syrie, L'État de barbarie*. Paris: Presses Universitaires de France.
Sheikh, Mona Kanwal (2022). "Transnational Jihad as a Bundled Conflict-Constellation." *Studies in Conflict and Terrorism*. Special Issue on Transnationalization of Jihadist Conflicts. April 6, 2022.
Shtuni, Adrian (2015). "Ethnic Albanian Foreign Fighters in Iraq and Syria." *CTC Sentinel*, *8*(4), 11–14.
——— (2016). "Dynamics of Radicalization and Violent Extremism in Kosovo." *US Institute of Peace Special Report*. https://www.usip.org/sites/default/files/SR397-Dynamics-of-Radicalization-and-Violent-Extremism-in-Kosovo.pdf.
——— (2019). "Western Balkans Foreign Fighters and Homegrown Jihadis: Trends and Implications." *CTC Sentinel*, *12*(7), 18–24.
Sifaoui, Mohamed (2010). *Al Qaida au Maghreb Islamique: le groupe terroriste qui menace la France*. Paris: Les Éditions Encre d'Orient.
Silber, Mitchell, and Arvin Bhatt (2007). *Radicalization in the West: The Homegrown Threat*. New York: NY Police Department.
Simoncini, Guendalina (2021). "Beyond the 'Epopee of Ben Guerdane': Exploring the Plurality of Resistance at the South-Eastern Tunisian Border." *Studi Magrebini*, *19*(1), 88–109.
——— (2024). "Counterterrorism in Transition: Post-2011 Tunisian Democracy and the War on Terror." Presentation of the volume, April 23, 2024. Department of Civilization and Shapes Knowledge. https://www.cfs.unipi.it/eventi/counterterrorism-in-transition-post-2011-tunisian-democracy-and-the-war-on-terror/.
Skare, Erik (2022). "Staying Safe by Being Good? The EU's Normative Decline as a Security Actor in the Middle East." *European Journal of International Security*, *8*(3), 337–353.
Skare, Erik, Ahmad Mhidi, Georges Fahmi, Nouran Ahmed, Kamaran Palani, Myriam Ababsa, Olivier Roy, and Dlawer Ala'Aldeen (2021a). "Enabling Environments, Drivers, and Occurrence/Non-Occurrence of Violent Extremism in the Region." PREVEX Working Paper D7.2. Oslo: PREVEX. https://www.prevex-balkan-mena.eu/wp-content/uploads/2022/01/D7.2_final.pdf.
——— (2021b). "Summarizing Lessons Learnt on the EU's Measures to Prevent Violent Extremism in the Region." PREVEX Policy Brief D7.5. https://www.prevex-balkan-mena.eu/wp-content/uploads/2021/12/D7.5_final.pdf.
Skretting, Vidar (2021). "Pragmatism and Purism in Jihadist Governance: The Islamic Emirate of Azawad Revisited." *Studies in Conflict and Terrorism*, *47*(7), 1–25.
Skrukwa, Grzegorz (2020). "Serbia's and Croatia's Struggles with the Past." *New Eastern Europe*, no. 6.

Social Cohesion Hub (n.d.). https://www.socialcohesion.info.
Spahiu, Ebi (2015). "Ethnic Albanian Foreign Fighters and the Islamic State." *Terrorism Monitor Volume*, *13*(10).
Stakić, Isidora (2016). "Serbian Nationalism and Right-Wing Extremism." In *Violent Extremism in the Western Balkans*, edited by Filip Ejdus and Predrag Jureković, 57–86. Vienna: Federal Ministry of Defence, Republic of Austria.
Stenersen, Anne (2020). "Jihadism After the 'Caliphate': Towards a New Typology." *British Journal of Middle Eastern Studies*, *47*(5), 774–793.
Stephens, William, Stijn Sieckelinc, and Hans Boutellier (2019). "Preventing Violent Extremism: A Review of the Literature." *Studies in Conflict and Terrorism*, *44*(4), 346–361.
Sterman, David, and Nate Rosenblatt (2018). "All Jihad Is Local: Volume II ISIS in North Africa and the Arabian Peninsula." Policy paper, April 5, 2018. Washington, DC: New America. https://www.newamerica.org/internationalsecurity/policy-papers/all-jihad-local.
Stevanovic, Nemanja (2021). "Experts Urge Improved Anti-Terrorism Strategy in Serbia." *Balkan Insight*, November 23, 2021. https://balkaninsight.com/2021/11/23/experts-urge-improved-anti-terrorism-strategy-in-serbia/.
Stimson Study Group on Counterterrorism Spending (2018). *Counterterrorism Spending: Protecting America While Promoting Efficiencies and Accountability*. Washington, DC: Stimson Center. https://www.stimson.org/wp-content/files/file-attachments/CT_Spending_Report_0.pdf.
Stojkovski, Filip, and Natasia Kalajdziovski (2018). *Community Perspectives on the Prevention of Violent Extremism in Macedonia: Country Case Study 1*. Berlin/Skopje: Berghof Foundation and Democracy Lab.
Strazzari, Francesco (2015). *Azawad and the Rights of Passage: The Role of Illicit Trade in the Logic of Armed Group Formation in Northern Mali*. Oslo: Norwegian Centre for Conflict Resolution (NOREF).
Strazzari, Francesco, and Bertine Kamphuis (2012). "Hybrid Economies and Statebuilding: On the Resilience of the Extralegal." *Global Governance*, *18*(1), 57–72.
Stronski, Paul, and Annie Himes (2019). *Russia's Game in the Balkans*. Washington, DC: Carnegie Endowment for International Peace.
Struwig, Jare, Yul Derek Davids, Benjamin Roberts, Moses Sithole, Virginia Tilley, Gina Weir-Smith, and Tholang Mokhele (2013). "Towards a Social Cohesion Barometer for South Africa." In *State of the Nation: South Africa: 2012–2013*, 399–421. Pretoria: HSRC Press.
Sven, Milekic, Marija Ristic, Maja Zivanovic, and Denis Dzidic Ristic (2017). "Far-Right Balkan Groups Flourish on the Net." Resonant Voices Initiative, May 5, 2017. https://resonantvoices.info/far-right-balkan-groups-flourish-on-the-net/806/.
Svensson, Isak, and Desiree Nilsson (2022). "Capitalizing on Cleavages: Transnational Jihadist Conflicts, Local Fault Lines and Cumulative Extremism." *Studies in Conflict, and Terrorism*. Special Issue on Transnationalization of Jihadist Conflicts, April 18, 2022.
Sweis, Rana F. (2016). "ISIS Is Said to Claim Responsibility for Deadly Attack in Jordan." *New York Times*, December 20, 2016.
Syrian Arab News Agency (2019). "President al-Asad Inaugurates the International Islamic Sham Center to Confront Terrorism and Extremism: The One Who Betrays Its Nation Cannot Be a True and Honest Believer." https://sana.sy/en/?p=166020.
Tahrir Institute for Middle East Policy (2019). "TIMEP Brief: Law No.19 of 2012: Counter-terrorism Law." Tahrir Institute for Middle East Policy, January 7, 2019.
Takvorian, Charles (2022). "A Bear in the Desert: How Putin Justified the Russian Military Intervention in Syria." Graduate School of Public and International Affairs, University of Ottawa.

Tawil, Camille (2010). *Brothers in Arms: The Story of Al Qaida and the Arab Jihadists*. London: Saqi.

Teets, Jessica C., and Erica Chenoweth (2009). "To Bribe or to Bomb: Do Corruption and Terrorism Go Together?" In *Corruption, Global Security, and World Order*, edited by Robert I. Rotberg, 167–193. Washington, DC: Brookings Institute Press.

Tella, Oluwaseun (2021). *Africa's Soft Power: Philosophies, Political Values, Foreign Policies and Cultural Exports*. London: Routledge.

Thurston, Alexander (2017). "Algeria's GIA: The First Major Armed Group to Fully Subordinate Jihadism to Salafism." *Islamic Law and Society*, 24, 412–436.

—— (2020). *Jihadists of North Africa and the Sahel: Local Politics and Rebel Groups*. Cambridge: Cambridge University Press.

—— (2021). "The Sahel's Oasis of Stability Isn't Really Stable." InkStick, March 3, 2021. https://inkstickmedia.com/the-sahels-oasis-of-stability-isnt-really-stable/.

Tönnies, Ferdinand (1887). *Gemeinschaft und Gesellschaft. Abhandlung des Communismus und des Socialismus als empirischer Culturformen*. Leipzig: Fues's Verlag.

Torelli, Sefano, Fabio Merone, and Francesco Cavatorta (2012). "Salafism in Tunisia: Challenges and Opportunities for Democratization." *Middle East Policy*, 19(4), 140–154.

Tozy, Mohammed (1999). *Monarchie et Islam Politique au Maroc*. Presses de Sciences Po.

Trošt, Tamara Pavasović, and Koen Slootmaeckers (2015). "Religion, Homosexuality and Nationalism in the Western Balkans: The Role of Religious Institutions in Defining the Nation." In *Religious and Sexual Nationalisms in Central and Eastern Europe: God, Gays and Governments*, edited by Srdjan Scremac and Ruard Ganzevoort, 154–180. Leiden: Brill.

Turčalo, Sead, and Hikmet Karčić (2021). "The Far Right in Bosnia and Herzegovina: Historical Revisionism and Genocide Denial." *Balkan Insight*. https://balkaninsight.com/wp-content/uploads/2021/08/The-Far-Right-in-Bosnia-and-Herzegovina_preview_without-IRI-logo.pdf.

UNDP (United Nations Development Programme) (2015). *Predicting Peace: The Social Cohesion and Reconciliation Index as a Tool for Conflict Transformation*. Nicosia: UNDP Action for Cooperation and Trust.

—— (2016). *Preventing Violent Extremism Through Promoting Inclusive Development, Tolerance and Respect for Diversity*. New York: UNDP.

—— (2017). *Journey to Extremism*. New York: UNDP.

—— (2020). *Strengthening Social Cohesion: Conceptual Framing and Programming Implications*. New York: UNDP.

—— (2022). *Prevention of Violent Extremism*. New York: UNDP.

—— (2023). *Journey to Extremism in Africa: Pathways to Recruitment and Disengagement*. New York: UNDP.

—— (n.d.). Human Development Index. https://hdr.undp.org/data-center/human-development-index#/indicies/HDI.

UNECA (United Nations Economic Commission for Africa) (2016). *Social Cohesion in Eastern Africa*. Addis Ababa: UNECA.

United Nations (2021). "Bosnia and Herzegovina Remains in Effect 'a Frozen Conflict' as Political Leaders Push Nationalistic Agendas, High Representative Tells Security Council." Press release, May 4, 2021. https://press.un.org/en/2021/sc14511.doc.htm.

United Nations and World Bank (2018). *Pathways for Peace: Inclusive Approaches to Preventing Violent Conflict*. Washington, DC: World Bank.

UNSC (United Nations Security Council) (2014). "Resolution 2178 (2014)." September 24, 2014. https://documents.un.org/doc/undoc/gen/n14/547/98/pdf/n1454798.pdf.

―――― (2020). *Final Report of the Panel of Experts on Mali Established Pursuant to Security Council Resolution 2374 (2017)*. New York: United Nations.

UNSG (United Nations Secretary-General) (2016). "Plan of Action to Prevent Violent Extremism." New York: United Nations.

USAID (United States Agency for International Development) (2011). *The Development Response to Violent Extremism And Insurgency: Putting Principles into Practice*. Washington, DC: USAID. https://2012-2017.usaid.gov/sites/default/files/documents/1870/VEI_Policy_Final.pdf.

―――― (2019). *USAID Policy Framework: Ending the Need for Foreign Assistance*. Washington, DC: USAID. https://www.usaid.gov/sites/default/files/2022-05/Web_PF-MINI_BOOKLET_10APRIL2019.pdf.

―――― (2020). *Policy for Countering Violent Extremism Through Development Assistance*. Washington, DC: USAID.https://www.usaid.gov/sites/default/files/2022-05/USAID-publication-Policy-for-Countering-Violent-Extremism-through-Development-Assistance-April2020.pdf.

―――― (2021). *Congressional Testimony: Statement of Robert W. Jenkins, Assistant to the Administrator for the Bureau of Conflict Prevention and Stabilization, before the House Foreign Affairs Committee Subcommittee on Middle East, North Africa, and Global Counterterrorism*. 118th Congress (September 29, 2021). https://www.usaid.gov/news-information/congressional-testimony/sep-28-2021-robert-w-jenkins-assistant-administrator-bureau-cps/.

US Department of State (2019). "Syria." In *Country Reports on Terrorism 2019*. Washington, DC: Bureau of Counterterrorism. https://www.state.gov/reports/country-reports-on-terrorism-2019/syria/.

―――― (2020). *Country Reports on Terrorism 2019*. Washington, DC: Bureau of Counterterrorism. https://www.state.gov/reports/country-reports-on-terrorism-2020/.

Utas, Mats, and Henrik Vigh (2017). "Radicalized Youth: Oppositional Poses and Positions." In *Africa's Insurgents: Navigating an Evolving Landscape*, edited by Morten Bøås and Kevin C. Dunn, 23–42. Boulder, CO: Lynne Rienner.

Van Bruinessen, Martin (1992). *Agha, Shaikh and State: Social and Political Structures of Kurdistan*. London: Zed Books.

Van Metre, Lauren, and Thomas Scherer (2023). *Preventing and Countering Violent Extremism: Assessing Missteps and Promising Community Approaches*. Washington, DC: United States Institute of Peace.

Veljan, Nejra, and Sead Turčalo (2018). *Community Perspectives on the Prevention of Violent Extremism in Bosnia and Herzegovina*. Berlin: Atlantic Initiative and Berghof Foundation.

Vigh, Henrik (2003). *Navigating Terrains of War: Youth and Soldiering in Guinea-Bissau*. New York: Berghahn Books.

―――― (2008). "Crisis and Chronicity: Anthropological Perspectives on Continuous Conflict and Decline." *Ethnos*, 73(1), 5–24.

Violations Documentation Center in Syria (2015). "Counter-terrorism Court: A Tool for War Crimes." Special Report on Counter-Terrorism Law No. 19 and the Counter-Terrorism Court in Syria. April 2015. https://syriaaccountability.org/counter-terrorism-court-as-a-tool-for-war-crimes-a-report-by-the-violations-documentation-center-in-syria/.

Visoka, Gezim (2017). *Shaping Peace in Kosovo*. Basingstoke, UK: Palgrave Macmillan.

Vladisavljevic, Anja (2018). "Croatian Activists Condemn Media Reporting on Migrants." *Balkan Insight*, November 12, 2018.
Voice of America (2010). "Tetovo: Six Killed During a Police Operation Against Armed Groups." https://www.zeriamerikes.com/a/a-30-2007-11-07-voa6-85721717/439773.html.
Vuksanovic, Vuk (2021). "Turkey's Pragmatic Policy in the Balkans Has Its Limits." *Balkan Insight*, November 11, 2021.
Vurmo, Gjergji (2018). *Transforming Albania's C/PVE Efforts into Community Resilience and Development Matrix*. Podgorica: British Council.
Wagemakers, Joas (2016). "Salafism." In *Oxford Research Encyclopedia of Religion*. https://doi.org/10.1093/acrefore/9780199340378.013.255.
Wainscott, Ann Marie (2017). *Bureaucratizing Islam: Morocco and the War on Terror*. Cambridge: Cambridge University Press.
Walkenhorst, Peter (2018). *What Holds Asian Societies Together?* Gütersloh: Bertelsmann Stiftung.
Waterbury, John (1970). *The Commander of the Faithful: The Moroccan Political Elite*. New York: Columbia University Press.
Watkins, Jessica (2022). *Creating Consent in an Illiberal Order: Policing Disputes in Jordan*. Cambridge: Cambridge University Press.
White House (1996). *A National Security Strategy of Engagement and Enlargement*. February 1996. https://history.defense.gov/Portals/70/Documents/nss/nss1996.pdf?ver=4f8riCrLnHIA-H0itYUp6A%3d%3d.
——— (2011). *National Strategy for Counterterrorism*. June 2011. https://obamawhitehouse.archives.gov/sites/default/files/counterterrorism_strategy.pdf.
Whiteside, Craig, and Anas Elallame (2020). "Accidental Ethnographers: The Islamic State's Tribal Engagement Experiment." *Small Wars and Insurgencies*, 31(2), 219–240.
Wilén, Nina (2023). *Here Are Four Things the West Gets Wrong About Africa*. Egmont Policy Brief 304. Brussels: Egmont Institute.
Williams, Brian, and Robert Souza (2016). "The Consequences of Russia's 'Counterterrorism' Campaign in Syria." *CTC Sentinel*, 9(11), 23–30.
Willis, Miachel (1999). *The Islamist Challenge in Algeria: A Political History*. New York: New York University Press.
——— (2012). *Politics and Power in the Maghreb—Algeria, Tunisia and Morocco from Independence to the Arab Spring*. London: Hurst.
Wolf, Anne (2013). "Tunisia: Signs of Domestic Radicalization Post-Revolution." ETH Zürich: Center for Security Studies. https://css.ethz.ch/en/services/digital-library/articles/article.html/157419.
World Bank (2022). *Understanding Poverty: Social Cohesion and Resilience*. https://www.worldbank.org/en/topic/social-cohesion-and-resilience#2.
——— (2023). *Towards Sustainable Growth: Western Balkans Regular Economic Report*. Washington, DC World Bank.
Wright-Neville, David, and Debra Smith (2009). "Political Rage: Terrorism and the Politics of Emotion." *Global Change, Peace, and Security*, 21(1), 85–98.
Yom, Sean (2023). "The Everyday Politics of Authoritarian Rule in Jordan." Middle East Research and Information Project (MERIP), January 3, 2023. https://merip.org/2023/03/the-everyday-politics-of-authoritarian-rule-in-jordan/.
Zelin, Anton (2020). *Your Sons Are at Your Service: Tunisia's Missionaries of Jihad*. New York: Columbia University Press.
Zollner, Barbra (2009). *The Muslim Brotherhood: Hasan al-Hudaybi and Ideology*. London: Routledge.

Contributors

Dlawer Ala'Aldeen, founding president of the Middle East Research Institute (MERI), was formerly a Kurdistan Regional Government (KRG) minister of higher education and scientific research and professor of medicine at Nottingham University, United Kingdom.

Edina Bećirevi is professor of security studies at the University of Sarajevo and cofounder of the Atlantic Initiative Center for Security and Justice Research. She has published extensively on transitional justice, genocide, and extremism.

Gilad Ben-Nun is senior researcher at Leipzig University's Centre for Area Studies, where he teaches global studies and the history of international law. His book *Seeking Asylum in Israel: Refugees and the History of Migration Law* (2017) was nominated for the 2017 US National Jewish Book Award.

Laura Berlingozzi is a postdoctoral researcher at the Sant'Anna School of Advanced Studies in Pisa. Drawing on insights from critical security studies and feminist approaches, she employs ethnographic methods in her research and focuses on conflict dynamics in West Africa, particularly jihadist insurgencies and counterinsurgency practices in the Sahel.

Steven Blockmans is a senior research fellow and previously director of research at the Centre for European Policy Studies (CEPS) in Brussels. He is also a senior fellow at the International Centre for Defence and Security

(ICDS), a visiting professor at the College of Europe (Bruges and Natolin), and editor in chief of *European Foreign Affairs Review*.

Morten Bøås is research professor at the Norwegian Institute of International Affairs (NUPI). Dr. Bøås has extensive fieldwork experience in several African countries and was the principal investigator of the EU Horizon 2020–funded project PREVEX: Preventing Violent Extremism in the Balkans and the MENA from 2020 to 2023.

Silvia Carenzi is a PhD candidate at Scuola Normale Superiore, Italy. She is an associate researcher at the Italian Institute for International Political Studies and her research interests include dynamics of political violence, armed groups, and Islamic movements, especially in Syria.

Abdoul Wakhab Cissé is coordinator of the ARDOA Institute, a research institute on trends in West Africa that consists of a network of researchers from Senegal, Mali, Niger, Burkina Faso, Ivory Coast, and Guinea. Dr. Cissé's research covers topics related to social contract building, violent extremism, political upheavals, the nexus between climate change, security, and migration, and political regime legitimacy.

Dylan Macchiarini Crosson is a researcher in the EU Foreign Policy Unit at Centre for European Policy Studies (CEPS). His main expertise is in EU foreign, security, and defense policies, transatlantic relations, and EU institutional and political dynamics in these areas.

Ulf Engel is professor of politics in Africa at the Institute of African Studies, Leipzig University, visiting professor at the Institute for Peace and Security Studies at Addis Ababa University, and professor in the Department of Political Science at Stellenbosch University. Since 2006, he has been advising the AU Department of Political Affairs, Peace and Security on conflict prevention, early warning, preventive diplomacy, and knowledge management.

Simeon Evstatiev is professor of Middle Eastern history and Islamic studies at Sofia University St. Kliment Ohridski, where he is head of the Department of Arabic and Semitic Studies, chair of the Center for the Study of Religions, and director of Graduate Studies, Middle East Studies. His publications include *Religion and Politics in the Arab World: Islam in Society* (2012), *Salafism in the Middle East and the Boundaries of Faith* (2018), and *Salafism, Belief and Unbelief: From the Middle East to the Balkans* (forthcoming).

Georges Fahmi is a research fellow at Sant'Anna School of Advanced Studies in Pisa. His research focuses on religious actors in democratic transitions, the interplay between state and religion, and violent radicalization in the Middle East and North Africa (MENA) region.

Elsa Lilja Gunnarsdottir is junior research fellow at Norwegian Institute of International Affairs (NUPI). She has worked at the European Free Trade Association (EFTA) Surveillance Authority (ESA) in Brussels and has taken part in intensive training on security, arms control, and disarmament agreement and institutions.

Andreas Lind Kroknes works as a junior researcher and advisor at the Norwegian Institute of International Affairs (NUPI) as part of the Research Group on Peace, Conflict, and Development. His interests include issues of peace and conflict, violent extremism, state building, unconstitutional changes in fragile states, migration, and great power rivalry in Africa, and his main geographic focus is the Sahel region.

Stéphane Lacroix is an associate professor of political science at Sciences Po, a senior researcher at Sciences Po's Centre de Recherches Internationales (CERI), and the codirector of Sciences Po's chair for the study of religion. His work deals with religion and politics, with a focus on the Gulf and Egypt.

Djallil Lounnas is associate professor of international relations at Al Akhawayn University, specializing in violent extremism in the North Africa and Sahel region. He is the author of the book *Le Djihadism en Afrique du Nord-Sahel: d'AQMI a Daech* (2019).

Nizar Messari is associate professor at Al Akhawayn University in Ifrane, Morocco. His areas of expertise are theories of international relations and critical security studies. He is coauthor, with João Pontes Nogueira, of the ninth edition of *Teoria das Relações Internacionais: Correntes e Debates* (2005).

Ahmad Mhidi is a researcher at the Centre for Humanitarian Dialogue. He has conducted extensive field research on tribes and the Islamic State in Syria since 2011 and has coauthored publications that appeared in *Foreign Affairs*, *Foreign Policy*, and *the Economist*.

Diana Mishkova is professor of history and academic director of the Centre for Advanced Study in Sofia, foreign corresponding member of the Austrian Academy of Sciences, and Doctor Honoris Causa of Södertörn University, Stockholm.

Daniela Musina is a PhD candidate in a joint program at the Scuola Normale Superiore (Florence) and the Sant'Anna School of Advanced Studies

(Pisa). Her research focuses on security governance and its effects on policing and institutional violence in Tunisia.

Kari M. Osland serves as director of the Norwegian Institute of International Affairs (NUPI). Her primary research areas include conflict dynamics, genocide, insurgencies, and governance in fragile states, as well as international crisis management and peacebuilding. She has conducted fieldwork in Afghanistan, the Western Balkans, the Sahel region, and several African countries.

Kamaran Palani is a research officer at the London School of Economics and Political Science's Middle East Centre. His research has been published in *International Peacekeeping*, *Third World Quarterly*, *Ethnopolitics*, *British Journal of Middle Eastern Studies*, and *International Migration*.

Predrag Petrovi is program director of the Belgrade Centre for Security Policy, where he has worked since 2006. His research focuses on new and inadequately researched topics such as the privatization of security, intelligence service reform, and violent extremism.

Colin Powers is a senior fellow and chief editor for the Noria MENA Program. He has more than a decade's worth of research experience in the Middle East and North Africa.

Luca Raineri is assistant professor in security studies at the Sant'Anna School of Advanced Studies in Pisa. His research draws on critical security and conflict studies and focuses on transnational (in)security in Africa and around European borders and EU external action in general.

Pernille Rieker is a research professor at the Norwegian Institute of International Affairs (NUPI) and part of the research group on security and defense. Her research interests include European integration and European foreign and security policies, including the foreign and security policies of France and the Nordic countries.

Kjetil Selvik is a research professor and head of the Norwegian Institute of International Affairs (NUPI) Research Group on Peace, Conflict and Development. His current research examines the struggles over states and regimes in the Middle East.

Tatjana Stankovic is a senior research fellow at NUPI. Her current research explores climate policy and international climate cooperation, and her research interests include political negotiations and the design of peace agreements.

Francesco Strazzari is professor of international relations at Sant'Anna School of Advanced Studies, Pisa. His main areas of expertise are European Union peripheries and extended neighborhoods, including the Balkans, North Africa and the Sahel, the Caucasus, the Black Sea.

Henrik Vigh is a professor in the Department of Anthropology at the University of Copenhagen. His main research lies within the field of political anthropology, with a special focus on crisis, conflict, and crime.

Index

Abdel Halim, Mahmud, 73
Abdul Latif Salafi, 170–171
African Union, 8
Afghanistan, 67, 70, 93
Ageidat, 174
Alawi, 156, 157; Shabbiha, 157
Albania, 122–123, 134–135, 164, 166
Algeria, 12, 67–75, 79–84, 130
Ansar Dine, 41
Ansar al-Shari'a in Tunisia (AST), 129–133, 187
"Arab Spring", 86, 97, 129, 132, 140, 156
Armé Islamique du salut (AIS), 67, 69–73, 74, 83–84
al-Assad, Bashar Hafiz, 155, 157, 191, 193–194, 196n5
al-Assad, Hafez, 156, 171, 191
Ayoub, Abu, 130
Azzam, Abdullah, 80

Baath, 96, 152, 155, 171, 192
al-Baghdadi, Abu Bakr, 134, 154
Bahrain, 193
Balkans. *See* Western Balkans
al-Banna, 73, 75–76
Bazoum, Mohamed, 184–185
Belaid, Choukri, 121
Belgium, 184
Ben Ali, Zine al-Abidine, 124, 130–131, 186
Ben Hassine, Seifallah, 129

Benhadjar, Ali, 72–73
Behrami, Bujar, 134
Bertelsmann Stiftung, 52, 55–56, 59, 64n2
Biden, Joseph, 209
bin Laden, Osama, 70
Black September, 96
Boko Haram, 42, 45, 146, 221
Bosnia and Herzegovina, 5, 9, 12–14, 28, 103–104, 109, 111–112, 122–123, 129, 134, 161–188; Bosnian Serb extremism 108–109
Bourguiba, Habuib, 124, 186
Brahmi, Mohamed, 121
Buchamel, 173
Burkina Faso, 11, 33–50, 143, 148, 151, 185, 227

Chahed, Youssef, 189
Chechnya, 129, 146
China, 56, 98, 116, 208, 218
conceptual Eurocentrism, 52, 58–59, 63–64
corruption, 24–29
Croatia, 106, 118n6; Catholic church 110–111; Croat nationalism, 109–111
counterterrorism, 3, 13–14, 18, 43, 45–46, 104, 107, 119, 121, 125–128, 150, 159, 179–181, 185–186, 188–194, 195, 200–201, 207–213, 221, 223n3

Daesh. *See* ISIS

Dayton Agreement, 104–105
Dicko, Jaffar, 41
Dicko, Malam, 41
Dodik, Milorad, 105
Dugin, Alexandar, 115
Durkheim, D. Émile, 53, 55–58

Egypt, 12, 67–69, 75–79, 79–84
enabling environments, 4, 11, 17–32
Ennahda, 121, 124, 129–131
entrepreneurs of violence, 5, 11, 23, 33–50
Essid, Habib, 189
ethnonationalism, 103–104, 105
European Union, 2, 3, 8, 10, 14–15, 57–58, 104, 115, 120, 125, 127–128, 179, 183–186, 189, 191, 195; CT–P/CVE 3, 197–199, 200–206; 215–221; CEPOL, 189; EUROPOL, 126, 189; European Peace Facility, 185; EUCAP Sahel Niger, 184, 186
extraversion, 181–182, 189
extremist order, 36–39
Ezzat, Mahmoud, 78

al-Filistini, Abu Qutada, 75, 94, 95, 130
foreign terrorist fighters (FTF), 3, 14, 28–29, 101, 103, 119–123, 128–129, 133–134, 164–165
France, 7, 150, 184–185, 194, 209, 277
Front Islamique du Salut (FIS), 67, 69–72
Frontex (European Border and Coast Guard Agency), 126

Germany, 109, 125, 134, 184
German Development Institute (DIE/IDOS), 52, 57, 60
Ghaliu, Iyafh, 41
Gharib, Tashin Hama, 169
al-Ghazali, Abu Hamid, 73–74
Goïta, Assimi, 185
Gousmi, Chérif, 71
governance, 4, 14–15, 24, 26–27, 37–39, 42, 49–51, 55–56, 59, 62, 81, 107, 117, 121, 127, 156, 172, 174–175, 179, 181–182, 195, 198–199, 202, 204, 206–207, 211, 214, 216–217, 220–222, 226–227, 230
Group for Preaching and Combat (GSPC), 75

Group for the Support of Islam and Muslims (JNIM), 41–42
Groupe Islamique Armé (GIA), 67–75, 83–84, 84n9
Groupes de Legitime Defences, 71
guardian state, 85–102

al-Hakim, Boubaker, 131
al-Hifl, Ibrahim, 174
al-Hifl, Motashar, 174
al-Hudaybi, Hassan, 76
al-Hummada, Abdelazziz, 173
al-Husseini, Haj Amin, 96
Hussein, Mahmoud, 78
Hussein, Saddam, 93, 152–153

al-Idrissi, Al Khatib, 130
International Criminal Tribunal for the former Yugoslavia (ICTY), 118n8
Iraq, 2, 13, 13–14, 26–28, 27, 100, 152–155, 165, 168, 170; Iraqi Islamic Party, 154, 159n1; Nineveh, 27–28
Islam, 9; Hanafi Sunni, 14, 30, 57; Salafism, 70–71, 74–75, 105, 111–112, 124, 152–153, 162–168, 170; Shia, 152; Sufism, 31, 40, 168, 175; Sunni, 9, 27, 28, 87–88, 90–91, 144, 152–153, 168; Wahhabism, 96, 104, 162, 164–165, 191
Islamic Action Front (IAF), 97
Islamic Community (IC), 166–168; Islamic Community in Serbia (ICiS), 166; Islamic Community of Servia (ICoS), 166
Islamic Fighting Group (TIFG), 129
Islamic Salvation Front (FIS), 130
Islamic State (IS), 2–3, 13, 18, 27–28, 151, 228; Islamic State in the Greater Sahara (ISGS), 41, 42; Islamic State in Iraq and Syria (ISIS), 75, 87, 92, 94, 95, 101, 103, 119, 121–122, 134, 152–158, 162, 169–171, 173–175, 187, 191–193, 197; Islamic State in the Levante (ISIL), 75; Islamic State Sahel Province (ISSP), 182–183; Islamic State West Africa Province (ISWAP), 182–183
Islamist groups, 39–43
Islamović, Sead, 167

Index 277

Issoufou, Mahamadou, 184
Italy, 125, 184
Iyadh, Abu, 131

Jama'at al Jihad, 128
Jama'at Nasr al-Islam wal Muslim (JNIM), 41–42, 150–151
Jabhat al-Nusra, 133–134, 157, 172–173
jihadism, 13, 15, 70–71, 74–75, 103–104, 120–121, 132–133, 143–158, 162, 165, 175, 182, 193
Jomaa, Mehdi, 189
Jordan, 12, 85–86, 93–99; indirect dialogue, 98–10

Kamal, Mohamed, 78
Karwani, Abubakir, 169
al-Kasasbeh, Moaz, 95
Katiba of Macina, 41
Kenya, 52, 62–63
Khaldūn, Ibn, 61
Knežević, Damnjan, 115
Kosovo, 12–13, 24, 27–28, 107, 122–123, 126–128, 133–136, 138–139, 164, 165; Islamic Community of Kosovo, 128, 135; Kosovo Liberation Army (KLA), 123
Kouffa, Hamadoun, 41
Kurdistan, 158, 161, 168–170, 176; Islamic Scholars' Union of Kurdistan, 169; Kurdistan Democratic Party (KDP), 169–171; Kurdish Democratic Union Party (PYD), 158; Kurdistan Region of Ira (KRI), 168–169, 171, 176; Ministry of Endowment, 169; Patriotic Union of Kurdistan (PUK), 169, 170–171
Kuwait, 93

Lefko-Everett, Kate, 65n12
Libya, 100–101, 121, 128–131, 136–137, 143, 147, 149, 201, 218–219, 222, 227

Maaroufi, Tarek, 129
Makhzen, 88, 102n2
Makić, Bekir, 167
Mali, 3, 13, 24–26, 29, 31, 33–50, 58, 148–152, 161–178, 185, 218–219, 222, 227

al-Maliki, Nouri, 154, 155
Maqdisi, Abu Muhammad, 94
al-Maqdisi, Abu Muhammad, 74–75, 95, 130
methodological approach, 6–8, 35–36, 68–69, 85–86, 145–146, 180, 225–226; comparative lessons, 226–227; future research, 229–231
Mezrag, Madani, 71, 73
Middle East and North Africa (MENA), 1–2, 5, 8, 12–15, 18–19, 22–24, 26, 28, 31, 57, 69, 86, 97, 101, 119–120, 122–123, 134, 138–140, 143, 164–165, 179–180, 182, 186, 191, 194, 201–202, 204–205, 210–211, 213, 216, 218, 221, 223n3, 225
Milošević, Slobodan, 106, 116
Mitchell, Mark, 208
Mokkdem, Mohamed, 74
Morocco, 12, 85–94, 100–101; King Mohammed VI, 88
Morsi, Mohamed, 76–77, 80, 97
al-Mourabitoune Katiba, 41
Moussalaha, 91–92
Movement of Justice and Misericord, 88
Mubarak, Husni, 76–77
Mukhabarat, 99
Muslim Brotherhood: Algeria, 12, 68; Egypt, 12, 69, 72–73, 75–84, 97–98, 138; Jordan, 93, 95–98; Tunisia, 124

Nabulsi, Suleiman, 96
Nasser, Gamal Abdel, 73, 76
Netherlands, 184
Niger, 14, 33–50, 151, 182–186, 194–195, 221, 227
nonoccurrence, 1, 4, 7, 11, 15, 18–21, 24, 26, 29–31, 36, 68, 119–120, 139, 140, 145, 159, 164–168, 198, 222, 230
North Atlantic Treaty Organization (NATO), 10, 24, 115, 227
North Macedonia, 115, 120, 123, 135, 139, 164, 168

Obama, Barack, 208
Organization for Security and Cooperation in Europe (OSCE), 114, 127

Ossama, Abu, 173
Ottoman empire, 8–9, 108, 164
Outb, Sayyid, 74, 76, 79–80, 82

al-Qaeda in the Islamic Maghreb (AQIM), 13, 18, 23, 41, 75, 94, 119, 121–122, 127, 129, 131–133, 149, 151, 162, 173, 200, 210, 228
Qatar, 230
al-Qunaybi, Iyad, 94

Palestine Liberation Organization (PLO), 96
Party of Justice and Development (PJD), 88
preventing violent extremism in the Balkans and the MENA (PREVEX), 1, 11, 15n1, 51, 60, 64n3, 65n14, 65n18, 86, 103, 145, 165, 180, 186, 195; policy implications, 228–229; political economy, 63, 121, 123, 136–137, 146, 156, 172, 226–227, 230
preventing and countering violent extremism (P/CVE). *See also* counterterrorism, violent extremism and terrorism, 2, 14, 125–128, 145, 181–182, 197–223; marketing P/CVE, 179–196
Putin, Vladimir, 115, 192

Rabita Mohamadia of Oulama, 87–89, 91–93, 101n1
radicalization, 1, 3–7, 11–12, 14–15, 19–21, 30, 33–34, 76, 79–80, 89, 92, 113–115, 119–142, 150–151, 164, 166–168, 170, 186, 188–189, 199–200, 204, 208–210, 216–217, 221–222, 229; de-radicalization, 12, 54, 89, 128, 133, 200–201, 219, 229
Rahman, Mohammed Abdel, 78
Reilly, Greg, 153
resilience, 4, 11, 32, 51–63, 64n3, 65, 136–139
Rouissi, Ahmed, 131
Russia, 10, 28, 104–105, 109, 115–117, 118n7, 158, 190, 192–193, 208, 218, 227, 230; Russian Orthodox Church, 104
Rwanda, 52, 62

Saddiq, Abdulrahman, 169
al-Saharaoui, Adnane Abou Walid, 41
Sahel, 3, 6, 9, 15, 18–19, 22–24, 26, 31, 33–50, 57–58, 122, 127, 148, 149–151, 182–186, 189, 194, 201–202, 205–206, 209–211, 214, 216, 218, 223n3
Saied, Kais, 121, 190
Saudi Arabia, 9, 40, 86, 111, 122–123, 129, 134, 164, 167, 230
al-Sayyed, Abdallah, 192
Schmidt, Christian, 116
sectarianism, 13, 27, 117, 143–158
self-defense groups, 43–46; Donzos, 47; Koglweogos, 47; Rougas, 46–47; Volunteers for the defense of the Homeland, 47–48
September 11, 2001, 1, 2, 14, 15, 18, 179, 186, 193, 197, 210, 211, 227
Serbia, 12, 103–118, 123, 164, 166–167; Serbian nationalism, 104–108; Serbian Orthodox Church, 107–108; Serbian Progressive Party (SNS), 116; Serbian Radical Party (SRS), 116
Sharifian kingdoms, 85–102
Shafiq, Ahmed, 76–77
Sharia, 25, 34, 37–39, 42, 70, 131, 135, 187
Sharif, Mohammad, 169
Sierra Leone, 65n8
Simmel, Georg, 53, 58
social cohesion, 11, 30–31, 44, 51–65, 99, 127, 138–40, 166, 186, 188, 199, 216, 220, 226–227, 230
social cleavages, 146–148
Social Cohesion and Reconciliation (SCORE), 52, 54, 59, 64
South Africa, 52–53, 55, 60–62, 65n8, 65n15
state, 8–10, 22, 159; state fragility, 24–29; 48–49; state weakness, 10, 143
al-Suri, Abu Mussab, 75
Syria, 2, 13–14, 100, 122, 155–160, 164–165–166, 168, 170–175, 190–194; Free Syrian Army (FSA), 157, 172; Syria Democratic Forces (SDF), 174

Tanzania, 65n15
Tönnies, Ferdinand, 53, 55–56, 58

Index 279

traditional authorities, 161–178
Trump, Donald, 207
Tuareg, 25, 147–152, 219
Tunisia, 12–14, 58, 120–122, 124–126, 128–133, 136–138, 186–190, 194
Turkey, 9–10, 116, 129, 206, 230; Diyanet, 127

Ubuntu, 61, 63
Ukraine, 104, 115–116
unemployment, 2, 18, 27, 122, 130, 180, 227
United Araba Emirates (UAE), 193, 230; Hedaya, 127
United Kingdom (UK), 184
United Nations Development Programme (UNDP), 8, 11, 52, 54–56, 60–62, 127, 183, 188
UN Secretary-General, 3
United States (USA), 2, 14–15, 120, 158, 167; CT–P/CVE 197–199, 206–215, 221–222; US Agency for International Development (USAID), 128, 209, 213

Velimirović, Nikolaj, 107–108
violent extremism and terrorism (VET). *See also* preventing and countering violent extremism, 2–4, 11, 17, 22–23, 36–43, 51, 95–98, 223n3, 225, 227–229
Vučić, Aleksandar, 107

Yacoubou, Ibrahim, 185
youth, 27, 31–33, 35, 39–40, 42, 49, 67, 69–70, 75, 78–83, 85, 87, 89, 91–92, 110, 122, 125, 126, 130–132, 136, 146, 162, 165–167, 170–171, 176, 180, 192, 201, 209, 216, 221, 227

Wagner group, 115
Weber, Max, 53, 57–58
Western Balkans, 1–2, 5, 7–9, 12–15, 18–19, 22–24, 28–32, 51, 57, 103–142, 161–178, 201–202, 204, 206–207, 210–211, 215–216, 218, 221, 223n3, 225, 227

Yassine, Abdelassam, 88
youth, 4, 79–81, 89
Yugoslav war, 28, 104, 106, 118n8, 120, 122, 164–165

al-Zarqawi, Abu Musab, 95, 152, 154
Zimbabwe, 65n15
Zukorlić, Muamer, 167

About the Book

Precarious living conditions across the Balkans, the Middle East, and North Africa create fertile ground for radical ideas. Yet, despite genuine grievances and legitimate grounds for anger, most people living in these regions are not radicalized and do not embrace ideas that lead to acts of violent extremism. Which raises the question . . . why?

To answer this question, the authors of *Resisting Radicalization* investigate the nonoccurrence of violent extremism in what they term enabling environments. Their work, the result of a multiyear international project, has critical implications for the future of P/CVE (Preventing and Countering Violent Extremism) programs.

Morten Bøås is research professor at the Norwegian Institute of International Affairs (NUPI). **Gilad Ben-Nun** is a senior lecturer in the Global and European Studies Institute at Leipzig University. **Ulf Engel** is professor of African politics at Leipzig University. **Kari Osland** is the director of NUPI.